Exam Ref AZ-103
Microsoft Azure
Administrator

Michael Washam
Jonathan Tuliani
Scott Hoag

Exam Ref AZ-103 Microsoft Azure Administrator

Published with the authorization of Microsoft Corporation by:
Pearson Education, Inc.

Copyright © 2019 by Pearson Education

ISBN-978-0-13-546658-2
ISBN-0-13-546658-X

Library of Congress Control Number: 2019937230

3 2019

Trademarks

Warning and Disclaimer

Special Sales

For information about buying this title in bulk quantities, or for special sales opportunities (which may include electronic versions; custom cover designs; and content particular to your business, training goals, marketing focus, or branding interests), please contact our corporate sales department at corpsales@pearsoned.com or (800) 382-3419.

For government sales inquiries, please contact governmentsales@pearsoned.com.

For questions about sales outside the U.S., please contact intlcs@pearson.com.

Editor-in-Chief	Brett Bartow
Executive Editor	Loretta Yates
Sponsoring Editor	Charvi Arora
Development Editor	Troy Mott
Managing Editor	Sandra Schroeder
Senior Project Editor	Tracey Croom
Editorial Production	Backstop Media
Copy Editor	Liv Bainbridge
Indexer	MAP Systems
Proofreader	Jana Gardner
Technical Editor	Jim Cheshire
Cover Designer	Twist Creative, Seattle

Contents at a glance

Contents

Acknowledgments

Michael Washam As a technologist, reading and writing books of this nature makes me appreciate how much I don't know and how challenging it is to keep up the pace of learning required to be successful in this industry. I want to acknowledge the readers of this book, and I hope it helps you all on your journey to certification. I also want to acknowledge the team at Pearson for the opportunity to help put a project like this together, as well as my team here at Opsgility for seeing it through to success.

Jonathan Tuliani I've enjoyed the rare privilege of spending part of my professional career as a member of the team that created Azure. It's inspiring to see how organizations all over the world are using what we built to deliver innovative services and greater efficiency. Special thanks go to all my former colleagues in the Azure networking team, for putting up with me and for everything I learned along the way.

Scott Hoag This could would not be possible without the team at Opsgility - co-authors including Jonathan Tuliani, Abu Zobayer, Michael Washam, and our wordsmith James Burleson. I'd also like to thank my family - my wife Amanda and two very understanding children. The long days and nights and poking away at the cloud are not possible without you.

About the Authors

MICHAEL WASHAM is CEO of Opsgility, a leading provider of IT training services that include both instructor-led and on-demand learning through their online learning platform SkillMeUp. com. Michael has extensive history in the IT Industry where he has worked as an IT Professional, Software Developer, Evangelist, and Program Manager before turning to his passion of enabling companies of all sizes make the digital transformation to the cloud.

JONATHAN TULIANI leads our European office and is responsible for managing our European clients. Prior to joining Opsgility, Jonathan was a 10-year Microsoft veteran, spending over 6 years in the Azure Engineering team where he was Principal Program Manager for both Azure DNS and Azure Traffic Manager. Jonathan has 20 years' experience in the IT industry, in roles spanning development, product management, technical pre-sales and program management.

SCOTT HOAG (MCITP, MCPD) is a Principal Cloud Solutions Architect with Opsgility where he drives adoption of Microsoft's cloud platforms for Opsgility's customers. Scott is a frequent speaker at SharePoint and Azure focused user groups and comes with a deep background in helping organizations deploy content management and collaboration systems. Scott has over 11 years of experience as both a developer and a system engineer delivering solutions from MCMS 2002 to SharePoint 2016 and Office 365 today. Scott also co-hosts the Microsoft Cloud IT Pro Podcast where he discusses the latest news and offerings with Office 365 and Azure. You can find him on twitter @ciphertxt and on the web at *psconfig.com*.

Introduction

The AZ-103 exam focuses on common tasks and concepts that an administrator needs to understand to deploy and manage infrastructure in Microsoft Azure. Managing Azure subscriptions and resources is a key topic on the exam, which includes configure cost center quotas, tagging, subscription level policies, as well as resource organization using resource groups. Another topic covered is implementing and managing storage; which includes creating and configuring storage accounts, implementing Azure backup, as well as configuring Azure files and understanding the services for importing and exporting data to Azure. A significant portion of the exam is focused on deploying and managing virtual machines, which includes configuring of networking, storage and monitoring, automated deployments and managing VM backups. Configuring, managing, and monitoring virtual networks is part of the exam, as-is configuring load balancing. This book covers the creation and managing of virtual networks, DNS, connectivity between virtual networks, and configuring network security groups. The final topic is managing identities, which includes topics on managing Azure Active Directory (AD) when creating users, groups, and devices. You will also find the configuring of hybrid identity using Azure AD Connect, multi-factor authentication, as well as configuring services such as identity protection and self-service password resets.

This book is geared toward Azure administrators who manage cloud services that span storage, security, networking and compute. It explains how to configure and deploy services across a broad range of related Azure services to help you prepare for the exam.

This book covers every major topic area found on the exam, but it does not cover every exam question. Only the Microsoft exam team has access to the exam questions, and Microsoft regularly adds new questions to the exam, making it impossible to cover specific questions. You should consider this book a supplement to your relevant real-world experience and other study materials. If you encounter a topic in this book that you do not feel completely comfortable with, use the "Need more review?" links you'll find in the text to find more information and take the time to research and study the topic. Great information is available on MSDN, TechNet, and in blogs and forums.

Organization of this book

This book is organized by the "Skills measured" list published for the exam. The "Skills measured" list is available for each exam on the Microsoft Learning website: *https://aka.ms/examlist*. Each chapter in this book corresponds to a major topic area in the list, and the technical tasks in each topic area determine a chapter's organization. If an exam covers six major topic areas, for example, the book will contain six chapters.

Microsoft certifications

Microsoft certifications distinguish you by proving your command of a broad set of skills and experience with current Microsoft products and technologies. The exams and corresponding certifications are developed to validate your mastery of critical competencies as you design and develop, or implement and support, solutions with Microsoft products and technologies both on-premises and in the cloud. Certification brings a variety of benefits to the individual and to employers and organizations.

> **MORE INFO** **ALL MICROSOFT CERTIFICATIONS**
>
> For information about Microsoft certifications, including a full list of available certifications, go to *http://www.microsoft.com/learning*.

Quick access to online references

Throughout this book are addresses to webpages that the author has recommended you visit for more information. Some of these addresses (also known as URLs) can be painstaking to type into a web browser, so we've compiled all of them into a single list that readers of the print edition can refer to while they read.

Download the list at *https://MicrosoftPressStore.com/ExamRefAZ103/downloads*

The URLs are organized by chapter and heading. Every time you come across a URL in the book, find the hyperlink in the list to go directly to the webpage.

Errata, updates, & book support

We've made every effort to ensure the accuracy of this book and its companion content. You can access updates to this book—in the form of a list of submitted errata and their related corrections—at:

https://MicrosoftPressStore.com/ExamRefAZ103/errata

If you discover an error that is not already listed, please submit it to us at the same page.

For additional book support and information, please visit
https://MicrosoftPressStore.com/Support.

Please note that product support for Microsoft software and hardware is not offered through the previous addresses. For help with Microsoft software or hardware, go to
http://support.microsoft.com.

Stay in touch

Let's keep the conversation going! We're on Twitter: *http://twitter.com/MicrosoftPress*.

Important: How to use this book to study for the exam

Certification exams validate your on-the-job experience and product knowledge. To gauge your readiness to take an exam, use this Exam Ref to help you check your understanding of the skills tested by the exam. Determine the topics you know well and the areas in which you need more experience. To help you refresh your skills in specific areas, we have also provided "Need more review?" pointers, which direct you to more in-depth information outside the book.

The Exam Ref is not a substitute for hands-on experience. This book is *not* designed to teach you new skills.

We recommend that you round out your exam preparation by using a combination of available study materials and courses. Learn more about available classroom training and find free online courses and live events at *http://microsoft.com/learn*. Microsoft Official Practice Tests are available for many exams at *http://aka.ms/practicetests*.

This book is organized by the "Skills measured" list published for the exam. The "Skills measured" list for each exam is available on the Microsoft Learn website: *http://aka.ms/examlist*.

Note that this Exam Ref is based on this publicly available information and the author's experience. To safeguard the integrity of the exam, authors do not have access to the exam questions.

## CHAPTER 1

Manage Azure subscriptions and resources

An Azure subscription, which forms the core of an Azure environment, is a foundational component of every Azure implementation. Every resource that you create in Azure resides in an Azure subscription, which is a billing boundary for Azure resources with per-resource role-based access controls.

IMPORTANT

Have you read page xix?

It contains valuable information regarding the skills you need to pass the exam.

In this chapter, you will learn how to manage Azure subscriptions. This includes how to:

- Assign permissions to Azure resources
- Govern cost through quotas and resource tags
- Configure Azure policy to ensure your Azure environment is governed in an effective way while maintaining the agility of the cloud

You will also learn how to analyze consumption and resource utilization within your subscriptions. This includes how to:

- View metrics for your Azure resources through Azure Monitor and create alerts based on metrics and logs
- Monitor and report on resource spend
- Perform deep analysis with Azure Log Analytics

Finally, you will learn how to manage Azure resource groups. This includes how to:

- Apply governance to Azure resource groups and their child resources through Azure policy
- Create and manage resource locks
- Manage the lifecycle of the resources that reside in resource groups

By understanding the controls that are available in Azure for subscription and resource management, you enable your organization for success across your Azure estate.

Skills covered in this chapter:

- Manage Azure subscriptions
- Analyze resource utilization and consumption
- Manage resource groups

Skill 1.1: Manage Azure Subscriptions

Azure subscriptions have controls available that govern access to the resources within a subscription, govern cost through quotas and tagging, and govern the resources that are allowed in an environment with Azure policy.

A subscription is a logical unit of Azure services linked to an Azure account, which is an identity in Azure Active Directory (Azure AD). Azure AD is an identity provider for Azure and provides authentication to resources in an Azure subscription. The resources themselves then have role-based access controls applied to them which provide authorization to the resources. (see Figure 1-1).

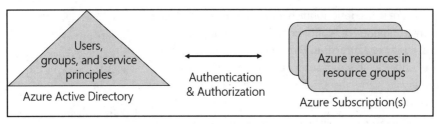

FIGURE 1-1 Azure AD and Azure Subscription relationship

There are multiple ways to obtain an Azure subscription, and a wide range of subscription types (or offers). Some of the cost common types include:

- Free trial
- Pay-As-You-Go/Web Direct
- Visual Studio/MSDN subscriptions
- Microsoft Resellers
- Cloud Solution Provider
- Microsoft Open Licensing
- Enterprise Agreements

The capabilities of each subscription are similar, in that each subscription type allows you to create and manage resources. Some subscription types have restrictions on supported resource types and locations. For example, Visual Studio subscriptions typically do not have a credit card associated with them, which prevents you from purchasing services from the Azure Marketplace, such as network virtual appliances. Visual Studio subscriptions for Azure only have access to a limited number of Azure regions. The regional restrictions for each offer can be viewed at *https://azure.microsoft.com/regions/offers/.*

This section covers how to:

- Assign administrator permissions
- Configure cost center quotas and tagging
- Configure Azure subscription policies

Assigning administrator permissions

Azure has many different roles for managing access to Azure resources. These include classic subscription administrative roles like Account Administrator, Service Administrator, or Co-Administrator, as well as Azure role-based access controls (RBAC) that are available in Azure Resource Manager (ARM). When managing access to Azure subscriptions and resources, it is recommended to use Azure RBAC roles whenever possible.

Classic subscription administrators have full access to an Azure subscription. They can manage resources through the Azure Portal, Resource Manager APIs (including through PowerShell and the CLI), and the classic deployment model APIs. By default, the account that is used to sign up for an Azure subscription is automatically set as both the Account Administrator and the Service Administrator. Once the subscription has been created, more Co-administrators can be added. Users assigned the Service Administrator and Co-administrator roles have the same access as a user who is assigned the Azure RBAC Owner role at the subscription scope (see Table 1-1).

TABLE 1-1 Azure subscription administrative roles

Administrative Role	Limit	Summary
Account Administrator	1 per Azure account	Authorized to access the Account Center (create subscriptions, cancel subscriptions, change billing for a subscription, change Service Administrator, and more).
Service Administrator	1 per Azure subscription	Authorized to access the Azure Management Portal for all subscriptions in the account. By default, it's the same as the Account Administrator when a subscription is created.
Co-administrator	200 per subscription	Same as the Service Administrator but cannot change the association of subscriptions to Azure directories.

In the Azure Portal, you can view the current assignments for the Account Administrator and Service Administrator roles by browsing to a subscription in the Azure Portal and selecting the **Properties** blade as seen in Figure 1-2.

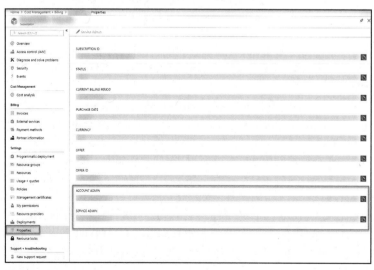

FIGURE 1-2 Azure subscription properties

Azure RBAC roles can also be used to grant rights to principals, including user and service principals. A user principal is an identity that is associated with a user, or a group of users. An example is a developer who is granted direct access to manage their web application. A service principal is an identity that exists in Azure AD that is associated with an application. Service principals allow applications in Azure AD to interact with Azure resources just a like a user principal. This can be beneficial when you have resources or applications that need to manage other resources in Azure. For example, an Azure Kubernetes Service (AKS) cluster needs to manage a load balancer and a VM scale set. The use of a service principal allows the cluster to manage the resources directly.

Azure RBAC roles are more flexible than classic administrator roles and allow for more fine-grained access management. Azure RBAC has more than 70 built-in roles, but there are four foundational roles, as shown in Table 1-2.

TABLE 1-2 Azure RBAC roles

Azure RBAC role	Permissions	Notes
Owner	■ Full access to all resources ■ Delegate access to others	■ The Service Administrator and Co-Administrators are assigned the Owner role at the subscription scope. ■ Applies to all resource types.
Contributor	■ Create and manage all of types of Azure resources ■ Cannot grant access to others	■ Applies to all resource types.
Reader	■ View Azure resources	■ Applies to all resource types.
User Access Administrator	■ Manage user access to Azure resources	

The Owner, Contributor, Reader, and User Access Administrator roles can be applied to all resource types. The other 70+ roles allow the management of specific Azure resources. It is also important to know that only the Azure Portal and the ARM APIs support Azure RBAC. User, groups, or service principals assigned to Azure RBAC roles cannot use the classic deployment APIs when only assigned to an Azure RBAC role as RBAC roles only exist in Azure Resource Manager. For example, to grant a user access to your subscription in the Classic deployment model, you would need to add that user as a Co-administrator, granting them rights to everything in the subscription.

When applying RBAC to Azure resources, access is applied (or granted) to a scope. Valid scopes include subscription, resource group, or a resource. RBAC in Azure is inherited from a parent resource. This means that if a principal is granted Contributor rights to a resource group, that principal would have Contributor rights on all of the child resources automatically.

To add a new administrator to an Azure subscription using Azure RBAC, browse to the Subscriptions blade in the Azure Portal (*https://portal.azure.com/#blade/Microsoft_Azure_Billing/SubscriptionsBlade*) and select the subscription that you want to grant access to. Open the **Access Control (IAM)** blade and click **Add Role Assignment**. Select the **Owner** role in the **Role** box and in the **Select** box type the user name or identifier for the target user, group, or service principal. When complete, click **Save**. An example is shown in Figure 1-3.

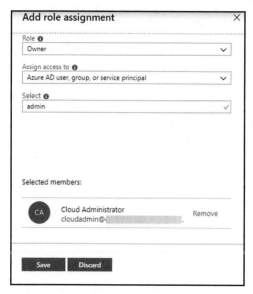

FIGURE 1-3 Add an Azure subscription Owner

If required, you can also grant Co-Administrator rights for the classic deployment model after adding an account as an Owner.

EXAM TIP

You would only make another user a Co-administrator of an Azure subscription if the needed to manage Classic resources. If all the resources you deploy are in the Resource Manager model, RBAC should be used to grant access to the appropriate scope.

Note that only accounts with Azure RBAC Owner rights can be granted Co-Administrator permissions. Users with the Contributor or Reader roles cannot be added as Co-Administrators to an Azure subscription.

To add a user as a Co-administrator, browse to the **Access Control (IAM)** blade of an Azure subscription. Click **+Add** and then **Add co-administrator** as shown in Figure 1-4.

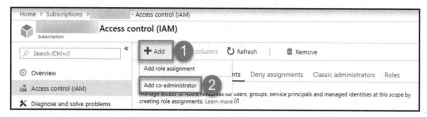

FIGURE 1-4 Add an Azure subscription Co-Administrator

In the blade that opens, select a user from the directory and click **Add**.

Management Groups can also be used to apply Azure RBAC to a subscription. Management Groups allow you to apply governance consistently across subscriptions, including the application of common RBAC controls and the application of Azure policy, as discussed later in this chapter.

Management groups allow subscriptions to be organized in a multi-level hierarchy, providing a number of tangible benefits:

- **Reduced overhead**   No need to apply governance on every subscription.
- **Enforcement**   Company admins can apply governance at the Management Group level, outside the control of the subscription admin and the controls implemented at the management group can be applied to both existing and new subscriptions. This eliminates inconsistencies in the application of governance as the same controls are applied the same way to the desired subscriptions.
- **Reporting**   The Standard tier SKU for Azure Policy provides reports of compliance; with Management Groups that reporting can span multiple/all subscriptions in an organization.

Management Groups form a hierarchy that is up to six levels deep, excluding the root and subscription levels. Each group has exactly one parent group and can have multiple child groups. An example hierarchy is shown in Figure 1-5. In such a hierarchy, one common set of policy could be applied at the root management group which all child management groups and subscriptions would inherit. Then, as needed, those children can have additional controls applies.

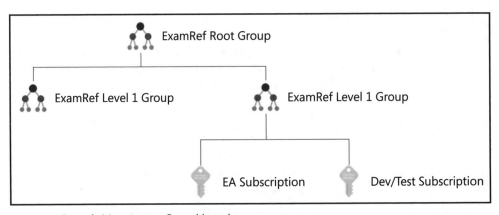

FIGURE 1-5 Example Management Group hierarchy

There is a single root Management Group at the root of the hierarchy. This management group is associated with the Azure AD tenant that is then associated with an Azure subscription. It cannot be moved or deleted. Individual subscriptions, including new subscriptions, are added to a Management Group.

In a manner similar to RBAC, Azure Policy is also applied at a scope. Recall that these are the subscription, a resource group, or an individual resource. For example, when Policy is applied at the subscription scope, it applies to all the resource groups and resources in the subscription as shown in Figure 1-6.

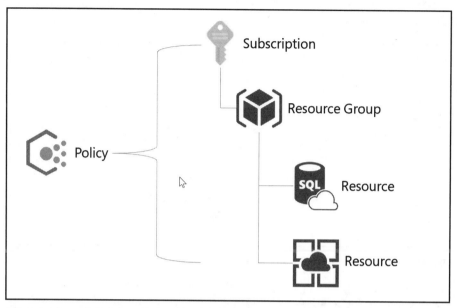

FIGURE 1-6 Example Policy applied at the subscription scope

Management Groups introduce an additional scope above a subscription. When applied at the Management Group scope, each subscription under the management group inherits the RBAC and Policy assignments of the management group as shown in Figure 1-7.

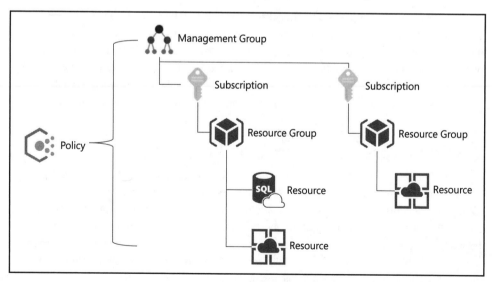

FIGURE 1-7 Example Policy applied at the management group scope

To add a role assignment to a Management Group, browse to the Management Groups service in the Azure Portal. Select a Management Group and then the Details of that group. Select the Access control (IAM) blade and add role assignments just as you would to an Azure subscription as shown in Figure 1-8.

FIGURE 1-8 Access control (IAM) blade for an Azure Management Group

---

IMPORTANT **RBAC AND MANAGEMENT GROUPS**

RBAC applied at the Management Group level is inherited by all of the child resources within the scope of the management group (subscriptions, resource groups, and resources). For instance, if you add a user as an Owner at the Management Group scope, that user will become an Owner in all the subscriptions associated with the Management Group.

When planning the application of RBAC and Policy through Management Groups, you should consider how administrative operations can be limited to privileged users by applying Owner rights through a Management Group. Also consider that there is a built-in role which can be used for managing Policy which is named Resource Policy Contributor. This role includes access to most Policy operations and should be considered privileged as well. By applying RBAC at the Management Group, you will ensure consistent application of tenant-wide security.

Configure cost center quotas and tagging

In Azure there are several types of quotas that are applicable to subscriptions, including resource quotas and spending quotas. With Azure resource quotas (or limits), Azure administrators can view the current consumption and usage of resources within an Azure subscription and understand how that consumption may be affected by Azure resource limits. Administrators can also request quota increases for certain resource types. For instance, the number of cores available for virtual machines is limited to 20 per region by default. This limit can be increased by submitting a request to Microsoft support.

There are also spending quotas in Azure. Spending quotas allow administrators to set alerts within an Azure subscription by configuring budgets to inform the business when their

Azure spending has hit a certain threshold. These differ slightly from limits. Where a resource limit can stop resources from being created (*e.g.* there are not enough cores available to the subscription in the desired region) a spending quota acts as an alerting mechanism and does not stop resources from being created or consumed. While an alert can be generated from a spending quota, resources can still be created and consumed which could cause the spending quota to be exceeded.

Tags in Azure Resource Manager allow consumers of Azure to logically categorize Azure resource groups and Azure resources. As resources are tagged, they can then be queried and tracked based on the associated tags. Tags are a crucial component to implementing charge-back (or showback) within an Azure subscription. For example in organizations where an Azure subscription is shared by multiple business units or departments there may be a need to understand how resources are used for individual departments and show the cost associated with each department, either to bill that department for their Azure consumption (chargeback) or to help that department understand their spend in Azure (showback).

Configure resource quotas

To view the existing resource quotas (or service limits) for your Azure subscription, browse to the Azure subscription in the Azure Portal and select the **Usage + quotas** blade. From this blade, you can view existing quotas by service, resource provider, and location. You also filter the list by resource types you have deployed.

To increase a quota, click the **Request Increase** button as shown in Figure 1-9.

FIGURE 1-9 Azure subscription resource quotas

Clicking the Request Increase button will begin the process to open a new support request. As a part of the request, you must select the quota type (e.g. Compute/VM cores or Machine Learning service) and provide a description of your request.

> **IMPORTANT QUOTA INCREASE**
>
> Submitting a request to increase a quota is only submitting a support request to Microsoft. Microsoft Support must respond to the request, and while most requests are granted, it is not guaranteed that a quota increase will be granted.

The consumption of resources within a subscription against a resource quota can also be viewed with PowerShell. There are multiple cmdlets available in the Az (formerly AzureRm) PowerShell modules for querying per-service quota usage. For example, to view the current usage of vCPU quotas, use the Get-AzVMUsage, and to view the current resource usage for the storage service use Get-AzStorageUsage.

EXAM TIP

In this chapter and throughout the remaining reference, PowerShell cmdlets are referenced using the new Az module. You may see examples on the web and in other reference materials that refer to the AzureRm cmdlets. The Az module can use AzureRm aliases with the command Enable-AzureRmAlias for compatibility with existing scripts. See: *https://docs. microsoft.com/powershell/azure/overview?#about-the-new-az-module* for more detail.

Configure cost center quotas

One of the key factors in managing an Azure subscription is being able to plan for and drive organizational accountability for Azure spend. One of the best ways to drive accountability is to make sure that the consumers of Azure resources understand their cost, including current usage and forecasting future spend based on current resource consumption.

Budgets in Azure Cost Management provide Azure customers subscriptions under many offer types with the ability to proactively manage cost and monitor Azure spend over time at a subscription level.

EXAM TIP

The full list of supported accounts and offers for Azure Cost Management can be found at: *https://docs.microsoft.com/ azure/cost-management/understand-cost-mgt-data*.

Budgets are a monitoring mechanism only, allowing users to create budgets with set thresholds and notification rules. When a budget threshold is exceeded a notification is triggered but resources continue to run.

To use Budgets with an Azure subscription, that subscription must be a supported offer type as previously stated. Users must have at least read access (Reader rights) to a subscription to view budgets and must have Contributor (or higher) rights to create and manage budgets. There are also specialized roles that can be used to grant principals access to Cost Management data including Cost Management contributor and Cost Management reader.

To create a budget in the Azure Portal, navigate to **Cost Management + Billing**, then **Subscriptions**, select a subscription, and then **Budgets**.

> **NOTE SUBSCRIPTION BUDGETS**
>
> By default, you will be creating a budget at the subscription scope, but budgets can also be created at the resource group scope as well if necessary. You must select the desired scope before clicking the **+Add** button.

Click **+Add** and in the Create budget blade, enter a budget name and budget amount. Choose the duration period (Monthly, Quarterly, or Annual) and an expiration date. Budgets require at least one cost threshold (% of budget) and an email address for the alert recipient. Figure 1-10 shows an example for a monthly budget for $10,000 with a threshold set at 90% of the budget ($9,000).

FIGURE 1-10 Azure budgets

> **NOTE BUDGET ALERTS**
>
> Budget alerts can also leverage the same Action Groups that Azure Monitor supports.

After your budgets have been created, they can be viewed through the Budgets blade. When viewing the subscription scope, you will see the budgets for both the subscription and any resource group scoped budgets in a single view as shown in Figure 1-11.

FIGURE 1-11 Azure budgets

For customers on non-EA subscriptions, Azure also has a Billing Alert Service, which can be configured by Account Administrators through the Account Portal at: *https://account.azure. com/subcriptions*. Select the desired subscription and then click on the **Alerts (preview)** tab as shown in Figure 1-12. You can create up to five billing alerts for a single subscription, each with a distinct threshold, and up to two email recipients per alert.

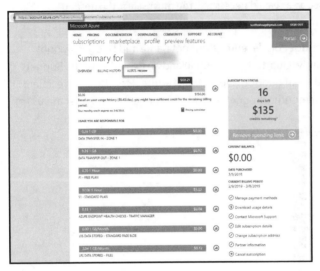

FIGURE 1-12 Azure Billing Alerts

When creating a billing alert, you can alert for either the billing total for the month or a monetary credit. For a billing total alert, an alert is sent when the subscription spend exceeds the threshold. For monetary credit alerts, an alert is sent when monetary credits drop below the defined limit (monetary credits usually apply to Visual Studio subscriptions and Free Trial subscriptions). An example of this screen is shown in Figure 1-13.

FIGURE 1-13 Azure Billing Alert creation

Configure resource tags

Resource tags allow you to apply custom metadata to your Azure resources to logically orga-nize them and build out custom taxonomies. A tag is a name and a value pair. For example, as you deploy resources in Azure, you want to track the environment the resource is associ-ated with. To do this, you can create a tag called Environment and the value Production to all resources in production. For downstream environments such as development or test, you can use the same Environment tag with the Dev/Test value. Common tags include the environment a resource is associated with, a cost center or billing code, and resource owner.

As tags are applied, you can query the resources in your subscription using your tags, even across resource groups. This allows you to understand related resources across resource groups for both billing and management. Tags are also included in the billing data for Azure EA subscriptions through the EA Portal, and for non-EA subscriptions through the Account Portal at: *https://account.azure.com/subscriptions*. Billing exports give clear line of sight for chargeback/showback to understand resource usage and cost. Figure 1-14 shows an example of an export with resource tags from an EA subscription.

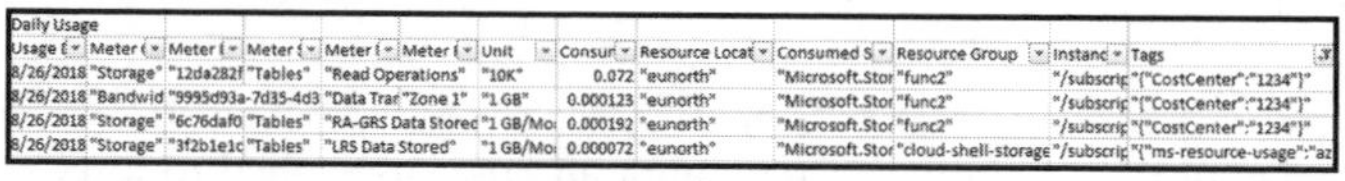

Daily Usage

Usage (	Meter (	Meter I	Meter {	Meter I	Meter I	Unit	Consum	Resource Locat	Consumed S	Resource Group	Instanc	Tags
8/26/2018	"Storage"	"12da282f	"Tables"	"Read Operations"		"10K"	0.072	"eunorth"	"Microsoft.Stor	"func2"	"/subscrip	"{"CostCenter":"1234"}"
8/26/2018	"Bandwid	"9995d93a-7d35-4d3		"Data Trar	"Zone 1"	"1 GB"	0.000123	"eunorth"	"Microsoft.Stor	"func2"	"/subscrip	"{"CostCenter":"1234"}"
8/26/2018	"Storage"	"6c76daf0	"Tables"	"RA-GRS Data Storec		"1 GB/Mo	0.000192	"eunorth"	"Microsoft.Stor	"func2"	"/subscrip	"{"CostCenter":"1234"}"
8/26/2018	"Storage"	"3f2b1e1c	"Tables"	"LRS Data Stored"		"1 GB/Mo	0.000072	"eunorth"	"Microsoft.Stor	"cloud-shell-storage	"/subscrip	"{"ms-resource-usage":"az

FIGURE 1-14 AZURE DETAILED USAGE CSV

> ***NOTE*** **TAGS AND USAGE REPORTS**
>
> **Tags must be applied at the resource scope to be visible in detailed usage exports. Tags applied at the resource group scope are not inherited by child resources. This means that as you are applying tags to your resources in Azure, you should think about applying tags to each individual resource to have the clearest line of sight into your usage based on your organizational tags.**

When planning for resource tags, any taxonomy should include a strategy for both on-demand (or self-service) tagging, as well as automatic tagging through Azure policy. In this section you will learn how to create tags and apply them to resources manually, while in Skill 1.3 you will learn how to automatically apply tags.

As you plan your tagging taxonomy, be mindful of the limitations of tags in Azure as detailed in Table 1-3.

TABLE 1-3 Azure Tag Limits

TaG LIMIT	Notes
Resource support	■ Not all resource types support tags. This means that you will not be able to apply tags to everything in Azure.
Number of tags	■ A resource or resource group is limited to 15 tags. Each resource can have different tags.
Tag name	■ Tag names cannot exceed 512 characters. For storage accounts, tag names are limited to 128 characters.
Tag value	■ Tag values cannot exceed 256 characters.
Virtual machine tags	■ VMs cannot exceed 2048 characters for all tag names and values combined.
Tag inheritance	■ Tags are not inherited by child resources. Tags applied to a resource group are not applied to resources in that resource group.
Classic resources	■ Tags cannot be applied to classic resources and are only available for resources created in the Resource Manager model.
Illegal characters	■ Tag names cannot contain the following characters: <, >, %, &, \, ?, /

To apply tags to a resource group or a resource, the user applying the tag must have *write* access to the resource (Contributor role or higher access).

Tags can be created and applied to Azure resources through:

- The Azure Portal
- Azure PowerShell
- The Azure CLI
- Resource Manager templates
- Resource Manager REST APIs

This means tags can be applied both in an imperative manner and declaratively through Resource Manager templates. When working with tags, especially for creation, it is often the case that many tags need to be created and applied at the same time. While this can be done through the Azure Portal, often at the time of resource creation, it is better suited to use PowerShell, the CLI, or Resource Manager templates.

Tags can be applied at the resource group and/or the resource level. Note again that there is no inheritance for tags. If you need a tag to be applied to all resources in a resource group, each resource must be tagged individually.

To apply a tag to a resource group with no existing tags with PowerShell, you can use the Set-AzResourceGroup cmdlet.

```
Set-AzResourceGroup -Name hrgroup -Tag @{ CostCode=1001; Environment=Production }
```

When applying tags to a resource group with existing tags, you can retrieve the Tags collection from the existing resource group and use the .Add() method to append a new tag.

```
$tags = (Get-AzResourceGroup -Name hrgroup).Tags
$tags.Add("Owner", "user@contoso.com")
Set-AzResourceGroup -Tag $tags -Name hrgroup
```

Working with resources in a resource group is similar. To tag a resource with no existing tags you can use the Set-AzResource cmdlet.

```
$r = Get-AzResource -ResourceName hrvm1 -ResourceGroupName hrgroup
Set-AzResource -Tag @{ CostCode="1001"; Environment="Production" } -ResourceId
$r.ResourceId -Force
```

To add tags to a resource with existing tags you can retrieve the existing tags and add to the Tags collection using the .Add() method.

```
$r = Get-AzResource -ResourceName hrvm1 -ResourceGroupName hrgroup
$r.Tags.Add("Owner", "user@contoso.com")
Set-AzResource -Tag $r.Tags -ResourceId $r.ResourceId -Force
```

To remove tags from an existing resource, pass an empty hash table to the -Tag switch with the Set-AzResourceGroup or Set-AzResource cmdlets.

```
Set-AzResourceGroup -Tag @{} -Name hrgroup
```

Once tags have been applied, you can query for resource groups and resources by tag. To retrieve all the resource groups with a specific tag, you can use the `Get-AzResourceGroup` cmdlet with the `-Tag` switch.

```
(Get-AzResourceGroup -Tag @{ Owner="user@contoso.com" }).ResourceGroupName
```

To retrieve resources with a specific tag, use:

```
(Get-AzResource -Tag @{ Owner="user@constoso.com"}).Name
```

You can also retrieve resources based on a tag name, and not a specific tag value. For example, to find all the resources with the tag *CostCode* applied, use:

```
(Get-AzResource -TagName CostCode).Name
```

Configure Azure subscription policies

Azure Policy is an Azure service that can be used to create, assign, and manage policies that enforce governance in your Azure environment. This includes the application of rules that allow or deny a given resource type, apply tags automatically, and even enforce data sovereignty. Where Azure RBAC controls individual user, group access, and rights to your Azure environments at a specific scope, Azure policy provides a mechanism to express how the environment is governed for all users at a specified scope regardless of any RBAC assignments. Another way to state this is that Azure RBAC is a default deny mechanism with explicit allow, whereas policy is a default allow with an explicit deny system.

To implement policy, a policy definition must first be authored. That policy definition is then assigned a specific scope using a policy assignment. Recall that scope refers to what your RBAC or Policy is assigned to with valid scopes including a management group, a subscription, a resource group, or a resource.

Policy definitions can also be packaged together using initiative definitions and applied to a scope using initiative assignments. Policy and initiative definitions both support parameter sets, which help simplify the re-use of policy at multiple scopes.

A policy definition describes your desired behavior for Azure resources at the time resources are created or updated. Through a policy definition, you declare what resources and resource features are considered compliant within your Azure environment and what should happen when a resource is non-compliant. For example, you can create a policy that states that resources can only be created in the East US and West US regions for an entire subscription. If a user attempts to create a resource in East US, Azure policy can deny the creation of the resource, because it does not meet the stated compliance goal for allowed regions. In this example, policy is used to deny the creation of a resource and enforce organizational standards. As we further explore policy, you will learn that policy can be used as not just a deny mechanism, but also an auditing and creation mechanism.

Policy definitions are authored in JSON. The schema for Azure Policy can be downloaded from: *https://schema.management.azure.com/schemas/2018-05-01/policyDefinition.json*. A policy definition contains elements for:

- mode
- parameters
- display name
- description
- policy rule
    - logical evaluation
    - effect

> **NOTE POLICY DEFNITION**
>
> While you do not need to memorize the schema, it is worthwhile to understand the elements of a policy definition and how to build your own policies from a blank template when necessary. Microsoft offers a number of built-in policy definitions and maintains a repository of samples at *https://docs.microsoft.com /azure/governance/policy/samples/* and *https://github.com/Azure/azure-policy*.

Policy definitions can be created through the Azure Portal by browsing to the Policy service at **All Services**, then **Policy**, and **Definitions**. From this blade you can manage both built-in policies and any custom policies that you create. Figure 1-15 shows an example of the Definitions blade.

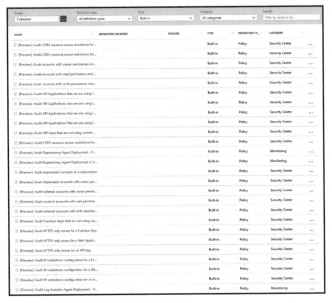

FIGURE 1-15 Azure Built-in Policies

For the remainder of this section, we will examine a basic policy that limits the creation of virtual machines to only a pre-determined list of virtual machine SKUs. Such a policy could be combined with a location policy to enforce data storage compliance based on geography (*e.g.* restrict the creation of resources such as storage accounts to only certain regions) and can be used as a cost control measure (*e.g.* restrict the creation of virtual machines to known sizes to prevent the creation of machines that are not needed or cost too much).

Note that the list of virtual machine SKUs is a parameter to the policy, allowing it to be dynamic in nature. For example, you may use virtual machines that are one set of sizes in one subscription (*e.g.* Production) and smaller machines in downstream environments (*e.g.* Dev/Test). With a single policy definition leveraging parameters, that list of allowed SKUs can be applied via the policy assignment. The use of parameters in policy reduces redundancy and simplifies policy management by allowing policy definitions to be re-used at multiple scopes.

```
{
    "mode": "all",
    "policyRule": {
        "if": {
            "allOf": [
                {
                    "field": "type",
                    "equals": "Microsoft.Compute/virtualMachines"
                },
                {
                    "not": {
                        "field": "Microsoft.Compute/virtualMachines/sku.name",
                        "in": "[parameters('listOfAllowedSKUs')]"
                    }
                }
            ]
        },
        "then": {
            "effect": "deny"
        }
    },
    "parameters": {
        "listOfAllowedSKUs": {
            "type": "array",
            "metadata": {
                "displayName": "Allowed VM SKUs",
                "description": "The list of allowed SKUs for virtual machines.",
                "strongType": "vmSKUs"
            }
        }
    }
}
```

The *mode* of this policy is set to *all*. The mode of a policy determines which resources are evaluated by the policy. A value of *all* evaluates both resource groups and all resource types while a value of *indexed* only evaluates resource types that support tags and location. If you are creating policies through the Azure Portal, they will default to *all* but can be changed to *indexed* later. The mode *indexed* is used when you are creating policies that enforce tags or locations. This is used for controlling which resources appear in any compliance reports. Recall that not all resources support tags, so you would not want a resource appearing on a compliance report as non-compliant if you do not actually have any control over the resource functionality. The same is true for location support. There are resources in Azure that are considered global and are not bound to a single region or geography.

Next is the *policyRule*. This is the heart of a policy definition–effectively "if this, then that" blocks. The "if" block defines one or more conditions with logical operators available for when more than one condition is required. The "then" block defines the effect if the conditions are fulfilled.

```
{
    "if": {
        <condition> | <logical operator>
    },
    "then": {
        "effect": "deny | audit | append | auditIfNotExists | deployIfNotExists |
 disabled"
    }
}
```

Supported logical operators are:

- "not": {condition or operator}
- "allOf": [{condition or operator},{condition or operator}]
- "anyOf": [{condition or operator},{condition or operator}]

A condition evaluates whether a field meets certain criteria. The supported conditions are:

- "equals": "value"
- "notEquals": "value"
- "like": "value"
- "notLike": "value"
- "match": "value"
- "notMatch": "value"
- "contains": "value"
- "notContains": "value"
- "in": ["value1","value2"]
- "notIn": ["value1","value2"]
- "containsKey": "keyName"
- "notContainsKey": "keyName"
- "exists": "bool"

You can nest multiple logical operators as well. For example, you could create a policy rule above to only allow the creation of virtual machines from a known set of images in an existing resource group.

```
"if": {
   "allOf": [
      {
         "field": "type",
         "equals": "Microsoft.Compute/virtualMachines"
      },
      {
         "not": {
            "field": "Microsoft.Compute/imageId",
            "contains": "[concat('resourceGroups/',parameters('resourceGroupName'))]"
         }
      }
   ]
},
"then": {
   "effect": "deny"
}
```

Conditions use fields to evaluate the type of resource in the request and the state of that resource. For example, the field *type* used in the preceding examples represents the type of resource being created based on the resource provider it belongs to. There are a number of fields that are supported in policy, including the resource name, the location of the resource, and the tags associated with a resource. These fields are used in combination with logical operators to define the logic for your policy.

> **NOTE SUPPORTED FIELDS**
>
> **The full list of supported fields can be found at:**
> *https://docs.microsoft.com/azure/governance/policy/concepts/definition-structure#fields.*

When conditions are fulfilled, effects are evaluated. Policy supports the following types of effect:

- **Deny** Generates an event in the activity log and fails the request
- **Audit** Generates a warning event in activity log but doesn't fail the request
- **Append** Adds the defined set of fields to the request
- **AuditIfNotExists** Enables auditing if a resource doesn't exist
- **DeployIfNotExists** Deploys a resource if it doesn't already exist
- **Disabled** Doesn't evaluate resources for compliance to the policy rule

In the example policy, a parameter is used to represent the list of allowed virtual machine SKUs ("[parameters('listOfAllowedSKUs')]").

Parameters make policy definitions reusable, which reduces the number of definitions that need to be managed. Parameter properties provide a single parameter's definition and a policy definition can have multiple parameters. An example parameter is provided:

```
"parameters": {
   "listOfAllowedSKUs": {
      "type": "array",
```

```
            "metadata": {
                "displayName": "Allowed VM SKUs",
                "description": "The list of allowed SKUs for virtual machines.",
                "strongType": "vmSKUs"
            },
            "defaultValue": "Standard_D2s_v3",
            "allowedValues": [
                "Standard_D2s_v3",
                "Standard_F2s_v2"
            ]
        }
    }
}
```

Parameters in a template are in the parameters property of a policy definition and each parameter is defined by a set of sub-properties that begins with a name (in the example above, listOfAllowedSKUs). The type property defines the if the parameter is a string or an array. For parameter validation, the sub-properties defaultValue and allowedValues are available. The metadata property is used by the Azure Portal display user-friendly information for parameters and has sub-properties where a displayName, description, and optional strongType can be defined. When strongType is defined, a multi-select list or options is generated with the Azure Portal when assigning the policy and the types are enforced when creating policies with PowerShell or the Azure CLI. In the example policy, the vmSKUs strongType has been defined which means when the policy is assigned in the Azure Portal a dynamically generated list of current virtual machine SKUs will be provided to select from.

The allowed values for strongType are:

- location
- resourceTypes
- storageSkus
- vmSKUs
- existingResourceGroups
- omsWorkspace

After a policy has been authored, you will need to determine where the policy will be stored (or located). Policy definitions can be located in a subscription or a Management Group, but not both. The location of the definition determines the scopes at which the policy can be assigned. If a definition is located in a subscription, only resources within that subscription can be assigned the policy. If the definition is in a Management Group, only resources within child management groups and child subscriptions can be assigned the policy. To re-use a policy across multiple subscriptions without duplicating the policy definition, the location must be a Management Group that contains the target subscriptions.

With the structure of a policy defined, you can then apply that policy through a policy assignment at a given scope. In this example, we'll use the Azure CLI to create a new policy, and then assign that policy to a subscription through a policy assignment.

Prior to creating a policy, make sure the Microsoft.PolicyInsights resource provider is registered in the target subscription. To register the provider, you can use the az provider register command.

```
az provider register --namespace 'Microsoft.PolicyInsights'
```

After the provider has been registered, the az policy definition create command can be used to create a policy.

```
az policy definition create --name 'allowedVMs' --description 'Only allow virtual
 machines in the defined SKUs' --mode All \
    --rules '{ \
      "if": { \
        "allOf": [ \
          { \
                    "field": "type", \
                    "equals": "Microsoft.Compute/virtualMachines" \
          }, \
          { \
            "not": { \
              "field": "Microsoft.Compute/virtualMachines/sku.name", \
              "in": "[parameters('"'"'listOfAllowedSKUs'"'"')]" \
            } \
          } \
        ] \
      }, \
      "then": { \
        "effect": "deny" \
      } \
    }' \
  --params '{ \
    "listOfAllowedSKUs": { \
      "type": "array", \
      "metadata": { \
        "displayName": "Allowed VM SKUs", \
        "description": "The list of allowed SKUs for virtual machines.", \
        "strongType": "vmSKUs" \
      } \
    } \
  }'
```

With the policy created, it can be applied to a scope through the az policy assignment create command. In this example, take the previously created policy definition and assign it to a subscription. Note that the -p parameter allows you to pass in parameters that are required by a policy definition. In this example, you will assign a policy that only allows two SKUs of virtual machines to be created in the target subscription.

```
az policy assignment create --policy allowedVMs --name 'deny-non-compliant-vms' --scope
 '/subscriptions/<Subscription ID>' -p '{ \
        "listOfAllowedSKUs": { \
          "value": [ \
            "Standard_D2s_v3", \
            "Standard_F2s_v2" \
```

```
            ] \
        } \
    }'
```

To delete the policy assignment, use az policy assignment delete.

```
az policy assignment delete --name deny-non-compliant-vms
```

Another common use case for Azure Policy is to apply default tags to the resources that are created in your Azure subscriptions. This means you can use Azure Policy to apply governance and ensure environmental compliance for resource metadata without user interaction. As previously stated, policy can be used to control what resources can be created and how those resources are modeled regardless of the user requesting the resource and their rights within the environment (see Figure 1-16).

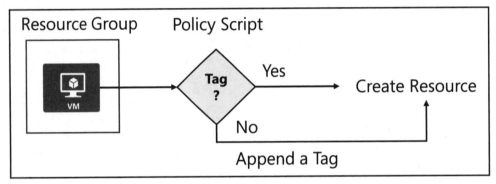

FIGURE 1-16 Policy flow chart

The logic for applying a default tag (or appending a tag) is shown in Figure 1-16. To create a policy to apply default tags, begin with the rules of the policy. To allow for flexibility in policy assignment, use parameters as needed. Note that in this example, the "effect" of the policy is an "append" action. This allows for the desired tag to be appended only when one has not been supplied at the time the resource is created. The following sample rules can be used with Azure PowerShell or the Azure CLI when automating policy creation.

To apply this policy with PowerShell, create a new file called AppendDefaultTag.json with the following content:

```
{
  "if": {
    "field": "[concat('tags[', parameters('tagName'), ']')]",
    "exists": "false"
  },
  "then": {
    "effect": "append",
    "details": [
      {
        "field": "[concat('tags[', parameters('tagName'), ']')]",
        "value": "[parameters('tagValue')]"
```

```
        }
      ]
    }
  }
}
```

The following is the JSON that defines the policy parameters used by Azure PowerShell and the CLI. Save the contents in a file called AppendDefaultTagParams.json.

```
{
    "tagName": {
        "type": "String",
        "metadata": {
            "description": "Name of the tag, such as Environment"
        }
    },
    "tagValue": {
        "type": "String",
        "metadata": {
            "description": "Value of the tag, such as Production"
        }
    }
}
```

To create add the new definition, use the New-AzPolicyDefinition cmdlet and make a policy assignment with New-AzPolicyAssignment. Note the use of the scope parameter. In this example, the scope is all resources in the subscription. The parameters for the assignment are passed in to the assignment definition using the -PolicyParameter parameter.

```
$definition = New-AzPolicyDefinition -Name 'appendEnvironmentTag' -DisplayName
'Append Environment Tag' -Policy 'AppendDefaultTag.json'
-Parameter 'AppendDefaultTagParams.json'

$scope = '/subscriptions/<Subscription ID>'

$policyparam = '{ "tagName": { "value": "Environment" }, "tagValue": { "value":
 "Production" } }'

$assignment = New-AzPolicyAssignment -Name 'append-environment-tag' -DisplayName
'Append Environment Tag' -Scope $scope -PolicyDefinition $definition
-PolicyParameter $policyparam
```

To remove the policy assignment and the definition, you can use the Remove-AzPolicyAssignment and Remove-AzPolicyDefinition cmdlets.

```
Remove-AzPolicyAssignment -Id $assignment.ResourceId
Remove-AzPolicyDefinition -Id $definition.ResourceId
```

Keep in mind that Policy can also be managed and applied at the Management Group scope. By associating policies with Management Groups, policy definitions and policy assignments can be shared across multiple subscriptions. This includes the ability to monitor multiple subscriptions for compliance when using the Standard tier of Azure Policy. It also allows you to secure the management of organization wide policy at a level above a single subscription.

Skill 1.2: Analyze resource utilization and consumption

As you being to deploy services into your Azure subscriptions, how the environment will be monitored is one of the first questions you will need to answer and to answer it you must think about all of the services in your deployment. You will most likely have a number of services deployed, including Infrastructure-as-a-Service services, such as virtual machines, which include compute, storage, and networking. And even without services deployed today, over time you may have Platform-as-a-Service services for hosting applications. You will also be using the services that drive your virtual machines in more meaningful ways, such as implementing advanced configurations in Azure storage and Azure identity.

You will need to account for all these services, along with the Azure platform itself in your monitoring strategy. This includes all of your infrastructure, applications, and networking.

By developing a proactive monitoring strategy, you will be able to understand the operation of your environment at a component level, including resource health, and resource spend. Implementing a robust strategy will help you increase your uptime through proactive notifications, so you can resolve issues before they become problems, and optimize your resources for optimal performance, allowing you to increase your ROI with the services you deploy.

As you develop your strategy, there are three areas you should consider:

- **Visibility into services and the Azure Platform**   This is all about understanding how an application or set of services is performing across the board. You will need to understand what metrics you need to monitor, and how those can be acted on in Azure through both alerts and visualizations in dashboards.
- **Deeper insights into applications**   This is particularly with service or dependency maps and advanced tracing. You may even use these insights to drive automation and remediations within your environments.
- **Resource optimization**   You need to understand which metrics are important to not just the health of your application, but also the impact to users or systems that consume those application. By using the visibility and insights you extract from the Azure platform, you can directly correlate the impact of remediations in your environment.

Azure includes multiple services that perform specific roles for monitoring and optimization. It is critical that you understand both the out-of-the-box monitoring capabilities of Azure and the scenario-specific monitoring capabilities within the platform. This section will focus on out-of-the-box monitoring and optimization through both Azure Monitor and Azure Advisor, as well as scenario-specific monitoring with Azure Monitor logs and log data that is stored in Log Analytics).

Azure Monitor helps you track performance, maintain security, and identify trends, by ingesting metrics and telemetry from multiple areas, including applications and the operating systems of virtual machines. It also allows you to query your Azure resources which emit performance counters, your Azure subscriptions, Azure AD tenant, and event custom sources.

The data from your Azure resources is ingested into either metrics stored within the Azure platform and accessible by the monitor service, or as logs into Log Analytics.

There is a difference between metric and logs. Metrics are always numerical values while logs are numerical or textual values that describe a resource at a point in time. Logs can be strongly typed (for example, a string or a datetime). Metrics are continuously collected provide near real-time access to performance data while logs can vary widely in the amount of time it takes for them to be collected and make available for query.

Once the data is collected, Azure Monitor provides a single pane of glass, or entry point, to interacting with your metrics and logs. Interactions can include querying and alerting, building visualizations and dashboards, or even automated responses based on telemetry for functionality like autoscaling in virtual machines. Querying data that is stored in a Log Analytics workspace through Azure Monitor is referred to as Azure Monitor logs.

Data stored in Log Analytics can also be queried directly through a Log Analytics workspace where you will have access to the same query interfaces as you have through Azure Monitor, but also the ability to make customizations to the configuration of the workspace and access workspace-specific solutions, including visualizations and queries.

All of the data that you can access through Azure Monitor can be used to create alerts within Azure Monitor with alert rules. Alert rules are built based on target resources or resource types such as virtual machines, storage account, and even PaaS services and your custom conditions. Alerts allow to be proactively notified of the health of the resources you deploy in Azure and you are not limited to notifications – alert rules leverage actions groups that allow you to even implement automation based on an alert condition.

Azure Advisor is a free, personalized guide to Azure best practices. It provides recommendations to help you optimize resources for high availability, security, performance, and cost. You can implement these recommendations easily right in the tool, and they're personalized based on the Azure workloads and configurations deployed within your subscriptions. The optimizations are available at no additional cost, although some recommendations do have cost implications. Figure 1-17 shows an example of the Azure Advisor primary dashboard.

FIGURE 1-17 Azure Advisor recommendations

This section covers how to:

- Configure diagnostic settings on resources
- Create and test alerts
- Create action groups
- Analyze alerts across subscriptions
- Analyze metrics across subscriptions
- Monitor for unused resources
- Utilize log search query functions
- View alerts in Log Analytics
- Monitor spend
- Report spend

Configure diagnostic settings on resources

While the resources you deploy in Azure create metrics automatically, many of them also offer richer diagnostics logs which can be configured to send their log data to another location such as a Storage Account or a Log Analytics workspace. In addition to resource logs, there are also tenant-level services such as Azure Active Directory which exist outside of a subscription from which you may need to collect log data.

Diagnostics logs are one type of log data. There is also log data within the Azure Activity log and there is log data that can be obtained from virtual machines with the use of diagnostics agents that is separate from diagnostic logs associated with a tenant-level service or an Azure resource. It is important to understand the differences between the types of log data that are available and where that log data can be stored.

> **IMPORTANT** **RESOURCE AND TENANT LOGS ARE DIAGNOSTIC LOGS**
>
> Both resource logs and tenant logs are considered diagnostics logs. Diagnostics logs that you configure for a tenant service or a resource are separate from the Azure Activity log and guest telemetry obtained with diagnostics agents.

The Azure Activity log surfaces data at the subscription level and can be useful for understanding actions that occur within your environment against the Resource Manager APIs. For example, when a new deployment is submitted, the events associated with that deployment such as the time it was submitted, the resources that were created, and the user that submitted the request are all tracked within the Activity Log. However, at the subscription level, you are missing any resource-level logs. For example, the Activity log can show when a Network Security Group (or NSG) was created, but it cannot show when an NSG rule was applied to traffic that was subject to the NSG such as when a port or protocol is blocked. Diagnostic logs are the feature that provide this functionality.

> **NOTE RETAINED FOR 90 DAYS**
>
> Events in the Activity Log are retained for 90 days. You can retain the data for a longer period by enabling archival and sending the logs to Azure storage and / or a Log Analytics workspace.

Diagnostic logs will need to be enabled for each resource that you wish to collect additional telemetry from. Note that metrics are resource-specific and captured automatically so you only need to enable diagnostic logs to capture log data or to send metrics to another service.

> **IMPORTANT SUPPORT FOR)DIAGNOSTIC LOGS**
>
> Not all Azure resource types support diagnostic logs. A full list of services that support logs and their service-specific log schemas can be found at:
> *https://docs.microsoft.com/azure/monitoring-and-diagnostics/monitoring-diagnostic-logs-schema*.

To enable diagnostic logs through the Azure Portal, you can browse to the resource itself to create the settings. The alternative and recommended method is to browse to the **Azure Monitor** and **Diagnostic Settings** blade. From this blade, you can view all the resource types eligible for diagnostic logs and view the status (Enabled or Disabled) for log collection on each resource. You also have options from this blade to filter by Subscription, Resource Group, Resource Type, and Resource. An example is shown in Figure 1-18.

FIGURE 1-18 Azure Monitor Diagnostic settings

To enable diagnostic settings, click on a resource with a status of Disabled. In the blade that opens, you will see a link to **Turn On Diagnostics** (see Figure 1-19).

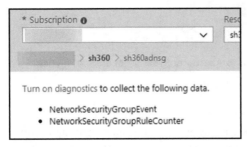

FIGURE 1-19 Azure Monitor Diagnostic settings for a resource

Click the link to open the configuration blade. Configure the settings as required and provide a Name for the setting. Click Save to persist the configuration. Note that retention can be configured independently for each log and the retention rule only applies to logs in storage as shown in Figure 1-20.

FIGURE 1-20 Azure Monitor Diagnostic settings configuration for a resource

> **NOTE DIAGNOSTIC LOGS**
>
> Each resource or tenant service that you enable diagnostic logs for will have varying controls (or settings). For example, not all resources support a retention policy in the diagnostic settings and not all resources support sending metric data to another location.

When configuration diagnostics settings, you will select where the logs (and optionally metrics) are sent. Valid locations to send data will be to Archive To A Storage Account, Stream To An Event Hub, or Send To Log Analytics. As you select each location, additional configuration will be required. For example, to Archive To A Storage Account, you will need to select an existing storage account or create a new storage account.

For diagnostics logs that support retention with storage, you will be able to select a retention period in days. A retention period of zero days means the logs will be retained forever. Valid numeric values for the number of days is any number between 1 and 2147483647. If you set the retention period and have only selected an Event Hub or a Log Analytics workspace but have not selected a storage account, the retention settings will be ignored.

As you configure each resource or service, you can send the data from multiple log sources to the same destination. For example, you can send the diagnostic logs from a tenant service like Azure Active Directory to a Log Analytics workspace and you can send the diagnostics logs from a resource like a Network Security Group to the same Log Analytics workspace.

It may take several moments for the setting to appear in the list of settings for the resource. Note that even though the setting has been configured, diagnostic data will not be collected until a new event is generated.

All of these settings can be configured through the Azure Portal, Azure PowerShell, the Azure CLI, or through the Azure Monitor REST API.

To enable collection of diagnostic logs with Azure PowerShell, use the `Set-AzDiagnostic-Setting` cmdlet. To use this cmdlet, you will need to know the resource ID of the resource you are enabling. You can find the resource ID with the `Get-AzResource` cmdlet. When sending diagnostics to storage, the `-StorageAccountId` parameter is used. This value will be the resource ID of the destination storage account which can also be found with `Get-AzResource`.

In the following example, diagnostic settings will be enabled for a Network Security Group and sent to Azure storage. Examples have also been provided for enabling streaming to an Event Hub and a Log Analytics workspace.

```
$resource = Get-AzResource -Name [resource name] -ResourceGroupName [resource group
  name]
$storage = Get-AzResource -Name [resource name] -ResourceGroupName [resource group name]
Set-AzDiagnosticSetting -ResourceId $resource.ResourceId -StorageAccountId
  $storage.ResourceId -Enabled $true
```

To enable streaming of diagnostic logs to an Event Hub:

```
$rule = Get-AzServiceBusRule -ResourceGroup [resource group name] -Namespace [namespace]
  -Topic [topic] -Subscription [subscription] -Name [rule name]
Set-AzureRmDiagnosticSetting -ResourceId $resource.ResourceId -ServiceBusRuleId
$rule.Id -Enabled $true
```

To enable streaming of diagnostic logs to a Log Analytics workspace:

```
$workspace = Get-AzOperationalInsightsWorkspace -Name [workspace name]
|-ResourceGroupName [resource group name]
Set-AzureRmDiagnosticSetting -ResourceId $resource.ResourceId -WorkspaceId
  $workspace.ResourceId -Enabled $true
```

The parameters for `-StorageAccountId`, `-ServiceBusRuleId`, and `-WorkspaceId` can be combined to enable any combination of the three.

When enabling diagnostic logs with the Azure CLI, you will use the `az monitor diagnostic-settings create` command. To obtain the Resource ID you can use the `az resource show` command and capture the resource identifier in a variable that you can use in your script. For example:

```
resourceId=$(az resource show –resource-group [resource group name] –name [resource name] --resource-type [resource type] --query id --output tsv)
```

> **NOTE RESOURCE TYPES**
>
> Note the use of the `resource-type` parameter in this command. You will need to know the Resource Provider and type of resource you are querying. You can query all your resources first with the `az resource list` command to find the resource type for your specific resource.

To enable collection with a storage account, implement the following:

```
  az monitor diagnostic-settings create --name <diagnostic name> \
 --storage-account <name or ID of storage account> \
 --resource <target resource object ID> \
 --resource-group <storage account resource group> \
 --logs '[
 {
     "category": "<category name>",
     "enabled": true,
     "retentionPolicy": {
         "days": "<# days to retain>",
         "enabled": true
     }
 }]'
```

To enable streaming to an Event Hub:

```
  az monitor diagnostic-settings create --name <diagnostic name> \
 --event-hub <event hub name> \
 --event-hub-rule <event hub rule ID> \
 --resource <target resource object ID> \
 --logs '[
 {
     "category": "<category name>",
     "enabled": true
 }
 ]'
```

To enable collection of diagnostic logs in a Log Analytics workspace:

```
  az monitor diagnostic-settings create --name <diagnostic name> \
 --workspace <log analytics name or object ID> \
 --resource <target resource object ID> \
 --resource-group <log analytics workspace resource group> \
 --logs '[
 {
     "category": "<category name>",
     "enabled": true
 }
 ]'
```

You can combine the `storage-account`, `event-hub`, and `workspace` parameters to enable multiple output options.

Tenant-level logs are enabled in each tenant service and cannot be configured from Azure Monitor. The configuration for each tenant service varies and you should refer to the service-specific documentation for detailed configuration instructions.

After you have captured the diagnostic logs, you will need to work with the data that is sent to your selected location. Each resource outputs different logs in varying formats based on the selected outputs, including the selection of categories.

> **NOTE SERVICE AND CATEGORY DIAGNOSTIC SCHEMAS**
>
> Service and category-specific diagnostic schemas can be found at:
> *https://docs.microsoft.com/azure/azure-monitor/platform/diagnostic-logs-schema#service-specific-schemas-for-resource-diagnostic-logs.*

Create and test alerts

Alerts proactively notify you when important conditions are found in your monitoring data. They allow you to identify and address issues before the users of your system notice them.

Azure Monitor brings a unified alerting experience to Azure, with a single pane of glass for interacting with metrics, the Activity Log, Log Analytics, service and resource health and service-specific insights that provide out-of-the-box dashboards with visualizations and queries for:

- Custom applications with Application Insights
- Virtual Machines (preview)
- Containers
- Networking
- Log Analytics monitoring solutions

> **EXAM TIP**
>
> Microsoft is adding new services and operational insights consistently. The current list of services can be found at: *https://docs.microsoft.com/ azure/azure-monitor/overview#insights.*

Alerts have multiple notification options, including:

- Email
- SMS
- Push notifications to the Azure mobile app
- Voice
- Integration with automation services.

Alerts that are generated within Azure Monitor alerts can invoke Azure Automation runbooks, Logic Apps, Azure Functions, and even generate incidents in third-party IT Service Management tools such as ServiceNow.

Alerts in Azure Monitor are centered around alert rules. Alert rules contain the following components:

- A target resource (or resource type)
- A signal emitted by the target
- Conditional logic for the alert with criteria based on the available signals for the target resource
- An action group, or what should happen when the alert rule condition is met
- A name and description for the alert rule
- A severity ranging from 0 to 4

> **NOTE AZURE MONITOR ALERT RULES**
>
> Alert rules in Azure Monitor are not the same as alerts. They are the criteria used to evaluate when an alert should be generated. An alert is generated based on the rule and then the alerts themselves are acted upon separately, even maintaining their own state (such as New or Closed).

An example of an alert rule being created is show in Figure 1-21 where you can see these components. In this example, an alert rule is being created to generate an alert for a target resource that is a virtual machine. The conditional logic for the alert is using a metric signal provided by the Azure platform called Percentage CPU.

FIGURE 1-21 Azure Monitor Create Alert Rule

The target resource defines the scope and signals available for the alert. A target resource is an Azure resource that generates signals (*e.g.* metrics or the Activity Log) such as a virtual machine or storage account. The signal types that are available for monitoring vary based on the selected target (or targets as you can select more than one target) and the available signal types are:

- Metrics
- Log search queries
- Activity logs

As you select your target resource, you will be able to view the signals that will be available for your conditional logic. In Figure 1-22, an example is provided where a virtual machine has been selected. Note that both Metric and Activity Log signals are available for this resource type.

FIGURE 1-22 Azure Monitor Target Selection

Target resources can also include a Log Analytics workspace or an Application Insights resource. Some resource types allow you to specify multiple resources as the target for an alert rule. For example, when you are configuring your target resource logic, you could construct an alert rule that will evaluate all the resources in all of the resource groups in a subscription, re-gardless of the resource type This would limit your condition logic to signals from the Activity Log but would allow you to create an alert across all of the resources in the subscription.

The condition, or criteria for an alert rule combine the signal and a logical test to the target resource(s). For example, if you had a critical service running a on virtual machine and wanted to be alerted when that virtual machine is stopped or restarted, you could use the *Restart Virtual Machine (virtualMachines)* signal from the *Administrative* category in the monitor service as your logic as shown in Figure 1-23.

Configure signal logic

Choose a signal below and configure the logic on the next screen to define the alert condition.

All signals (75)

Signal type ❶ | Monitor service ❶
Activity Log ⌄ | All ⌄

🔍 Restart

SIGNAL NAME	SIGNAL TYPE	MONITOR SERVICE
Restart Virtual Machine (virtualMachines)	Activity Log	Administrative
Restart Virtual Machine (virtualMachines)	Activity Log	Security
Restart Virtual Machine (virtualMachines)	Activity Log	Recommendation
Restart Virtual Machine (virtualMachines)	Activity Log	Policy
Restart Virtual Machine (virtualMachines)	Activity Log	Autoscale

FIGURE 1-23 Azure Monitor Condition Logic

Alert rules also have an alert name, an alert description, a severity ranging from 0 to 4, and define the action that is taken when the alert fires through one or more Action Groups that are associated with the alert rule.

An Action Group provides the definition for what will happen when the conditional logic of the alert rule is met by grouping together one or more actions. Each action group is an Azure resource itself (meaning it is located in an Azure subscription and a resource group) and has a:

- **Name**   This is the name of the Action Group resource in the Resource Group. Action Group names must be unique within a Resource Group.

- **Short name**   The short name is used to identify the Action Group in emails and SMS messages and is limited to 12 characters.

- **Actions**   Actions define the configuration for a specific action type.

Each action has a type with each type having a specific configuration. For example, using the type Email/SMS/Push/Voice means that generated alerts can be sent to any (or all) of those endpoints.

Available action types include:

- Email/SMS/Push/Voice
- Azure Function
- Logic App
- Webhook
- ITSM
- Automation Runbook

> **NOTE ACTION GROUPS**
> Action groups are separate resources and are independent of the alert rule. This means that the same action group can be used across multiple alert rules.

To create an alert rule, browse to Azure Monitor in the Azure Portal, select the **Alerts** blade and select **+New Alert Rule** as shown in Figure 1-24.

> **NOTE AZURE MONITOR SERVICES**
> The Azure Monitor service can be found in the list of services in the left-navigation of the Azure Portal. If you do not see Monitor in the default list of services, browse to All services and search for Monitor.

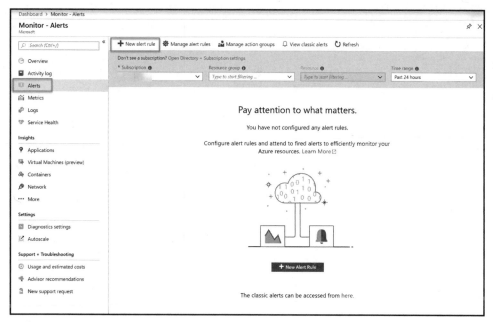

FIGURE 1-24 Azure Monitor Alerts

Pick the target for the alert, which determines the available signals by clicking the **Select** button as shown in Figure 1-25.

FIGURE 1-25 Azure Monitor Create alert rule

For instance, selecting Subscription will allow you to select Activity Log signals. Selecting a single resource like a virtual machine will allow you to select signals that include both the Activity Log and metrics as shown in Figure 1-26.

FIGURE 1-26 Azure Monitor alert target

Next, add a condition using the **Add condition** button as shown in Figure 1-27.

FIGURE 1-27 Azure Monitor Add condition

The condition will allow you to select the signal from the available signals for the target and define the logic test that will be applied to the data from the signal. For example, for a virtual machine you can use the Percentage CPU metric to generate an alert based on a custom threshold for CPU usage as shown in Figure 1-28. The alert logic conditions are different for Activity Log signals or metric signals.

Configure signal logic

Show history

Over the last 6 hours ⌄

```
100%

80% ━━━━━━━━━━━━━━━━━━━━━━━━━━━━━━━━━╱╲╱╲━━━ ■
60%
40%
20%
0% ┄┄┄┄┄┄┄┄┄┄┄┄┄┄┄┄┄┄┄┄┄┄┄┄┄┄┄┄┄┄┄
   4 am    5 am    6 am    7 am    8 am    9 am
```
Percentage CPU (Avg)
ExamRefVM1
71.8%

Alert logic

Condition ❶	* Time Aggregation	* Threshold ❶
Greater than ⌄	Average ⌄	75 ✓
		%

Condition preview

Whenever the percentage cpu is greater than 75 percent

Evaluated based on

Period (grain) ❶	Frequency ❶
Over the last 5 minutes ⌄	Every 1 Minute ⌄

Done

FIGURE 1-28 Azure Monitor alert condition

Configure one or more conditions for the alert rule. After the conditions are defined, proceed to Actions Groups and use the **Select existing** button if you have an existing action group you want to use or the **Create New** button to create a new action group as shown in Figure 1-29.

FIGURE 1-29 Azure Monitor Action Groups

When creating a new Action Group, define the Action Group Name, a Short Name, Subscription, and Resource Group the Action Group will be created in (Figure 1-30).

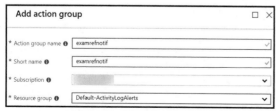

FIGURE 1-30 Azure Monitor new action group blade

The group's short name is included in Email and SMS notifications to identify which Action group was the source of the notification. If a user unsubscribes, they are unsubscribing from the specific Action Group identified by the Short Name. When an action is configured to notify a person by Email or SMS, the person will receive a confirmation indicating that he or she has been added to the action group as shown in Figure 1-31.

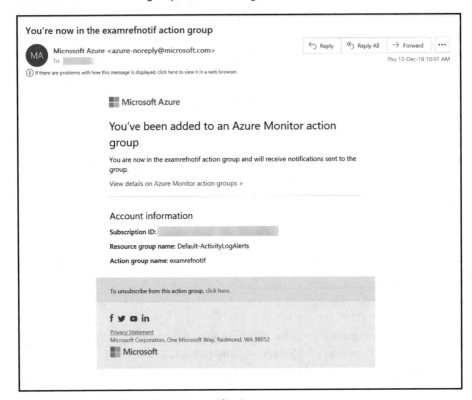

FIGURE 1-31 Azure Monitor action group notification

You can now define a list of actions for the action group. Each action has a name, an action type (Email/SMS/Push/Voice, Logic App, Webhook, ITSM, or Automation Runbook), and details (see Figure 1-32).

FIGURE 1-32 Azure Monitor new action group blade Email/SMS/Push/Voice configuration

Define one or more actions to complete the configuration of the action group. You can now specify the remaining alert details, including the Alert Rule Name, Alert Description, Severity, and whether the rule will be enabled upon creation as shown in Figure 1-33.

> **IMPORTANT ACTIVE ALERTS**
>
> When creating a new alert rule based on a metric signal, it can take up to 10 minutes for the alert rule to become active.

ALERT DETAILS

* Alert rule name ❶

Percentage CPU greater than 75 percent for ExamRefVM1

* Description

Percentage CPU greater than 75% for ExamRefVM1

* Severity ❶

Sev 1

Enable rule upon creation

Yes   No

ℹ It can take up to 10 minutes for a metric alert rule to become active.

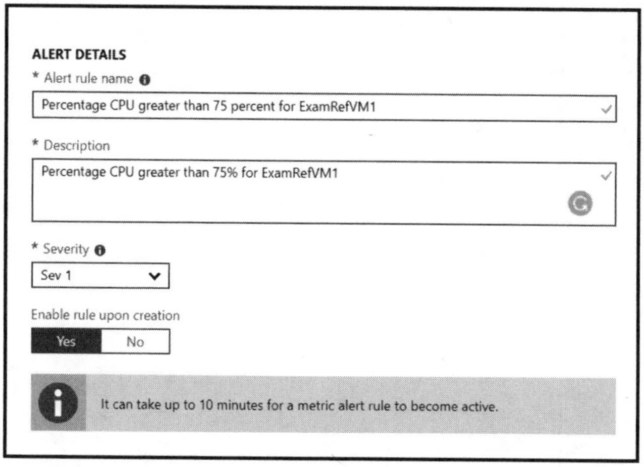

FIGURE 1-33 Azure Monitor new action alert rule details

After an alert rule has been created, the alert rule and action group can be managed through Azure Monitor from the Alerts blade by selecting **Manage Alert Rules**. Alerts can be managed across multiple subscriptions and can be filtered by Resource Group, Resource Type, Signal Type, and Status (see Figure 1-34).

FIGURE 1-34 Azure Monitor new action alert rule details

Recall that alert rules do not generate alerts immediately and can take up to 10 minutes in the case of metric alerts. When alerts are generated, they will be distributed based on the actions defined in the action group. For example, when an email is sent, the defined users will receive a message with the alert details and a link to view the alert in the Azure Portal as shown in Figure 1-35.

Microsoft Azure

⚠ Your Azure Monitor alert was triggered

Azure monitor alert rule Percentage CPU greater than 75 percent for ExamRefVM1 was triggered for ExamRefVM1 at December 13, 2018 15:20 UTC.

Rule description	Percentage CPU greater than 75% for ExamRefVM1
Rule ID	/subscriptions//r esourceGroups/ExamRefRG/providers/microsoft.insights/ metricAlerts/Percentage%20CPU%20greater%20than%20 75%20percent%20for%20ExamRefVM1 View Rule >
Resource ID	/subscriptions//r esourceGroups/ExamRefRG/providers/Microsoft.Compute /virtualMachines/ExamRefVM1 View Resource >

Alert Activated Because:

Metric name	Percentage CPU
Metric namespace	virtualMachines/ExamRefVM1
Dimensions	ResourceId = 5
Time Aggregation	Average
Period	Over the last 5 mins
Value	77.855
Operator	GreaterThan
Threshold	75
Criterion Type	StaticThresholdCriterion

FIGURE 1-35 Azure Monitor alert notification email

When an alert is resolved by the state of the monitor condition and changed to Resolved, notifications are sent as well. An example of a resolution email is shown in Figure 1-36.

FIGURE 1-36 Azure Monitor alert resolution email

Analyze alerts across subscriptions

When an alert rule is created, the alert rule targets resources in a single subscription and the alerts that are generated based on the alert rules are associated with the subscription they are generated from. Azure operators are not limited to viewing alerts from only a single subscription through Azure Monitor which again provides a single pane of glass for not only managing alert rules across multiple subscriptions, but also managing the generated alerts as well.

Recall that alert rules and action groups are separate entities. The alerts that are generated based on the conditional logic of an alert rule are separate entities as well. This means that they are managed independently of alert rules and maintain their own state.

Alerts can have one of three states:

- **New** The alert is new and has not been reviewed
- **Acknowledged** The issue that generated the alert is being actioned by an administrator
- **Closed** The issue that generated the alert has been resolved and the alert has been marked as closed

The state of an alert is updated by the user who is interacting with the alert and is not updated automatically by the Azure platform.

> **NOTE ALERT STATE**
>
> Alert state is not the same as the monitor condition of an alert. When the Azure platform generates an alert based on an alert rule, the alert's monitor condition is set to *fired* and when the underlying condition clears, the monitor condition is set to *resolved*.

As alerts are generated, they will appear on the Alerts blade in Azure Monitor. From the Alerts blade can you view alerts for all subscriptions, and drill into one or more specific Subscriptions, Resource Groups, and Resources. You can also filter by time range with supported values of the Past Hour, the Past 24 Hours, the Past 7 Days, and the Past 30 Days (see Figure 1-37).

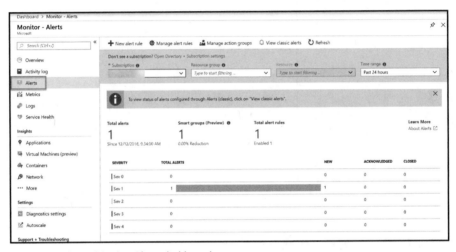

FIGURE 1-37 Azure Monitor Alerts dashboard

Selecting one of the links on the dashboard (e.g. Total Alerts) will open the **All Alerts** blade as shown in Figure 1-38.

FIGURE 1-38 Azure Monitor All alerts blade

The view on this page can be filtered through the dropdowns on the page and you can also filter, sort, and edit the columns that are displayed with the following limitations:

- When you filter by subscription, you are limited to selecting a maximum of 5 subscriptions
- When filtering by resource group, you can only select one resource group at a time
- The Resource Type filter is dynamic and is based on the selection of the resource group. You will not be able to select resource types that are not deployed to the selected resource group you are filtering with.
- The time range filter shows only alerts fired within the selected time window and supported values are the past hour, the past 24 hours, the past 7 days, and the past 30 days.

Selecting an alert will open the alert details (see Figure 1-39). From this blade you can view Alert History, including any changes to monitor condition state. This is also where you can alter the alert state to New, Acknowledged, or Closed. If the state of an alert is changed, that change is included in the alert history for audit purposes.

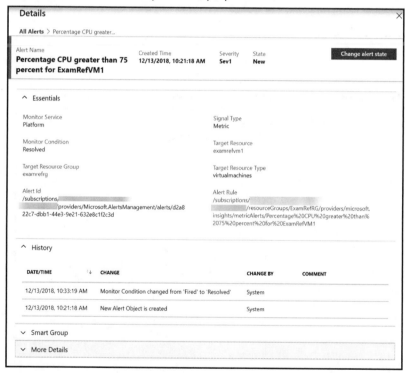

FIGURE 1-39 Azure Monitor alert details

Analyze metrics across subscriptions

Recall that metrics are the numerical values output by resources and services within Azure. Metrics are available for a number of Azure resources, but not all resources support metrics at this time.

Metrics includes platform metrics, which are created by Azure resources and made available in Azure Monitor for querying and alerting. You can also query application metrics from Application Insights if the service is enabled and you have instrumented your applications, whether that application is hosted on a virtual machine or even a PaaS service such as Azure App Service. Virtual machines in Azure can also push custom metrics to the monitor service using the Windows Diagnostic extension on Windows servers and Linux VMs through the InfluxData Telegraf Agent. There is also an opportunity to push custom metrics from other sources through a REST API.

An example of a metrics chart displaying Percentage CPU for a virtual machine is shown in Figure 1-40.

> **IMPORTANT NUMERICAL VALUES IN AZURE**
>
> In this case, we are only referring to the numerical values that the resources in Azure generates, not the logs, or text-based values, such as the value of an event log that may be stored in a storage account or a Log Analytics workspace.

FIGURE 1-40 Azure Metrics

Azure metrics are collected at one-minute intervals (unless otherwise specified) and are identified by a metric name and a namespace (or category). Azure metrics are retained for 93 days within Azure Monitor.

EXAM TIP

For longer term retention, metrics can optionally be sent to Azure storage for select resources and retained up to the configured retention policy or the storage limits of the account. They can also be sent to Log Analytics and stored for up to two years.

As metrics are collected, each metric has the following properties:

- The time the value was collected.
- The type of measurement the value represents.
- The resource the value is associated with.
- The value itself.

Metrics can be one dimensional or multi-dimensional with up to 10 dimensions. A non-dimensional metric can be thought of as the metric name and the value of the metric output and collected in the Monitor service over time. A multi-dimensional metric (both from an Azure resource or a custom metric) is the metric name and an additional name-value pair with additional data. For example, imagine a storage account with multiple blob containers where you need to track the consumption of storage by container. A non-dimensional metric would provide only the total consumed storage for the blob service in the storage account where a multi-dimensional metric would provide the consumption by container as it has the additional data stored in the metric record.

To interact with metrics, browse to the Metrics blade of Azure Monitor in the Azure Portal. You will be presented with a blank chart (see Figure 1-41).

FIGURE 1-41 Azure Metrics blank chart

To begin populating the chart, you need to select a metric. To select a metric, you must select a subscription and a resource group. You can optionally filter by resource type as well. Selecting a resource will then allow you to select a metric namespace (or category), a metric, and an aggregation if applicable. For example, to view the Ingress metric for a storage account, select the storage account, the Metric Namespace **Account**, the Metric **Ingress**, and the Aggregation **Sum** as shown in Figure 1-42.

FIGURE 1-42 Azure Metrics selection

You can add multiple metrics to the chart, even mixing Resources, Namespaces, Sums, and Aggregations as required (see Figure 1-43).

FIGURE 1-43 Azure Metrics selection for multiple resources

The chart will be rendered as you complete your resource selection. The period for the query can be changed, up to the retention limits of the metrics service, and the chart can be rendered as a Line Chart (default), Area Chart, Bar Chart, or Scatter Chart. An example of a line chart is shown in Figure 1-44.

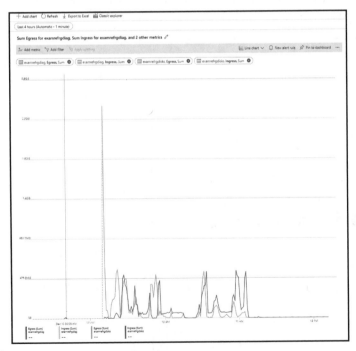

FIGURE 1-44 Azure Metrics line chart

Note that you are not limited to charting resources from the same subscription. You can select metrics for resources of any available type across all of the subscriptions you have access to.

From the Metrics blade, you can also create a new Alert Rule based on the metric query that is visualized. If you need to perform deeper analysis, the raw metric data can also be exported to Excel.

> **NOTE AZURE DASHBOARDS**
>
> Each chart or visualization that you create in Azure Monitor can also be pinned to an Azure Dashboard. You can have multiple Dashboards in Azure and you can even share a Dashboard with others in your organization.

You also are not limited to creating a single chart. Selecting the Add Chart button in the Metrics explorer will allow you to stack multiple charts, so existing charts can be cloned and then customized.

> **NOTE METRICS AND VISUAL RESPONSE TIMES**
>
> If you are evaluating a web application, you may want to use multiple charts for visualization response times (in milliseconds) and response size (in kilobytes). This is especially useful when you are working with metrics that have different units of measure of where the scale of the metrics you are evaluating varies widely.

Utilize log search query functions

Azure Monitor stores and surfaces two types of data: metrics and logs. Metrics are numerical values such as performance counters, while logs can be either numerical data or text. For instance, the full text of an exception that is raised in an application or even the text of an application log from a Windows or Linux server is one example.

Comparing metrics and logs surfaces some key differentiators:

- **Retention** Metrics are retained for 93 days within the Azure service, while logs stored in Log Analytics can be retained for up to two years. There are opportunities to do long term retention of metrics by storing metrics in Log Analytics as well.

- **Properties** Metrics have a fixed set of properties (or attributes). These are time, type, resource, value, and dimensions (optional). Logs have different properties for each log type and even support rich data types such as date and time.

- **Data availability** Metrics are gathered over time (like once a minute) and available for immediate query. Logs are often gathered after being triggered by an event (such as an event is written to an application log) and can take time to process before they are available for query. While both offer near real-time query capabilities, metrics will typically be used for fast alerts, and logs used for more complex analysis.

Before you can interact with resource logs and tenant logs in Azure Monitor, you must configure Log Analytics. Log Analytics helps you collect, correlate, search, and act on log and performance data generated by operating systems, applications, and Azure services. It gives you operational insights using rich search and visualizations. Log Analytics provides a single pane of glass for interacting with the data from the entire platform and the workloads you host on it including both Linux and Windows servers.

A Log Analytics workspace is where logs are collected and aggregated. The logs can also be queried and visualized through Log Analytics or through Azure Monitor. A workspace is an Azure resource, meaning that RBAC can be applied for granular access to the service and the data stored within it. This also means that workspaces can be in regions that meet your organization's regulatory requirements, data isolation, and scope. You can create multiple workspaces in a single subscription.

A workspace can be created through the Azure Portal, Azure PowerShell, the Azure CLI, and Resource Manager templates. To create a workspace through the Azure Portal, browse to the Azure Marketplace and search for **Log Analytics**. Select **Create** to open the workspace configuration blade (see Figure 1-45).

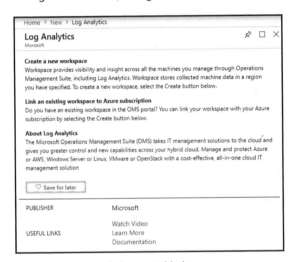

FIGURE 1-45 Log Analytics create blade

To configure a workspace, you will need to provide (Figure 1-46):

- A name for the workspace
- The subscription the workspace will be associated with
- A resource group
- A location
- A selection for pricing tier

> *NOTE* **LOG ANALTICS PRICING**
>
> Details on pricing for Log Analytics can be found at *https://azure.microsoft.com/pricing/details/monitor/*. This page also includes the pricing details for other services related to Azure Monitor such as Application Insights and Alert rules.

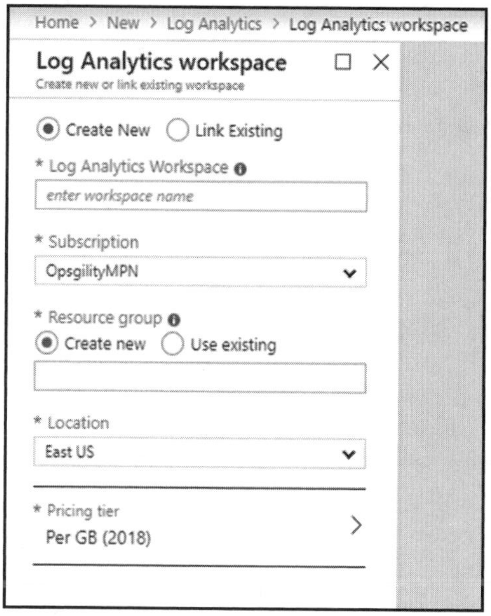

FIGURE 1-46 Log Analytics workspace configuration

Note that Log Analytics is not available in all regions. You can use the Azure Products by Region documentation, at *https://azure.microsoft.com/global-infrastructure/services/,* to select an appropriate region.

To select the appropriate pricing tier, review the pricing documentation at *https://azure.microsoft.com/pricing/details/monitor/.* A new workspace will default to the Free tier which includes 5 GB of log storage per month (31 days) with per GB pricing and per GB charges for additional storage and retention.

To create a workspace with Azure PowerShell or the Azure CLI you can use a Resource Manager template. For example,, the sample template provided below will create a new Log Analytics workspace in the region selected through the location parameter and with the pricing tier selecting through the sku parameter.

```
{
"$schema": "http://schema.management.azure.com/schemas/2014-04-01-
preview/deploymentTemplate.json#",
"contentVersion": "1.0.0.0",
"parameters": {
    "workspaceName": {
        "type": "String",
        "metadata": {
          "description": "Specifies the name of the workspace."
        }
    },
    "location": {
        "type": "String",
        "allowedValues": [
          "eastus",
```

```
          "westus2"
        ],
        "defaultValue": "eastus",
        "metadata": {
          "description": "Specifies the location in which to create the workspace."
        }
      },
      "sku": {
        "type": "String",
        "allowedValues": [
          "Standalone",
          "PerNode",
          "PerGB2018"
        ],
        "defaultValue": "PerGB2018",
        "metadata": {
          "description": "Specifies the service tier of the workspace: Standalone,
PerNode, Per-GB"
        }
      }
    },
    "resources": [
      {
        "type": "Microsoft.OperationalInsights/workspaces",
        "name": "[parameters('workspaceName')]",
        "apiVersion": "2017-03-15-preview",
        "location": "[parameters('location')]",
        "properties": {
          "sku": {
            "Name": "[parameters('sku')]"
          },
          "features": {
            "searchVersion": 1
          }


        }
      }
    ]
  }
}
```

The template above when used with the New-AzResourceGroupDeployment cmdlet or the az group deployment command will provision a new workspace based on the supplied parameters. Save the template above as azuredeploy.json and execute the following script to create a new Log Analytics workspace with the Per GB pricing model in the East US region:

```
$params = @{
    workspaceName = "ExampleLA"
    location = "eastus"
    sku = "PerGB2018"
}

New-AzResourceGroup -Name ExamRefRG -Location "East US"
New-AzResourceGroupDeployment -ResourceGroupName ExamRefRG -TemplateFile
'azuredeploy.json' -TemplateParameterObject $params -Verbose
```

After a workspace has been provisioned, you must enable data collection and configure both resource and tenant logs to store their logs within the service.

To collect event and performance data from Windows and Linux machines, open the workspace and configure the Advanced settings (see Figure 1-47). From this blade, you can obtain the Workspace ID, Primary Key, and Secondary Key for associating machines with the service through the monitoring agent. You can use this information when onboarding clients manually to the workspace.

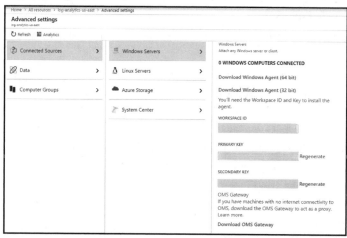

FIGURE 1-47 Log Analytics workspace advanced settings

From the Data settings you can configure the Windows Event Logs, Windows Performance Counters, Linux Performance Counters, Syslog, IIS Logs, and Custom Fields and Custom Logs (see Figure 1-48).

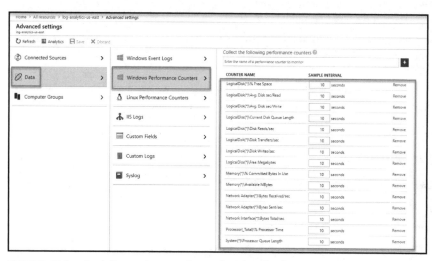

FIGURE 1-48 Log Analytics workspace advanced settings for data

After the workspace has been configured, you can begin to onboard machines. For machines to report telemetry to Log Analytics, they must be running the Azure Log Analytics (OMS) agent. This agent was previously referred to as the Microsoft Monitoring Agent (MMA) or the OMS Linux agent. The agent binds to a workspace to collect the data defined in the workspace settings or any installed solutions.

The method for installing the agent varies based on the machine operating system, where it is hosted, and how it is managed.

- Azure Virtual Machines can be onboarded manually through the Azure Portal, automatically through a Log Analytics workspace associated with Azure Security Center, or programmatically through the Log Analytics VM extension for Windows or Linux using Azure PowerShell, the Azure CLI, or a Resource Manager template.

- Hybrid Windows computers (server or client) can be onboarded manually by downloading the agent and installing locally or through Azure Automation DSC when using hybrid workers.

- Hybrid Linux computers (server only) can by onboarded manually by downloading the agent and installing locally.

- Machines managed with System Center Operations Manager (SCOM) can be integrated directly with Log Analytics by configuring SCOM to forward logs to the service.

You must also ensure that the required ports are available and required URIs are whitelisted for the agent to send telemetry. The agent utilizes port 443 for all outbound communication. The required URIs are shown in Table 1-4.

TABLE 1-4 Log Analytics Agent ports and protocols

Agent Resource	Ports	Direction	Bypass HTTPS inspection
*.ods.opinsights.azure.com	Port 443	Inbound and outbound	Yes
*.oms.opinsights.azure.com	Port 443	Inbound and outbound	Yes
*.blob.core.windows.net	Port 443	Inbound and outbound	Yes
*.azure-automation.net	Port 443	Inbound and outbound	Yes

After the workspace has been configured, tenant logs, resource logs, and machines have been onboarded, you can begin to analyze and visualize data. To interact with the data in Log Analytics you use log queries, which are used to:

- Perform interactive analysis of log data through the Azure Portal in Azure Monitor and a Log Analytics workspace.
- Build custom alert rules based on the logs in a workspace.
- Generate visualizations to can be shared through Azure Dashboards.
- Export custom data sets to Excel or Power BI.
- Perform automation based on log data with PowerShell or the Azure CLI.

> **NOTE LOG QUERY USAGE**
>
> To learn more about all the ways that log queries can be used, refer to the documentation at: *https://docs.microsoft.com/ azure/azure-monitor/log-query/log-query-overview#where-log-queries-are-used.*

The query language used by Log Analytics is called Kusto. Kusto queries are used to generate read-only requests to process data and return results. This means that the logs stored in Log Analytics are immutable and are only removed from a workspace based on the retention configuration. Queries are authored in plain-text and the schema used by Log Analytics is like SQL's with databases and tables composed of columns and rows. In each table, data is organized in columns with different data types as indicated by icons next to the column name. Column data types include text, numbers, and datetime.

Authored queries in Log Analytics can take many forms, from basic queries to very advanced queries with multiple aggregates and summarizations. Queries can be used to search terms, identify trends, analyze patterns, and provide many other insights. Queries search tables and can start with either a table name or a search command that defines scope. The pipe (|) character separates commands, and you can add as many commands as required.

In the following example query the Heartbeat table is queried to summarize the count of computers (by IP) and by a time value (TimeGenerated) to render a chart to track the number of computers reporting a workspace each hour.

```
// Chart the number of reporting computers each hour
Heartbeat
| summarize dcount(ComputerIP) by bin(TimeGenerated, 1h)
| render timechart
```

To run this query, browse to Azure Monitor and select Logs to open the query interface. This query will not return data if you do not have any virtual machines deployed and running. Those machines must also be associated with the Log Analytics workspace you are querying.

The query shown above is a table-based query. Queries always begin with a scope—either a table or search-based query. Kusto queries are case-sensitive. Language keywords are typically written in lower-case. When using the names of tables and columns in queries, you must ensure you are using the correct case. Table-based queries target a single table in a Log Analytics workspace (or database) while search-based queries target all tables by default.

Table-based queries start by scoping the query, and therefore tend to be very efficient and generally faster than search queries. Search queries are less structured by nature, which makes them the better choice when searching for a specific value across columns or tables. In other words, search can scan all columns in a given table, or in all tables across an entire workspace, for the defined value.

The amount of data being processed by a query could be enormous, which is why these queries can take longer to complete and might return large result sets which are limited by the Log Analytics service to 10,000 results.

To author queries in the Azure Portal, browse to Azure Monitor and select the **Logs** blade. From this blade, you can access all the subscriptions and workspaces you have rights to read from. Azure Monitor offers many sample queries for heartbeats, performance, and usage across your machines and services tracked in Log Analytics (see Figure 1-49).

FIGURE 1-49 Azure Monitor logs

In addition to sample queries, you can browse the schema for the currently selected work-space. This is useful for determining the proper case for table and column names as Kusto is a case-sensitive query language. Authored queries can be saved for later and/or favorited where they can be retrieved later using the Query explorer.

The query interface also gives to the ability to easily create alert rules based on your query logic. Using the **+New alert rule** button will pre-populate an alert rule with the resource target already configured and a single condition pre-populated as well (see Figure 1-50). The condition log can be refined, and the query can be updated if needed.

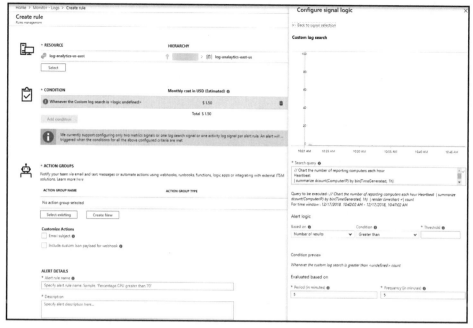

FIGURE 1-50 Azure Monitor Log Analytics new alert rule

Monitor for unused resources

There are several approaches to monitoring for unused resources in Azure. You can use a service like Azure Monitor and Alerts to monitor for resource consumption below a threshold to use your own logic criteria or you can leverage Azure Advisor and its built-in optimization recommendations.

Azure Advisor is a service in Azure that offers personalized recommendations to consumers of Azure based on the resources that are used in your subscriptions. An example of the Azure Advisor dashboard is shown in Figure 1-51.

Azure Advisor creates recommendations across four domains:

- **High availability**   To improve the high-availability and business continuity of your applications hosted on Azure.

- **Security**   To detect configurations that may lead to breaches.

- **Performance**   To improve the speed of your applications.

- **Cost**   To optimize and reduce your overall Azure spending by identifying underused and idle resources like virtual machines.

FIGURE 1-51 Azure Advisor

As the recommendations in Azure Advisor are personalized, the value gained from Azure Advisor depends on the services you deploy and how those services and resources are configured.

Azure Advisor cost recommendations can help you with optimizing the cost and resource consumption for virtual machines, ExpressRoute circuits, and virtual network gateways.

Virtual machines can be one of the most expensive resources in a cloud implementation and are also one of the easiest resources to control for cost. There are several ways to accomplish this:

- Deallocating compute when it is not in use or not needed. For example, shutting down and deallocating development virtual machines in off-hours means you will not be charged for the CPU and RAM consumption normally associated with running a virtual machine.

- Deleting unused virtual machines. It may sound obvious, but many organizations leave virtual machines in place. If you take the time to automate the provisioning and configuration of your environments, you can tear them down when not needed and stand them up on demand. For example, if you have a user-acceptance environment that is short-lived, it should only be allocated when testing is occurring.

- Right-sizing virtual machines to ensure full-utilization of virtual machine resources such as CPU.

Azure Advisor monitors your virtual machines through Azure metrics to identify low-utilization VMs. This is done by monitoring CPU usage over 14 days and identifying VMs whose CPU consumption is 5 percent or less, and network usage is 7 MB or less for four or more days. Advisors shows under-utilized VMs on the Cost Recommendations blade with an estimated cost to continue running the machine.

The CPU utilization rule can be customized to 5, 10, 15, or 20 percent. In Figure 1-52, you can see the configuration of a custom CPU utilization rule within Azure Advisor. This rule is subscription-specific allowing you to have different utilization rules based on the workloads you deploy. Right-sizing your virtual machines can lead to a significant reduction in cost for underutilized servers.

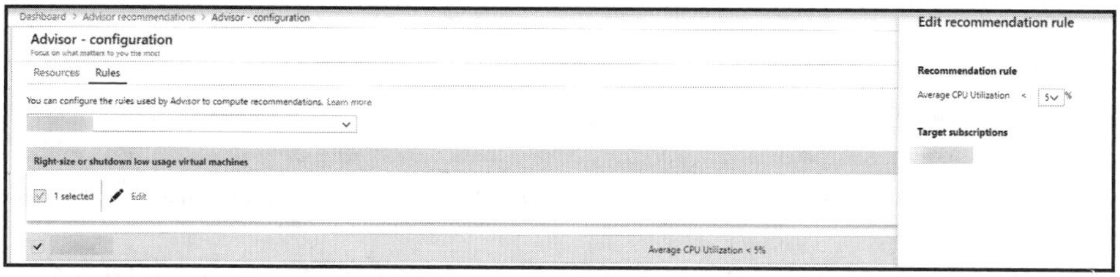

FIGURE 1-52 Azure Advisor CPU utilization rule

Advisor can also identify ExpressRoute circuits that have been in the provider status of Not Provisioned for more than 30 days and will recommend deleting the circuit if you are not planning to finalize provisioning the circuit with your network service provider.

Advisor will also identify virtual network gateways that have been idle for more than 90 days. Gateways are currently billed hourly, and you can recognize savings quickly by eliminating unused gateways.

Monitor and report spend

While Azure Advisor and its cost recommendations provide one method for monitoring spend and unused resources, Azure has many other tools that can help you monitor the cost of your resources and report on that cost.

There are several considerations that you must account for when reporting on the cost associated with your Azure resources:

- Azure services are available to customers in 140 countries worldwide.
- Billing is supported across 24 major currencies.
- Azure subscriptions are billed monthly. If paying by credit card, note that pre-paid cards and virtual credit cards are not accepted.
- You can also pay for Azure by monthly invoice. To apply for invoice payment, raise an appropriate billing support ticket from the Azure management portal. Processing the request takes 5-7 days, depending on the time required for the necessary credit checks. Invoice payment is only available to business customers, and once a subscription has been moved to invoice payment, it cannot be moved back to credit card payment.
- Customers on an Enterprise Agreement (EA) can add up-front commitments to Azure and then create multiple subscriptions under the agreement, which draw from the monetary commitment.
  - EA commitments are billed immediately, and then consumed throughout the year against the Azure resources consumed.
  - If the committed spend is exceeded, the extra spend, or 'overage,' is billed at the same discounted EA rate. Billing for overage is annual if the overspend is under 50% of the commitment, or quarterly if over 50%.

- Azure Marketplace services are billed separately with a potentially different billing period, separate invoice, and separate credit card charge. Each service has its own billing model, which will be described in the Azure Portal at the time of purchase. These range from pay-as-you-go per-minute billing to fixed monthly charges. Some services also offer a 'bring your own license' model, which must provide a license purchased separately prior to using the service.

There are three portals that are used to manage Azure subscriptions that are relevant for billing and cost management. They are:

- The EA Portal available at *https://ea.azure.com*. This is available only to customers with an Enterprise Agreement and is used for managing spend across one or more subscriptions.
- The Account Portal at *https://account.azure.com/subscriptions*. This is available for all subscriptions and accessible by Account owners. It is used to manage subscriptions, payment methods, and spending limits.
- The Azure Portal at *https://portal.azure.com*. This is available for all subscriptions and includes Azure Cost Management.

The EA Portal can be used to monitor spend across multiple subscriptions with the ability to view costs by the entire organization or by the business unit. Organizations can view historical spending, broken out by commitment, and overage or third-party Azure Marketplace consumption (see Figure 1-53). They can also download their current price sheet to see their EA discount rates, which often differ from the public pricing shown in the Azure Portal and in the pricing calculator.

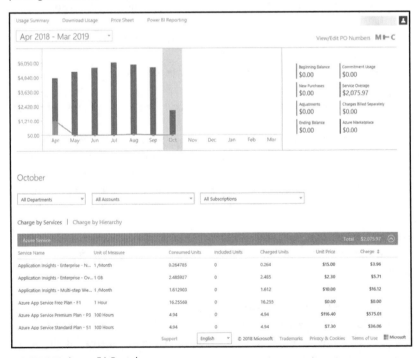

FIGURE 1-53 Azure EA Portal

EA customers can create spending quotas and set notification thresholds through the EA Portal. This is in addition to the budget alerts available through Azure Cost Management and Billing Alerts found in the Account Portal. An advantage of using the EA portal to configure spending notifications is that a quota alert can be triggered based on aggregate spending across all of the subscriptions within a department. Cost centers can be assigned to the departments that accounts and subscriptions roll up to for EA customers, making it easier to track cost by business unit and operate a showback or chargeback model.

Within the Azure Portal, EA customers can also use Azure Cost Management for tracking cost for individual subscriptions. Cost Management includes features for performing cost analysis, setting per-subscription budgets and alerts, setting recommendations for optimization, and exporting cost management data to perform deeper analysis.

Access to the Cost Management service is dictated by scopes. A user must have at least read access to one of the following scopes shown in Table 1-5 to view data in Cost Management.

TABLE 1-5 Cost Management access scopes

Scope	Defined at	Required access to view data	Prerequisite EA setting	Consolidates data to
Billing account	https://ea.azure.com	Enterprise Admin	None	All subscriptions from the enterprise agreement
Department	https://ea.azure.com	Department Admin	DA view charges enabled	All subscriptions belonging to an enrollment account that is linked to the department
Enrollment account	https://ea.azure.com	Account Owner	AO view charges enabled	All subscriptions from the enrollment account
Management group	https://portal.azure.com	Cost Management Reader (or Reader)	AO view charges enabled	All subscriptions below the management group
Subscription	https://portal.azure.com	Cost Management Reader (or Reader)	AO view charges enabled	All resources/resource groups in the subscription
Resource group	https://portal.azure.com	Cost Management Reader (or Reader)	AO view charges enabled	All resources in the resource group

To access Cost Management, in the Azure Portal browse to **Cost Management + Billing**, then **Cost Management**, and then select **Cost Analysis** as shown in Figure 1-54.

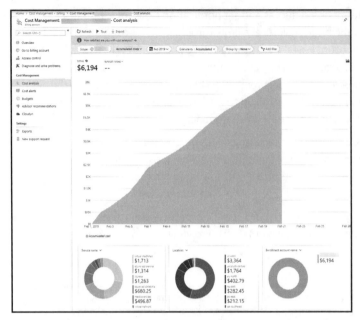

FIGURE 1-54 Azure Cost Management cost analysis

If you have access to more than one scope, you can filter by scope and begin interacting with the data. From cost analysis, you can view the total costs for the current month, view the budget (if available), set the granularity (Accumulated, Daily, or Monthly), and set the pivot. You can pivot by Department Name, Enrollment Account Name, Location, Meter, Meter Category, Meter Subcategory, Resource, Resource Group Name, Resource Type, Service Name, Service Tier, Subscription ID, Subscription Name, and Tag.

The data in a view can be downloaded from Cost analysis as a CSV. Any filtering that you have applied, including groupings, are applied to the file.

Cloudyn is an Azure service that is related to Cost Management, which can track resource cost for Azure resources. Cloudyn can also track resource usage for AWS and Google. Cloudyn also supports non-EA accounts including Pay-As-You-Go and Cloud Solution Provider. Cloudyn can be used to monitor usage and spending after it has been configured by tenant owner.

To enable Cloudyn, in the Azure Portal browse to **Cost Management + Billing**, followed by **Cost Management**, and then **Cloudyn**. Click the **Go to Cloudyn** button to open a new window and finish registration (see Figure 1-55). You must be signed in as a user with permission to register the *CloudynCollector* application with your Azure AD tenant, and the ability to assign the application to a role in your Azure subscriptions. In your Azure subscriptions, your accounts must have *Microsoft.Authorization/*/Write* access to assign the *CloudynCollector* application. This action is granted through the Owner role or User Access Administrator role. Contributors do not have permission to assign the application.

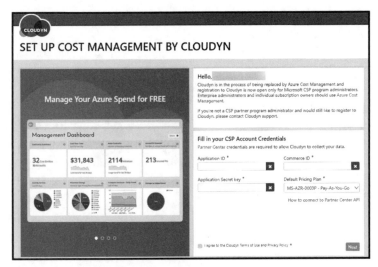

FIGURE 1-55 Cloudyn registration

The Offer ID for your subscription can be found in the Account Portal. In the upper-right of the Azure portal, click your user information and then click View My Bill (may be behind an ellipsis). Under Billing, click Subscriptions. Under My subscriptions, select the subscription. Your Offer ID is shown under Offer ID (see Figure 1-56).

FIGURE 1-56 Azure subscription offer ID

After the application has been provisioned, it may take some time for the dashboards and reports in Cloudyn to show data (see Figure 1-57).

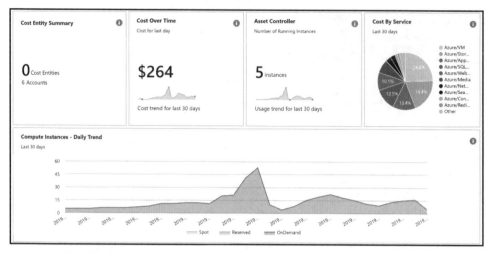

FIGURE 1-57 Cloudyn dashboard

Skill 1.3: Manage resource groups

As you build and deploy services in Azure you will create many types of resources. For instance, when creating your first virtual machine you will also deploy many other resources including:

- A disk for the OS
- A network interface for the VM
- A virtual network and subnet for that network interface to bind to
- A network security group (in a default portal configuration)

It is important to understand that many services in Azure create multiple resources and how you manage those resources will be driven by organizational policy and the lifecycle of your infrastructure hosted in Azure.

A resource in Azure is a single service instance, which can be a virtual machine, a virtual network, a storage account, or any other Azure service (Figure 1-58).

FIGURE 1-58 Azure resource

Resource groups are logical groupings of resources, or those single service instances (Figure 1-59).

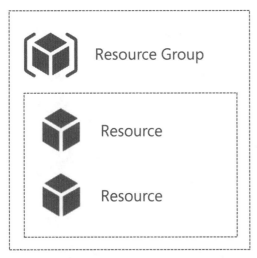

FIGURE 1-59 Azure hierarchy

Using a virtual machine, which is many individual service instances, you can group the instances together and manage them as one unit. Each resource in Azure can only exist in one resource group, and resource groups cannot be renamed. There are no limitations to the types of resources that can be logically contained within a resource group, and there are no limitations on the regions that resources must reside in when in a resource group.

Figure 1-60 shows this hierarchy with an Azure subscription, multiple resource groups, and the resources that reside within those resource groups.

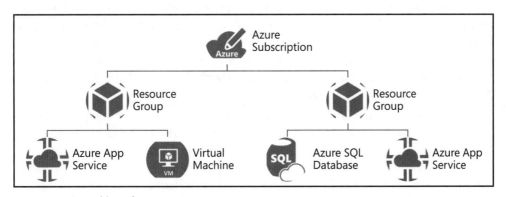

FIGURE 1-60 Azure hierarchy

When creating resource groups, it is import that you consider the factors noted above such as a single resource being associated with only one resource group at a time and the following:

- A resource group cannot be nested in another resource group.
- You can add or remove a resource from a resource group at any time.

- You can move a resource from one resource group to another.
- A resource group can be used to scope access control.
- A resource group can be used to scope policy.
- A resource in a resource group can interact with resources in another resource group.
- A resource group is created in a location. The location of a resource group specifies where the metadata for the resource group is stored. If you have compliance constraints, this is an important consideration.

> **This section covers how to:**
> - Create baseline for resources
> - Use Azure policies for resource groups
> - Configure resource locks
> - Configure resource policies
> - Implement and set tagging on resource groups
> - Move resources across resource groups
> - Remove resource groups

Create baseline for resources

Automating the creation and configuration of your resources will lead to consistent environments through idempotent deployments.

To automate the creation of Azure resources in a declarative manner you can use Azure Resource Manager templates. Resource Manager templates are JSON files that define the infrastructure and configuration of resources in Azure. When a Resource Manager template is used to create resources in Azure, it is submitted to the Resource Manager API as a deployment. Azure tooling, including the Azure Portal, also create and submit Resource Manager deployments as resources are created. In this sense, you can think of the Azure Portal as a Resource Manager template expression generator.

Templates define the resources that will be created or updated in one or more resource groups. This includes the basic metadata associated with every resource, such as name and location, resource-specific properties and configuration, and resource dependencies. For example, a template can be used to create a resource group, a virtual network with a subnet, a network interface, and a virtual machine. The virtual machine cannot be created until the network interface has been created, and the network interface cannot be created until the virtual network and subnet have been created. This dependency chain can be defined within the template (see Figure 1-61).

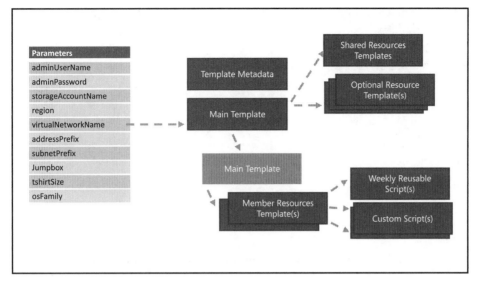

FIGURE 1-61 Resource Manager Template Diagram

Declarative deployments with Resource Manager templates have a number of advantages over imperative deployments with PowerShell or the CLI. These include:

- Simple orchestration of complex environments
- Deploy multiple resources in parallel
- Use parameters, variables, and functions for dynamic deployments and templates can be reused multiple times
- Templates are text files and can easily be used source control management systems and treated as formal artifacts

Resource Manager templates have a set schema. The required properties for a Resource Manager template are:

- $schema
- contentVersion
- resources

And the following optional properties:

- parameters
- variables
- functions
- outputs

A blank template takes the following form. In this example, parameters, variables, and outputs are included. While not required, you will see these properties used in most templates, especially as you move beyond basic templates and your deployments and deployment logic become more complex.

```
{
    "$schema": "https://schema.management.azure.com/schemas/2015-01
-01/deploymentTemplate.json#",
    "contentVersion": "1.0.0.0",
    "parameters": {
    },
    "variables": {
    },
    "resources": [
    ],
    "outputs": {
    }
}
```

Where:

- $schema is the URL to the JSON schema that defines the version of the template language.

- contentVersion is the version of your template. This is useful to ensure you are deploying the correct version of the template.

- parameters define inputs for the template.

- variables are custom values usually created from parameters or output from other templates.

- resources are the resources in Azure the template defines.

- outputs return values (if any) that the template produces.

The following is an example of a complete Resource Manager template that creates a storage account. Note that properties like output are present even if no values are returned. While this is not required per the schema it is still valid and, in some cases, can make it easier to extend your template at a later time.

```
{
    "$schema": "http://schema.management.azure.com/schemas/2015-01-01/
deploymentTemplate.json#",
    "contentVersion": "1.0.0.0",
    "parameters": {
        "location": {
            "type": "string"
        },
        "accountType": {
            "type": "string"
        },
        "kind": {
```

```
                "type": "string"
            },
            "accessTier": {
                "type": "string"
            },
            "supportsHttpsTrafficOnly": {
                "type": "bool"
            }
        },
        "variables": {
            "storageAccountName": "[concat(uniquestring(resourceGroup().id), 'standardsa')]"
        },
        "resources": [
            {
                "name": "[variables('storageAccountName')]",
                "type": "Microsoft.Storage/storageAccounts",
                "apiVersion": "2018-07-01",
                "location": "[parameters('location')]",
                "properties": {
                    "accessTier": "[parameters('accessTier')]",
                    "supportsHttpsTrafficOnly": "[parameters('supportsHttpsTrafficOnly')]"
                },
                "dependsOn": [],
                "sku": {
                    "name": "[parameters('accountType')]"
                },
                "kind": "[parameters('kind')]"
            }
        ],
        "outputs": {}
}
```

When you are creating templates, you will need to know the types of resources that are available and the values to use in your templates. The reference documentation for all valid resource types can be found at *https://docs.microsoft.com/azure/templates/*. If you know the resource type, you can browse directly to the documentation by using the URL format *https://docs.microsoft.com/azure/templates/<provider-namespace>/<resource-type>*. For example, to browse to the documentation for storage accounts, use the **Microsoft.Storage** resource provider and the storageAccounts resource type, making the URL *https://docs.microsoft.com/azure/templates/Microsoft.Storage/storageAccounts*.

There are several ways to get started with Resource Manager templates. For any resource group or resource deployed through the Azure Portal you can browse to the Automation script blade of the resource as shown in Figure 1-62.

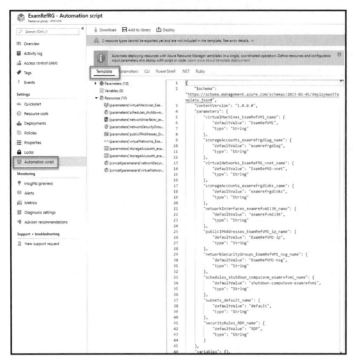

FIGURE 1-62 Automation script blade

From this blade you redeploy the template, add the template to a library that can secured with RBAC, or download the template to make modifications to it or store it in another location such as a source control provider. Note that the entire template is provided, including pre-defined parameters, variables, resources, and outputs (if any exist).

Microsoft also maintains a repository with more than 700 example templates known as the Azure Quickstart Templates, which can be found at *https://azure.microsoft.com/resources/ templates/*. The templates found at that location are hosted in a public GitHub repository that can be found at *https://github.com/Azure/azure-quickstart-templates*. The GitHub repository is useful if you want to clone or download the repository to have a local copy.

To deploy a Resource Manager template, you can use the Azure Portal, Azure PowerShell, the Azure CLI, and the REST API. With any of these tools, templates can be deployed from a local source (a template that is uploaded to the Portal from a local machine) or from an external source (a publicly accessible template file in a GitHub repository).

To deploy a Resource Manager template using the Azure Portal, select **+Create A Resource** and search the Azure Marketplace for **Template Deployment** and click **Create**. Note that from the Custom deployment blade you can elect to Build your own template in the editor, select from a list of common templates, or search the Azure Quickstart Template repository as shown in Figure1-63.

FIGURE 1-63 Custom template deployment blade

After selecting a starter template or building your own, you will be presented with a blade to input the Basics for your deployment, including the selection of a Subscription, the selection or creation of a resource group, and the Location for the deployment. Any parameters from the source template will be presented under Settings, offering the opportunity to supply any runtime values prior to submitting the deployment. Figure 1-64 shows an example of this blade.

FIGURE 1-64 Custom template configuration blade

After you have submitted the deployment by clicking **Purchase** you will be able to track the deployment progress by browsing the resource group and clicking the link under Deployments on the Overview blade (see Figure 1-65).

When you are deploying resources to Azure using a template, those resources could be from Microsoft or from a third-party publisher which may have its own payment terms (for instance, if you deploy a third-party network virtual appliance). This is why the button says Purchase, instead of Create.

FIGURE 1-65 Resource group overview blade

Clicking through to the deployment will open the Overview for the blade where you can view the deployment history, see the status for any resources that were included in the deployment, and drill into operation details as needed. From this screen you can also once again download the template as well (see Figure 1-66).

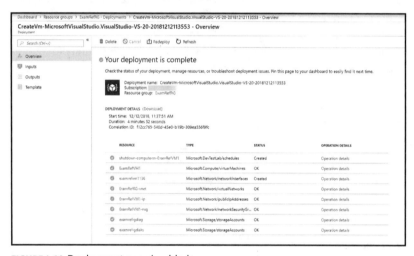

FIGURE 1-66 Deployment overview blade

To deploy a template with Azure PowerShell, you can use the New-AzResourceGroupDeployment cmdlet. Note that deployments are submitted to resource groups, so if you do not have an existing resource group to deploy to, you will need to create one first with the New-AzResourceGroup cmdlet.

To deploy a template from a local source:

```
Connect-AzAccount
Select-AzSubscription -SubscriptionName <yourSubscriptionName>

New-AzResourceGroup -Name ExamRefRG -Location "East US 2"
New-AzResourceGroupDeployment -Name ExamRefDeployment -ResourceGroupName ExamRefRG `
    -TemplateFile c:\MyTemplates\azuredeploy.json -storageAccountType Standard_GRS
```

To deploy a template from an external source:

```
New-AzResourceGroupDeployment -Name ExamRefDeployment -ResourceGroupName ExamRefRG `
  -TemplateUri https://raw.githubusercontent.com/Azure/azure-quickstart-templates/
master/101-storage-account-create/azuredeploy.json `
  -storageAccountType Standard_GRS
```

There are cmdlets within Azure PowerShell which will allow you to validate your templates without deploying them as well. To test a template without deploying it, use the `Test-AzResourceGroupDeployment` cmdlet.

```
Test-AzResourceGroupDeployment -ResourceGroupName ExamRefRG `
  -TemplateFile c:\MyTemplates\azuredeploy.json -storageAccountType Standard_GRS
```

If the deployment passes validation, the command will return with no output. If a deployment does not pass validation, the output will be display. For example, using the same template we can pass in a value for the `storageAccountType` parameter that is not allowed:

```
Test-AzResourceGroupDeployment -ResourceGroupName ExamRefRg `
  -TemplateFile c:\MyTemplates\azuredeploy.json -storageAccountType unknownSKU
Code    : InvalidTemplate
Message : Deployment template validation failed: 'The provided value 'unkownSKU' for
 the template parameter 'storageAccountType'
          at line '15' and column '24' is not valid. The parameter value is not
part of the allowed value(s):
          'Standard_LRS,Standard_ZRS,Standard_GRS,Standard_RAGRS,Premium_LRS'.'.
Details :
```

To deploy a template with the Azure CLI, you can use the `az group deployment create` command. Just as with PowerShell, your deployment is submitted against a resource group. If the resource group does not exist, you must create one first with the `az group create` command.

```
az group create --name ExamRefRg --location "East US 2"
az group deployment create \
  --name ExamRefDeployment \
  --resource-group ExamRefRg \
  --template-file azuredeploy.json \
  --parameters storageAccountType=Standard_GRS
```

The Azure CLI can also be used to execute deployments from external sources:

```
az group deployment create \
  --name ExamRefDeployment \
  --resource-group ExamRefRg \
  --template-uri "https://raw.githubusercontent.com/Azure/azure-quickstart-
templates/master/101-storage-account-create/azuredeploy.json" \
  --parameters storageAccountType=Standard_GRS
```

To test a deployment, use the `az group deployment validate` command:

```
az group deployment validate \
  --resource-group ExamRefRg \
  --template-file azuredeploy.json \
  --parameters @storage.parameters.json
```

Regardless of whether the template deployment succeeds or fails, the command will always return a value. If an error is found, it will be shown in the "error" object in the returned JSON.

```
{
  "error": {
    "code": "InvalidTemplate",
    "details": null,
    "message": "Deployment template validation failed: 'The provided value
'unknownSKU' for the template parameter
    'storageAccountType' at line '13' and column '20' is not valid. The
parameter value is not part of the allowed
    value(s): 'Standard_LRS,Standard_ZRS,Standard_GRS,Standard_RAGRS,Premium_LRS'.'.",
    "target": null
  },
  "properties": null
}
```

Use Azure policies for resource groups

When managing resource groups, and in many cases the multiple Azure services that reside within them, both Azure Policy with policy definitions and policy assignments can be used to govern those resources. Initiative definitions and initiative assignments can be used to govern those same resources, but instead of applying multiple policy definitions and making multiple policy assignments, you can package or group multiple definitions into a single initiative and then assign that initiative to your desired scope.

Controlling resource groups with Azure Policy is done by scoping the assignment of policy and initiatives. Recall that Azure Policy supports multiple scopes:

- **Management Group**   Assignments scoped at the Management Group (either the Tenant Root Group or a child group) apply to all child resources in the Management Group–subscriptions, resource groups, and resources.

- **Subscription**   Assignments scoped to a subscription apply to all child resources in the subscription–resource groups and resources.

- **Resource Group**   Assignments scoped to a resource group apply to all child resources in the resource group.

When creating assignments, it is also possible to configure excluded scopes. The ability to configure exclusions in an assignment is determined by the scope of the policy. For example, when scoping an assignment to a Management Group, any subscriptions, resource groups, or even resources that are children of the Management Group, can be excluded. When scoping an assignment to a subscription, child resource groups and resources can be excluded. When scoping an assignment to a resource group, only child resources can be excluded.

The flexibility of policy scoping is a powerful feature of Azure Policy. This allows you to model your environments with rich declarations in the form of policy definitions that are applied exactly as required by your organization's governance needs.

Imagine you have an environment with the following requirements :

- All resources should be tagged with the tag "Environment" and the value "Dev/Test."

- Only A-Series and D-Services virtual machines can be created, specifically Standard A0, A1, and D2 virtual machines that are not promotional.

- Resources in the rgCoreNetwork resource group are exempt from these policies.

To model this environment with Azure Policy, you can create two policy definitions (or use built-in policy definitions where applicable) as shown in Table 1-6.

TABLE 1-6 Azure policy definitions example

Policy Field	Policy Effect	Description
Type	deny	If virtual machines are not in the required SKU in the A-Series or D-Series prevent their creation
tags	append	Append tag name "Environment" and tag value "Dev/Test" to all resources

In the Azure Portal, browse to the Policy service and select the Definitions blade. To reduce administrative overhead, a new initiative definition will be created. Initiative definitions are a collection of policy definitions that are focused on the same goal. They allow for a set of policies to be grouped as a single item.

From the Definitions blade, select **+Initiative Definition**, as shown in Figure 1-67.

FIGURE 1-67 Azure Policy Definitions blade

Name the initiative Dev/Test Compliance and set the category to (create new) Custom (Figure 1-68).

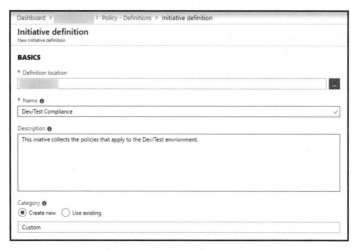

FIGURE 1-68 Azure Policy new initiative definition

Add the following built-in policies to the definition and set the values as noted (see Figure 1-69):

- Apply tag and its default value
  - **Tag Name**   Environment
  - **Tag Value**   Dev/Test
- Allowed virtual machine SKUs
  - **Allows SKUs**   Standard_A0, Standard_A1, Standard_A1_v2, Standard_D2, Standard_D2_v2, Standard_D2_v3, Standard_D2s_v3

FIGURE 1-69 Azure Policy new initiative definition policies and parameters

Save the definition so it can be used in an initiative assignment. Browse to the Assignments blade and select **Assign Initiative** (see Figure 1-70).

FIGURE 1-70 Azure Policy Assignments blade

To meet the environmental requirements, set the Scope of the assignment to the target subscription and configure the exclusions to exclude the rgCoreNetwork resource group. Configure the rest of the assignment and click **Assign** (see Figure 1-71).

FIGURE 1-71 Azure Policy Assign initiative blade

After policy definitions have been assigned, either through policy assignments or initiative assignments, the effects of the policy will be immediately applicable. Policy evaluation for compliance, however, happens about once an hour which means you may not be able to view the compliance state of a new assignment immediately.

Compliance state can be viewed on the Compliance blade of the Azure Policy service as shown in Figure 1-72.

FIGURE 1-72 Azure Policy Compliance blade

Configure resource locks

Azure resource locks (sometimes called management locks) are used to prevent the accidental deletion or modification of critical resources with two types of locks available:

- **CanNotDelete**   Locks prevent the deletion of a resource. A CanNotDelete lock only prevents deletion of a resource and does not impede the modification of a resource.
- **ReadOnly**   Locks prevent users from modifying a resource, which includes updating or deleting a resource.

Note that both types of resource locks allow for authorized users to read resources and resource locks apply across all users and roles, even custom and privileged roles.

Resource locks, regardless of type, can be applied at the subscription, resource group, and resource scopes. When you apply a lock at a scope, the resources within that scope inherit the lock. This means that a lock applied at the resource group scope applies to all the resources in the resource group. Resource locks apply to all service instances and resources within a scope.

Lock inheritance varies based on the type of lock that is applied. ReadOnly locks are inherited by child resources, while CanNotDelete locks are inherited by child resources and also pushed up to parent resources up and down. For example, a CanNotDelete lock applied to a DNS A record would prevent the deletion of the DNS zone that record resides in as well as the resource group the zone is located in.

It is also important to note that resource locks apply to the management plane of Azure, specifically operations sent to *https://management.azure.com*. This means they only affect interactions with Azure resources and not how those resources perform their own functions. For example, a ReadOnly lock applied to an Azure App Service would prevent users from updating configuration settings such as adding or updating an application setting or configuring an SSL certificate as show in Figure 1-73.

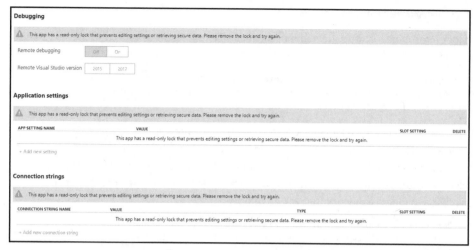

FIGURE 1-73 Read-only management lock applied to Azure App Service

When creating locks, you should exercise caution because they can have unexpected results. Many operations appearing to be a read operation require *write* access within the Azure management plane. For example, the same **ReadOnly** lock on an Azure App Service prevents Visual Studio from displaying files for the resource because the action requires *write* access.

Once you have determined the type of lock you will apply based on your requirements, you can apply the lock through the Azure Portal, Azure PowerShell, the Azure CLI, Resource Manager templates, or the REST API.

To create a lock through the Azure Portal, browse to the desired scope and select the Locks blade. From the blade, select **+Add** to create a new lock. Give the lock a name, select the lock type, and add a note that describes the lock as shown in Figure 1-74.

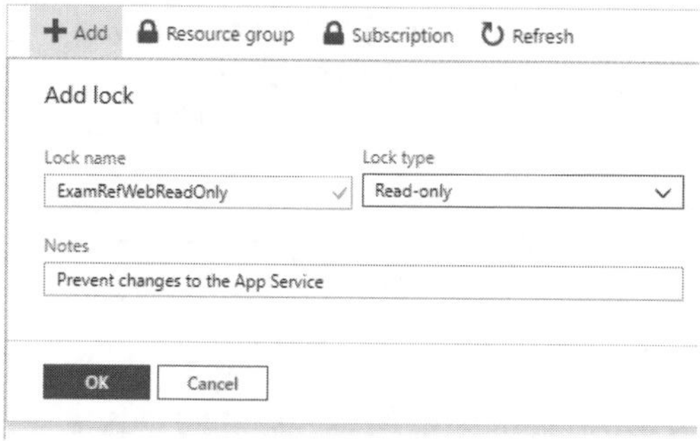

FIGURE 1-74 Management locks blade

When working with PowerShell, the parameter set of the New-AzResourceLock cmdlet varies based on the scope of the lock.

To lock a resource group, provide the name of the resource group with the Name parameter and the lock type with the LockLevel parameter.

```
New-AzResourceLock -LockName rgCoreNetworkLock -LockLevel CanNotDelete
```

```
-ResourceGroupName rgCoreNetwork
```

To lock a resource, provide the name of the resource, the resource type, and the resource group name.

```
New-AzResourceLock -LockLevel CanNotDelete -LockName CoreNetworkERCircuitLock
-ResourceName erCircuitCore -ResourceType Microsoft.Network/expressRouteCircuits
-ResourceGroupName rgCoreNetwork
```

Management of resource locks include removing locks when appropriate. For instance, if you have a CanNotDelete lock on a resource that is no longer needed, the lock can be deleted so the resource can be deleted so you are no longer billed for it. To delete a lock with PowerShell you will use the `Remove-AzResourceLock` cmdlet. This cmdlet has a parameter `LockId`, which is used to identify the lock that will be removed.

```
$id = (Get-AzResourceLock -ResourceGroupName rgCoreNetwork -ResourceName erCircuitCore
-ResourceType Microsoft.Network/expressRouteCircuits).LockId
Remove-AzResourceLock -LockId $lockId
```

Implement and set tagging on resource groups

Recall that resource tags can be applied at the resource group and/or the resource scopes. Also recall that there is no inheritance model for tags when they are applied at a resource group scope. If you need a tag to be applied to all resources in a resource group, each resource must be tagged individually.

Even with this limitation, it can be advantageous to tag resource groups. You may want to do this to be able to make inferences about child resources based on metadata associated with the parent resource group, or even just to store additional metadata if you need to apply more than 15 tags per resource.

Managing tags for resource groups uses the same tools as when working with tags with resources–the Azure Portal, Azure PowerShell, the Azure CLI, Resource Manager templates, and the REST APIs. In Skill 1.1 you learned how to manage tags with Azure PowerShell. In this section, you'll use the Azure CLI to manage tags.

To add tags to a resource group without existing tags, you will use the `az group update` command.

```
az group update -n hrgroup --set tags.Environment=Production tags.CostCode=1001
```

To add tags to a resource group with existing tags you must retrieve the existing tags, reformat the value, and then reapply the tags to the resource group with the new values.

```
jsonrtag=$(az group show -n hrgroup --query tags)
rt=$(echo $jsonrtag | tr -d '"{}, ' | sed 's/: /=/g')
az group update -n hrgroup --tags $rt Owner=user@contoso.com
```

The `az group show` command can be used to retrieve the existing tags for a resource group. Note that the output of the command is returned in JSON, which is why it had to be formatted in the example above.

```
az group show -n hrgroup --query tags
```

To retrieve all the resource groups with a particular tag you can use the `az group list` command. For example, to retrieve all the groups with the tag CostCode=1001, you can use the following:

```
az group list --tag CostCode=1001
```

Move resources across resource groups

Some resources in Azure can be moved between resource groups and even across subscriptions, but support for move operations does vary based on the service. A reference of services that can be moved can be found at *https://docs.microsoft.com/ azure/azure-resource-manager/move-support-resources. Figure 1-75* shows a resource group with a virtual machine and the ability for that virtual machine to be moved both within the same subscription and even to another subscription within the same Azure Active Directory tenant.

> **IMPORTANT MOVE OPERATIONS**
>
> Even if a resource states that it supports move operations, there may be other factors that prevent the resource from moving.

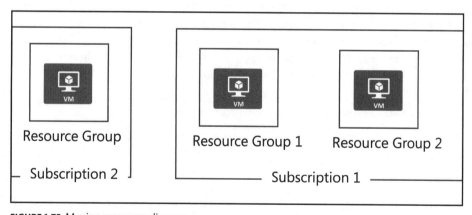

FIGURE 1-75 Moving resources diagram

During a move operation your resources will be locked. Both write and delete operations to the Azure resource will be blocked, but the underlying service will continue to function. For example, if you move an Azure App Service, the service will continue to serve web requests to visitors.

You cannot change the location of a resource as a part of a move operation. If you need to change the location of a resource after it has been deployed, the service will need to be deleted and recreated or created with a new name if the existing service cannot be deleted.

To move resources between subscriptions, both subscriptions must be associated with the same Azure AD tenant. If the subscriptions do not belong to the same tenant, you can update the target subscription to use the source Azure AD tenant by transferring ownership of the subscription to another account. Note that this operation can have unexpected impacts, because the Azure AD tenant associated with a subscription is used for RBAC to any currently deployed Azure services.

When moving resources between subscriptions, the resource provider of the source resource must also be registered in the target subscription. This is not a concern when moving resources within the same subscription, because the resource provider will already be registered.

If you are moving resources between subscriptions, you must also be mindful of resource quotas. For example, if you are moving many virtual machines, you will need to make sure that the target subscription has enough vCPUs available or the move operation will fail. Make sure you validate any quotas prior to moving a resource.

Finally, there are limitations in Azure Resource Manager that impact the number of resources you can move in a single operation. A single move operation in Resource Manager cannot move more than 800 resources in a single operation. With this constraint, it is recommended that you break large operations into smaller batches. Note that even if you are moving less than 800 resources in a single move request, the operation may still fail by timing out.

Once you have met the stated prerequisites to a move operation, it is critical that you validate the move operation through the REST API with the `validateMoveResources` method. This API validates whether resources can be moved from one resource group to another resource group. If validation succeeds, an HTTP 204 will be returned, and if it fails an HTTP 409 with an error message will be returned in the response. This method can be called with a POST request to:

```
https://management.azure.com/subscriptions/{subscriptionId}/resourceGroups/
{sourceResourceGroupName}/validateMoveResources?api-version=2018-05-01
```

In a POST request, include a request body with "resources" and "targetResourceGroup" properties:

```
{
  "resources": ["<resource-id-1>", "<resource-id-2>"],
  "targetResourceGroup": "/subscriptions/<subscription-id>/resourceGroups/<target-group>"
}
```

If the request is properly formatted, the operation will return output like the following:

```
Response Code: 202
cache-control: no-cache
pragma: no-cache
expires: -1
```

```
location: https://management.azure.com/subscriptions/<subscription-id>/
operationresults/<operation-id>?api-version=2018-02-01
retry-after: 15
...
```

The HTTP 202 response code shows the request was accepted. The location URI can be used in an HTTP GET that you can use to check the status of the long running operation for the final HTTP 204 or HTTP 409 status code. Figure 1-76 shows the output of an operation to validate a move request for an Azure Automation account associated with a Log Analytics workspace. As expected, the validation operation returned an HTTP 409, since this move request cannot be executed.

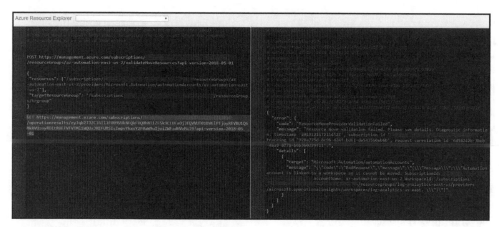

FIGURE 1-76 ValidateMoveResources API Response

After you have validated your resources are valid for a move operation, you can move the resources with the Azure Portal, Azure PowerShell, the Azure CLI, or the REST API.

To use the Azure Portal, browse to the resource group containing the resources and select the move button as showing in Figure 1-77.

FIGURE 1-77 Move button in the Azure Portal

You can now select the resources to move and select the destination resource group. Note that you must acknowledge that you may need to update existing tools or scripts to account for the changes in resource IDs (see Figure 1-78).

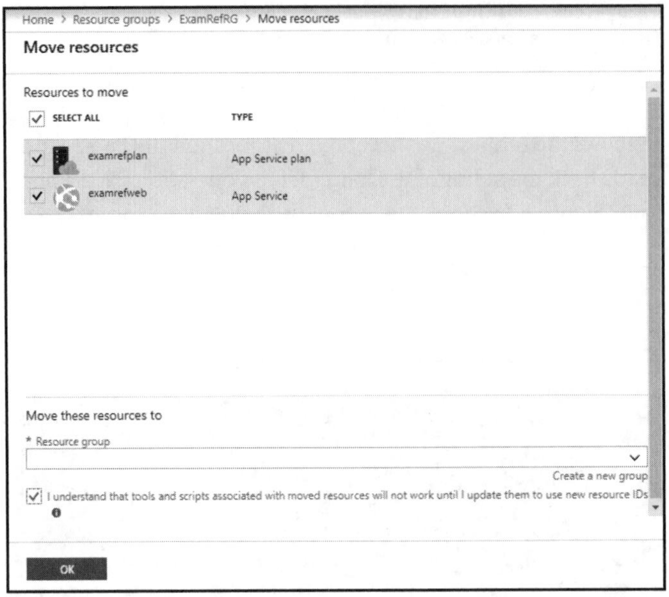

FIGURE 1-78 Move resources blade

To move resources with Azure PowerShell you can use the `Move-AzResource` cmdlet. When executing the cmdlet, the `ResourceId` parameter accepts an array of resource IDs for the source resources. When moving resources between subscriptions, you must also use the `Destination-SubscriptionId` parameter.

```
$webapp = Get-AzResource -ResourceGroupName ExamRegRG -ResourceName examrefweb
$plan = Get-AzResource -ResourceGroupName ExamRefRG -ResourceName examrefplan
Move-AzResource -DestinationResourceGroupName NewRG -ResourceId $webapp.ResourceId,
 $plan.ResourceId
```

To use the Azure CLI to move resources you can use the `az resource move` command. The ids parameter accepts a space-separated list of resource IDs to move. To move resources between subscriptions you must also supply the `destination-subscription-id` parameter.

```
webapp=$(az resource show -g ExamRefRG -n examrefweb --resource-type "Microsoft.Web/
sites"
 --query id --output tsv)
plan=$(az resource show -g ExamRefRG -n examrefplan --resource-type
 "Microsoft.Web/serverfarms" --query id --output tsv)
az resource move --destination-group NewRG --ids $webapp $plan
```

After a resource has been moved, you should validate that the resource is available and reconfigure any RBAC, resource locks, or policies. Also remember to update any scripts that interacted with the resources to account for the new resource IDs, resource group name, and potentially a different subscription.

Remove resource groups

In Azure, you can delete individual resources in a resource group, or delete a resource group and all of its resources. Deleting a resource group removes all the resources contained within it in one operation. When deleting resource groups, exercise caution because the resource group may contain resources that other resources you have deployed depend on. For example, if you delete a storage account that is used by an application to store application data, the Azure platform will not recognize that dependency and will allow the storage account to be deleted.

For resources that do support dependencies, you will not be able to delete the target resource until the dependencies have been cleared. For example, to do delete an App Service Plan, you must first remove or disassociate any App Services that depend on that plan. An example of attempting to delete an App Service Plan with existing App Service associations is shown in Figure 1-79.

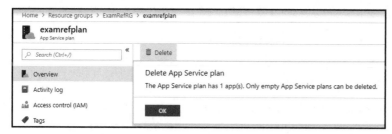

FIGURE 1-79 Delete an Azure resource with dependencies

To delete a resource group or an individual resource, you can use the Azure Portal, Azure PowerShell, the Azure CLI, or the REST API.

To delete a resource group in the Azure Portal, browse to the resource group and select the Delete Resource Group button (see Figure 1-80).

FIGURE 1-80 Delete an Azure resource group

In the **Are you sure you want to delete?** blade that opens you will need to type the resource group name to confirm that you want to delete the resource group. The blade will also show the affected resources and warn you that the operation is irreversible. An example is shown in Figure 1-81.

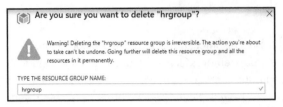

FIGURE 1-81 Delete an Azure resource group

Selecting Delete will begin deleting resources immediately. Note that it can take several minutes for a resource group to be deleted because each resource is deleted individually.

To delete a resource group with Azure PowerShell, use the `Remove-AzResourceGroup` cmdlet. To delete a resource group with a confirmation prompt, execute the cmdlet with the `Name` parameter:

```
Remove-AzResourceGroup -Name "hrgroup"
```

To delete a resource group without confirmation, use the execute the cmdlet with the `-Force` switch.

```
Remove-AzResourceGroup -Name "hrgroup" -Force
```

To delete a resource group with the Azure CLI, use the `az group delete` command. To delete a resource group with a confirmation prompt, execute the command with the `name` parameter:

```
az group delete --name hrgroup
```

To delete a resource group without confirmation, execute the command with the `--yes` switch.

```
az group delete --name hrgroup --yes
```

Skill 1.4: Manage role-based access control (RBAC)

Access control in Microsoft Azure is an important part of an organization's security and compliance requirements. Implementing Role-Based Access Control (RBAC) provides the capability within Azure to define access rights at a very granular level, based on each user's assigned tasks or the activities they need to perform day-to-day in their role. This ensures that each person can perform the task they need to accomplish.

Role-Based Access Control

Role-Based Access Control (RBAC) allows you to manage the entities, also referred to as security principals, that have access to Azure resources and the actions that those entities can perform. In addition to determining who can do what, Azure RBAC is also applied at a scope that dictates the areas they have access to. In Azure, access to can be granted to users, groups, service principals, and managed identities through role assignments, which are then applied at a scope such as a subscription, a resource group, or even an individual resource. Azure RBAC is applicable to the management of resources created in the Azure Resource Manager (ARM) deployment model.

A role is the definition of what actions are allowed and/or denied. RBAC is configured by selecting a role and associating the role with a security principal such as a user, a group, or a service identity. Then, this combination of role and security principal is applied to a scope of a subscription, a resource group, or a specific resource through a role assignment.

In Azure, there is also role inheritance where child resources inherit the role assignments of any parents. For example, if a user is granted read access to a subscription, that user will have read access to all the resource groups and resources in that subscription. If a managed identity is granted contributor rights for a single resource group, that security principal can only interact with that resource group and its child resources, but it cannot create new resource groups or access resources in other resource groups unless an explicit role assignment is made.

Before a security principal such as a user or group can interact with Azure resources, they must be granted access at a scope through a role assignment. Once a security principal has been granted access, it can perform any action that is has rights to perform. It is always recommended to provide the minimum privileges to an object or user to perform their actions as needed. Figure 1-82 shows a suggested access pattern that adheres to the principles of least privilege. In this example, a security group in Azure Active Directory (Azure AD), called IT Audit, is granted Reader access rights at the subscription scope, granting them read access to all resource groups and resources in the subscription. A security group called Application Admins is granted Contributor access rights to only select resource groups. Another security group called Application Owners is granted Owner access rights to select resource groups as well. By using multiple security groups and role assignments at the proper scope, access can be granted in the future just by updating the security group membership in Azure AD.

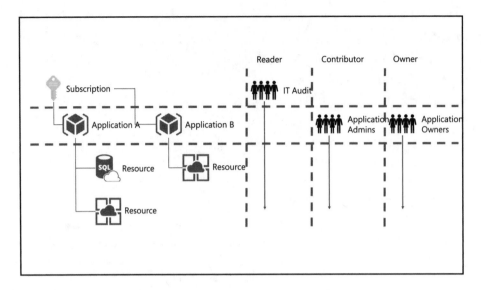

FIGURE 1-82 Azure RBAC Role Assignments

How RBAC works

Role assignments are the mechanism to control access to Azure resources using RBAC. This is a key concept to understand, because it is how permissions are enforced. A role assignment consists of three elements:

- A security principal
- A role definition
- A scope

Security principals

Security principals are the objects that are associated with a role definition and a scope to apply RBAC to Azure resources. A security principal can be:

- A user, or an individual identity that resides in Azure AD.
- A group, which is composed of one or more users that reside in Azure AD.
- A service principal, which is an application registered with Azure AD.
- A managed identity, which is a security principal in the form of an application registration that is managed automatically by Azure and an Azure service.

Role definition

The specific permissions that are applied to a resource with RBAC are defined in a role definition. A role definition contains the list of permissions, or declared permissions, and those permissions define what actions can or cannot be performed against a type of resource, such as read, write, or delete.

Role definitions, or roles, can be either built-in or custom. There are a number of built-in role definitions in Azure. Some of the built-in roles in Azure grant privileged rights, such as the Owner role, with includes permissions not only managing resources, but also permissions manage security and the application of role assignments. There are also built-in roles with limited permission sets, such as a Virtual Machine Contributor, which allows the assigned security principal to manage a virtual machine and some, but not all, of its associated resources.

There are many built-in roles in Azure, but there are four built-in roles that are considered foundational in Azure:

- **Owner**   Owners have full access to all resources, including the ability to alter security, or access rights, for the resources they manage.
- **Contributor**   Contributors can create and manage resources, but they don't have the ability to manage access rights to resources.
- **Reader**   Readers can view resources, but cannot create, manage, or alter access rights to resources.
- **User Access Administrator**   Principals assigned the User Access Administrator role manage access rights to Azure resources.

The remaining built-in roles can be found at *https://docs.microsoft.com/azure/role-based-access-control/built-in-roles*. Microsoft consistently adds new built-in roles as services evolve, or as new services are introduced.

While the built-in roles in Azure provide a great deal of flexibility and choice, there are times when a custom permission set needs to be defined. In Azure, custom roles are defined and stored in Azure AD, where they can then be shared across all of the subscriptions that are associated with the Azure AD tenant.

> **IMPORTANT CREATING CUSTOM ROLES**
>
> Custom roles cannot be created through the Azure Portal, but they can be assigned after they are created using the Portal. Custom roles can be created using Azure PowerShell, the Azure CLI, and through the REST API.

Custom roles are defined using JSON, or JavaScript Object Notation. A role definition includes:

- A name represented by the Name attribute
- An identifier represented by the Id attribute
- A description represented by the Description attribute
- A flag that denotes if the role is custom or built-in represented by the IsCustom attribute, which is set to false for built-in roles, and should be set to true when authoring custom roles
- The actions that can or cannot be performed within the Azure management plane represented by the Actions[] and NotActions[] attributes
- Optionally the scopes at which the role is available through the AssignableScopes[] attribute

To better understand roles (or role definitions), consider the Virtual Machine Contributor built-in role. To retrieve the definition of any role, you can use the Get-AzRoleDefintion cmdlet available in Azure PowerShell or az role definition list in the Azure CLI. For example, to retrieve the definition of the Virtual Machine Contributor role with Azure PowerShell, use the following:

```
Get-AzRoleDefinition -Name "Virtual Machine Contributor" | ConvertTo-Json
```

To retrieve the output of the same role using the Azure CLI, use the following:

```
az role definition list -n "Virtual Machine Contributor"
```

For both commands, the output of the command will be like the following:

```
{
  "Name": "Virtual Machine Contributor",
  "Id": "9980e02c-c2be-4d73-94e8-173b1dc7cf3c",
  "IsCustom": false,
  "Description": "Lets you manage virtual machines, but not access to them, and
 not the virtual network or storage account they're connected to.",
  "Actions": [
    "Microsoft.Authorization/*/read",
    "Microsoft.Compute/availabilitySets/*",
    "Microsoft.Compute/locations/*",
    "Microsoft.Compute/virtualMachines/*",
```

```
        "Microsoft.Compute/virtualMachineScaleSets/*",
        "Microsoft.DevTestLab/schedules/*",
        "Microsoft.Insights/alertRules/*",
        "Microsoft.Network/applicationGateways/backendAddressPools/join/action",
        "Microsoft.Network/loadBalancers/backendAddressPools/join/action",
        "Microsoft.Network/loadBalancers/inboundNatPools/join/action",
        "Microsoft.Network/loadBalancers/inboundNatRules/join/action",
        "Microsoft.Network/loadBalancers/probes/join/action",
        "Microsoft.Network/loadBalancers/read",
        "Microsoft.Network/locations/*",
        "Microsoft.Network/networkInterfaces/*",
        "Microsoft.Network/networkSecurityGroups/join/action",
        "Microsoft.Network/networkSecurityGroups/read",
        "Microsoft.Network/publicIPAddresses/join/action",
        "Microsoft.Network/publicIPAddresses/read",
        "Microsoft.Network/virtualNetworks/read",
        "Microsoft.Network/virtualNetworks/subnets/join/action",
        "Microsoft.RecoveryServices/locations/*",
        "Microsoft.RecoveryServices/Vaults/backupFabrics/backupProtectionIntent/write",
        "Microsoft.RecoveryServices/Vaults/backupFabrics/protectionContainers/
protectedItems/*/read",
        "Microsoft.RecoveryServices/Vaults/backupFabrics/protectionContainers/
protectedItems/read",
        "Microsoft.RecoveryServices/Vaults/backupFabrics/protectionContainers/
protectedItems/write",
        "Microsoft.RecoveryServices/Vaults/backupPolicies/read",
        "Microsoft.RecoveryServices/Vaults/backupPolicies/write",
        "Microsoft.RecoveryServices/Vaults/read",
        "Microsoft.RecoveryServices/Vaults/usages/read",
        "Microsoft.RecoveryServices/Vaults/write",
        "Microsoft.ResourceHealth/availabilityStatuses/read",
        "Microsoft.Resources/deployments/*",
        "Microsoft.Resources/subscriptions/resourceGroups/read",
        "Microsoft.SqlVirtualMachine/*",
        "Microsoft.Storage/storageAccounts/listKeys/action",
        "Microsoft.Storage/storageAccounts/read",
        "Microsoft.Support/*"
    ],
    "NotActions": [],
    "DataActions": [],
    "NotDataActions": [],
    "AssignableScopes": [
      "/"
    ]
}
```

The permissions for management of Azure resources are defined in the Actions and NotActions portions of the role definition. Actions define the management operations that can be performed. NotActions define the management operations that are excluded from any of the allowed actions. Sometimes it can be easier to define a role by excluding operations rather that defining multiple allow operations. In the case of NotActions, it is not an explicit deny rule. If a user is granted access rights in an Action, they will have the ability to perform the operation.

Actions and NotActions always include a resource provider and a permission at a minimum. For example, to grant rights to all of the operations for all of the resource types in the

`Microsoft.Compute` resource provider, a valid `Action` would be `Microsoft.Compute/*`. The same type of wildcard permission can be used to only grant access to virtual machines. For example, to grant all rights for the virtual machines resource type, a valid `Action` would be `Microsoft.Compute/virtualMachines/*`. To grant read rights to just virtual machines, the full resource provider, resource type, and permission can be defined. For example, to grant read rights to virtual machines, a valid `Action` would be `Microsoft.Compute/virtualMachines/read`.

Operations support wildcards as well. This allows you to specify all permissions, all resource types, or all resource providers. For example, to grant read, write, and delete permissions to virtual machines, you can use Microsoft.Compute/virtualMachines/*, or to create read access to all resource types in the Microsoft.Compute resource provider you can use Microsoft.Compute/*/read.

`DataActions` and `NotDataActions` are related to a preview capability in Azure RBAC where RBAC can be extended beyond the management plane to the data plane of select Azure resources. The management plane of Azure refers to the management of Azure resources through the Azure Resource Manager APIs, while the data plane refers specifically to a security principal that can interact with the data stored in a service. For example, storage accounts have both a management plane and a data plane. When a security principal is granted access to the management plane of a storage account, it can access all of the components of that storage account, including blobs, tables, files, and queues. By extending RBAC to the data plan, it is possible to create custom roles in Azure that grant access to only blob containers, and not the other capabilities of the storage account.

To retrieve the current resource providers and resource provider operations that support `DataActions` and `NotDataActions`, you can use the `Get-AzProviderOperation` cmdlet with Azure PowerShell and `az provider operation list` with the Azure CLI.

For example, to retrieve only the operations that support `DataActions` and `NotDataActions` with Azure PowerShell, use the following:

```
Get-AzProviderOperation * | ? { $_.IsDataAction -eq $true }
```

The `AssignableScopes` property can be used to limit the scopes to which a custom role can be assigned. If this property is not set, the role is available for assignment in all of the subscriptions associated with the Azure AD tenant, and all of the scopes within a subscription – namely all resources groups and resources. By setting the `AssignableScopes` property for custom roles, you can ensure that the role is available for assignment with any scopes that are not specified, and that the Portal UI displays customer roles that are not applicable.

Scope

Scope is a logical boundary where access rights apply. For example, to grant a group Contribute rights to all of the resources in a resource group, the Contributor role can be assigned to the group at the resource group scope where it is then inherited by all of the resources in the resource group.

There are four scopes at which RBAC can be applied, and scopes are structured in a parent-child relationship where RBAC is inherited by any child scopes. The highest scope, or top-most parent scope, is a management group.

EXAM TIP

Management groups are not applicable in all scenarios and in some cases a subscription will be the highest scope you will work with when applying role assignments.

Under the management group are subscriptions, under subscriptions are resource groups, and under resource groups are resources. Figure 1-83 shows a sample hierarchy with a parent management group, and two subscriptions, each with a resource group and child resources.

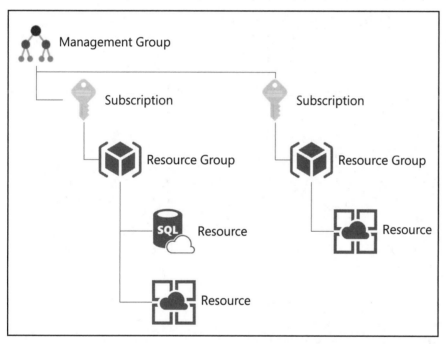

FIGURE 1-83 Scope Hierarchy

IMPORTANT   RBAC INHERITANCE

The concept of RBAC inheritance is critical. Granting a user access to the Owner role at the Management group scope will grant that user Owner rights to all of the subscriptions under the management group, and inclusive of all of the resource groups and resources within them.

Role assignment

After you have identified the role, security principal, and scope at which the role will be as-signed, you can make the assignment. Remember that security principals do not have access to Azure until a role assignment is made, and that access can be revoked by removing a role assignment.

> **IMPORTANT ROLE ASSIGNMENT SUBSCRIPTION LIMITS**
>
> You can have up to 2000 role assignments in each subscription.

To create and remove role assignments, you must have `Microsoft.Authorization/roleAs-signments/*` permission at the necessary scope. This permission is granted through the Owner or User Access Administrator built-in roles, or it can be included in custom roles.

As you begin to apply roles to security principals in Azure, it is not uncommon to have overlapping assignments where a security principal is assigned a different role assignment at both a parent and a child scope. For example, if a user is granted Contribute rights at the Man-agement group scope, and then Reader rights in a subscription, they will still have Contribute rights across the subscription along with Contribute rights to any other subscriptions under the Management group. Another way to think of this is that the most privileged access right takes precedence.

> **NOTE AZURE ROLE ASSIGNMENTS**
>
> With Azure role assignments there is no way to revoke access rights at a child scope through the application of a more restrictive role assignment, because the role assignment is inher-ited from the parent. It is, however, possible to apply a deny assignment at a scope when using Azure Blueprints and resource locks. Deny assignments are evaluated before role assignments and can be used to exclude service principals from accessing child scopes. For more information, see: *https://docs.microsoft.com/azure/governance/blueprints/tutorials/protect-new-resources*.

Implementing RBAC using the portal

To manage role assignments, you can use the Azure Portal, the Azure CLI, Azure PowerShell, Azure SDKs, or the Resource Manager REST APIs. In the following section, we will walk through how to manage role assignments using the Azure Portal.

In the Azure Portal, the Access Control (IAM) blade is used to manage access to resources. It is where role assignments are applied or removed. The Access Control (IAM) blade is available at any scope where role assignments can be made (Management group, subscription, resource group, and resource). To find the Access Control (IAM) blade, navigate to the resource or ser-vice where you want to manage role assignments.

In the following example, the Virtual Machine Contributor built-in role will be assigned to a user at the resource group scope.

In the Azure Portal, navigate to a resource group by selecting Resource groups in the left navigation, selecting a resource group, and then selecting the Access Control (IAM) blade as shown in Figure 1-84.

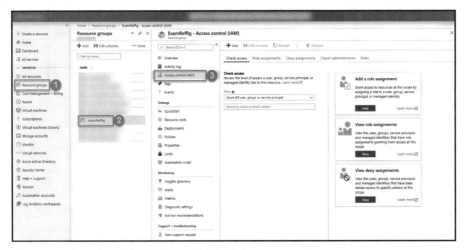

FIGURE 1-84 Azure Portal Access Control (IAM) blade

From the Access control (IAM) blade you can:

- Check the effective access rights for a security principal at the current scope through the Check access tab, including being able to view access rights inheritance from a parent scope.

- Edit role assignments, both granting and revoking access rights through the Role Assignments tab.

- View deny assignments, which are controlled by Microsoft, through the Deny assignments tab.

- View and manage permissions to classic resources through the Classic Administrators tab.

- View the available roles, both built-in and custom, through the Roles tab.

> **IMPORTANT** **DENY ASSIGNMENTS IN THE IAM BLADES**
>
> The Deny Assignments tab of the Access Control (IAM) blade cannot be used to make or alter deny assignments. Deny assignments are only supported in a limited capacity, and are set and controlled by Microsoft, or through the application of a resource lock for resources created through Azure Blueprints.

To assign permissions, navigate to the Role Assignments tab and click Add, as shown in Figure 1-85.

FIGURE 1-85 Role assignments tab on the Access control (IAM) blade

After clicking Add, select Add Role Assignment, as shown in Figure 1-86.

FIGURE 1-86 Add role assignment

In the Add Role Assignment blade, select the role and the security principal you want to assign the role to. The **Select** dropdown can be used to filter users, groups, or service principals found in the Azure AD tenant associated with the Azure subscription. Click **Save** when complete. Figure 1-87 shows an example, where the user, cloudadmin@opsgility.onmicrosoft.com, is being granted access to the Virtual Machine Contributor role. In the example directory, two security principals were returned from the filtered list using the search term "cloud" (CloudynAzureCollected and cloudadmin@opsgility.onmicrosoft.com), and a single principal was selected (Selected Members) to apply to the Virtual Machine Contributor role assignment.

FIGURE 1-87 Add role assignment blade

After clicking **Save**, you will see the role assignment on the Role Assignments blade, as shown in Figure 1-88.

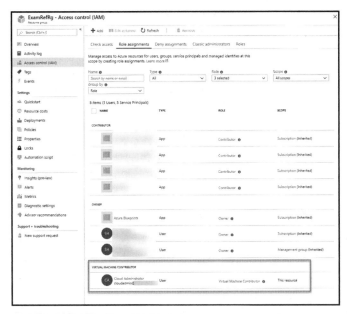

FIGURE 1-88 Role Assignments blade

To remove a role assignment, from the Role Assignments tab, select one or more security principals and click **Remove**. An example is shown in Figure 1-89.

FIGURE 1-89 Remove a role assignment

Azure PowerShell and the Azure CLI can also be used to manage Azure RBAC. In the following section, we will explore how to manage role assignments from the command line using these tools.

To list the roles that are available for assignment with PowerShell, the `Get-AzRoleDefintion` cmdlet can be used. For example, to return a list of custom roles available for assignment, use the following:

```
Get-AzRoleDefinition | Where-Object { $_.IsCustom -eq $true }
```

The `Get-AzRoleDefinition` cmdlet includes parameters such as `Scope`, which can be used to filter for available role assignments at a supplied scope. To work with a single definition, use the cmdlet with the `Name` parameter.

```
Get-AzRoleDefinition -Name "Virtual Machine Contributor"
```

The Azure CLI can be used to obtain the same information us the `az role` command group and its subcommands. For example, to return a list of custom roles available for assignment in a table, use the following:

```
az role definition list --custom-role-only -o table
```

To list a single role, use the `az role definition list` command with the `--name` parameter:

```
az role definition list --name "Virtual Machine Contributor"
```

Azure PowerShell and the CLI can be used to check the existing role assignments at a particular scope as well. For example, to view all the role assignments in a subscription, use the `Get-AzRoleAssignment` cmdlet to return all of the role assignments in a subscription. With the `Get-AzRoleAssignment` cmdlet it is also possible to filter for assignments at a scope of subscription, resource group, or even an individual resource or resource type. The equivalent command in the Azure CLI is `az role assignment list`. By default, the command returns only assignments scope to a subscription, but using the `--all` parameter will also return role assignments scoped to a resource group or a resource.

```
az role assignment list --all
```

Assigning roles with PowerShell and the Azure CLI requires several pieces of information:

- The sign-in name of the user when granting access to a user or the object identifier when granting access to a security group or service principal.
- The name of the role, either custom or built-in which you want to assign to the security principal.
- The scope at which you are making the role assignment.

To assign a role using Azure PowerShell for a user, use the `New-AzRoleAssignment` cmdlet with the `-SignInName` parameter, where the value of the parameter is the user principal name of the user in Azure AD. For example, to grant the user cloudadmin@opgility.onmicrosoft.com Virtual Machine Contributor rights at the ExamRefRG resource group scope, use the following:

```
New-AzRoleAssignment -SignInName cloudadmin@opsgility.onmicrosoft.com
-RoleDefinitionName "Virtual Machine Contributor" -ResourceGroupName ExamRefRG
```

To make the same assignment using the Azure CLI, the `az role assignment create` command group can be used:

```
az role assignment create --role "Virtual Machine Contributor" --assignee cloudadmin@
opsgility.onmicrosoft.com --resource-group ExamRefRG
```

To grant the same role to a security group, you need to first retrieve the object identifier of the security principal. In this example, to grant the Virtual Machine Contributor role to a security group called Cloud Admins at the ExamRefRG resource group scope, use the following:

```
$group = Get-AzADGroup -SearchString "Cloud Admins"
New-AzRoleAssignment -ObjectId $group.Id -RoleDefinitionName "Virtual Machine
Contributor" -ResourceGroupName ExamRefRG
```

To make the assignment using the Azure CLI from Bash, use the following:

```
groupid=$(az ad group list --query "[?displayName=='Cloud Admins'].objectId" -o tsv)
az role assignment create --role "Virtual Machine Contributor" -assignee-object-id
$groupid --resource-group ExamRefRG
```

To remove assignments using Azure Power, The `Remove-AzRoleAssignment` cmdlet can be used. This cmdlet has a similar parameter set to the `New-AzRoleAssignment` cmdlet and can be used to revoke permissions for a user when used with the `-SignInName` parameter, or for a security group or service principal with the `-ObjectId` parameter. Use the following to remove the access rights for a user:

```
Remove-AzRoleAssignment -SignInName cloudadmin@opsgility.onmicrosoft.com
-RoleDefinitionName "Virtual Machine Contributor" -ResourceGroupName ExamRefRG
```

And for a group:

```
$group = Get-AzADGroup -SearchString "Cloud Admins"
Remove-AzRoleAssignment -ObjectId $group.Id -RoleDefinitionName "Virtual Machine
Contributor" -ResourceGroupName ExamRefRG
```

The Azure CLI offers the same flexibility. To remove a role assignment from a user, use az `role assignment delete`:

```
az role assignment delete --role "Virtual Machine Contributor" --assignee cloudadmin@
opsgility.onmicrosoft.com --resource-group ExamRefRG
```

And to remove access for a group:

```
groupid=$(az ad group list --query "[?displayName=='Cloud Admins'].objectId" -o tsv)
az role assignment delete --role "Virtual Machine Contributor" -assignee-object-id
$groupid --resource-group ExamRefRG
```

Thought experiment

In this thought experiment, apply what you have learned. You can find answers to these questions in the next section.

You are responsible for creating and tracking resources in Azure for two business units within your organization: HR and Marketing. Your organization has an Enterprise Agreement (EA). Each business unit needs to deploy their own resources. Your Finance department needs to be able to understand the consumption of resources for each business unit for chargeback purposes. Finance would also like to be able to receive a notification when a defined monetary threshold is reached for each business unit.

The resources that each business unit will deploy are from a known set of resources and users should be prevented from creating unapproved resources. There will be resources within a subscription that are not billed back directly to the business units, but will be billed to IT. These resources must be differentiated for Finance.

1. How will you ensure that users can only create approved resources in Azure?

2. How will you grant access to create resources and restrict each business unit's users from impacting the other business units?

3. How will Finance access billing data for Azure and how will they be able to tell where each cost is coming from?

4. How will Finance be notified when each business unit is nearing their spending threshold?

Thought experiment answers

This section contains the solution to the thought experiment for the chapter.

For each business unit, HR and Marketing, a separate subscription can be created. This will allow for the separation of resources by business unit and allow for segregated and aggregated cost reporting and monitoring for Finance through the EA Portal.

1. To ensure users can only create approved resources, Azure Policies should be defined that can be assigned to each subscription. The policies will deny the creation of any unapproved resources and compliance can be monitored through Azure Policy as well.

2. Each business unit will be placed into its own subscription. Within a subscription, resource groups will be created, and users will be granted appropriate rights at the resource group level. As RBAC is inherited by child resources, with the appropriate rights granted, users will be able to create and manage resources as needed without impact others in the subscription. This will be layered with Azure Policy to ensure that only allowed resources can be created. This can be extended further by creating Azure Resource Manager templates, which can be used by business unit users to deploy their resources with well-known configurations.

3. Users in the Finance department can be granted access to the EA Portal and/or Cost Azure Cost Management by configuring access through the required scopes. To make sure that they can tell where each resource cost is coming from, tags should be applied to all resources using a taxonomy defined by Finance. For example, "BusinessUnit" can be a tag with the allowed values "HR," "Marketing," and "IT." That taxonomy should be

governed through Azure Policy to ensure that all resources are tagged with required and valid tags.

4. To manage thresholds, Department quotas can be configured in the EA Portal. In addition, Budgets can be created in Cost Management. Budgets in Cost Management can provide more flexibility has multiple notification thresholds can be set and each notification can have a different receiver. This would allow a single budget to send notifications to both business unit owners and Finance.

Chapter summary

Here are some of the key takeaways from this chapter:

- Azure offers a rich ecosystem of governance controls with user-level and platform-level controls in the form of role-based access control (RBAC) and Azure Policy.

- Azure Management Groups can be used to control policy and RBAC for multiple subscriptions. Management groups enable organizational alignment for your Azure subscriptions through custom hierarchies and groupings.

- Tags in Azure can be used to logically organize resources by categories. Each tag is a name and a value pair. Tags can be shared across multiple resources and enforced with Azure Policy.

- Azure Policy is a service that lets you create, manage, and apply policy to Azure resources at a subscription, resource group, or resource level. Policies enforce different rules over your Azure resources, so those resources remain compliant with your organization's standards.

- Role-based access control allows you to grant users, groups, and service principals access to Azure resources at the subscription, resource group, or resource scopes with RBAC inheritance. The three core roles are Owner, Contributor, and Reader.

- Azure Monitor is a single-pane of glass for accessing Azure metrics, tenant and resource diagnostic logs, Log Analytics, service health, and alerts.

- You can configure alerts based on metric alerts (captured from Azure Metrics) to Activity Log alerts that can notify by email, web hook, SMS, Logic Apps, or even an Azure Automation Runbook.

- Azure Log Analytics can consolidate machine data from on-premises and cloud-based workloads and this data is indexed and categorized for quick searching. Data can be collected from both Windows and Linux machines.

- Azure Log Analytics has many management solutions that help administrators gain value out of complex machine data. These solutions contain pre-built visualizations and queries that help surface insights quickly.

- Queries in Log Analytics can be saved for quick access and visualized and shared using Azure Dashboards. To analyze data outside of Log Analytics you can export the data to Excel and Power BI.

- You can create resources from the portal, PowerShell, the CLI tools, and Azure Resource Manager templates. You should understand when to use which tool and how to configure the resource during provisioning and after provisioning.

- A resource is simply a single service instance in Azure. Most services in Azure can be represented as a resource. For example, a Web App instance is a resource. An App Service Plan is also a resource. Even a SQL Database instance is a resource.

- A resource group is a logical grouping of resources. For example, a Resource Group where you deploy a VM compute instance may be composed of a Network Interface Card (NIC), a Virtual Machine, a Virtual Network, and a Public IP Address.

- A resource group template is a JSON file that allows you to declaratively describe a set of resources. These resources can then be added to a new or existing resource group. For example, a template can contain the configuration necessary to create two API App instances, a Mobile App instance, and a Document DB instance.

- A template can simplify orchestration because you only need to deploy the template to deploy all of your resources.

- A template allows you to configure multiple resources simultaneously and use variables/parameters/functions to create dependencies between resources.

## CHAPTER 2

Implement and manage storage

Implementing and managing storage is one of the most important aspects of building or deploying a new solution using Azure. There are several services and features available for use, and each has their own place. Azure Storage is the underlying storage for most of the services in Azure. It provides service for the storage and retrieval of files, and has services that are available for storing large volumes of data through tables, as well as a fast and reliable messaging service for application developers with queues. Azure Backup is another critical service that enables simplified disaster recovery for virtual machines by ensuring that data is securely backed up and easily restorable. In this chapter we'll review how to implement and manage storage with an emphasis on the Azure Storage and Azure Backup services.

We'll also discuss related services such as Azure Content Delivery Network (CDN), Import/Export, Azure Data Box, and many of the tools that simplify the management of these services.

Skills covered in this chapter:
- Create and configure storage accounts
- Import and export data to Azure
- Configure Azure files
- Implement Azure backup

Skill 2.1: Create and configure storage accounts

An Azure storage account is an entity you create that is used to store Azure Storage data objects such as blobs, files, queues, tables, and disks. Data in an Azure storage account is durable and highly available, secure, massively scalable, and accessible from anywhere in the world over HTTP or HTTPS.

This section covers how to:

- Create and configure a storage account
- Install and use Azure Storage Explorer
- Implement Azure storage replication
- Manage access keys
- Generate shared access signatures
- Monitor activity log by using Log Analytics
- Configure network access to the storage account

Create and configure a storage account

Azure storage accounts provide a cloud-based storage service that is highly scalable, available, performant and durable. Within each storage account, a number of separate storage services are provided. These services are:

- **Blobs**   Provides a highly scalable service for storing arbitrary data objects, such as text or binary data.
- **Tables**   Provides a NoSQL-style store for storing structured data. Unlike a relational database, tables in Azure storage do not require a fixed schema, so different entries in the same table can have different fields.
- **Queues**   Provides reliable message queueing between application components
- **Files**   Provides managed file shares that can be used by Azure VMs or on-premises servers

There are three types of storage blobs: block blobs, append blobs, and page blobs. Page blobs are used to store VHD files when deploying unmanaged disks. (Unmanaged disks are an older disk storage technology for Azure virtual machines. Managed disks are recommended for new deployments.)

When creating a storage account, there are several options that must be selected. These are the performance tier, account kind, replication option and access tier. There are some interactions between these settings, for example only the Standard performance tier allows you to choose the access tier. The following sections describe each of these settings. We then describe how to create storage accounts using the Azure portal, PowerShell, and Azure CLI.

Performance Tiers

When creating a storage account, you must choose between the Standard and Premium performance tiers. This setting cannot be changed later.

- **Standard**   This tier supports all storage services: blobs, tables, files, queues, and unmanaged Azure virtual machine disks. It uses magnetic disks to provide cost-efficient and reliable storage.

- **Premium** This tier is designed to support workloads with greater demands on I/O and is backed by high performance SSD disks. They only support page blobs, and do not support the other storage services. In addition, Premium storage accounts only support the locally-redundant (LRS) replication option, and do not support access tiers.

Replication options

When you create a storage account, you can also specify how your data will be replicated for redundancy and resistance to failure. There are four options, as described in Table 2-1.

TABLE 2-1 Storage account replication options

Account Type	Description
Locally redundant storage (LRS)	Makes three synchronous copies of your data within a single datacenter. Available for general purpose or blob storage accounts, at both the Standard and Premium performance tiers.
Zone redundant storage (ZRS)	Makes three synchronous copies of your data across multiple availability zones within a region. Available for general purpose v2 storage accounts only, at the Standard performance tier only.
Geographically redundant storage (GRS)	Same as LRS (three copies local), plus three additional asynchronous copies to a second data center hundreds of miles away from the primary region. Data replication typically occurs within 15 minutes, although no SLA is provided. Available for general purpose or blob storage accounts, at the Standard performance tier only.
Read-access geographically redundant storage (RA-GRS)	Same capabilities as GRS, plus you have read-only access to the data in the secondary data center. Available for general purpose or blob storage accounts, at the Standard performance tier only.

> **NOTE** **SPECIFYING REPLICATION AND PERFORMANCE TIER SETTINGS**
>
> When creating a storage account via the Azure portal, the replication and performance tier options are specified using separate settings. When creating an account using Azure PowerShell, the Azure CLI, or via a template, these settings are combined within the Sku setting.
>
> For example, to specify a Standard storage account using locally-redundant storage using the Azure CLI, use --sku Standard_LRS.

Access tiers

Azure blob storage supports three access tiers: Hot, Cool, and Archive. Each represents a trade-off of performance, availability, and cost. There is no trade-off on the durability (probability of data loss) which is extremely high across all tiers.

The tiers are as follows:

- **Hot** This access tier is optimized for the frequent access of objects in the storage account. Relative to other tiers, data access costs are low while storage costs are higher.

- **Cool** This access tier is optimized for storing large amounts of data that is infrequently accessed and stored for at least 30 days. The availability SLA is lower than for the hot tier. Relative to the Hot tier, data access costs are higher and storage costs are lower.

- **Archive** This access tier is designed for long-term archiving of infrequently-used data that can tolerate several hours of retrieval latency, and will remain in the Archive tier for at least 180 days. This tier is the most cost-effective option for storing data, but accessing that data is more expensive than accessing data in the Hot or Cool tiers.

There is a fourth tier, Premium, providing high-performance access for frequently-used data, based on solid-state disks. This tier is now available at: *https://azure.microsoft.com/blog/azure-premium-block-blob-storage-is-now-generally-available/.* It is only available from the Block Blob storage account type.

Table 2-2 compares the key features of each of the Hot, Cool, and Archive blob storage access tiers.

TABLE 2-2 Blob storage access tiers

	Hot tier	Cool tier	Archive tier
Availability SLA	99.9% (99.99% RA-GRS reads)	99% (99.9% RA-GRS reads)	N/A
Costs	Higher storage costs, lower access costs	Lower storage costs, higher access costs	Lowest storage costs, highest access costs
Latency	milliseconds	milliseconds	Up to 15 hours
Minimum storage duration	N/A	30 days	180 days

When using Azure storage, a default access tier is defined at the storage account level. This default must be either the Hot or Cool tier (not the Archive tier). Individual blobs can be assigned to any access tier, regardless of the account-level default. For Archive, there is only support for block blobs without any snapshots (A blob block that has snapshots cannot be re-tiered).

Account Kind

Another storage account setting is the account kind. There are three possible values: general-purpose v1, general-purpose v2, and blob storage. The features of each kind of account are listed in Table 2-3. Key points to remember are:

- The blob storage account is a specialized storage account used to store block blobs and append blobs. You can't store page blobs in these accounts, therefore you can't use them for unmanaged disks.

- Only general-purpose v2 and blob storage accounts support the hot, cool and archive access tiers.

- Only general-purpose v2 accounts support zone-redundant (ZRS) storage.

General-purpose v1 and blob storage accounts can both be upgraded to a general-purpose v2 account. This operation is irreversible. No other changes to the account kind are supported.

TABLE 2-3 Storage account types and their supported features

	General-purpose V2	General-purpose V1	Blob storage
Services supported	Blob, File, Queue, Table	Blob, File, Queue, Table	Blob (block blobs and append blobs only)
Unmanaged DIsk (page blob) support	Yes	Yes	No
Supported Performance Tiers	Standard, Premium	Standard, Premium	Standard
Supported Access Tiers	Hot, Cool, Archive	N/A	Hot, Cool, Archive
Replication Options	LRS, ZRS, GRS, RA-GRS	LRS, GRS, RA-GRS	LRS, GRS, RA-GRS

Creating an Azure Storage Account (Portal)

To create a storage account by using the Azure portal, first click **Create a resource** and then select **Storage**. Next click **Storage account**, which will open the Create storage account blade (Figure 2-1). You must choose a unique name for the storage account name. Storage account names are more restrictive than for other resources types—the name must be globally unique, and can contain lower-case characters and digits only. Select the Azure region (Location), the performance tier, the kind of storage account, the replication mode, and the access tier. The blade adjusts based on the settings you choose so that you cannot select an unsupported feature combination.

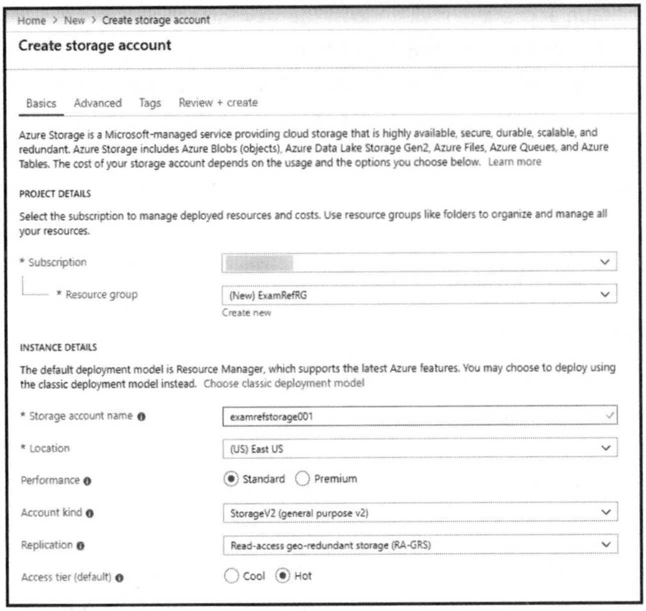

FIGURE 2-1 Creating an Azure Storage account using the Azure portal

The Advanced tab of the Create storage account blade is shown in Figure 2-2. This tab allows you to specify whether SSL is required for accessing objects in storage, access from all or a specific virtual network, as well as a preview feature for Data Lake Storage integration. Clicking the Tags tab allows you to specify tags on the storage account resource.

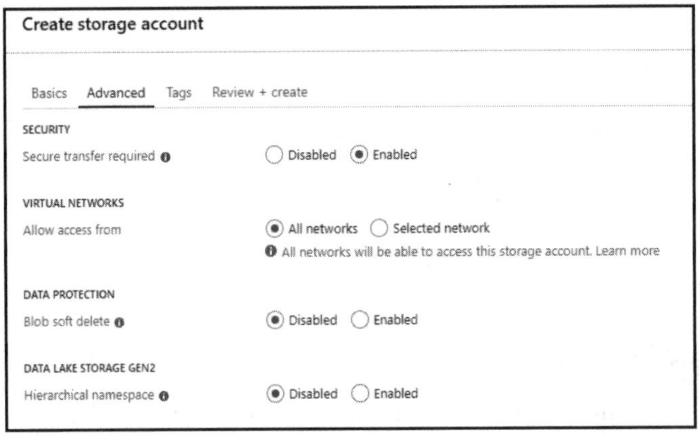

FIGURE 2-2 The advanced properties that can be set when creating an Azure Storage Account using the portal

Creating an Azure Storage Account (PowerShell)

The `New-AzStorageAccount` cmdlet is used to create a new storage account using Azure PowerShell. The cmdlet requires the `ResourceGroupName`, `Location`, and `SkuName` parameters to be specified, although you can also specify the account kind and access tier using the `Kind` and `AccessTier` parameters. If `Kind` is not specified, a general purpose v1 account is created by default.

The following PowerShell script creates a new resource group called ExamRefRG using the `New-AzResourceGroup` cmdlet and then creates a new storage account using the `New-AzStorageAccount` cmdlet.

```
$resourceGroup = "ExamRefRG"
$accountName   = "mystorage112300"
$location      = "WestUS"
$sku           = "Standard_LRS"
$kind          = "StorageV2"
$tier          = "Hot"
New-AzResourceGroup -Name $resourceGroup -Location $location
New-AzStorageAccount -ResourceGroupName $resourceGroup `
            -Name $accountName `
            -SkuName Standard_LRS `
            -Location $location `
            -Kind $kind `
            -AccessTier $tier
```

When creating a storage account with PowerShell you can specify several additional options such as custom domains using the `CustomDomainName` parameter, and optionally also the `UseSubDomain` switch if using the intermediary method of registering custom domains (for further information, see: *https://docs.microsoft.com/azure/storage/blobs/storage-custom-domain-name*). You can also specify whether to require HTTPS/SSL by specifying `EnableHttpsTrafficOnly`, assign a network rule set for virtual network access by passing a set of firewall and network rules using the `NetworkRuleSet` parameter, and automatically create and assign an identity to manage keys in Azure KeyVault using the `AssignIdentity` parameter.

> **MORE INFO   CREATING A STORAGE ACCOUNT WITH POWERSHELL**
>
> You can learn more about the additional parameters here:
> *https://docs.microsoft.com/powershell/module/az.storage/new-azstorageaccount*.

The `Set-AzStorageAccount` cmdlet is used to update an existing storage account. In this next example the storage account access tier is changed to `Cool`. The `Force` parameter is specified to avoid a prompt notifying that changing the access tier may result in price changes.

```
Set-AzStorageAccount -ResourceGroupName $resourceGroup `
            -Name $accountName `
            -AccessTier Cool `
            -Force
```

Creating an Azure Storage Account (CLI)

The `az storage account create` command is used to create an Azure Storage Account using the Azure CLI. This next example shows an Azure CLI script which creates a new resource group called `ExamRefRG` using the `az group create` command and then creates a new storage account using the `az storage account create` command. Note that this won't run in a PowerShell prompt with the Azure CLI installed without Bash variables.

```
resourceGroup="ExamRefRG"
accountName="mystorage112301"
location="WestUS"
sku="Standard_LRS"
kind="StorageV2"
tier="Hot"
az group create -l $location --name $resourceGroup
az storage account create --name $accountName -resourceg-roup $resourceGroup --location
$location --sku $sku
```

Similar to creating a storage account using PowerShell, there are several optional parameters that allow you to control additional account options such as custom domains using the `custom-domain` parameter, whether to require HTTPS/SSL by specifying `https-only`, and to automatically create and assign an identity to manage keys in Azure KeyVault using the `assign-identity` parameter.

> **MORE INFO** **CREATING A STORAGE ACCOUNT WITH THE AZURE CLI**
>
> You can learn more about the additional parameters here: *https://docs.microsoft.com/cli/azure/storage/account#az-storage-account-create*.

Install and use Azure Storage Explorer.

Azure Storage Explorer is a cross-platform application designed to help you quickly manage one or more Azure storage accounts. It can be used with all storage services: blobs, tables, queues and files. In addition, Azure Storage Explorer also supports the CosmosDB and Azure Data Lake Storage services

You can install Azure Storage Explorer by navigating to its landing page on *https://azure.microsoft.com/features/storage-explorer/* and selecting your operating system choice out of Windows, macOS, or Linux.

In addition, a version of Storage Explorer with similar functionality is integrated into the Azure portal. To access, simply click **Storage Explorer (Preview)** from the storage account blade.

Connecting Storage Explorer to Storage Accounts

After Storage Explorer is installed, you can connect to Azure storage in one of five different ways (shown in Figure 2-3):

- **Add an Azure Account**   This option allows you to sign in using a work or Microsoft account and access all of your storage accounts via role-based access control.
- **Using a connection string**   This option requires you to have access to the connection string of the storage account. The connection string is retrievable by opening the storage account blade in the Azure portal and clicking on Access keys.
- **Using a storage account name and key**   This option requires you to have access to the storage account name and key. These values can also be accessed from the Azure portal under Access keys.
- **User a shared access signature URI**   A shared access signature provides access to a storage account without requiring an account key to be shared. Access can be restricted, for example to read-only access for blob storage for one week only.
- **Attach to a local emulator**   Allows you to connect to the local Azure storage emulator as part of the Microsoft Azure SDK.

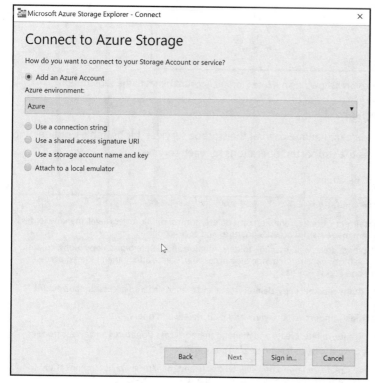

FIGURE 2-3 Connecting to an Azure Storage Account using Azure Storage Explorer

After connecting, you then filter on which subscriptions to use. Once you select a subscription, all of the supported services within the subscriptions will be made available. Figure 2-4 shows an expanded Azure Storage Account named mystorage112300.

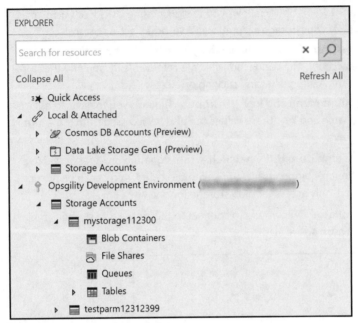

FIGURE 2-4 Azure Storage Explorer showing an Azure Storage Account beneath the subscription

Using Storage Explorer

Using Storage Explorer, you can manage each of the storage services: blobs, tables, queues and files. Table 2-4 summarizes the supported operations for each service.

TABLE 2-4 Storage Explorer Operations

Storage Service	Supported Operations
Blob	**Blob containers** Create, rename, copy, delete, control public access level, manage leases, create and manage shared access signatures and access policies **Blobs** Upload, download, manage folders, rename and delete blobs, copy blobs, create and manage blob snapshots, change blob access tier, create and manage shared access signatures and access policies
Table	**Tables** Create, rename, copy, delete, create and manage shared access signatures and access policies **Table entities** Import, export, view, add, edit, delete and query
Queue	**Queues** Create, delete, create and manage shared access signatures and access policies **Messages** Add, view, dequeue, clear all messages
Files	**File shares** Create, rename, copy, delete, create and manage snapshots, connect VM to file share, create and manage shared access signatures and access policies **Files** Upload folders or files, download folders or files, manage folders, copy, rename, delete

In each case Azure Storage Explorer provides an intuitive GUI interface for each operation.

Configure network access to the storage account

Storage accounts are managed through Azure Resource Manager. Management operations are authenticated and authorized using Azure Active Directory and role-based access control. Each storage account service exposes its own endpoint used to manage the data in that storage service (blobs in blob storage, entities in tables, and so on). These service-specific endpoints are not exposed through Azure Resource Manager, instead they are (by default) Internet-facing endpoints.

Access to these Internet-facing storage endpoints must be secured, and Azure Storage provides several ways to do so. In this section, we will review the network-level access controls: the storage firewall and service endpoints. We also discuss blob storage access levels. The following two sections then describe the application-level controls: access keys and shared access signatures.

Storage Firewall

The storage firewall is used to control which IP address and virtual networks can access the storage account. It applies to all storage account services (blobs, tables, queues and files). For example, by limiting access to the IP address range of your company, access from other locations will be blocked.

To configure the storage firewall using the Azure portal, open the storage account blade and click **Firewalls And Virtual Networks**. Click to allow access from **Selected Networks** to reveal the firewall and virtual network settings, as shown in Figure 2-5.

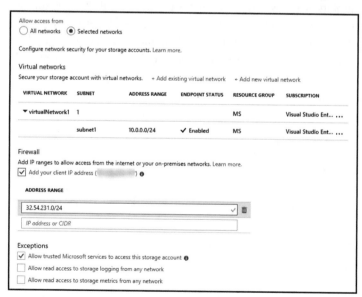

FIGURE 2-5 Configuring a Storage account firewall and virtual network service endpoint access

When accessing the storage account via the Internet, use the storage firewall to specify the Internet-facing source IP addresses that will make the storage requests. You can specify a list of either individual IPv4 addresses or IPv4 CIDR address ranges (CIDR notation is explained in the chapter on Azure Networking).

The storage firewall includes an option to allow access from trusted Microsoft services. These services include Azure Backup, Azure Site Recovery, and Azure Networking, for example to allow access to storage for NSG flow logs. There are also options to allow read-only access to storage metrics and logs.

Virtual Network Service Endpoints

In some scenarios, a storage account is only accessed from within an Azure virtual network. In this case, it is desirable from a security standpoint to block all Internet access. Configuring Virtual Network Service Endpoints for your Azure storage accounts allows you to remove access from the public Internet, and only allow traffic from a virtual network for improved security.

Another benefit of using service endpoints is optimized routing. Service endpoints create a direct network route from the virtual network to the storage service. This is important when forced tunneling is used to direct outbound Internet traffic from the virtual network via an on-premises network security device. Without service endpoints, access from the virtual network to the storage account would also be routed via the on-premises network, adding significant latency. With service endpoints, the direct route to the storage account takes precedence over the on-premises route, so no additional latency is incurred.

Configuring service endpoints requires two steps. First, from the virtual network subnet, specify Microsoft.Storage in the service endpoint settings. This creates the route from the subnet to the storage service but does not restrict which storage account the virtual network can use. Figure 2-6 shows the subnet settings, including the service endpoint configuration.

FIGURE 2-6 Configuring a subnet with a service endpoint for Azure storage

The second step is to configure which virtual networks can access a particular storage account. From the storage account blade click **Firewalls And Virtual Networks**. Click to allow access from **Selected Networks** to reveal the firewall and virtual network settings, as already seen in Figure 2-5. Under Virtual networks, select the virtual networks and subnets which should have access to this storage account. To further restrict access, the storage firewall can be configured with private IP addresses of specific virtual machines.

Blob storage access levels

Storage accounts support an additional access control mechanism, limited only to blob storage. By default, no public read access is enabled for anonymous users, and only users with rights granted through role-based access control (RBAC), or with the storage account name and key, will have access to the stored blobs. To enable anonymous user access, you must change the container access level. The supported levels are as follows:

- **No public read access** The container and its blobs can be accessed only by the storage account owner. This is the default for all new containers.
- **Public read-only access for blobs only** Blobs within the container can be read by anonymous request, but container data is not available. Anonymous clients cannot enumerate the blobs within the container.
- **Full public read-only access** All container and blob data can be read by anonymous request. Clients can enumerate blobs within the container by anonymous request but cannot enumerate containers within the storage account.

You can change the access level through the Azure portal, Azure PowerShell, Azure CLI, programmatically using the REST API, or using Azure Storage Explorer. The access level is configured separately on each blob container.

A Shared Access Signature token (SAS token) is a URI query string parameter that grants access to specific containers, blob, queues, and tables. Use a SAS tokens to grant access to a client that should not have access to the entire contents of the storage account (and therefore should not have access to the storage account keys), but still requires secure authentication. By distributing a SAS URI to these clients, you can grant them access to a specific resource, for a specified period of time, with a specified set of permissions.

Manage access keys

The simplest, and most powerful control over access to a storage is account is via the access keys. With the storage account name and an access key of the Azure Storage Account, you have full access to all data in all services within the storage account. You can create, read, update, and delete containers, blobs, tables, queues, and file shares. In addition, you have full administrative access to everything other than the storage account itself (you cannot delete the storage account or change settings on the storage account, such as its type).

Applications will often use the storage account name and key for access to Azure storage. Sometimes this is to grant access by generating a Shared Access Signature token, and sometimes for direct access with the name and key.

To access the storage account name and key, open the storage account from within the Azure portal and click **Access keys**. Figure 2-7 shows the primary and secondary access keys for the mystorage112300 storage account.

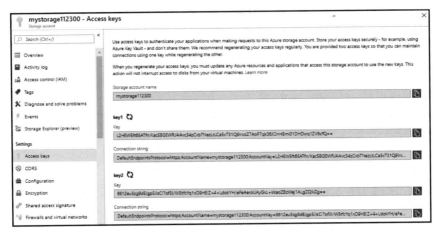

FIGURE 2-7 Access keys for an Azure storage account

Each storage account has two access keys. This allows you to modify applications to use the second key instead of the first, and then regenerate the first key. This technique is known as key rolling, and it allows you to reset the primary key with no downtime for applications that access storage directly using an access key.

Storage account access keys can be regenerated using the Azure portal or the command line tools. In PowerShell, this is accomplished with the `New-AzStorageAccountKey` cmdlet, and for the Azure CLI you will use the `az storage account keys renew` command.

> **NOTE ACCESS KEYS AND SAS TOKENS**
> Rolling a storage account access key will invalidate any Shared Access Signature tokens that were generated using that key.

Managing Access Keys in Azure Key Vault

It is important to protect the storage account access keys because they provide full access to the storage account. Azure Key Vault helps safeguard cryptographic keys and secrets used by cloud applications and services, such as authentication keys, storage account keys, data encryption keys and certificate private keys.

The following example shows how to create an Azure Key Vault and then securely store the key in Azure Key Vault (using software protected keys) using PowerShell.

```
$vaultName = "[key vault name]"
$rgName = "[resource group name]"
$location = "[location]"
$keyName = "[key name]"
$secretName = "[secret name]"
$storageAccount = "[storage account]"
# create the key vault
New-AzKeyVault -VaultName $vaultName -ResourceGroupName $rgName -Location $location
# create a software managed key
$key = Add-AzKeyVaultKey -VaultName $vaultName -Name $keyName -Destination 'Software'
# retrieve the storage account key (the secret)
$storageKey = Get-AzStorageAccountKey -ResourceGroupName $rgName -Name $storageAccount
# convert the secret to a secure string
$secretvalue = ConvertTo-SecureString $storageKey[0].Value -AsPlainText -Force
# set the secret value
$secret = Set-AzKeyVaultSecret -VaultName $vaultName -Name $secretName -SecretValue
$secretvalue
```

The same capabilities exist with the Azure CLI tools. In the following example, the az keyvault create command is used to create the Azure KeyVault. From there, the az keyvault key create command is used to create the key. Finally, the az keyvault secret set command is used to set the secret value.

```
vaultName="[key vault name]"
rgName="[resource group name]"
location="[location]"
keyName="[key name]"
secretName="[secret name]"
storageAccount="[storage account]"
secretValue="[storage account key]"
# create the key vault
az keyvault create --name "$vaultName" --resource-group "$rgName" --location "$location"
# create a software managed key
az keyvault key create --vault-name "$vaultName" --name $keyName --protection "software"
# set the secret value
az keyvault secret set --vault-name "$vaultName" --name "$secretName" --value
"$secretValue"
```

Keys in Azure Key Vault can be protected in software or by using hardware security modules (HSMs). HSM keys can be generated in place or imported. Importing keys is often referred to as bring your own key, or BYOK.

MORE INFO **USING HSM-PROTECTED KEYS FOR AZURE KEY VAULT**

You can learn more about the bring your own key (BYOK) scenario here:
https://docs.microsoft.com/azure/key-vault/key-vault-hsm-protected-keys.

Accessing and unencrypting the stored keys is typically done by a developer, although keys from Key Vault can also be accessed from ARM templates during deployment.

Generate a shared access signature

You can create SAS tokens using Storage Explorer or the command line tools (or programmatically using the REST APIs/SDK). Figure 2-8 demonstrates how to create a SAS token using Azure Storage Explorer.

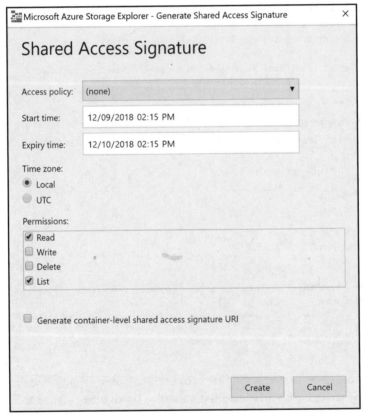

FIGURE 2-8 Creating a Shared Access Signature using Azure Storage Explorer

The following example shows how to create a SAS token for a specific storage blob using the Azure PowerShell cmdlets. The example creates a storage context using the storage account name and key that is used for authentication, and to specify the storage account to use. The context is passed the New-AzStorageBlobSASToken cmdlet, which is also passed the container, blob, and permissions (read, write, and delete), along with the start and end time that the SAS token is valid for. There are alternative cmdlets, such as New-AzStorageAccountSASToken, New-AzStorageContainerSASToken, New-AzStorageTableSASToken, New-AzStorageFileSASToken, New-AzStorageShareSASToken, and New-AzStorageQueueSASToken, to generate SAS tokens for other storage services.

```
$accountName = "[storage account]"
$rgName = "[resource group name]"
$container = "[storage container name]"
$blob = "[blob path]"

$storageKey = Get-AzStorageAccountKey `
    -ResourceGroupName $rgName `
    -Name $accountName

$context = New-AzStorageContext `
    -StorageAccountName $accountName `
    -StorageAccountKey $storageKey[0].Value

$startTime = Get-Date
$endTime = $startTime.AddHours(4)

New-AzStorageBlobSASToken `
    -Container $container `
    -Blob $blob `
    -Permission "rwd" `
    -StartTime $startTime `
    -ExpiryTime $endTime `
    -Context $context
```

Figure 2-9 shows the output of the script. After the script executes, notice the SAS token output to the screen.

```
?sv=2018-03-28&sr=b&sig=%2B6TEOoJyT5EAL3HF9ohApxnPOXNwHUeAPZosRaBZBG4%3D&st=2018-12-09T20%3A37%3A01Z&se=2018-12-10T00%3A37%3A01Z&sp=rwd
```

FIGURE 2-9 Creating a Shared Access Token

The Azure CLI tools can also be used to create SAS tokens. For example, to create a SAS token for a specific blob, use the az storage blob generate-sas command.

```
storageAccount="[storage account name]"
container="[storage container name]"
storageAccountKey="[storage account key]"
blobName="[blob name]"
```

```
az storage blob generate-sas \
   --account-name "storageAccount" \
   --account-key "$storageAccountKey" \
   --container-name "$container" \
   --name "$blobName" \
   --permissions r \
   --expiry "2019-05-31"
```

Using shared access signatures

Each SAS token is a query string parameter that can be appended to the full URI of the blob or other storage resource the SAS token was created for. Create the SAS URI by appending the SAS token to the full URI of the blob or other storage resource.

The following example shows the combination in more detail. Suppose the storage account name is 'examrefstorage', the blob container name is 'examrefcontainer1', and the blob path is 'sample-file.png'. The full URI to the blob in storage is then:

```
https://examrefstorage.blob.core.windows.net/examrefcontainer1/sample-file.png
```

The combined URI with the generated SAS token is:

```
https://examrefstorage.blob.core.windows.net/examrefcontainer/sample-file.png?sv=2018-
03-28&sr=b&sig=%2B6TEOoJyT5EAL3HF9OhApxnPOXNWHUeAPZosRaBZBG4%3D&st=2018-12-
09T20%3A37%3A01Z&se=2018-12-10T00%3A37%3A01Z&sp=rwd
```

Using a stored access policy

A standard SAS token incorporates the access parameters (start and end time, permissions, etc) as part of the token. The parameters cannot be changed without generating a new token, and the only way to revoke an existing token before its expiry time is to roll over the storage account key used to generate the token Or to delete the blob. These limitations can make standard SAS tokens difficult to manage in practice.

Stored access policies allow the parameters for a SAS token to be decoupled from the token itself. The access policy specifies the start time, end time and access permissions, and is created independently of the SAS tokens. SAS tokens are generated that reference the stored access policy instead of embedding the access parameters explicitly.

With this arrangement, the parameters of existing tokens can be modified by simply editing the stored access policy. Existing SAS tokens remain valid, and use the updated parameters. An existing token can be deactivated by simply setting the expiry time in the access policy to a time in the past.

Figure 2-10 shows the Azure Storage Explorer creating two stored access policies.

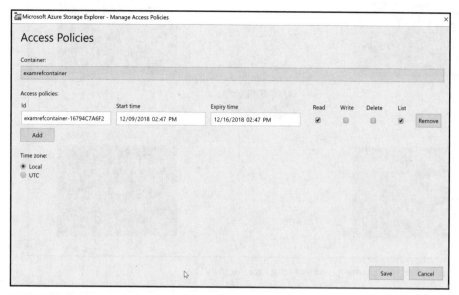

FIGURE 2-10 Creating stored access policies using Azure Storage Explorer

To use the created policies, reference them by name during creation of a SAS token using Storage Explorer, or when creating a SAS token using PowerShell or the CLI tools.

Monitor activity log by using Log Analytics

The Azure Activity log is a subscription level log that captures events that range from operational data such as resource creation or deletion, to service health events for a subscription.

> **MORE INFO** **MONITOR SUBSCRIPTION ACTIVITY WITH THE AZURE ACTIVITY LOG**
>
> You can learn more about what can be captured and analyzed for your Azure subscriptions here: *https://docs.microsoft.com/azure/monitoring-and-diagnostics/monitoring-overview-activity-logs*.

There are many options for capturing and analyzing data from the activity log. Figure 2-11 demonstrates several options.

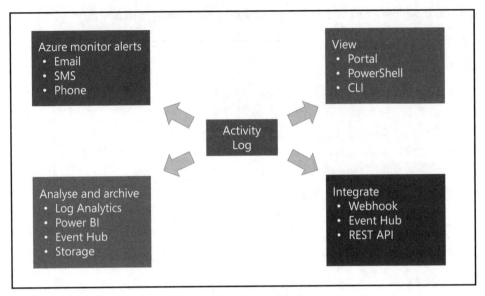

FIGURE 2-11 Options for extracting data from the Azure Activity Log

For the exam it is important that you understand how to archive Activity Log data to Azure Storage, and then use the Azure Log Analytics service to analyze the resulting Activity Log records.

To get started, access the Activity Log for your subscription by clicking on **All Services** in the Azure portal. In the resulting view you can find the **Activity Log In The Management + Governance** section, or you can search for **Activity Log** in the search box.

In the Activity Log view you will be able to see the recent subscription level events for the subscription, the time, the status, and the user who initiated the event. Clicking on either event allows you to view more about it, such as the reason it failed. In Figure 2-12 you can see that the Delete Virtual Machine event failed and then immediately after a Delete Management Locks event occurred.

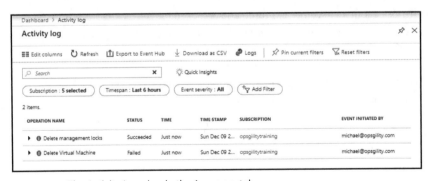

FIGURE 2-12 The Activity Log view in the Azure portal

Clicking the Logs icon at the top of the Activity Log view allows you to select an existing Log Analytics (OMS) workspace or create a new one. Figure 2-13 demonstrates creating the Azure Log Analytics workspace from the Activity Log view.

FIGURE 2-13 Creating a log analytics workspace

After the workspace is created, you are prompted to create the Log Analytics solution. The solution is a set of pre-configured views and queries designed to help analyze your log activity. The solution will automatically import the Activity Log data into the workspace after it is created.

After the data is imported, the Overview Page shows several views of your activity log data, grouping them by status, resource, and resource provider, as shown in Table 2-5.

TABLE 2-5 Azure Activity Log Blades and what data they contain

View	Description
Azure Activity Log Entries	A bar chart shows the number of activity log entries over time. Beneath the bar chart, a table shows the top 10 callers (the accounts initiating the actions recorded in the activity log). Clicking the bar chart opens a log search blade pre-populated with a query to show the activity log entries for the selected date range. Clicking a caller opens a log search blade pre-populated with a query to show the log entries for that caller.
Activity Logs by Status	A doughnut chart shows a breakdown of the activity log entry status—succeeded, failed, and so on. Beneath the bar chart, a table lists the same breakdown. Clicking on the chart opens a log search blade pre-populated with a query to show the activity log entries grouped by status. Clicking on an entry in the table opens a log search blade pre-populated with a query to show the activity log entries with that status.
Activity Logs by Resource	The number of unique resources with activity log entries is shown, followed by a table listing the top 10 resource by number of activity log entries. Clicking the number opens a log search blade pre-populated with a query to show the log entries grouped by resource. Clicking a row in the table opens a log search blade pre-populated with a query to show the log entries for that resource.
Azure Logs by Resource Provider	The number of resource providers with activity log entries is shown, followed by a table listing the top 10 resource providers by number of activity log entries. Clicking the number opens a log search blade pre-populated with a query to show the log entries grouped by resource provider. Clicking a row in the table opens a log search blade pre-populated with a query to show the log entries for that resource provider.

FIGURE 2-14 Shows the Activity Log Overview blade in the Azure portal.

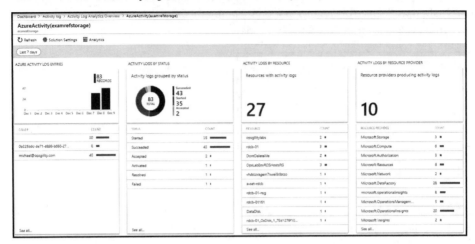

FIGURE 2-14 The Azure Activity Log Analytics overview

To view the activity related to Azure storage, click the Microsoft.Storage resource provider. The resulting view shows all related activity, such as creating or deleting storage accounts, accessing keys, and so on. Figure 2-15 shows the resulting view, including the query that was used to generate the view. You can modify the query or click Advanced Analytics to go to the full editor.

FIGURE 2-15 Analyzing data from the Microsoft.Storage resource provider using Log Analytics

You can enable alerts on data from the provider by providing your own query or building off the existing view. For example, to create a new alert when the Delete Storage Account action happens again, click the **Delete Storage Account** operation name and then click **New Alert Rule** from the top of the screen and configure the alert.

> **MORE INFO   ACTIVITY LOG WITH LOG ANALYTICS**
>
> You can learn more about what about configuring the Log Analytics Activity Log Solution and creating alerts here:
>
> *https://docs.microsoft.com/azure/azure-monitor/platform/collect-activity-logs.*

Implement Azure storage replication

The data in your Azure storage accounts is always replicated for durability and high availability. The built-in storage replication options were discussed at a high level in Table 2-1. It's important to understand when each replication option should be used and at what level of availability you require for your scenario. Table 2-6 describes the scenarios and expected availability for each of the replication options.

TABLE 2-6 Durability and availability for the LRS and ZRS replication options.

Scenario	LRS	ZRS	GRS	RA-GRS
Supported storage account types	GPv21, GPv12, Blob	GPv2	GPv1, GPv2, Blob	GPv1, GPv2, Blob
Server or other failure within a data center	Available	Available	Available	Available
Failure impacting an entire data center (e.g. fire)	Not available	Available	Available	Available
Failure impacting all data centers in a region (e.g. major hurricane)	Not available	Not available	Microsoft controlled failover	Read access only until failed over
Designed durability (probability of data loss)	At least 99.999999999% (11 9's)	At least 99.9999999999% (12 9's)	At least 99.99999999999999% (16 9's)	At least 99.99999999999999% (16 9's)
Availability SLA for read requests	At least 99.9% (99% for cool access tier)	At least 99.9% (99% for cool access tier)	At least 99.9% (99% for cool access tier)	At least 99.99% (99.9% for cool access Tier)
Availability SLA for write requests	At least 99.9% (99% for cool access tier)	At least 99.9% (99% for cool access tier)	At least 99.9% (99% for cool access tier)	At least 99.9% (99% for cool access tier)

Changing storage account replication mode

Storage accounts can be moved freely between the LRS, GRS, and RA-GRS replication modes. Azure will replicate the data asynchronously in the background as required.

Migrating to or from the ZRS replication mode works differently. The recommended approach is to simply copy the data to a new storage account with the desired replication mode, using a tool such as AzCopy. This may require application downtime. Alternatively, you can request a live data migration via Azure Support.

You can set the replication mode for a storage account after it is created through the Azure portal by clicking the **Configuration** link on the storage account and selecting the **Replication Type** (see Figure 2-16).

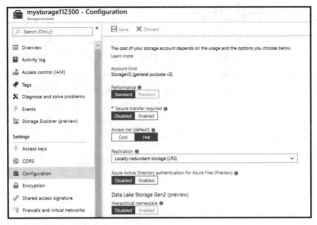

FIGURE 2-16 The configuration blade of an Azure Storage account

To change replication mode using the Azure PowerShell cmdlets, use the Type Inline code parameter of New-AzStorageAccount (at creation) or the Set-AzStorageAccount cmdlets (after creation), as shown:

```
$resourceGroup = "[resource group name]"
$accountName = "[storage account name]"
$type        = "Standard_RAGRS"
Set-AzStorageAccount -ResourceGroupName $resourceGroup `
                     -Name $accountName `
                     -SkuName $type
```

Using the async blob copy service

The async blob copy service is a server-side based service that can copy files you specify from a source location to a destination in an Azure Storage account. The source blob can be located in another Azure Storage account, or it can even be outside of Azure, as long as the storage service can access the blob directly for it to copy. This service does not offer an SLA on when the copy will complete. There are several ways to initiate a blob copy using the async blob copy service.

Async blob copy (PowerShell)

Use the Start-AzStorageBlobCopy cmdlet to copy a file using PowerShell. This cmdlet accepts either the source URI (if it is external), or as the next example next shows, the blob name, container, and storage context to access the source blob in an Azure Storage account. The destination requires the container name, blob name, and a storage context for the destination storage account.

```
$blobCopyState = Start-AzStorageBlobCopy -SrcBlob $blobName `
                 -SrcContainer $srcContainer `
                 -Context $srcContext `
                 -DestContainer $destContainer `
                 -DestBlob $vhdName `
```

```
-DestContext $destContext
```

Let's review the parameters in the preceding example:

- **SrcBlob**   Expects the file name of source file to start copying.
- **SrcContainer**   Is the container the source file resides in.
- **Context**   Accepts a context object created by the `New-AzStorageContext` cmdlet. The context has the storage account name and key for the source storage account and is used for authentication.
- **DestContainer**   Is the destination container to copy the blob to. The call will fail if this container does not exist on the destination storage account.
- **DestBlob**   Is the filename of the blob on the destination storage account. The destination blob name does not have to be the same as the source.
- **DestContext**   Also accepts a context object created with the details of the destination storage account, including the authentication key.

Here is a complete example of how to use the Start-AzStorageBlob copy cmdlet to copy a blob between two storage accounts:

```
# Copy blob between storage accounts
# Source account, blob container, and blob must exist
# Destination account must exist. Destination blob container will be created
$blobName          = "[blob name]"
$srcContainer      = "[source container]"
$destContainer     = "[destination container]"
$srcStorageAccount = "[source storage]"
$destStorageAccount = "[dest storage]"
$sourceRGName      = "[source resource group name]"
$destRGName        = "[destination resource group name]"
# Get storage account keys (both accounts)
$srcStorageKey = Get-AzStorageAccountKey `
  -ResourceGroupName $sourceRGName `
  -Name $srcStorageAccount

$destStorageKey = Get-AzStorageAccountKey `
  -ResourceGroupName $destRGName `
  -Name $destStorageAccount

# Create storage account context (both accounts)
$srcContext = New-AzStorageContext `
  -StorageAccountName $srcStorageAccount `
  -StorageAccountKey $srcStorageKey.Value[0]

$destContext = New-AzStorageContext `
  -StorageAccountName $destStorageAccount `
  -StorageAccountKey $destStorageKey.Value[0]

# Create new container in destination account
New-AzStorageContainer `
  -Name $destContainer `
  -Context $destContext
```

```
# Make the copy
$copiedBlob = Start-AzStorageBlobCopy `
  -SrcBlob $blobName `
  -SrcContainer $srcContainer `
  -Context $srcContext `
  -DestContainer $destContainer `
  -DestBlob $blobName `
  -DestContext $destContext
```

There are several cmdlets in this example. The `Get-AzStorageKey` cmdlet accepts the name of a storage account and the resource group it resides in. The return value contains the storage account's primary and secondary authentication keys in the `.Value` array of the returned object. These values are passed to the `New-AzStorageContext` cmdlet, including the storage account name, and the creation of the context object. The `New-AzStorageContainer` cmdlet is used to create the storage container on the destination storage account. The cmdlet is passed the destination storage account's context object (`$destContext`) for authentication.

The final call in the example is the call to `Start-AzStorageBlobCopy`. To initiate the copy this cmdlet uses the source (`$srcContext`) and destination context objects (`$destContext`) for authentication. The return value is a reference to the new blob object on the destination storage account.

Pipe the copied blob object to the `Get-AzStorageBlobCopyState` cmdlet to monitor the progress of the copy as shown in the following example.

```
$copiedBlob | Get-AzStorageBlobCopyState
```

The return value of `Get-AzStorageBlobCopyState` contains the CopyId, Status, Source, Bytes-Copied, CompletionTime, StatusDescription, and TotalBytes properties. Use these properties to write logic to monitor the status of the copy operation.

> **MORE INFO**   **MORE EXAMPLES WITH POWERSHELL**
>
> There are many variations for using the async copy service with PowerShell. For more information see the following:
> *https://docs.microsoft.com/powershell/module/az.storage/start-azstorageblobcopy.*

Async blob copy (CLI)

The Azure CLI tools support copying data to storage accounts using the async blob copy service. The following example uses the `az storage blob copy start` command to copy a blob from one storage account to another. The following script gives an example. For authentication, the command requires the storage account name and key for the source (if the blob is not available via public access) and the destination. The storage account key is retrieved using the `az storage account keys list` command.

```
# Copy blob between storage accounts
# Source account, blob container, and blob must exist
# Destination account and blob container must exist
blobName="[file name]"
srcContainer="[source container]"
destContainer="[destination container]"
srcStorageAccount="[source storage]"
destStorageAccount="[destination storage]"
$srcStorageKey="[source account key]"
$destStorageKey="[destination account key]"
az storage blob copy start \
   --account-name "$destStorageAccount" \
   --account-key "$destStorageKey" \
   --destination-blob "$blobName" \
   --destination-container "$destContainer" \
   --source-account-name "$srcStorageAccount" \
   --source-container "$srcContainer" \
   --source-blob "$blobName" \
     --source-account-key "$srcStorageKey"
```

After the copy is started, you can monitor the status using the az storage blob show command as shown here:

```
az storage blob show \
   --account-name "$destStorageAccount" --account-key "$destStorageKey" \
   --container-name "$destContainer" --name "$blobName"
```

> **MORE INFO** **MORE EXAMPLES WITH CLI**
>
> There are many variations for using the async copy service with the Azure CLI. For more information see the following: *https://docs.microsoft.com/cli/azure/storage/blob/copy.*

Async blob copy (AzCopy)

The AzCopy application can also be used to copy between storage accounts. The following example shows how to specify the source storage account using the /source parameter and /sourcekey, and the destination storage account and container using the /Dest parameter and /DestKey.

```
AzCopy /Source:https://[source storage].blob.core.windows.net/[source container]/
/Dest:https://[destination storage].blob.core.windows.net/[destination container]/
/SourceKey:[source key] /DestKey:[destination key] /Pattern:disk1.vhd
```

AzCopy offers a feature to mitigate the lack of SLA with the async copy service. The /Sync-Copy parameter ensures that the copy operation gets consistent speed during a copy. AzCopy performs the synchronous copy by downloading the blobs to copy from the specified source to local memory, and then uploading them to the Blob storage destination.

```
AzCopy /Source:https://[source storage].blob.core.windows.net/[source container]/
/Dest:https://[destination storage].blob.core.windows.net/[destination container]/
/SourceKey:[source key] /DestKey:[destination key] /Pattern:disk1.vhd /SyncCopy
```

> **MORE INFO   AZCOPY**
>
> **AzCopy version 10 (in preview) is multi-platform, and works with Windows, Linux and macOS.**
>
> For more information on AzCopy see the following:
>
> *https://docs.microsoft.com/azure/storage/common/storage-use-azcopy.*

Async blob copy (Storage Explorer)

The Azure Storage Explorer application can also take advantage of the async blob copy service. To copy between storage accounts, navigate to the source storage account, select one or more files and click the copy button on the tool bar. Then navigate to the destination storage account, expand the container to copy to, and click **Paste** from the toolbar. In Figure 2-17, the Workshop List – 2017.xlsx blob was copied from examrefstorage\srccontainer to examrefstorage2\destcontainer using this technique.

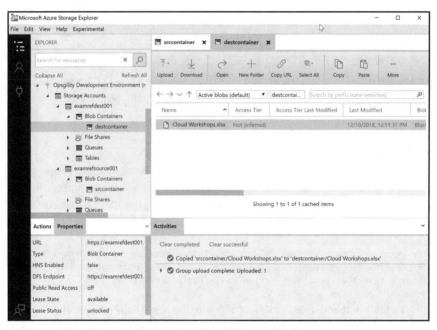

FIGURE 2-17 Using the async blob copy service with Storage Explorer

Skill 2.2: Import and export data to Azure

If your dataset is large enough, or you have limited or no connectivity from your data to the Internet, you may want to physically ship the data and import it into Microsoft Azure instead of uploading it. There are two solutions that enable this scenario. The first solution is the Azure Import and Export service, which allows you to ship data into or out of an Azure Storage account by physically shipping disks to an Azure datacenter. This service is ideal when it is either not possible, or prohibitively expensive, to upload or download the data directly. The second solution is Azure Data Box, which is a device that Microsoft will send to you that allows you to copy your data to it and then ship it back to Microsoft for uploading to Azure.

> **This section covers how to:**
> - Configure and use Azure blob storage
> - Create export from Azure job
> - Create import into Azure job
> - Use Azure Data Box
> - Configure Azure content delivery network (CDN) endpoints

Configure and use Azure blob storage

This section describes the key features of the blob storage service provided by each storage account. Blob storage is used for large-scale storage of arbitrary data objects, such as media files, log files, or any other objects.

Blob containers

Figure 2-18 shows the layout of the blob storage service. Each storage account can have one or more blob containers and all blobs must be stored within a container. Containers are similar in concept to a hard drive on your computer, in that they provide a storage space for data in your storage account. Within each container you can store blobs, much as you would store files on a hard drive. Blobs can be placed at the root of the container or organized into a folder hierarchy.

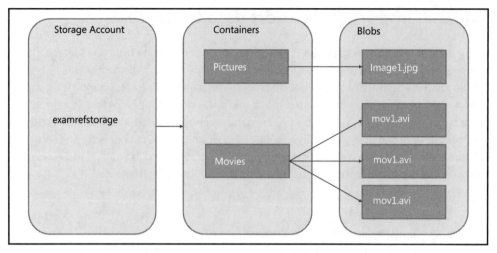

FIGURE 2-18 Azure Storage account entities and hierarchy relationships

Each blob has a unique URL. The format of this URL is as follows:
https://[account name].blob.core.windows.net/[container name]/[blob path and name].

Optionally, you can create a container at the root of the storage account, by specifying the special name $root for the container name. This allows you to store blobs in the root of the storage account and reference them with URLs such as:
https://[account name].blob.core.windows.net/fileinroot.txt.

Understanding blob types

Blobs come in three types, and it is important to understand when each type of blob should be used and what the limitations are for each.

- **Page blobs**   A Optimized for random-access read and write operations. Page blobs are used to store virtual disk (VHD) files which using unmanaged disks with Azure virtual machines. The maximize page blob size is 8 TB.
- **Block blobs**   Optimized for efficient uploads and downloads, for video, image and other general-purpose file storage. The maximum block blob size is slightly over 4.75 TB.
- **Append blobs**   Optimized for append operations, and do not support modification of existing blob contents. Page blobs are most commonly used for log files. Up to 50,000 blocks can be added to each append blob, and each block can be up to 4MB in size, giving a maximum append blob size of slightly over 195 GB.

Blobs of all three types can share a single blob container.

EXAM TIP

The type of the blob is set at creation and cannot be changed after the fact. A common problem that may show up on the exam is if a .vhd file was accidently uploaded as a block blob instead of a page blob. The blob must be deleted first and reuploaded as a page blob before it can be mounted as an OS or Data Disk to an Azure VM.

MORE INFO   BLOB TYPES

You can learn more about the intricacies of each blob type here: https://docs.microsoft.com/rest/api/storageservices/understanding-block-blobs--append-blobs--and-page-blobs.

Managing blobs and containers (Azure portal)

You can create and manage containers through the Azure Management Portal, Azure Storage Explorer, third-party storage tools, or through the command line tools. To create a container in the Azure Management Portal, open a storage account by clicking **All Services**, then **Storage Accounts**, and choose your storage account. Within the storage account blade, click the **Blobs** tile, and then click the **+ Container** button, as shown in Figure 2-19. See Skill 2.1 for more information on setting the public access level.

FIGURE 2-19 Creating a container using the Azure Management Portal

After a container is created, you can also use the portal to upload blobs to the container as demonstrated in Figure 2-20. Click the **Upload** button in the container and then browse to the blob to upload. If you click the **Advanced** button you can select the blob type (Blob, Page or Append), the block size, and optionally a folder to upload the blob to.

FIGURE 2-20 The Azure Management Portal uploads a blob to a storage account container

Managing blobs and containers (PowerShell)

To create a container using the Azure PowerShell cmdlets, use the `New-AzStorageContainer` cmdlet. The access tier is specified using the `Permission` parameter.

To create a blob within an existing container, use the `Set-AzStorageBlobContent` cmdlet.

Both `New-AzStorageContainer` and `Set-AzStorageBlobContent` require a storage context, which specifies the storage account name and authentication credentials (for example access keys or SAS token). A storage context can be created using the `New-AzStorageContext` cmdlet. The context then can be passed explicitly when accessing the storage account, or implicitly by storing the context using the `Set-AzCurrentStorageAccount` cmdlet.

The following PowerShell script shows how to use these cmdlets to get the account key, create and store the storage context, then create a container and upload a local file as a blob.

```
$storageAccount = "[storage account name]"
$resourceGroup = "[resource group name]"
$container = "[blob container name]"
$localFile = "[path to local file]"
$blobName = "[blob path]"

# Get account key
$storageKey = Get-AzStorageAccountKey `
  -Name $storageAccount `
  -ResourceGroupName $resourceGroup

# Create and store the storage context
$context = New-AzStorageContext `
  -StorageAccountName $storageAccount `
  -StorageAccountKey $storageKey.Value[0]

Set-AzCurrentStorageAccount -Context $context

# Create storage container
New-AzStorageContainer -Name $container `
  -Permission Off

# Create storage blob
Set-AzStorageBlobContent -File $localFile `
  -Container $container `
  -Blob $blobName
```

> **MORE INFO**   **MANAGING BLOB STORAGE WITH POWERSHELL**
>
> The Azure PowerShell cmdlets offer a rich set of capabilities for managing blobs in storage. You can learn more about their capabilities here:
>
> *https://docs.microsoft.com/azure/storage/blobs/storage-how-to-use-blobs-powershell.*

Managing blobs and containers (CLI)

The Azure CLI tools can also be used to create a storage account container with the `az storage container create` command. The public-access parameter is used to set the permissions. The supported values are off, blob, and container.

```
storageaccount="[storage account name]"
containername="[blob container]"
az storage container create --account-name $storageaccount --name $containername
--public-access off
```

You can use the Azure CLI to upload a file as well using the `az storage blob upload` command as shown next

```
container_name="[blob container]"

account_name="[storage account name]"
account_key="[storage account key]"
file_to_upload="[path to local file]"
blob_name="[blob name]"
az storage blob upload --container-name $container_name --account-name $account_name
--account-key $account_key --file $file_to_upload --name $blob_name
```

> **MORE INFO** **MANAGING BLOB STORAGE WITH THE AZURE CLI**
>
> The Azure CLI also offers a rich set of capabilities for managing blobs in storage. You can learn more about their capabilities here:
>
> *https://docs.microsoft.com/azure/storage/common/storage-azure-cli.*

Managing blobs and containers (Storage Explorer)

Azure Storage Explorer provides rich functionality for managing storage data, including blobs and containers. To create a container, expand the Storage Accounts node, and expand the storage account you want to use, right-clicking on the Blob Containers node. This will open a new menu item where you can create a blob container as shown in Figure 2-21.

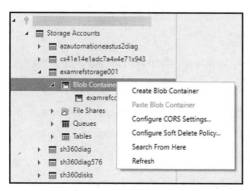

FIGURE 2-21 Creating a container using the Azure Storage Explorer

Azure Storage Explorer provides the ability to upload a single file or multiple files at once. The Upload Folder feature provides the ability to upload the entire contents of a local folder, recreating the hierarchy in the Azure Storage Account. Figure 2-22 shows the two upload options.

FIGURE 2-22 Uploading files and folders using Azure Storage Explorer

Managing blobs and containers (AzCopy)

AzCopy is a command line utility that can be used to copy data to and from blob, file, and table storage, and also provides support for copying data between storage accounts. AzCopy is designed for optimal performance, so it is commonly used to automate large transfers of files and folders.

There are currently two versions of AzCopy: one for Windows and one for Linux. The latest preview version, v10, combines Windows, Linux and macOS support in a single release. For more information, see *https://docs.microsoft.com/azure/storage/common/storage-use-azcopy-v10*.

The following example shows how you can use AzCopy (v10) to download a single blob from a container to a local folder. In this example, a SAS token is used to authorize access.

```
AzCopy  copy "https://[source storage].blob.core.windows.net/[source container]/
[path-to-blob]?[SAS]" "[local file path]"
```

This example shows how you can switch the order of the source and destination parameters to upload the file instead.

```
AzCopy  copy "[local file path]" "https://[destination storage]
.blob.core.windows.net/[destination container]/[path-to-blob]?[SAS]"
```

> **MORE INFO   AZCOPY EXAMPLES**
>
> AzCopy provides many capabilities beyond simple uploading and downloading of files. For more information see the following:
>
> - **AzCopy v8** *https://docs.microsoft.com/azure/storage/common/storage-use-azcopy*
> - **AzCopy v10** *https://docs.microsoft.com/azure/storage/common/storage-use-azcopy-v10*

Soft delete for Azure storage blobs

The default behavior of deleting a blob is that the blob is deleted and lost forever. Soft delete is a feature that allows you to save and recover your data when blobs or blob snapshots are deleted even in the event of an overwrite. This feature must be enabled on the Azure Storage account and a retention period set for how long the deleted data is available (see Figure 2-23).

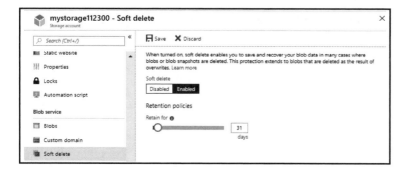

FIGURE 2-23 Enabling soft delete on an Azure storage account

EXAM TIP

The maximum retention period for soft delete is 365 days.

MORE INFO   SOFT DELETE FOR AZURE STORAGE BLOBS

You can learn more about using soft delete with Azure blob storage here: *https://docs.microsoft.comazure/storage/blobs/storage-blob-soft-delete.*

Create export from Azure job

An export job allows you to export large volumes of data from Azure storage to your on-premises environment, by shipping you the data on disk.

To export data, create an export job on the storage account using the management portal. To create an export job, do the following:

1. Log in to the Azure portal and click **All Services** then search for and select **Import/ Export Jobs**.

2. Click **Create Import/Export Job**.

3. On the **Basics** tab (as shown in Figure 2-24), choose **Export From Azure** and specify the job name and the resource group to contain the created job.

4. On the **Job Details** tab, choose which storage account to export from and choose the blobs to export. You have the following options.

- Export All

- Selected Containers And Blobs

- Export From Blob List file (XML Format)

5. On the **Return Shipping Info** tab, specify your carrier information and the address for the disks to be shipped to.

6. On the **Summary** tab, click the **OK** button after confirming the export job.

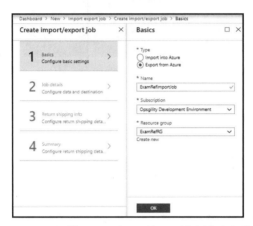

FIGURE 2-24 The create import/export job blade in the Azure portal

---

> **MORE INFO** **WALKTHROUGH CREATING A DATA EXPORT JOB**
>
> To learn more about creating an import job see the following:
> *https://docs.microsoft.com/azure/storage/common/storage-import-export-data-from-blobs*.

After you receive the disks from Microsoft you will need to retrieve the BitLocker keys from the Azure portal to unlock the disks.

Create import into Azure job

An import job allows you to import large volumes of data to Azure by shipping the data on disk to Microsoft.

The first step to import data using the Azure Import/Export service is to install the Microsoft Azure Import/Export tool.

Additional requirements and limitations of the Azure Import/Export tool include:

- A Windows 7, Windows Server 2008 R2, or a later OS version is required
- The tool also requires .NET Framework 4.5.1 and BitLocker
- All storage account types are supported (general purpose v1, general purpose v2, and blob storage)
- Block, Page, and append blobs are supported for both import and export
- The Azure Files service is only supported for import jobs but not export jobs

Table 2-7 lists the disks requirements for sending data to the Import/Export service.

TABLE 2-7 Supported disks for the Import/Export service

Disk Type	Size	Supported	Not Supported
SSD	2.5″		
HDD	3.5″	SATA II, SATA III	External HDD with built-in USB adaptor Disk inside the casing of an external HDD

EXAM TIP

A single import/export job can have a maximum of 10 HDD/SSDs and a mix of HDD/SSD of any size.

The second step to import data is to prepare your drives using the Microsoft Azure Import/Export tool (WAImportExport.exe), and copy the data to transfer to the drives.

The first session, when preparing the drive, requires several parameters, such as the destination storage account key, the BitLocker key, and the log directory. The following example (for the v1 tool) shows the syntax of using the Azure Import/Export tool with the PrepImport parameter to prepare the disk for an import job for the first session.

```
WAImportExport.exe PrepImport /j:<JournalFile> /id:<SessionId> [/logdir:<LogDirectory>]
[/sk:<StorageAccountKey>] /t:<source drive letter> /srcdir:<source folder> /
dstdir:<destination path>
```

The Azure Import/Export tool creates a journal file that contains the information necessary to restore the files on the drive to the Azure Storage account, such as mapping a folder/file to a container/blob or files. Each drive used in the import job will have a unique journal file on it created by the tool.

> **NOTE USING THE IMPORT/EXPORT TOOL**
>
> To add a single file to the drive and journal file, use the /srcfile parameter instead of the / srcdir parameter.
>
> The Azure Import/Export tool supports a number of other parameters. For a full list, see:
>
> - Version 1: *https://docs.microsoft.com/azure/storage/common/storage-import-export-tool-preparing-hard-drives-import-v1*
> - Version 2: *https://docs.microsoft.com/azure/storage/common/storage-import-export-tool-preparing-hard-drives-import*

Once drive preparation is complete, the third step in the import process is to create an import job through the Azure portal. To create an import job, do the following:

1. Log in to the Azure portal and click **All Services**, then **Storage**, followed by **Import/ Export Jobs**.

2. Click **Create Import/Export Job**.

3. On the **Basics** tab, choose **Import into Azure** and specify the job name and the resource group to contain the created job.

4. On the **Job Details** tab, choose the journal file created with the WAImportExport.exe tool and select the destination storage account.

5. On the **Return Shipping Info** tab, specify your carrier information and return address for the return disks.

6. On the **Summary** tab, click the OK button after confirming the import job.

Having created the import job, the fourth step in the import process is to physically ship the disks to Microsoft and add the courier tracking number to the existing import job. The drives will be returned using the courier information provided in the import job.

Check the job status regularly until it is completed. You can then verify that the data has been uploaded to Azure.

MORE INFO **WALKTHROUGH CREATING A DATA IMPORT JOB**

To learn more about creating an import job see the following:

- Version 1 (blobs)   *https://docs.microsoft.com/azure/storage/common/storage-import-export-data-to-blobs*

- Version 2 (files)   *https://docs.microsoft.com/azure/storage/common/storage-import-export-data-to-files*

Use Azure Data Box

Azure Data Box is a service that provides a device that Microsoft will send to you via a regional courrier that allows you to send terabytes of on-premises data to Azure in a quick, inexpensive, reliable, and secure way.

Like the Import/Export service, use Azure Data Box when you have limited to no connectivity and it is more feasible to ship the data to Azure instead of uploading it directly. Common scenarios include one-time or periodic data migrations, as well as initial data transfers which are followed by incremental updates over the network.

There are three types of Data Box available. The key features of each type are described in Table 2-8.

TABLE 2-8 Azure Data Box variations

	Data Box Disk	Data Box	Data Box Heavy
Format	Standalone SSDs	Rugged device	Large rugged device
Capacity	Up to 35 TB usable	80 TB usable	800 TB usable
Support	Blobs	Blobs and Files	Blobs and Files
Destination storage accounts	1 only	Up to 10	Up to 10

The workflow to use Azure Data Box is simple:

- **Order**   Use the Azure portal to initiate the data box order by creating an Azure Data Box resource. Specify your shipping address and destination storage account. You will receive a shipping tracking ID once the device ships.

- **Receive**   Once the device is received, connect it to your network, power on.

- **Copy data**   Mount your file shares and copy your data to the device. The client used to copy data will need to run Windows 7 or later, Windows Server 2008 R2 SP1 or later, or a Linux OS supporting NFS4.1 or SMB 2.0 or higher.

- **Return**   Prepare the device, and ship it back to Microsoft.

- **Upload**   Your data will be uploaded to your storage account and securely erased from the device.

Configure Azure content delivery network (CDN) endpoints

A content delivery network (CDN) is a global network of servers, placed in key locations to provide fast, local access for the majority of Internet users. Web applications use CDNs to cache static content, such as images, at locations close to each user. The CDN retrieves content from origin servers provided by the web application, caching that content for fast delivery.

By retrieving this content from the CDN cache, users benefit from reduced download times and a faster browsing experience. In addition, each request that is served from the Azure CDN means it is not served from your website, which can remove a significant amount of load.

Configuring CDN endpoints

To publish content in a CDN endpoint, first create a new CDN profile. To do this using the Azure portal click **Create a resource**, then click **Web**, then select **CDN** to open the create CDN profile blade (Figure 2-25). Provide a name for the CDN profile, the name of the resource group, along with the region and pricing tier.

FIGURE 2-25 Creating a CDN profile using the Azure portal

After the CDN profile is created, add an endpoint to the profile. Add an Endpoint by opening the CDN profile in the portal and click the **+ Endpoint** button. On the creation dialog, specify a unique name for the CDN endpoint, and the configuration for the origin settings, including the type (Storage, Web App, Cloud Service, or Custom), the host header and the origin port for HTTP and HTTPS), and then click the Add button. Figure 2-26 shows an endpoint using an Azure Storage account as the origin type. An endpoint can also be created when creating the CDN profile, and also directly from the blob storage settings of a storage account.

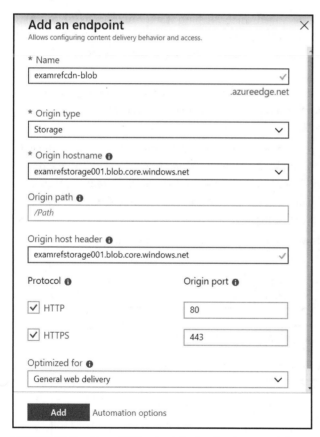

FIGURE 2-26 Creating a CDN endpoint using the Azure portal

Blobs stored in public access enabled containers are cached in the CDN edge endpoints. To access the content via the CDN, instead of directly from your storage account, change the URL used to access the content to reference the CDN endpoint, as shown in the following example:

- Original URL within storage:
  - *http://storageaccount.blob.core.windows.net/imgs/logo.png*
- New URL accessed through CDN:
  - *http://examrefcdn-blob.azureedge.net/imgs/logo.png*

How the Azure CDN Works

Figure 2-27 shows how CDN caching works at a high level. In this example, the file logo.png has been hosted in blob storage in West US. A user in the UK can access the file, but due to the physical distance, the user experiences a high latency which slows down their browsing experience.

To address this, a CDN endpoint is deployed, using the blob storage account as the origin. To access the logo.png from the CDN, the URL for the file is changed from *http://storageaccount.blob.core.windows.net/imgs/logo.png* to *http://examrefcdnh.azureedge.net/imgs/logo.png*.

The CDN provides a worldwide network of caching servers. Users accessing the 'examrefcnd.azureedge.net' domain are automatically routed to their closest available server cluster, providing low-latency access to the CDN.

When a request for logo.png is received by a CDN server, the server checks to see if the file is available in its local cache. If not, this is called a cache miss, and the CDN will retrieve the file from the origin. The file is then cached locally and returned to the client. Subsequent requests for the same file will result in a 'cache hit', and the cached file is returned to the client directly from the CDN, avoiding a round-trip to the origin.

This local caching provides for lower latency and a faster browsing experience for the user.

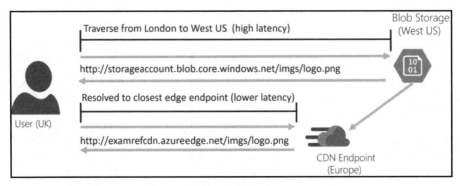

FIGURE 2-27 Accessing content from a CDN instead of a storage account

Cache duration

Content is cached by the CDN until its time-to-live (TTL) elapses. The TTL is determined by the Cache-Control header in the HTTP response from the origin server. You can set the Cache-Control header programmatically in web apps by specifying it in the HTTP header. This setting can be set programmatically when serving up the content, or by setting the configuration of the web app.

You can manage the content expiration directly for blobs served directly from an Azure storage account by setting the time-to-live (TTL) period of the blob itself. Figure 2-28 demonstrates how to use Storage Explorer to set the CacheControl property on the blob files directly. You can also set the property using Windows PowerShell or the CLI tools when uploading to storage.

FIGURE 2-28 Setting the CacheControl property of a blob using Azure Storage Explorer

You can also control the TTL for your blobs using the Azure portal depending on the type of CDN endpoint created (see *https://docs.microsoft.com/azure/cdn/cdn-features* to compare the different SKU feature sets). In Figure 2-29 you can see the options for setting the cache duration of the Standard Verizon CDN endpoint.

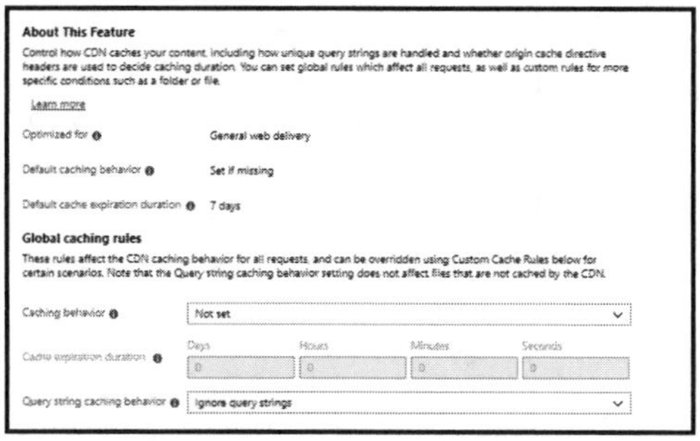

FIGURE 2-29 Setting global caching rules for the Standard Verizon CDN endpoint

MORE INFO **MANAGING THE TIME-TO-LIVE (TTL) OF CDN CONTENT**

You can learn more about how to programmatically set the CacheControl HTTP header for web apps here: *https://docs.microsoft.com/azure/cdn/cdn-manage-expiration-of-cloud-service-content*. And learn about using PowerShell and the CLI tools here: *https://docs.microsoft.com/azure/cdn/cdn-manage-expiration-of-blob-content*.

Versioning assets using query string parameters

To permanently remove content from the Azure CDN, it should first be removed from the origin servers. If the content is stored in storage, you can set the container to private, or delete the content from the container, or even delete the container itself. If the content is in an Azure web app, you can modify the application to no longer serve the content.

Keep in mind that even if the content is deleted from storage, or if it is no longer accessible from your web application, cached copies may remain in the CDN endpoint until the TTL has expired. To immediately remove it from the CDN, purge the content as shown in Figure 2-30.

FIGURE 2-30 Purging a file from the Azure CDN

Purging content is also used when the content in the origin has changed. Purging the CDN cache of the old content means the CDN will pick up the new content from the origin when the next request for that content is received.

Using query strings is another technique for controlling information cached in the CDN. For instance, suppose your application hosted in Azure cloud services or Azure web apps has a page that generates content dynamically, such as: *http://[CDN Endpoint].azureedge.net/chart.aspx*. You can configure query string handling to cache multiple versions, depending on the query string that is passed in. The Azure CDN supports three different modes of query string caching:

- **Ignore query strings**   This is the default mode. The CDN edge node will pass the query string from the requestor to the origin on the first request and cache the asset. All subsequent requests for that asset that are served from the edge node will ignore the query string until the cached asset expires.

- **Bypass caching for URL with query strings**   In this mode, requests with query strings are not cached at the CDN edge node. The edge node retrieves the asset directly from the origin and passes it to the requestor with each request.

- **Cache every unique URL**   This mode treats each request with a query string as a unique asset with its own cache. For example, the response from the origin for a request for foo.ashx?q=bar is cached at the edge node and returned for subsequent caches with that same query string. A request for foo.ashx?q=somethingelse is cached as a separate asset with its own time to live.

Configuring custom domains for storage and CDN

Both an Azure storage account and an Azure CDN endpoint allow you to specify a custom do-main for accessing blob content instead of using the default domain name (<account name>. blob.core.windows.net). To configure either service, you must create a new CNAME record with the DNS provider that is hosting your DNS records.

For example, to enable a custom domain blobs.contoso.com foran Azure storage account, create a CNAME record that points from blobs.contoso.com to the Azure storage account [storage account].blob.core.windows.net. Table 2-10 shows an example mapping in DNS.

TABLE 2-9 Mapping a domain to an Azure Storage account in DNS

CNAME RECORD	TARGET
blobs.contoso.com	contosoblobs.blob.core.windows.net

Mapping a domain that is already in use within Azure may result in minor downtime as the DNS entry must be updated before it is registered with the storage account. If necessary, you can avoid the downtime by using a second option to validate the domain. In this approach, you create the DNS record asverify.<your domain> to verify your ownership of your domain, allowing you to register your domain with your storage account without impacting your application. You can then modify the DNS record for your domain to point to the storage account. Because the domain name is already registered with the storage account, traffic will be accepted immediately, avoiding any downtime. The asverify record can then be deleted.

Table 2-11 shows the example DNS records created when using the asverify method.

TABLE 2-10 Mapping a domain to an Azure Storage account in DNS with the asverify intermediary domain

CNAME RECORD	TARGET
asverify.blobs.contoso.com	asverify.contosoblobs.blob.core.windows.net
blobs.contoso.com	contosoblobs.blob.core.windows.net

To enable a custom domain for an Azure CDN endpoint, the process is almost identical. Create a CNAME record that points from cdn.contoso.com to the Azure CDN endpoint [CDN endpoint]. azureedge.net. Table 2-12 shows mapping a custom CNAME DNS record to the CDN endpoint.

TABLE 2-11 Mapping a domain to an Azure CDN endpoint in DNS

CNAME RECORD	TARGET
cdncontent.contoso.com	examrefcdn.azureedge.net

The cdnverify intermediate domain can be used just like asverify for storage. Use this intermediate validation if you're already using the domain with an application because updating the DNS directly can result in downtime. Table 2-13 shows the CNAME DNS records needed for verifying your domain using the cdnverify subdomain.

TABLE 2-12 Mapping a domain to an Azure CDN endpoint in DNS with the cdn intermediary domain

CNAME RECORD	TARGET
cdnverify.cdncontent.contoso.com	cdnverify.examrefcdn.azureedge.net
cdncontent.contoso.com	examrefcdn.azureedge.net

After the DNS records are created and verified you then associate the custom domain with your CDN endpoint or blob storage account.

EXAM TIP

Azure Storage does not yet natively support HTTPS with custom domains. You can currently use the Azure CDN to access blobs with custom domains over HTTPS.

> **MORE INFO   CONFIGURING CUSTOM DOMAINS FOR STORAGE AND CDN**
>
> You can learn more about configuring custom domains for storage here:
> *https://docs.microsoft.com/azure/storage/blobs/storage-custom-domain-name.*
>
> You can learn more about using customer domains with the Azure CDN here:
> *https://docs.microsoft.com/azure/cdn/cdn-map-content-to-custom-domain.*

Skill 2.3: Configure Azure files

Azure File Service is a fully managed file share service that offers endpoints for the Server Messaging Block (SMB) protocol, also known as Common Internet File System or CIFS 2.1 and 3.0. This allows you to create one or more file shares in the cloud (up to 5 TB per share) and use the share for similar uses as a regular Windows File Server, such as shared storage or for new uses such as part of a lift and shift migration strategy.

> **This section covers how to:**
> - Create Azure file share
> - Create Azure File Sync service
> - Create Azure sync group
> - Troubleshoot Azure File Sync

Using the Azure File Service

Common use cases for using Azure Files are:

- **Replace or supplement on-premises file servers**   In some cases Azure files can be used to completely replace an existing file server. Azure File shares can also be replicated with Azure File Sync to Windows Servers, either on-premises or in the cloud, for performant and distributed caching of the data where it's being used.

- **"Lift and shift" migrations**   In many cases migrating all workloads that use data on an existing on-premises file share to Azure File Service at the same time is not a viable option. Azure File Service with File Sync makes it easy to replicate the data on-premises and in the Azure File Service so it is easily accessible to both on-premises and cloud workloads without the need to reconfigure the on-premises systems until they are migrated.

- **Simplify cloud development and management** Storing common configuration files, installation media and tools, as well as a central repository for application logging, are all great use cases for Azure File Service.

Figure 2-31 shows the hierarchy of files stored in Azure files.

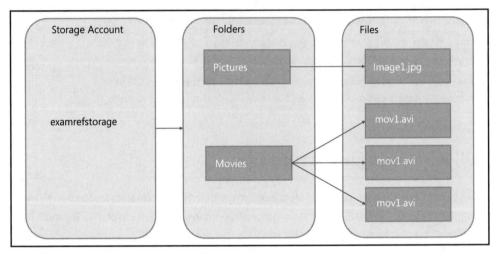

FIGURE 2-31 Azure files entities and relationship hierarchy

There are several common use cases for using Azure files. A few examples include the following:

- Migration of existing applications that require a file share for storage.
- Shared storage of files such as web content, log files, application configuration files, or even installation media.

Creating an Azure File Share (Azure portal)

To create a new Azure File using the Azure portal, open a Standard Azure storage account (Premium is not supported), click the **Files** link, and then click the **+ File Share** button. On the dialog shown in figure 2-32, you must provide the file share name and the quota size, which can go up to 5120 GB.

FIGURE 2-32 Adding a new share with Azure files

Creating an Azure File Share (PowerShell)

To create a share, first create an Azure Storage context object using the `New-AzStorageContext` cmdlet. This cmdlet requires the name of the storage key, and the access key for the storage account, which is retrieved by calling the `Get-AzStoragerAccountKey` cmdlet or copying it from the Azure portal. Pass the context object to the `New-AzStorageShare` cmdlet along with the name of the share to create, as the next example shows.

To create a share using the Azure PowerShell cmdlets, use the following code:

```
$storageAccount = "[storage account]"
$rgName = "[resource group name]"
$shareName = "contosoweb"
$storageKey = Get-AzStorageAccountKey `
    -ResourceGroupName $rgName `
    -Name $storageAccount
$ctx = New-AzStorageContext -StorageAccountName $storageAccount `
                        -StorageAccountKey $storageKey.Value[0]
New-AzStorageShare -Name $shareName -Context $ctx
```

Creating an Azure File Share (CLI)

To create an Azure File Share using the CLI, first retrieve the connection string using the `az show connection string` command, and pass that value to the `az storage share create` command, as the following example demonstrates.

```
rgName="[resource group name]"
storageAccountName="[storage account]"
shareName="contosoweb"
constring=$(az storage account show-connection-string -n $storageAccountName
-g $rgName --query 'connectionString' -o tsv)
az storage share create --name $shareName --quota 2048 --connection-string $constring
```

Connecting to Azure File Service outside of Azure

Because Azure File Service provides support for SMB 3.0 it is possible to connect directly to an Azure File Share from a computer running outside of Azure. In this case, remember to open outbound TCP port 445 in your local network. Some Internet service providers may block port 445, so check with your service provider for details if you have problems connecting.

Connect and mount with Windows File Explorer

There are several ways to mount an Azure File Share from Windows. The first is to use the Map network drive feature within Windows File Explorer. Open File Explorer and find the This PC Node in the explorer view. Right-click **This PC**, and you can then click the **Map Network Drive** option, as shown in Figure 2-33.

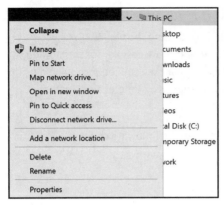

FIGURE 2-33 The Map Network Drive option from This PC

When the dialog opens, specify the following configuration options, as shown in Figure 2-34:

- **Folder**   \\[name of storage account].files.core.windows.net\[name of share]
- **Connect Using Different Credentials**   Checked

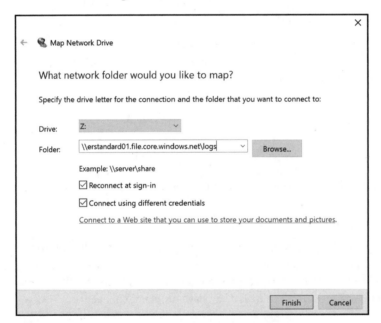

FIGURE 2-34 Mapping a Network Drive to an Azure File Share

When you click Finish, you see another dialog like the one shown in Figure 2-35 requesting the user name and password to access the file share. The user name should be in the following format: Azure\[name of storage account], and the password should be the access key for the Azure storage account.

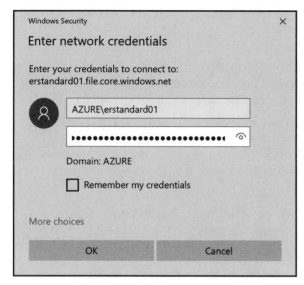

FIGURE 2-35 Specifying credentials to the Azure File Share

Connect and mount with the net use command

You can also mount the Azure File Share using the Windows net use command as the following example demonstrates.

```
net use x \\erstandard01.file.core.windows.net\logs  /u:AZURE\erstandard01
r21Dk4qgY1HpcbriySWrBxnXnbedZLmnRK3N49PfaiL1t3ragpQaIB7FqK5zbez/sMnDEzEu/dgA9Nq/W7IF4A==
```

Connect and mount with PowerShell

You can connect and mount an Azure File using the Azure PowerShell cmdlets. In this example, the storage account key is retrieved using the Get-AzStorageAccountKey cmdlet. The account key is the password to the ConvertTo-SecureString cmdlet to create a secure string, which is required for the PSCredential object. From there, the credentials are passed to the New-PSDrive cmdlet, which maps the drive.

```
$rgName = "[resource group name]"
$storageName = "[storage account name]"
$storageKey = (Get-AzStorageAccountKey -ResourceGroupName $rgName
-Name $storageName).Value[0]
$acctKey = ConvertTo-SecureString -String "$storageKey" -AsPlainText -Force
$credential = New-Object System.Management.Automation.PSCredential
-ArgumentList "Azure\$storageName", $acctKey
New-PSDrive -Name "Z" -PSProvider FileSystem -Root
"\\$storageName.file.core.windows.net\$shareName" -Credential $credential
```

Automatically reconnect after reboot in Windows

To make the file share automatically reconnect and map to the drive after Windows is rebooted, use the following command (ensuring you replace the place holder values):

```
cmdkey /add:<storage-account-name>.file.core.windows.net /user:AZURE\<storage-
account-name> /pass:<storage-account-key>
```

Connect and mount from Linux

Use the mount command (elevated with sudo) to mount an Azure File Share on a Linux virtual machine. In this example, the logs file share would be mapped to the /logs mount point.

```
sudo mount -t cifs //<storage-account-name>.file.core.windows.net/logs /logs -o
vers=3.0,username=<storage-account-name>.,password=<storage-account
-key>,dir_mode=0777,file_mode=0777,sec=ntlmssp
```

Create Azure File Sync service

Azure File Sync extends the Azure File service to allow on-premises file services to be extended to Azure while maintaining performance and compatibility.

Some of the key functionality Azure File Sync provides:

- **Multi-site access**   The ability to write files across Windows and Azure Files.
- **Cloud tiering**   Storage only recently accessed data on local servers.
- **Azure Backup integration**   Backup in the cloud.
- **Fast disaster recovery**   Restore file metadata immediately and recall as needed.

Create the Azure File Sync Service in the portal by navigating to **Create A Resource**, then **Storage**, then **Azure File Sync**. The creation blade requires the name of the Sync Service, the Subscription, Resource Group, and the region to create as Figure 2-36 demonstrates.

FIGURE 2-36 Specifying credentials to the Azure File Share

Create Azure sync group

Create a sync group to define the topology for how your file synchronization will take place. Within a sync group you will add server endpoints, which are file servers and paths within the file server you want the sync group to sync with each other. Figure 2-37 shows the settings for creating a sync group using the Azure portal.

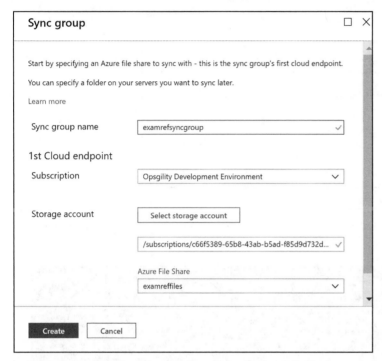

FIGURE 2-37 Creating a Sync Group and specifying the Azure file share

Deploying the Azure File Sync agent

To add endpoints to your Azure File Sync Group you first need to register a server to the sync group by installing the Azure File Sync agent on each server. The agent can be downloaded from the Microsoft Download Center: *https://go.microsoft.com/fwlink/?linkid=858257*. The installer is pictured in Figure 2-38.

Prerequisites

- Internet Explorer Enhanced Security configuration must be disabled before installing the agent. It can be re-enabled after the initial install.
- Install the latest Azure PowerShell module on the server. See the following for installation instructions: *https://go.microsoft.com/fwlink/?linkid=856959*.

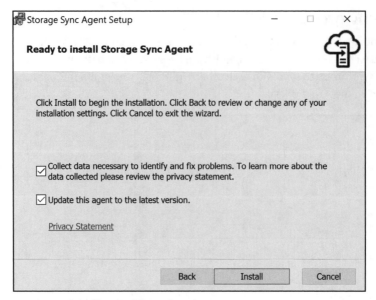

FIGURE 2-38 Installing the Storage Sync Agent

After the agent is installed, sign in with the Azure credentials for your subscription, as shown in Figure 2-39.

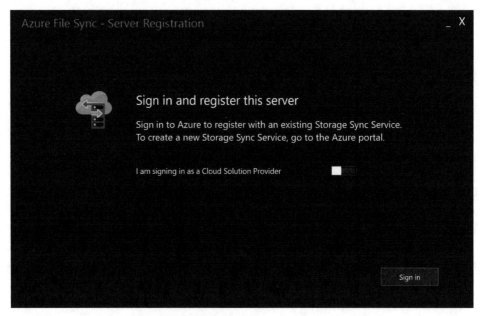

FIGURE 2-39 Signing into the Azure Storage Sync Agent

Next, register the server with the storage sync service, as shown in Figure 2-40.

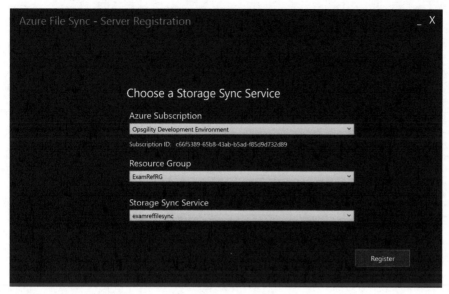

FIGURE 2-40 Registering the server with the Storage Sync Service

Adding a server endpoint

After the server is registered, you must navigate back to the sync group in the Azure portal and click on **Add Server Endpoint**. In the registered server dropdown, you will find all the servers that have the agent installed and associated with this sync service.

Enable cloud tiering to only store frequently accessed files locally on the server while all your other files are stored in Azure files. This is an optional feature that is configured by a policy.

> **MORE INFO   CLOUD TIERING OVERVIEW**
>
> You can learn more about configuring cloud tiering here:
> *https://docs.microsoft.com/azure/storage/files/storage-sync-cloud-tiering.*

Figure 2-41 shows the blade in the Azure portal to add the server endpoint. Ensure that you are only synching the location to one sync group at a time and that the path entered exists on the server.

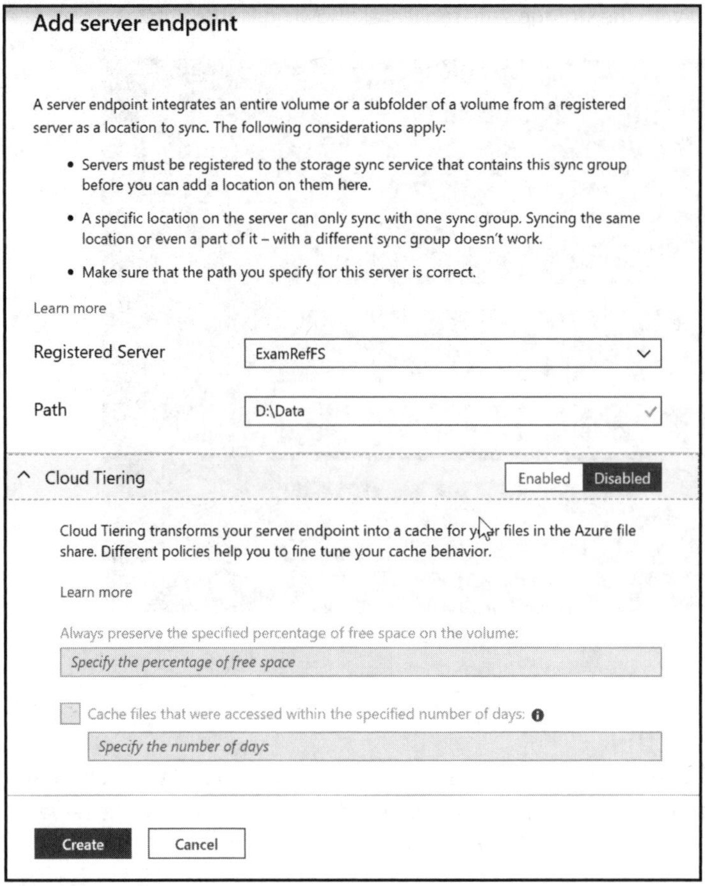

FIGURE 2-41 Adding a server endpoint to the Azure Storage Sync Service.

Troubleshoot Azure File Sync

In this section we will cover some key topics for collecting logs to identify problems, and some of the common issues and troubleshooting techniques you may run into with Azure File Sync.

Agent installation and server registration

If you run into issues installing the storage sync agent run the following command to generate a log file that may give you better insight into what the failure is:

```
StorageSyncAgent.msi /l*v AFSInstaller.log
```

Agent installation fails on Active Director Domain Controller

If you try to install the sync agent on an Active Directory domain controller where the PDC role owner is on a Windows Server 2008R2 or below OS version, you may hit an issue where the sync agent will fail to install. To resolve this, transfer the PDC role to another domain controller running Windows Server 2012R2 or a more recent OS, then install sync.

This server is already registered error

If you need to move the server to a different sync group, or you are troubleshooting why the server does not appear in the list, you may receive the error "This server is already registered during registration." Run the following commands from PowerShell to remove the server:

```
Import-Module "C:\Program Files
\Azure\StorageSyncAgent\StorageSync.Management.ServerCmdlets.dll"
Reset-StorageSyncServer
```

EXAM TIP

If the agent is on a cluster, there is a separate command to clean up the cluster configuration during agent removal: `Reset-StorageSyncServer -CleanClusterRegistration`.

AuthorizationFailed or other permissions issues

If you receive errors creating a cloud endpoint that point to a permissions related problem, ensure that your user account has the following Microsoft.Authorization permissions:

- **Read**   Get role definition
- **Write**   Create or update custom role definition
- **Read**   Get role assignment
- **Write**   Create role assignment

The Owner and User Access Administrator roles both have the correct permissions.

Server endpoint creation fails, with this error: "MgmtServerJobFailed" (Error code: -2134375898)

This error occurs because you are enabling cloud tiering on the system volume. Cloud tiering is not supported on the system volume.

Server endpoint deletion fails, with this error: "MgmtServerJobExpired"

This error occurs because the sync service can no longer reach the server due to network connectivity or the server is just offline. See the following for details on removing servers that are no longer available: *https://docs.microsoft.com/azure/storage/files/storage-sync-files-server-registration#unregister-the-server-with-storage-sync-service*.

Unable to open server endpoint properties page or update cloud tiering policy.

This issue can occur if a management operation on the server endpoint fails. You can update the server endpoint configuration by executing the following PowerShell code from the server:

```
Import-Module "C:\Program Files
\Azure\StorageSyncAgent\StorageSync.Management.PowerShell.Cmdlets.dll"
# Get the server endpoint id based on the server endpoint DisplayName property
Get-AzureRmStorageSyncServerEndpoint `
    -SubscriptionId mysubguid `
    -ResourceGroupName myrgname `
    -StorageSyncServiceName storagesvcname `
    -SyncGroupName mysyncgroup
# Update the free space percent policy for the server endpoint
Set-AzureRmStorageSyncServerEndpoint `
    -Id serverendpointid `
    -CloudTiering true `
    -VolumeFreeSpacePercent 60
```

Server endpoint has a health status of "No Activity" or "Pending" and the server state on the registered server's blade is "Appears offline"

This issue occurs when the Storage Sync Monitor process is not able to communicate with the Azure File Sync service. It could be caused by the process is not running, or a proxy or firewall is blocking communication. The following steps can help you resolve this issue:

- Ensure that the AzureStorageSyncMonitor.exe process is running by looking in Task Manager on the server. If it is not running try to restart the server or use Microsoft Update to update the Azure File Sync Agent.

- If the server is behind a firewall you can use the following code to set application specific proxy settings if you are using version 4.0.1.0 or later:

  ```
  Import-Module "C:\Program Files
  \Azure\StorageSyncAgent\StorageSync.Management.ServerCmdlets.dll"
  Set-StorageSyncProxyConfiguration -Address <url> -Port <port number>
  -ProxyCredential <credentials>
  ```

- You can set machine-wide proxy settings for earlier versions. For more information on machine-wide proxy settings see the following: *https://docs.microsoft.com/azure/storage/files/storage-sync-files-firewall-and-proxy#proxy.*

- For troubleshooting firewalls, ensure that outbound port 433 (HTTPS) is open and the endpoints documented here are not blocked: *https://docs.microsoft.com/azure/storage/files/storage-sync-files-firewall-and-proxy#firewall.*

Server endpoint has a health status of "No Activity" and the server state on the registered servers blade is "Online"

This issue occurs because there is a delay when changes occur because the service is still scanning for changes. Wait for the job to complete and the status should change.

Monitoring synchronization health

Open the sync group in the Azure portal. A health indicator is displayed by each of the server endpoints with green indicating a healthy status. Click on the endpoint to drill in to see stats such as the number of files remaining, size, and any resulting errors.

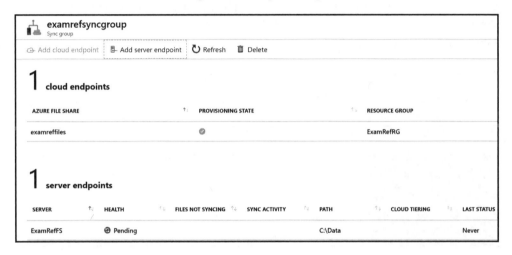

FIGURE 2-42 Monitoring the health of a new server endpoint

> **MORE INFO TROUBLESHOOTING AZURE FILE SYNC**
>
> Keep up with the latest issues and learn more about troubleshooting Azure File Sync here:
> *https://docs.microsoft.com/azure/storage/files/storage-sync-files-troubleshoot.*

Skill 2.4: Implement Azure Backup

Azure Backup is a service that allows you to backup on-premises servers, cloud-based virtual machines, and virtualized workloads such as SQL Server and SharePoint to Microsoft Azure. It also supports backup of Azure storage file shares.

Create Recovery Services Vault

Within Azure, a single resource is provisioned for either Azure Backup or Azure Site Recovery. This resource is called a Recovery Services vault. It is also the resource that is used for configuration and management of both Backup and Site Recovery.

Create a Recovery Services vault (Azure portal)

To create a Recovery Services vault from the Azure portal, click Create a resource, and in the marketplace search dialog box enter Backup and Site Recovery (OMS), and click the **Backup And Site Recovery (OMS)** option. Figure 2-43 shows the search box to find the service.

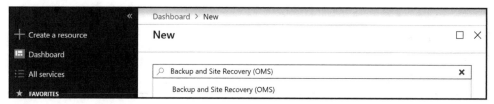

FIGURE 2-43 Creating a Recovery Services vault

Within the marketplace page for **Backup And Site Recovery (OMS)**, click **Create**. Enter the name of the vault and choose or create the resource group where it resides. Next, choose the region where you want to create the resource, and click **Create** as shown in Figure 2-44.

> **NOTE   OPERATIONS MANAGEMENT SUITE (OMS)**
> Operations Management Suite is a collection of features that are licensed together as a unit, including Azure Monitoring and Log Analytics, Azure Automation, Azure Security Center, Azure Backup, and Azure Site Recovery.

FIGURE 2-44 Completing the creation of the vault

Create a Recovery Services vault (PowerShell)

To create a Recovery Services vault with PowerShell, start by creating the resource group it should reside in.

```
New-AzResourceGroup -Name 'ExamRefRG' -Location 'WestUS'
```

Next, create the vault.

```
New-AzRecoveryServicesVault -Name 'MyRSVault' -ResourceGroupName 'ExamRefRG' -Location
'WestUS'
```

The storage redundancy type should be set at this point. The options are Locally Redundant Storage or Geo Redundant Storage. It is a good idea to use Geo Redundant Storage when protecting IaaS virtual machines, because the vault must be in the same region as the VM being backed up. Having the only backup copy in the same region as the item being protected is not wise, so Geo Redundant storage gives you three additional copies of the backed-up data in the sister (paired) region.

```
$vault1 = Get-AzRecoveryServicesVault -Name 'MyRSVault'
Set-AzRecoveryServicesBackupProperties -Vault $vault1 -BackupStorageRedundancy
GeoRedundant
```

Create a Recovery Services vault (CLI)

To create a Recovery Services vault with CLI, start by creating the resource group it should reside in.

```
az group create --location $location --name 'ExamRefRG'
```

Next, create the vault.

```
az backup vault create --name 'MyRSVault' --resource-group 'ExamRefRG'
--Location 'WestUS'
```

Backup and restore data

Having seen how to create a recovery services vault in the previous section, we now look at how to backup and restore data using the vault.

Using a Backup Agent

There are different types of backup agents you can use with Azure Backup. There is the Microsoft Azure Recovery Services (MARS) agent, which is a stand-alone agent used to protect files and folders. There is also the DPM protection agent that is used with Microsoft Azure Backup Server and with System Center Data Protection Manager. Finally, there is the VMSnapshot extension that is installed on Azure VMs to allow snapshots to be taken for full VM backups. The deployment of the DPM protection agent can be automated with either the use of System Center Data Protection Manager or Azure Backup Server. The VMSnapshot or VMSnapshot-Linux extensions are also automatically deployed by the Azure fabric controller. The remainder of this section focuses on deploying the MARS agent.

The MARS agent is available for install from within the Recovery Services vault. Click Backup under Getting Started. Under the **Where Is Your Workload Running?** drop-down menu, select **On-Premises**, and under **What Do You Want To Backup?**, choose **Files And Folders**. Next, click **Prepare Infrastructure**, and the Recovery Services agent is made available, as shown in Figure 2-45.

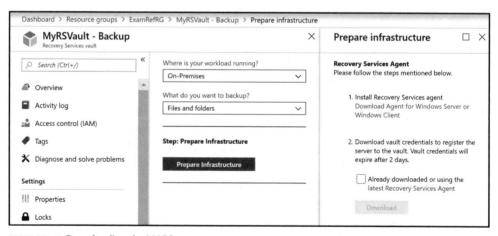

FIGURE 2-45 Downloading the MARS agent

Notice there is only a Windows agent because the backup of files and folders is only supported on Windows computers. Click the link to download the agent. Before initiating the installation of the MARS agent, also download the vault credentials file, which is right under the download links for the Recovery Services agent. The vault credentials file is needed during the installation of the MARS agent.

During the MARS agent installation, a cache location must be specified. There must be free disk space within this cache location that is equal to or greater than five percent of the total amount of data to be protected. These configuration options are shown in Figure 2-46.

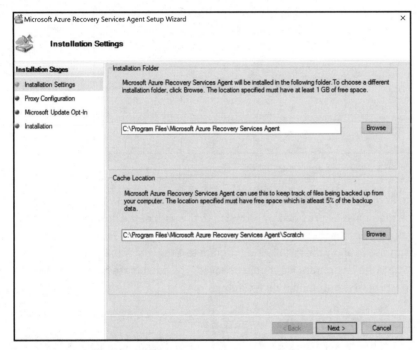

FIGURE 2-46 Installing the MARS agent

The agent needs to communicate to the Azure Backup service on the Internet, so on the next setup screen, configure any required proxy settings. On the last installation screen, any required Windows features are added to the system where the agent is being installed. After it is complete, the installation prompts you to Proceed to Registration, as shown in Figure 2-47.

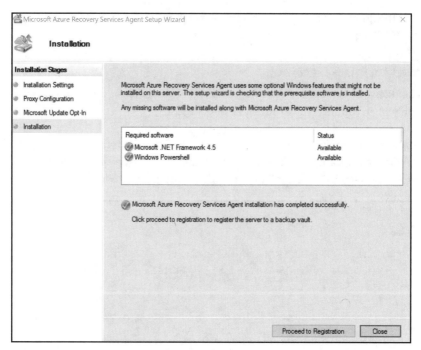

FIGURE 2-47 Final screen of the MARS agent installation

Click Proceed to Registration to open the agent registration dialog box. Within this dialog box the vault credentials must be provided by browsing to the path of the downloaded file. The next dialog box is one of the most important ones. On the Encryption Settings screen, either specify a passphrase or allow the installation program to generate one. Enter this in twice, and then specify where the passphrase file should be saved. The passphrase file is a text file that contains the passphrase, so store this file securely.

> *NOTE* **AZURE BACKUP ENCRYPTION PASSPHRASE**
>
> Data protected by Azure Backup is encrypted using the supplied passphrase. If the passphrase is lost or forgotten, any data protected by Azure Backup is not able to be recovered and is lost.

After the agent is registered with the Azure Backup service, it can then be configured to begin protecting data.

In the last section, the MARS agent was installed and registered with the Azure Backup vault. Before data can be protected with the agent, it must be configured with settings such as, when the backups occur, how often they occur, how long the data is retained, and what data is protected. Within the MARS agent interface, click **Schedule Backup** to begin this configuration process.

Click to move past the Getting Started screen and click **Add Items** to add files and folders. Exclusions can also be set so that certain file types are not protected, as shown in Figure 2-48.

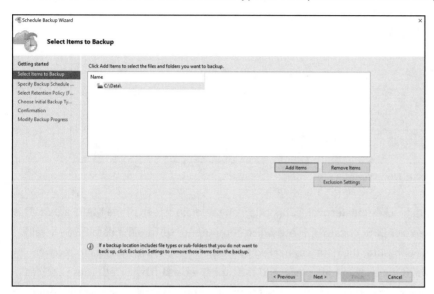

FIGURE 2-48 Configuring the MARS agent to protect data

Next, schedule how often backups should occur. The agent can be configured to back up daily or weekly, with a maximum of three backups taken per day. Specify the retention you want, and the initial backup type (Over the network or Offline). Confirm the settings to complete the wizard. Backups are now scheduled to occur, but they can also be initiated at any time by clicking Back up now on the main screen of the agent. The dialog showing an active backup is shown in Figure 2-49.

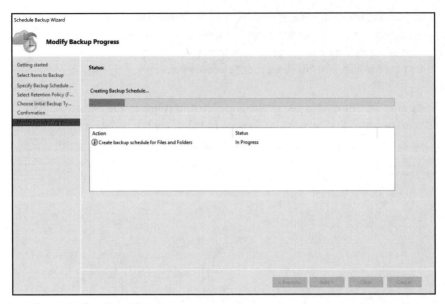

FIGURE 2-49 Backup Now Wizard

To recover data, click the Recover Data option on the main screen of the MARS agent. This initiates the Recover Data Wizard. Choose which computer to restore the data to. Generally, this is the same computer the data was backed up from. Next, choose the data to recover, the date on which the backup took place, and the time the backup occurred. These choices comprise the recovery point to restore. Click **Mount** to mount the selected recovery point as a volume, and then choose the location to recover the data. Confirm the options selected and the recovery begins.

Backing up and Restoring an Azure Virtual Machine

In addition to the MARS agent and protecting files and folders with Azure Backup, it is also possible to back up IaaS virtual machines in Azure. This solution provides a way to restore an entire virtual machine, or individual files from the virtual machine, and it is quite easy to set up. To backup an IaaS VM in Azure with Azure backup, navigate to the Recovery Service vault and under **Getting Started**, click **Backup**. Select Azure as the location where the workload is running, and Virtual machine as the workload to backup and click **Backup**, as shown in Figure 2-50.

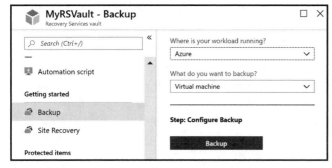

FIGURE 2-50 Configuring Azure Backup to protect IaaS VMs

The next item to configure is the Backup policy. This policy defines how often backups occur and how long the backups are retained. The default policy accomplishes a daily backup at 06:00am and retains backups for 30 days. No more than one backup can be taken daily and a VM can only be associated with one policy at a time. It is also possible to configure custom Backup policies. In this example, a custom Backup policy is configured that includes daily, weekly, monthly, and yearly backups, each with their own retention values. Figure 2-51 shows the creation of a custom backup policy.

Backup policy

Choose backup policy ⓘ
Create New ⌄

* Policy name ⓘ
MyBackupPolicy ✓

Backup schedule

| * Frequency | * Time | * Timezone |
| Daily ⌄ | 6:30 AM ⌄ | (UTC-06:00) Central Time (US & Canada) ⌄ |

Retention range

☑ Retention of daily backup point.

| * At | For | |
| 6:30 AM ⌄ | 180 ✓ | Day(s) |

☑ Retention of weekly backup point.

| * On | * At | For | |
| Sunday ⌄ | 6:30 AM ⌄ | 52 ✓ | Week(s) |

☑ Retention of monthly backup point.

[Week Based] [Day Based]

| * On | * Day | * At | For | |
| First ⌄ | Sunday ⌄ | 6:30 AM ⌄ | 60 | Month(s) |

☑ Retention of yearly backup point.

[Week Based] [Day Based]

| * In | * On | * Day | * At | For | |
| January ⌄ | First ⌄ | Sunday ⌄ | 6:30 AM ⌄ | 10 ✓ | Year(s) |

FIGURE 2-51 Configuring a custom backup policy

Next, choose the VMs to backup. Only VMs within the same region as the Recovery Services vault are available for backup.

> **NOTE** **AZURE IAAS VM PROTECTION AND VAULT STORAGE REDUNDANCY TYPE**
> When protecting IaaS VMs by using Azure Backup, only VMs in the same region as the vault are available for backup. Because of this, it is a best practice to choose Geo-Redundant storage or Read Access Geo-Redundant storage to be associated with the vault. This ensures that, in the case of a regional outage affecting VM access, there is a replicated copy of back-ups in another region that can be used to restore from.

After the VMs are selected, click Enable Backup, as shown in Figure 2-52.

FIGURE 2-52 Enabling VM backups

When you click the Enable Backup button, behind the scenes the VMSnapshot (for Windows) or VMSnapshotLinux (for Linux) extension is automatically deployed by the Azure fabric controller to the VMs. This allows for snapshot-based backups to occur, meaning that first a snapshot of the VM is taken, and then this snapshot is streamed to the Azure storage associated with the Recovery Services vault. The initial backup is not taken until the day/time configured in the backup policy, however an ad-hock backup can be initiated at any time. To do so, navigate to the Protected Items section of the vault properties, and click Backup items. Then, click Azure Virtual Machine under Backup Management type. The VMs that are enabled for backup are listed here. To begin an ad-hock backup, right-click on a VM and select **Backup Now**, as shown in Figure 2-53.

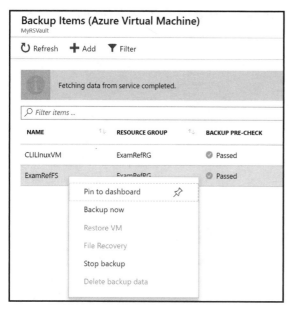

FIGURE 2-53 Starting an ad-hock backup

Preview Features: Backup support for Azure Files and SQL Server in an Azure VM

Azure Backup also directly supports the ability to backup and restore data from Azure Files and SQL Server in an Azure virtual machine. These two features are currently in preview, but it is still a good idea to have a basic understanding of the capabilities as they may eventually appear on the exam.

> **MORE INFO** **AZURE FILES AND SQL SERVER IN AN AZURE VM**
>
> Learn about the current capabilities of Azure Backup support for Azure Files here: *https://docs.microsoft.com/azure/backup/backup-azure-files* and SQL Server in an Azure VM here: *https://docs.microsoft.com/azure/virtual-machines/windows/sql/virtual-machines-windows-sql-backup-recovery*.

When to use Azure Backup Server

Azure Backup Server is a stand-alone service that you install on a Windows Server operating system that stores the backed-up data in a Microsoft Azure Recovery Vault. Azure Backup Server inherits much of the workload backup functionality from Data Protection Manager (DPM). Though Azure Backup Server shares much of the same functionality as DPM, Azure Backup Server does not back up to tape and it does not integrate with System Center.

You should consider using Azure Backup server when you have a requirement to back up the following supported workloads:

- Windows Client
- Windows Server
- Linux Servers
- VMWare VMs
- Exchange
- SharePoint
- SQL Server
- System State and Bare Metal Recovery

> **MORE INFO** **AZURE BACKUP SERVER PROTECTION MATRIX**
>
> The entire list of supported workloads and the versions supported for Azure Backup Server can be found here: *https://docs.microsoft.com/azure/backup/backup-mabs-protection-matrix*.

Configure and review backup reports

Azure Backup Reports provide data visualization from within Power BI from across your Recovery Service vaults and Azure subscriptions to provide insight into your backup activity. This service is currently in preview and at this time reports are supported for Azure virtual machine backup and file and folder backup scenarios when using the MARS agent.

Prerequisites

- Create an Azure Storage account that will contain the report related data.
- Create a Power BI account if you do not already have one at the following URL: *https://powerbi.microsoft.com/landing/signin/*. With this account you can view, customize, and create your own reports in the Power BI portal.
- Register the Microsoft.Insights resource provider for your subscription if it's not already registered. To do this using the Azure portal navigate to **All Services**, **Subscriptions**, your subscription, then **Resource Providers**.
- After you enable the prerequisites, click **Backup Reports**, then **Turn On Diagnostics** to configure diagnostics for the recovery vault (Figure 2-54).

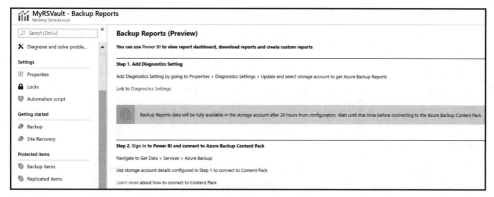

FIGURE 2-54 Configuring backup reports in the Azure portal

The diagnostics configuration allows you to storage diagnostics data in Azure Storage, Event Hubs or Log Analytics. In Figure 2-55 a storage account is selected and AzureBackupReport data is configured for 30 days retention.

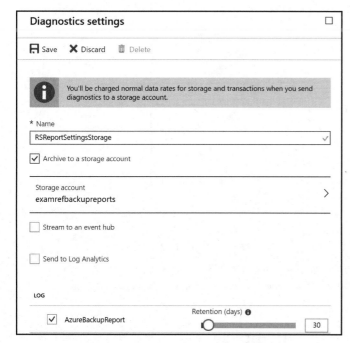

FIGURE 2-55 Diagnostic settings for the Azure Recovery Vault

Backup report data is not available until 24 hours after configuring the storage account.

View Reports in Power BI

After your data has synchronized you can then login to Power BI at the following URL: *https://powerbi.microsoft.com/landing/signin/*. After you are signed in, select **Get Data** and in the More Ways To Create Your Own Content section select **Service Content Packs**. Search for Azure Backup and then click **Get It Now** on the returned result.

After selecting **Azure Backup**, you will be prompted for the storage account name and key created in the previous step. Retrieve these from the Azure portal by navigating to your storage account blade, then **Keys**.

Having completed the Power BI configuration for Azure Backup, you can now navigate to Power BI to review the status of your backups (Figure 2-56).

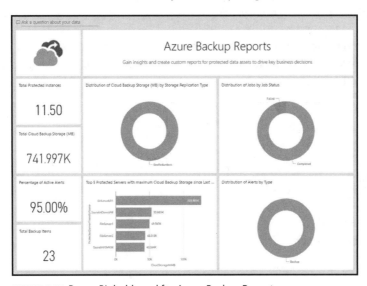

FIGURE 2-56 Power BI dashboard for Azure Backup Reports

MORE INFO   CONFIGURING AND CONNECTING WITH POWER BI

You can learn more about connecting to Azure Backup Reports with Power BI here: *https://docs.microsoft.com/azure/backup/backup-azure-configure-reports*.

Create and configure backup policy

In the Backup and restore data section a backup policy was created while performing an ad-hoc backup of an Azure Virtual Machine. You can edit a policy, associate more virtual machines to a policy, and delete unnecessary policies to meet compliance requirements.

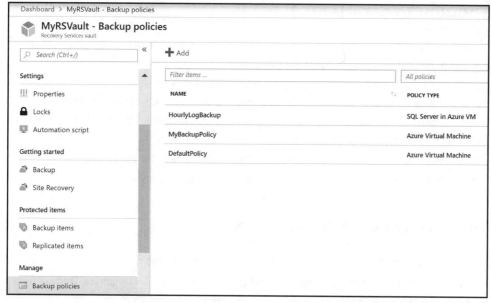

FIGURE 2-57 Backup policies in a Recovery Services Vault

To view your current backup policies in the Azure portal, navigate to the recovery services vault blade, then click **Backup policies** (Figure 2-57). Click on an existing policy to view the policy details or click **Add** to create a new policy. You can create three different types of policies from this view, as depicted in Figure 2-58.

- **Azure Virtual Machine**   Depicted in Figure 2-51 it allows you to specify the backup frequency, retention period, and the backup point on a weekly, monthly and yearly schedule.

- **Azure File Share**   Allows you to schedule a daily backup for an Azure File Share.

- **SQL Server in Azure VM**   Allows you to use SQL Server specific backup technology such as full, differential, and log backup with an associated schedule for each option. You can also specify that SQL Backup compression be enabled on the backups.

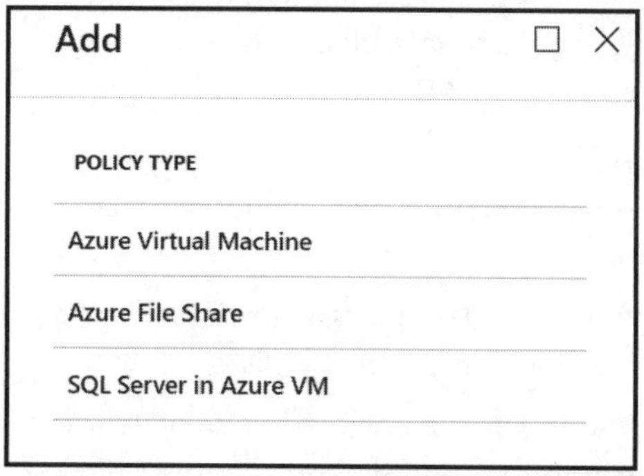

```
Add                          □  ×

    POLICY TYPE

    Azure Virtual Machine

    Azure File Share

    SQL Server in Azure VM
```

FIGURE 2-58 Available backup policy options in the Azure portal

Thought experiment

In this thought experiment, apply what you have learned about this objective. You can find answers to these questions in the next section.

You are the web administrator for www.contoso.com, which is hosted in virtual machines in the West US Azure region. Several customers from England and China complain that the PDF files for your product brochures take too long to download. Currently, the PDF files are served from the /brochures folder of your website.

1. What steps should you take to mitigate the download time for your PDFs?

2. What changes need to happen on the www.contoso.com web site?

Thought experiment answers

This section contains the solution to the thought experiment for the chapter.

To mitigate this problem, move the PDF files closer to the customer locations. This can be solved by moving the PDF files to Azure Storage and then enabling them for CDN.

1. Create an Azure Storage account and move the PDF files to a container named bro-chures and enable public access (blob) on the container. Next, you should create a new CDN profile and an endpoint that originates from the blob storage account. From there, pre-load the PDF files into CDN to minimize the content being delayed when the first user requests it.

2. The website pages will need to change to refer to the URL of the CDN endpoint. For example, if the PDF was previously referenced by *www.contoso.com/brochures/product1.pdf*, it would now be referenced by *contosocdn.azureedge.net/brochures/product1.pdf* unless the CDN endpoint was configured for custom domains.

Chapter summary

This chapter covered several key services related to implementing storage in Microsoft Azure. Topics included how to create and manage Azure Storage Accounts, blob storage, files, backup, import and exporting data, Azure Data Box and Azure CDN.

Below are some of the key takeaways from this chapter:

- Azure storage accounts provide 4 separate services: blobs, tables, queues and files. Understand the usage scenarios of each service.

- The Standard performance tier uses magnetic disks and supports all services. The Premium tier uses solid-state disks and is only used for unmanaged VM disks.

- Storage accounts must specify a replication mode. Options are locally-redundant, zone-redundant, geo-redundant and read-access geo-redundant storage.

- Blob storage supports three types of blobs (block, page and append blobs), and three access tiers (hot, cool, and archive).

- There are 3 kinds of storage account: general purpose v1, general purpose v2 and blob storage. The availability of features varies between storage account kinds.

- Azure storage can be managed through several tools directly from Microsoft: the Azure portal, PowerShell, CLI, Storage Explorer, and AzCopy. It's important to know when to use each tool.

- Access to storage accounts can be controlled using several techniques. Among them are: storage account name and key, shared access signature (SAS), SAS with access policy, and using the storage firewalland virtual network service endpoints. Access to blob storage can also be controlled using the public access level of the blob container.

- You can also use the async blob copy service to copy files between storage accounts or from outside publicly accessible locations to your Azure storage account.

- Azure CDN can be used to improve web site performance by caching static data close to the end users. Blob storage can be used as a CDN origin.

- Storage accounts and CDN both support custom domains. Enabling SSL is only supported on custom domains when the blob is accessed via CDN.

- Enable diagnostics and alerts to monitor the status of your storage accounts.

- Data can be imported into Azure storage when on-premises locations have limited or no connectivity using the Azure Import/Export service or Azure Data Box.

- Azure Backup can be used to protect files and folders, applications, and IaaS virtual machines. This cloud-based data protection service helps organizations by providing offsite backups of on-premises servers and protection of VM workloads they have already moved to the cloud.

## CHAPTER 3

Deploy and manage virtual machines (VMs)

Microsoft Azure offers many features and services that can be used to create inventive solutions for almost any IT problem. Two of the most common services for designing these solutions are Microsoft Azure Virtual Machines (VM) and VM scale sets. Virtual machines are one of the key compute options for deploying workloads in Microsoft Azure. Virtual machines can provide the on-ramp for migrating workloads from on-premises (or other cloud providers) to Azure, because they are usually the most compatible with existing solutions.

The flexibility of virtual machines makes them a key scenario for many workloads. For example, you have a choice of server operating systems with various supported versions of Windows and Linux distributions. Azure Virtual Machines also provide you full control over the operating system along with advanced configuration options for networking and storage. VM Scale Sets provide similar capabilities to VMs. They provide the ability to scale out certain types of workloads to handle large processing problems, and they optimize cost by only running instances when needed.

In this chapter, you will learn the ins-and-outs of deploying and managing virtual machines in Azure as we cover creation through the portal and the command line tools, automation with templates, as well as core management tasks.

Skills covered in this chapter:

- Create and configure a VM for Windows and Linux
- Automate deployment of VMs
- Manage Azure VMs
- Manage VM backups

Skill 3.1: Create and configure a VM for Windows and Linux

Microsoft Azure Virtual Machines are a flexible and powerful option for deploying workloads into the cloud. The support of both Windows and Linux-based operating systems allows for the deployment of a wide variety of workloads that traditionally run in an on-premises environment. This section will cover how to create and configure virtual machines and virtual machine scale sets including configuring for high availability.

> **This section covers how to:**
> - Configuring virtual machine size
> - Configure high availability
> - Configure monitoring
> - Configure networking
> - Configure storage
> - Deploy and configure scale sets

Creating virtual machines

There are multiple ways to create virtual machines, depending on your intended use. The easiest way to create an individual virtual machine is to use the Azure portal. If you have a need for automated provisioning (or you just enjoy the command line), the Azure PowerShell cmdlets and the Azure cross-platform command-line tools (CLI) are a good fit. For more advanced automation, that can even include orchestration of multiple virtual machines, Azure Resource Manager templates can also be used. Each method brings its own capabilities and tradeoffs, and it is important to understand which tool should be used in the right scenario.

Create an Azure VM (Azure Portal)

To create a virtual machine using the Azure portal, click the Create Resource button, and you can then either search for an image or solution, or you can browse by clicking Compute, as shown in Figure 3-1. Within the Compute category, you will see the featured images, and if one of those images is not appropriate, you can click the See All option to view a larger selection.

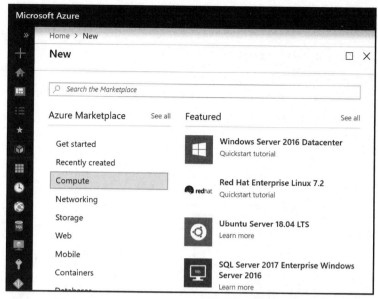

FIGURE 3-1 The Azure Marketplace view for virtual machines

The Azure portal allows you to provision virtual machines from a wide variety of virtual machine images and pre-defined templates for entire solutions such as SQL Server Always On, or even a complete SharePoint farm using only your web browser. For individual virtual machines you can specify some, but not all, configuration options at creation time.

Using the Azure portal, you can create virtual machines individually or you can deploy an ARM template that can deploy many virtual machines (including other Azure resources as well). You can even use the Azure portal to export an ARM template from an existing deployed resource. Through the integrated Azure Cloud Shell, you can also execute commands from the command line that can be used to provision virtual machines. After an image is selected, you can navigate through several screens to configure the virtual machine.

The first blade to complete is the Basics blade, as shown in Figure 3-2, which allows you to set the following configuration options:

- The Azure subscription to create the VM in (if you have more than one)
- The resource group name to deploy the virtual machine and its related resources in, such as network interface or public IP
- The name of the virtual machine
- The Azure region the virtual machine is created in
- The availability options needed for the virtual machine
- The administrator credentials

- The operating system image name
- The virtual machine size
- User name and password for Windows and Linux
- An SSH key for Linux VMs
- Inbound port rules such as port 3389 for RDP or 22 for SSH
- Choose to use the hybrid use benefit if you already have licenses for Windows Server

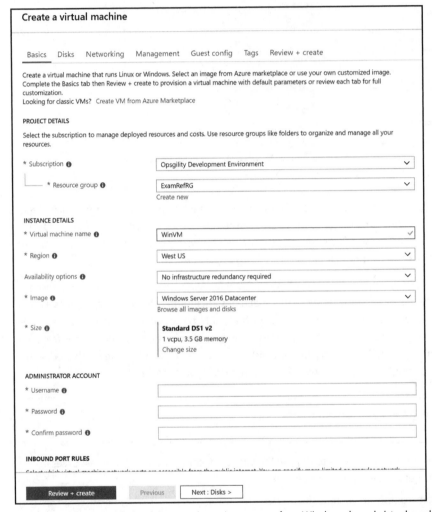

FIGURE 3-2 The Basics blade of the portal creation process for a Windows-based virtual machine

Create an Azure VM (PowerShell)

The PowerShell cmdlets are commonly used for automating common tasks such as stopping and starting virtual machines, deploying ARM templates, or for making configuration settings on a vast number of resources at the same time. Using the Azure PowerShell cmdlets, you can also create virtual machines imperatively and declaratively.

The approach we'll use is to programmatically create the resources needed for the virtual machine such as storage, networking, availability sets and so on, and then associate them with the virtual machine at creation time.

Before you can create or manage any resources in your Azure subscription using the Azure PowerShell cmdlets, you must login by executing the Connect-AzAccount.

```
Connect-AzAccount
```

A virtual machine and all its related resources such as network interfaces, disks, and so on must be created inside of an Azure Resource Group. Using PowerShell, you can create a new resource group with the New-AzResourceGroup cmdlet.

```
$rgName     = "ExamRefRG"
$location   = "West US"
New-AzResourceGroup -Name $rgName -Location $location
```

This cmdlet requires you to specify the resource group name, and the name of the Azure region. These values are defined in the variables $rgName, and $location. You can use the Get-AzResourceGroup cmdlet to see if the resource group already exists or not, and you can use the Get-AzLocation cmdlet to view the list of available regions.

Azure virtual machines must be created inside of a virtual network. In the portal example, networking was not mentioned. Should probably remove this here, OR show the networking and disk tabs in the Portal example above, using PowerShell you can specify an existing virtual network, or you can create a new one. In the code example next, the New-AzVirtualNetwork-SubnetConfig cmdlet is used to create two local objects that represent two subnets in the virtual network. The virtual network is actually created within the call to New-AzVirtualNetwork. It is passed in the address space of 10.0.0.0/16, and you can also pass in multiple address spaces similar to how the subnets are passed in using an array.

```
$subnets = @()
$subnet1Name = "Subnet-1"
$subnet2Name = "Subnet-2"
$subnet1AddressPrefix = "10.0.0.0/24"
$subnet2AddressPrefix = "10.0.1.0/24"
$vnetAddresssSpace = "10.0.0.0/16"
$VNETName = "ExamRefVNET-PS"
$subnets += New-AzVirtualNetworkSubnetConfig -Name $subnet1Name `
                -AddressPrefix $subnet1AddressPrefix
$subnets += New-AzVirtualNetworkSubnetConfig -Name $subnet2Name `
                -AddressPrefix $subnet2AddressPrefix
$vnet = New-AzVirtualNetwork -Name $VNETName `
                -ResourceGroupName $rgName `
                -Location $location `
                -AddressPrefix $vnetAddresssSpace `
                -Subnet $subnets
```

To connect to the virtual machine from the public Internet, create a public IP address resource.

```
$ipName = "examRefIP"
$pip = New-AzPublicIpAddress -Name $ipName `
                -ResourceGroupName $rgName `
                -Location $location `
                -AllocationMethod Dynamic `
                -DomainNameLabel $dnsName
```

By default, adding a public IP to a VM's network interface will allow in all traffic regardless of the destination port. To control this, create a network security group and only open the ports you will use. The next example creates an array that will be used for the rules and populates the array with the New-AzNetworkSecurityRuleConfig cmdlet.

```
# Add a rule to the network security group to allow RDP in
$nsgRules = @()
$nsgRules += New-AzNetworkSecurityRuleConfig -Name "RDP" `
                -Description "RemoteDesktop" `
                -Protocol Tcp `
                -SourcePortRange "*" `
                -DestinationPortRange "3389" `
                -SourceAddressPrefix "*" `
                -DestinationAddressPrefix "*" `
                -Access Allow `
                -Priority 110 `
                -Direction Inbound
```

The New-AzNetworkSecurityGroup cmdlet creates the network security group. The rules are passed in using the SecurityRules parameter.

```
$nsgName    = "ExamRefNSG"
$nsg = New-AzNetworkSecurityGroup -ResourceGroupName $rgName `
                -Name $nsgName `
                -SecurityRules $nsgRules `
                -Location $location
```

Now that all the resources are created that the virtual machine requires, use the New-Az-VMConfig cmdlet to instantiate a local configuration object that represents a virtual machine to associate them together. The virtual machine's size and the availability set are specified during this call.

```
$vmSize = "Standard_DS1_V2"
$vmName = "ExamRefVM"
$vm = New-AzVMConfig -VMName $vmName -VMSize $vmSize
```

After the virtual machine configuration object is created there are several configuration options that must be set. This example shows how to set the operating system and the credentials using the Set-AzVMOperatingSystem cmdlet. The operating system is specified by using either the Windows or the Linux parameter. The `ProvisionVMAgent` parameter tells Azure to automatically install the VM agent on the virtual machine when it is provisioned. The `Credential` parameter specifies the local administrator username and password with the values passed to the $cred object.

```
$cred = Get-Credential
Set-AzVMOperatingSystem -Windows `
            -ComputerName $vmName `
            -Credential $cred `
            -ProvisionVMAgent `
            -VM $vm
```

The operating system image (or existing VHD) must be specified for the VM to boot. Setting the image is accomplished by calling the Set-AzVMSourceImage cmdlet and specifying the Image publisher, offer, and SKU. These values can be retrieved by calling the cmdlets Get-Az-VMImagePublisher, Get-AzVMImageOffer, and Get-AzVMImageSku.

```
$pubName   = "MicrosoftWindowsServer"
$offerName = "WindowsServer"
$skuName   = "2019-Datacenter"
Set-AzVMSourceImage -PublisherName $pubName `
            -Offer $offerName `
            -Skus $skuName `
            -Version "latest" `
            -VM $vm
Set-AzVMOSDisk -CreateOption fromImage -VM $vm
```

EXAM TIP

In the previous example of creating a virtual machine, managed disks were used to create the virtual machine by omitting two parameters. For unmanaged disks the Set-AzOSDisk cmdlet would have also required the -VhdUri and -Name parameters. The -VhdUri would point to the Uri of where the disk would be created in an Azure storage account.

Use the New-AzNetworkInterface cmdlet to create the network interface for the VM. This cmdlet accepts the unique ID for the subnet, public IP, and the network security group for configuration.

```
$nicName   = "ExamRefVM-NIC"
$nic = New-AzNetworkInterface -Name $nicName `
            -ResourceGroupName $rgName `
```

```
            -Location $location `
            -SubnetId $vnet.Subnets[0].Id `
            -PublicIpAddressId $pip.Id `
            -NetworkSecurityGroupId $nsg.ID

Add-AzVMNetworkInterface -VM $vm `
            -NetworkInterface $nic
```

EXAM TIP

In addition to knowing how to provision a virtual machine from an image, it is also important to understand how to create from an existing disk using the `Set-AzVMOSDisk` and the -CreateOption attach parameter (for more information see: *https://docs.microsoft.com/powershell/module/az.compute/set-azvmosdisk*)

The final step is to provision the virtual machine by calling the New-AzVMConfig cmdlet. This cmdlet requires you to specify the resource group name to create the virtual machine in and the virtual machine configuration, which is in the $vm variable.

```
New-AzVM -ResourceGroupName $rgName -Location $location -VM $vm
```

It is also possible to create a virtual machine with just the New-AzVM cmdlet. This is useful to quickly spin up a VM for testing or demonstration purposes where you don't need to set the individual characteristics of the virtual machine. See the following for more examples: *https://docs.microsoft.com/powershell/module/azurerm.compute/new-Azvm.*

Create an Azure VM (CLI)

The Azure CLI tools are used in a similar fashion to the PowerShell cmdlets. They are built to run cross platform on Windows, Mac, or Linux. The syntax of the CLI tools is designed to be familiar to users of a Bash scripting environment. Let's walk through an example that creates the same resources as the previous PowerShell example, except creating a Linux-based virtual machine instead.

Like the PowerShell cmdlets, you first must login to access Azure using the CLI tools. The approach is slightly different, after executing the command `az login`, the tools provide you with a link to navigate to in the browser, and a code to enter. After entering the code and your credentials you are logged in to the command line.

```
az login
```

Create a new resource group by executing the `az group create` command and specifying a unique name and the region.

```
rgName="ExamRefRG"
location="WestUS"
az group create --name $rgName --location $location
```

The following command can be used to identify available regions that you can create resources and resource groups in.

```
az account list-locations
```

From here you have two options. You can create a virtual machine with a very simple syntax that generates much of the underlying configuration for you such as a virtual network, public IP address, storage account, and so on, or you can create and configure each resource and link to the virtual machine at creation time. Here is an example of the syntax to create a simple stand-alone virtual machine:

```
# Creating a simple virtual machine
vmName="myUbuntuVM"
imageName="UbuntuLTS"
az vm create --resource-group $rgName --name $vmName --image $imageName
--generate-ssh-keys
```

> **NOTE SSH KEYS**
>
> The generate-ssh-keys parameter dynamically generates keys to connect to the Linux virtual machine for you if they are missing. The new keys are stored in ~/.ssh. You can also specify a user name and password using the admin-username and admin-password parameters if you set the authentication-type parameter to password (default is ssh).

To create all the resources from scratch, as shown in the section on creating a virtual machine using the PowerShell cmdlets, you can start with the virtual network. Use the az network vnet create command to create the virtual network. This command requires the name of the virtual network, a list of address prefixes, and the location to create the virtual network in.

```
vnetName="ExamRefVNET-CLI"
vnetAddressPrefix="10.0.0.0/16"
az network vnet create --resource-group $rgName -n ExamRefVNET-CLI --address-prefixes
 $vnetAddressPrefix -l $location
```

The az network vnet subnet create command is used to add additional subnets to the virtual network. This command requires the resource group name, the name of the virtual network, the subnet name, and the address prefix for the subnet to create.

```
Subnet1Name="Subnet-1"
Subnet2Name="Subnet-2"
Subnet1Prefix="10.0.1.0/24"
Subnet2Prefix="10.0.2.0/24"
az network vnet subnet create --resource-group $rgName --vnet-name $vnetName
 -n $Subnet1Name --address-prefix $Subnet1Prefix
az network vnet subnet create --resource-group $rgName --vnet-name $vnetName
 -n $Subnet2Name --address-prefix $Subnet2Prefix
```

The az network public-ip create command is used to create a public IP resource. The allocation-method parameter can be set to dynamic or static.

```
dnsRecord="examrefdns123123"
ipName="ExamRefCLI-IP"
az network public-ip create -n $ipName -g $rgName --allocation-method Dynamic
--dns-name $dnsRecord -l $location
```

The az network nsg create command is used to create a network security group.

```
nsgName="webnsg"
az network nsg create -n $nsgName -g $rgName -l $location
```

After the network security group is created, use the `az network rule create` command to add rules. In this example, the rule allows inbound connections on port 22 for SSH and another rule is created to allow in HTTP port 80.

```
# Create a rule to allow in SSH
az network nsg rule create -n SSH --nsg-name $nsgName --priority 100 -g $rgName
--access Allow --description "SSH Access" --direction Inbound --protocol Tcp
--destination-address-prefix "*" --destination-port-range 22
--source-address-prefix "*" --source-port-range "*"
# Create a rule to allow in HTTP
az network nsg rule create -n HTTP --nsg-name webnsg --priority 101 -g $rgName
--access Allow --description "Web Access" --direction Inbound --protocol Tcp
--destination-address-prefix "*" --destination-port-range 80
--source-address-prefix "*" --source-port-range "*"
```

The network interface for the virtual machine is created using the `az network nic create` command.

```
nicname="WebVMNic1"
az network nic create -n $nicname -g $rgName --subnet $Subnet1Name
--network-security-group $nsgName --vnet-name $vnetName
--public-ip-address $ipName -l $location
```

To create a virtual machine, you must specify whether it will boot from a custom image, a marketplace image, or an existing VHD. You can retrieve a list of marketplace images by executing the following command:

```
az vm image list --all
```

The command `az image list` is used to retrieve any of your own custom images you have captured.

Another important piece of metadata needed to create a virtual machine is the VM size. You can retrieve the available form factors that can be created in each region by executing the following command:

```
az vm list-sizes --location $location
```

The last step is to use the `az vm create` command to create the virtual machine. This command allows you to pass the virtual machine size, the image the virtual machine should boot from, and other configuration data such as the username and password, availability and storage configuration.

```
imageName="Canonical:UbuntuServer:16.04-LTS:latest"
vmSize="Standard_DS1_V2"
user=demouser
vmName="WebVM"
```

```
az vm create -n $vmName -g $rgName -l $location --size $vmSize
--nics $nicname --image $imageName
--generate-ssh-keys
```

EXAM TIP

To use unmanaged disks with the Azure CLI you will need to specify the use-unmanaged-disk
parameter and specify the disk name, the storage account name, and the storage container.

Stopping a virtual machine from the Azure portal, Windows PowerShell with the Stop-Az-
VM cmdlet, or the az vm deallocate command puts the virtual machine in the Stopped (deallocated) state (az vm stop puts the VM in the Stopped state). It is important to understand the
difference between Stopped (deallocated) and just Stopped. In the Stopped state a virtual machine is still allocated in Azure, and the operating system is simply shut down. You will still be
billed for the compute time for a virtual machine in this state. A virtual machine in the Stopped
(deallocated) state is no longer occupying physical hardware in the Azure region, and you will
not be billed for the compute time (you are still billed for the underlying storage).

Operating system images

In addition to using the VM images from the Azure Marketplace, Azure also provides the ability
to upload your own image or create a custom image directly in the cloud.

VM images are captured from an existing VM that has been prepared using the Windows
program sysprep.exe or the Microsoft Azure Linux Agent (waagent) to make the operating
system generalized. Generalized means that unique settings such as hostname, security IDs,
personal information, user accounts, domain join information, and so on are removed from the
operating system, so it is in a state to be provisioned on a new VM. Generalization does not remove customizations, such as installation of software, patches, additional files, and folders. This
capability is what makes VM images a great solution for providing pre-configured and tested
solutions for VMs or VM scale sets.

There are two types of VM image types available: managed and unmanaged where managed is the recommended option. Prior to the launch of Azure Managed Disks, unmanaged
images were your only option. With unmanaged images, you can only create a new VM in the
same storage account that the image resides in. This means that if you want to use the image in
another storage account you have to use one of the storage tools to copy it to the new storage
account first and then create the VM from it. Managed images solve this problem by removing
the direct dependency on the storage account. Once a managed image exists you can create a
VM based on it without worrying about the storage account configuration. This applies only to
VMs created in the same region. If you want to create the VM in a remote region you must still
copy the managed image to the remote region first.

MORE INFO **SHARED IMAGE GALLERY**

Using virtual machine images across regions will be simplified using a shared image gallery which is currently in preview. You can learn more about shared image galleries here: *https://docs.microsoft.com/azure/virtual-machines/windows/shared-image-galleries/*.

Preparing the operating system for capture

To create a VM image you first generalize the operating system. In Windows this is using the sysprep.exe tool as shown in Figure 3-3. After this tool has completed execution, the VM is in a generalized state and it's shut down.

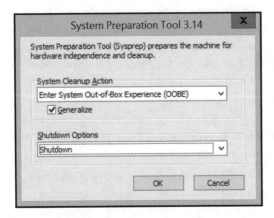

FIGURE 3-3 Using the System Preparation tool to generalize a Windows VM

Here is the command to generalize a Linux VM using the waagent program that you would execute from the Linux command line:

```
sudo waagent –deprovision+user
```

MORE INFO **GENERALIZING A VM CANNOT BE UNDONE**

A virtual machine can no longer be used after it is generalized. Make sure you make a copy of the VM prior to generalization if you need it.

Capturing a managed VM image (Azure portal)

After the virtual machine is generalized, you can capture the image. The image can be captured using the Azure portal, PowerShell, or the CLI. To capture the virtual machine in the portal, click the Capture button at the top of the Virtual Machine blade. This will open a dialog box, shown in Figure 3-4, where you can specify the image Name and the Resource Group to store the image in. You can also specify to delete the virtual machine after the image is created since it has been generalized.

FIGURE 3-4 Creating an image using the Azure portal

Capturing a managed VM image (PowerShell)

This example shows how to create a managed VM image using PowerShell. This snippet uses the New-AzImageConfig and New-AzImage cmdlets.

```
$rgName = "Contoso"
$vmName = "ImageVM"
$location = "WestUS"
# Set the status of the virtual machine to Generalized
Set-AzVm -ResourceGroupName $rgName -Name $vmName -Generalized
# Create a managed VM from a VM
$imageName = "WinVMImage"
$vm = Get-AzVM -ResourceGroupName $rgName -Name $vmName
$image = New-AzImageConfig -Location $location -SourceVirtualMachineId $vm.ID
New-AzImage -Image $image -ImageName $imageName -ResourceGroupName $rgName
```

Capturing a managed VM image (CLI)

This example uses the `az vm generalize` and `az image` commands from the CLI tools to create a managed VM image.

```
# Create a Managed Image
rgName="Contoso"
vmName="ImageVM"
imageName="LinuxImage"
# Deallocate the VM
az vm deallocate --resource-group $rgName --name $vmName
# Set the status of the virtual machine to Generalized
az vm generalize --resource-group $rgName --name $vmName
az image create --resource-group $rgName --name $imageName --source $vmName
```

Creating a VM from an image

Creating a VM from an image is very similar to creating an image using an Azure Marketplace image. There are differences depending on if you start with an unmanaged image or a managed image. You can create a virtual machine from a managed image with the Azure portal by navigating to **Images**, selecting your image, and then Create Virtual Machine, **Create Virtual Machine**.

If you have a legacy unmanaged image you can only provision virtual machines using the command line. To do so you must ensure that the destination operating system and data disk URIs for your VM references the same storage account that your image resides in, and then reference the operating system image by its URI in the storage account and this is only available from the command line tools since it is no longer recommended.

To specify a legacy unmanaged image using PowerShell, set the SourceImageUri parameter of the Set-AzOsDisk cmdlet to the full URI of VHD in an Azure Storage account in the same region.

```
# In this example, $vm was a variable you created earlier using New-AzConfig
# This example is not meant to run directly on its own since the VM creation process
 has already been shown
$osDiskUri = "https://examrefstorage.blob.core.windows.net/vhd/os-disk"
$imageUri  = "https://examrefstorage.blob.core.windows.net/images/legacy-image.vhd"
$vm = Set-AzVMOSDisk -VM $vm -Name $osDiskName -VhdUri $osDiskUri `
    -CreateOption fromImage -SourceImageUri $imageURI -Windows
```

Using the CLI tools, specify the URI using the image parameter of the az vm create command.

```
az vm create --resource-group $rgName --name $vmName --image $osDiskUri
--generate-ssh-keys
```

To create using a manage image with PowerShell, you first retrieve the image ID and pass it to Set-AzVMOSDisk instead.

```
$image = Get-AzImage -ImageName $imageName -ResourceGroupName $rgName
$vmConfig = Set-AzVMSourceImage -VM $vmConfig -Id $image.Id
```

Using the CLI tools saves a step because it retrieves the image ID for you, as long as you specify the name of your managed image.

```
az vm create -g $rgName -n $vmName --image $imageName
```

Configuring high availability

Resiliency is a critical part of any application architecture. Azure provides several features and capabilities to make it easier to design resilient solutions. The platform helps you to avoid a single point of failure at the physical hardware level and provides techniques to avoid downtime during host updates. Using features like availability zones, availability sets, and load balancers provides you the capabilities to build highly resilient and available systems.

Availability zones

At a high level, availability zones help to protect you from datacenter-level failures. They are located inside an Azure region, and each zone has its own independent power source, network, and cooling. To ensure resiliency, there's a minimum of three separate zones in all enabled regions. The physical and logical separation of availability zones within a region protects applications and data from zone-level failures. Availability zones provide a 99.99 percent SLA uptime when two or more VMs are deployed. Figure 3-5 demonstrates how a 3-tier application can be deployed with a virtual machine from each tier deployed in each of the three zones for increased availability.

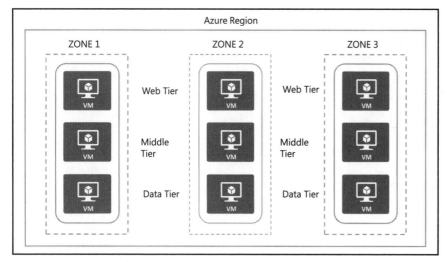

FIGURE 3-5 Architectural view of an availability zone

To deploy a VM to an availability zone, select the zone you want to use on the Basics blade of the virtual machine creation dialog, as shown in Figure 3-6. If you add a virtual machine to an availability zone, you cannot also join it to an availability set.

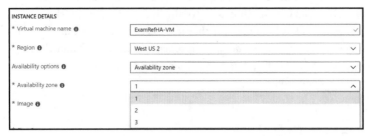

FIGURE 3-6 Specifying the availability zone for a VM

At the time of this writing the following services are supported with availability zones (see: *https://docs.microsoft.com/azure/availability-zones/az-overview#services-that-support-availability-zones* for more information):

- Linux Virtual Machines
- Windows Virtual Machines
- Virtual Machine Scale Sets
- Managed Disks
- Load Balancer
- Public IP address
- Zone-redundant storage
- SQL Database
- Event Hubs
- Service Bus
- VPN Gateway
- ExpressRoute
- Application Gateway (preview)

Currently supported regions :

- Central US
- East US 2
- France Central
- North Europe
- Southeast Asia
- West Europe
- West US 2

Availability sets

Availability sets are used to control availability for multiple virtual machines in the same application tier. To provide redundancy for your virtual machines, it is least two virtual machines in an availability set. This configuration ensures that at least one virtual machine is available in the event of a host update, or a problem with the physical hardware the virtual machines are hosted on. Having at least two virtual machines in an availability set is a requirement for the service level agreement (SLA) for virtual machines of 99.95 percent.

Virtual machines should be deployed into availability sets according to their workload or application tier. For instance, if you are deploying a three-tier solution that consists of web servers, a middle tier, and a database tier, each tier would have its own availability set, as Figure 3-7 demonstrates.

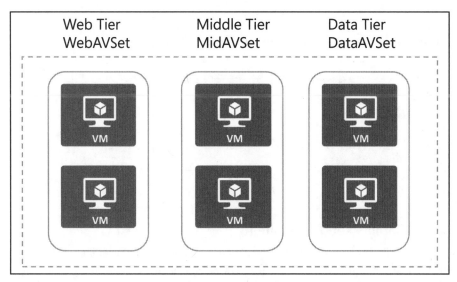

FIGURE 3-7 Availability set configurations for a multi-tier solution

Each virtual machine in your availability set is assigned a fault domain and an update domain. Each availability set has up to 20 update domains available, which indicates the groups of virtual machines and the underlying physical hardware that can be rebooted at the same time for host updates. Each availability set is also comprised of up to three fault domains, which represent which virtual machines will be on separate physical racks in the datacenter for redundancy. This limits the impact of physical hardware failures such as server, network, or power interruptions. It is important to understand that the availability set must be set at creation time of the virtual machine.

Create an availability set (Azure portal)

To create an availability set, specify a name for the availability set that is not in use by any other availability sets within the resource group, along with the number of fault and updates domains, as well as whether you will use managed disks with the availability set or not. Figure 3-8 demonstrates the Create Availability Set blade in the portal.

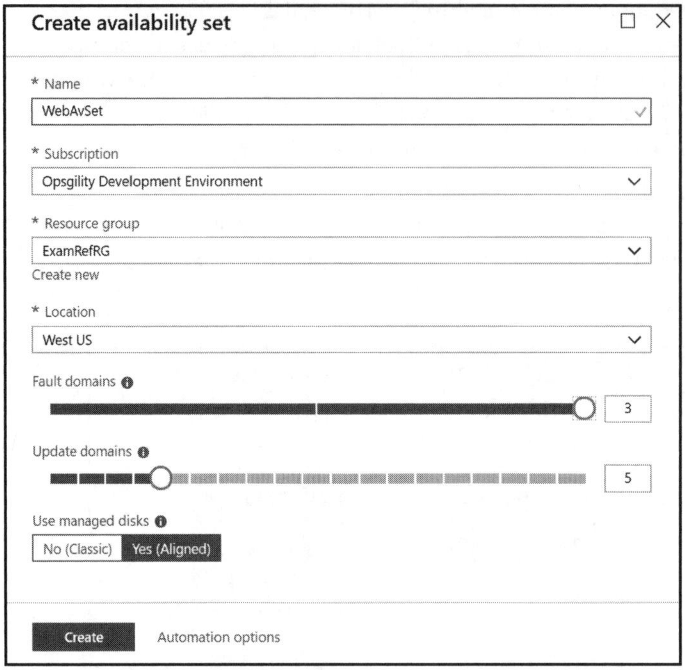

FIGURE 3-8 Creating an availability set

Create an availability set (PowerShell)

The New-AzAvailabilitySet cmdlet is used to create an availability set in PowerShell. The PlatformUpdateDomainCount and PlatformFaultDomainCount parameters control the number of fault domains and upgrade domains. The Sku parameter should be set to Aligned if you intend to deploy VMs that use managed disks. The following example shows how to create the availability set using PowerShell. The example assumes the resource group already exists.

```
# Create an availability set

$rgName     = "ExamRefRG"
$avSetName  = "WebAVSet"
$location   = "West US"
New-AzAvailabilitySet -ResourceGroupName $rgName `
                      -Name $avSetName `
                      -Location $location `
                      -PlatformUpdateDomainCount 10 `
                      -PlatformFaultDomainCount 3 `
                      -Sku "Aligned"
```

Create an availability set (CLI)

The `az vm availability-set create` command is used to create an availability set using the CLI tools. The `platform-update-domain-count` and `platform-fault-domain-count` parameters are used to control the number of fault and upgrade domains. By default, an availability set is created as aligned unless you pass the parameter unmanaged. The following example shows how to create the availability set using CLI. The example assumes the resource group already exists.

```
# Create an availability set
rgName="ExamRefRGCLI"
avSetName="WebAVSet"
location="WestUS"
az vm availability-set create --name $avSetName --resource-group $rgName
--platform-fault-domain-count 3 --platform-update-domain-count 10
```

Availability sets and managed disks

For VMs that use Azure Managed Disks, VMs are aligned with managed disk fault domains when using an aligned availability set, as shown in Figure 3-9. This alignment ensures that all the managed disks attached to a VM are within the same managed disk fault domain. Only VMs with managed disks can be created in a managed availability set. The number of managed disk fault domains varies by region, with either two or three managed disk fault domains per region.

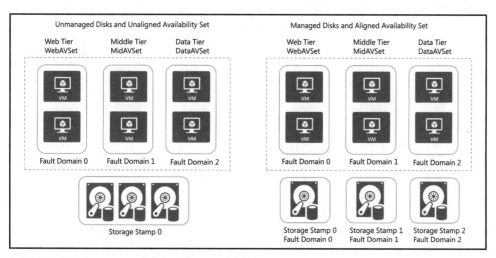

FIGURE 3-9 Aligning managed disks with an availability set

> **MORE INFO** **UNDERSTANDING AVAILABILITY IN AZURE VMS**
>
> You can learn more about update and fault domains and how to manage availability of your Azure VMs here:
>
> *https://docs.microsoft.com/azure/virtual-machines/windows/manage-availability.*

Configure virtual machine size

There are many situations where the amount of compute processing your workload needs varies dramatically from day to day or even hour to hour. For example, in many organizations line of business (LOB) applications are used heavily during the workweek, but on the weekends, they see little actual usage. Other examples are workloads that require more processing time due to scheduled events such as backups or maintenance windows where having more compute time may make it faster to complete these tasks. Azure Resource Manager-based VMs make it relatively easy to change the size of a virtual machine even after it has been deployed. There are a few things to consider with this approach.

The first consideration is to ensure that the region your VM is deployed to supports the instance size that you want to change the VM to. In most cases this is not an issue, but if you have a use case where the desired size isn't in the region the existing VM is deployed to, your only options are to either wait for the size to be supported in the region, or to move the existing VM to a region that already supports it.

The second consideration is if the new size is supported in the current hardware cluster your VM is deployed to. This can be determined by clicking the Size link in the virtual machine configuration blade in the Azure portal of a running virtual machine, as Figure 3-10 demonstrates. If the size is available, you can select it. Changing the size reboots the virtual machine. It also reallocates it as you're pushed to a new host so it's slower than a reboot where you stay on the same host.

FIGURE 3-10 Changing the size of a virtual machine using the Azure portal

A third consideration is the form factor of the new size compared to the old size. Consider scaling from a DS3_V2 to a DS2_V2. A DS3_V2 supports up to eight data disks and up to four network interfaces. A DS2_V2 supports up to four data disks and up to two network interfaces. If the VM you are sizing from (DS3_V2) is using more disks or network interfaces than the target size, the resize operation will fail.

Resizing a VM (PowerShell)

Use the Get-AzVMSize cmdlet and pass the name of the region to the location parameter to view all the available sizes in your region to ensure the new size is available. If you specify the resource group and the VM name, it returns the available sizes in the current hardware cluster.

```
# View available sizes
$location = "WestUS"
```

```
Get-AzVMSize -Location $location
```

After you have identified the available size, use the following code to change the VM to the new size.

```
$rgName = "ExamRefRG"
$vmName = "Web1"
$size = "Standard_DS2_V2"
$vm = Get-AzVM -ResourceGroupName $rgName -VMName $vmName
$vm.HardwareProfile.VmSize = $size
Update-AzVM -VM $vm -ResourceGroupName $rgName
```

If the virtual machine(s) are part of an availability set, the following code can be used to shut them all down at the same time and restart them using the new size.

```
$rgName = "ExamRefRG"
$vmName = "Web1"
$size = "Standard_DS2_V2"
$avSet = "WebAVSet"
```

Resizing a VM (CLI)

The `az vm list-vm-resize-options` command can be used to see which VM sizes are available in the current hardware cluster.

```
rgName="ExamRefRG"
vmName="Web1"
az vm list-vm-resize-options --resource-group $rgName --name $vmName --output table
```

The `az vm list-sizes` command is used to view all sizes in the region.

```
az vm list-sizes --location westus
```

The `az vm resize` command is used to change the size of an individual VM.

```
az vm resize --resource-group $rgName --name $vmName --size Standard_DS3_v2
```

Authentication options

For Windows-based virtual machines usernames can be a maximum of 20 characters in length and cannot end in a period (".") and many common usernames are blocked during the creation process. Examples of blocked account names include: 1, 123, a, admin, administrator, john and several other easily guessable names. Passwords must be between 12 and 123 characters in length and meet several complexity requirements.

For Linux-based virtual machines, you can specify an existing SSH public key or a password when creating a Linux VM. Linux usernames must be between 1 and 32 characters in length and passwords must be between 6 and 72 characters. Like Windows, certain easily guessable usernames and passwords are automatically when creating through the Portal.

If you choose to use the SSH public key option, you must paste in the public key for your SSH certificate. You can create the SSH certificate using the following command:

```
ssh-keygen -t rsa -b 2048
```

To retrieve the public key for your new certificate, run the following command in a bash console:

`cat ~/.ssh/id_rsa.pub`

From there, copy all of the data starting with ssh-rsa and ending with the last character on the screen, pasting it into the SSH public key box, as shown on the Create a virtual machine blade in the Azure portal.. Ensure you don't include any extra spaces.

FIGURE 3-11 The Basics blade of the portal creation process for a Linux-based virtual machine

MORE INFO **LEARN MORE ABOUT USERNAME AND PASSWORD REQUIREMENTS**

For information on username and password requirements on Windows VMs, see: *https://docs.microsoft.com/azure/virtual-machines/windows/faq,* or for Linux-based VM requirements, see: *https://docs.microsoft.com/azure/virtual-machines/linux/faq.*

Configure storage

The storage subsystem for virtual machines is configured using Azure virtual machine disks. There are many options and features to consider when configuring disks. Options such as whether to use managed or unmanaged disks, which disk types (Premium SSD, Standard SSD, and Standard HDD, Ultimate SSD), as well as when and how to take advantage of disk read/write caching.

Azure virtual machine disks

Each Azure virtual machine can have three different type of disks:

- **Operating System Disk (OS Disk)**   The C drive in Windows or /dev/sda on Linux. This disk is registered as a SATA drive and has a maximum capacity of 2048 gigabytes (GB). This disk is persistent and stored in Azure Storage.

- **Temporary Disk**   The D drive in Windows or /dev/sdb on Linux. This disk is used for short term storage for applications or the system. Data on this drive can be lost during a maintenance event and if the VM is moved to a different host because the data is stored on the local disk.

- **Data Disk**   Registered as a SCSI drive. These disks can be attached to a virtual machine, the number of which depends on the VM instance size. Data disks have a maximum capacity of 4095 gigabytes (GB) currently, No longer in preview. GA'd on 3/25 *https://azure.microsoft.com/blog/larger-more-powerful-managed-disks-for-azure-virtual-machines/.* These disks are persistent and stored in Azure Storage.

MORE INFO DISKS AND VHDS

See the following for more information on Disks and VHDs:
https://docs.microsoft.com/azure/virtual-machines/windows/about-disks-and-vhds.

OS disks and data disks can be created as managed or an unmanaged disk.

MANAGED DISKS

Managed disks handle storage for you by automatically distributing your disks in storage accounts for capacity and by integrating with Azure Availability Sets to provide isolation for your storage just like availability sets do for virtual machines. Managed disks also make it easy to change between Standard and Premium storage (HDD to SSD) without the need to write conversion scripts.

UNMANAGED DISKS

With unmanaged disks you are responsible for ensuring for the correct distribution of your VM disks in storage accounts for capacity planning as well as availability. An unmanaged disk is also not a separate manageable entity. This means that you cannot take advantage of features like role-based access control (RBAC) or resource locks at the disk level. Managed disks are recommended for all new workloads and suggests migrating existing workloads to managed as well.

CHOOSING THE RIGHT DISK TYPE

Table 3-1 provides a summary of when to use which disk type, including the suggested work-load types, max IOPS and throughput.

TABLE 3-1 Summary of performance and recommended workloads per disk type

Disk Type	Premium SSD	Standard SSD	Standard HDD
Summary	Designed for IO intensive enterprise workloads. Delivers consistent performance with low latency and high availability.	Designed to provide consistent performance for low IOPS workloads. Delivers better availability and latency compared to HDD Disks.	Optimized for low-cost mass storage with infrequent access. Can exhibit some variability in performance.
Workload	Demanding enterprise workloads such as SQL Server, Oracle, Dynamics, Exchange Server, MySQL, Cassandra, MongoDB, SAP Business Suite, and other production workloads.	Web servers, low IOPS application servers, lightly used enterprise applications, and Dev/Test.	Backup storage.
Max IOPS	7,500 IOPS provisioned	Up to 500 IOPS	Up to 500 IOPS
Max Throughput	250 MBPS provisioned	Up to 60 MBPS	Up to 60 MBPS

EXAM TIP

Ultra and Standard SSD disks are only creatable as managed disks.

Using the Azure portal on the Disks configuration blade, you can specify the OS disk type to Standard SSD, Standard HDD, or Premium SSD when provisioning a virtual machine. You can also attach additional data disks and specify whether the disks are managed or unmanaged during the provisioning process or after the virtual machine is provisioned.

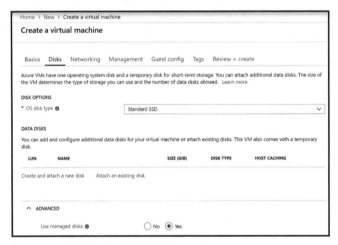

FIGURE 3-12 Configuring disks during creation

Planning for storage capacity

Planning for storage capacity is a key exercise when you are deploying a new workload or migrating an existing workload. For an Azure virtual machine, the maximum capacity of a disk is 4095 GB (4 TB). Disk sizes larger than 4095 GB are currently available: *https://azure.microsoft.com/blog/larger-more-powerful-managed-disks-for-azure-virtual-machines/.*

Virtual machine disk caching

Azure disks (operating system and data) have configurable cache settings that you can configure that affects durability and performance. The caching behavior differs whether you are using Standard storage or Premium storage.

Caching works on Standard HDD storage by buffering the reads and write on the local physical disk on the host server the virtual machine is running on. Virtual machines that use SSD-based storage have a multi-tier caching technology called BlobCache. BlobCache uses a combination of the Virtual Machine RAM and local SSD for caching. This cache is available for Standard and Premium SSD. By default, this cache setting is set to Read/Write for operating system disks and Read Only for data disks hosted on SSD storage. With disk caching enabled on storage disks, virtual machines can achieve extremely high levels of performance that exceed the underlying disk performance.

There are three settings that can be applied to your disks:

- **None**   Configure host-cache as None for write-only and write-heavy disks (data disk only).

- **Read Only**   Configure host-cache as ReadOnly for read-only and read-write disks (OS and data disk).

- **Read Write**   Configure host-cache as ReadWrite only if your application properly handles writing cached data to persistent disks when needed (OS and data disk).

You can set the host caching setting at any time, but understand that when the cache setting is changed that the disk will be unattached and then reattached to the virtual machine. For best practice, you should ensure that none of your applications are actively using the disk when you change the cache setting. Changing the operating system disk's host cache setting, results in the virtual machine being rebooted.

The host cache setting can be modified for a disk by using the Azure portal as shown in Figure 3-13. This setting can also be modified using the command line tools, a template, or a call to the Azure REST API.

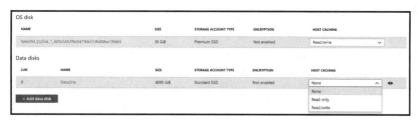

FIGURE 3-13 Setting the Host Caching options

With PowerShell, use the Set-AzVMDataDisk cmdlet to modify the cache setting of a disk. In the following example, an existing virtual machine configuration is returned using the Get-AzVM cmdlet, the disk configuration is modified using Set-AzVMDataDisk, and then the virtual machine is updated using the Update-AzVM cmdlet. Use the Set-AzVMOSDisk cmdlet instead to update the operating system disk. The Set-AzVMDataDisk cmdlet also supports a Name parameter if you would rather update the disk by name instead of using the LUN.

```
$rgName = "ExamRefRG"
$vmName = "ExamRefVM"
$vm = Get-AzVM -ResourceGroupName $rgName -Name $vmName
Set-AzVMDataDisk -VM $vm -Lun 0 -Caching ReadOnly
Update-AzVM -ResourceGroupName $rgName -VM $vm
```

There are two commands to use with Azure CLI, depending on whether the virtual machine is an unmanaged or a managed disk. Also, the host cache setting can only be specified when attaching a disk using the az vm unmanaged-disk for unmanaged disks, or az vm disk attach for managed, specifying the caching parameter. This means you detach and then attach an existing VHD to modify the cache setting, or you can specify it during the creation of a new disk as the following example demonstrates.

```
rgName="StorageRG"
vmName="StandardVM"
diskName="ManagedDisk"
az vm disk attach --vm-name $vmName --resource-group $rgName --size-gb 128
--disk $diskName --caching ReadWrite –new
```

To configure the disk cache setting using a resource manager template specify the caching property of the OSDisk, or each disk in the dataDisks collection of the virtual machine's OSProfile configuration. The following example shows how to set the cache setting on a data disk for an unmanaged disk.

```
"dataDisks": [
  {
    "name": "datadisk1",
    "diskSizeGB": "1023",
    "lun": 0,
    "caching": "ReadOnly",
    "vhd": { "uri": "[variables('DISKURI')]" },
    "createOption": "Empty"
  }
]
```

Capacity planning with unmanaged disks

A Standard Azure Storage account supports a maximum of 20,000 IOPS. A Standard Tier Azure Virtual Machine using Standard storage supports 500 IOPS per disk, and basic tier supports 300 IOPS per disk. If the disks are used at maximum capacity, a single Azure Storage account can handle 40 disks hosted on standard virtual machines, or 66 disks on basic virtual machines. Storage accounts also have a maximum storage capacity of 2 PB for US and Europe and 500 TB for all other regions. When performing capacity planning, the number of Azure Storage accounts per the number of virtual machines can be derived from these numbers. Table 3-2 provides the disk and storage account limits for basic and standard tier virtual machines using standard storage.

TABLE 3-2 Standard unmanaged virtual machine disks: per disk and account limits

VM Tier	Basic Tier VM	Standard Tier VM
Disk size	4095 GB	4095 GB
Max 8 KB IOPS per persistent disk	300	500
Max number of disks performing max IOPS (per storage account)	66	40

A premium Azure storage account supports a maximum of 35 TB of total disk capacity, with up to 10 TB of capacity for snapshots. The maximum bandwidth per account (ingress + egress) is <= 50 Gbps. Table 3-3 lists the storage account limits when using premium unmanaged disks.

TABLE 3-3 Premium storage account limits when using unmanaged disks

Resource	Default Limit
Total disk capacity per account	35 TB
Total snapshot capacity per account	10 TB
Max bandwidth per account (ingress + egress1)	<=50 Gbps

This means that just like when using standard storage, you must carefully plan how many disks you create in each storage account. You should also consider the maximum throughput per Premium disk type, because each type has a different max throughput, which affects the overall max throughput for the storage account. Table 3-4 shows the disk and storage account capacity limits for unmanaged Premium disks.

TABLE 3-4 Premium unmanaged virtual machine disks: per disk limits

Type	Size	IOPS per disk	Throughput	MAX DISKS/Account
P10	128 GiB	500	100 MB/s	280
P20	512 GiB	2300	150 MB/s	70
P30	1024 GiB	5000	200 MB/s	35
P40	2048 GiB	7500	250 MB/s	17
P50	4095 GiB	7500	250 MB/s	8

Capacity planning with managed disks

A significant difference for managed disks over unmanaged disks is there no requirement for managing the underlying storage account for managed disks. This simplifies capacity planning because you must only consider the storage capacity size, IOPS, and overall throughput, and not how many disks per storage account. There are four types of managed disks to understand: Standard HDD, Standard SDD, Premium SDD, and the new Ultra SSD, which is currently in preview. Table 3-5 shows the disk sizes, IOPS, and throughput per disk for Standard HDD managed disks.

TABLE 3-5 Standard HDD managed virtual machine disks

Type	Size	IOPS per disk	Throughput
S4	32 GB	500	60 MB/sec
S6	64 GB	500	60 MB/sec
S10	128 GB	500	60 MB/sec
S30	1024 GB	500	60 MB/sec
S40	2048 GB	500	60 MB/sec

TABLE 3-5 Continued

Type	Size	IOPS per disk	Throughput
S50	4095 GB	500	60 MB/sec
S60	8 TiB	1,300	300 MB/sec
S70	16 TiB	2,000	500 MB/sec
S80	32 TiB	2,000	500 MB/sec

Table 3-6 shows the disk sizes, IOPS, and throughput per disk for Standard SSD managed disks.

TABLE 3-6 Standard SSD managed virtual machine disks: per disk limits

Type	Size	IOPS per disk	Throughput
E10	128 GiB	Up to 500	Up to 60 MiB per second
E15	256 GiB	Up to 500	Up to 60 MiB per second
E20	512 GiB	Up to 500	Up to 60 MiB per second
E30	1,024 GiB	Up to 500	Up to 60 MiB per second
E40	2,048 GiB	Up to 500	Up to 60 MiB per second
E50	4,095 GiB	Up to 500	Up to 60 MiB per second
E60	8,192 GiB	Up to 1,300	Up to 300 MiB per second
E70	16,384 GiB	Up to 2,000	Up to 500 MiB per second
E80	32,767 GiB	Up to 2,000	Up to 500 MiB per second

Table 3-7 shows the disk sizes, IOPS, and throughput per disk for Premium SSD managed disks.

TABLE 3-7 Premium SSD managed virtual machine disks: per disk limits

Type	Size	IOPS per disk	Throughput
P4	32 GB	120	25 MB/sec
P6	64 GB	240	50 MB/sec
P10	128 GB	500	100 MB/sec
P15	256 GB	1100	125 MB/sec
P20	512 GB	2300	150 MB/sec
P30	1024 GB	5000	200 MB/sec
P40	2048 GB	7500	250 MB/sec
P50	4095 GB	7500	250 MB/sec
P60	8 TiB	12,500	480 MB/sec
P70	16 TiB	15,000	750 MB/sec
P80	32 TiB	20,000	750 MB/sec

Each SSD backed storage-supported virtual machine size has scale limits and performance specifications for IOPS, bandwidth, and the number of disks that can be attached per VM.

When you use SSD disks with VMs, make sure that there is enough IOPS and bandwidth on your VM to drive disk traffic.

> **MORE INFO**   **VIRTUAL MACHINE SCALE LIMITS FOR STORAGE**
>
> For the most up-to-date information about maximum IOPS and throughput (bandwidth) for Premium storage-supported VMs, see Windows VM sizes at: *https://docs.microsoft.com/azure/virtual-machines/windows/sizes* or Linux VM sizes: *https://docs.microsoft.com/azure/virtual-machines/linux/sizes.*

Implementing disk redundancy for performance

If your workload throughput requirements exceed the maximum IOPS capabilities of a single disk or your storage requirements are greater than the size of a single disk you do have options. The first option is to add multiple data disks (depending on the virtual machine size) and implement RAID 0 disk striping, and create one or more volumes with multiple data disks. Be sure to only use RAID 0 striping or you will see performance degradation. This provides increased capacity and increased throughput.

If your virtual machine is hosted on Windows Server 2012 or above, you can use storage pools to virtualize storage by grouping industry-standard disks into pools, and then create virtual disks called Storage Spaces from the available capacity in the storage pools. You can then configure these virtual disks to provide striping capabilities across all disks in the pool, combining good performance characteristics. Storage pools make it easy to grow or shrink volumes depending on your needs (and the capacity of the Azure data disks you have attached).

This next example creates a new storage pool named VMStoragePool with all of the available data disks configured as part of the pool. The code identifies the available data disks using the Get-PhysicalDisk cmdlet and creates the virtual disk using the New-VirtualDisk cmdlet.

```
# Create a new storage pool using all available disks
New-StoragePool -FriendlyName "VMStoragePool" `
        -StorageSubsystemFriendlyName "Windows Storage*" `
        -PhysicalDisks (Get-PhysicalDisk -CanPool $True)
# Return all disks in the new pool
$disks = Get-StoragePool -FriendlyName "VMStoragePool" `
            -IsPrimordial $false |
            Get-PhysicalDisk
# Create a new virtual disk
New-VirtualDisk -FriendlyName "DataDisk" `
        -ResiliencySettingName Simple `
        -NumberOfColumns $disks.Count `
        -UseMaximumSize -Interleave 256KB `
        -StoragePoolFriendlyName "VMStoragePool"
```

The NumberOfColumns parameter of New-VirtualDisk should be set to the number of data disks utilized to create the underlying storage pool. This allows IO requests to be evenly distributed against all data disks in the pool. The Interleave parameter enables you to specify the number of bytes written in each underlying data disk in a virtual disk. Microsoft recommends in general that you use 256 KB for all workloads. After the virtual disk is created, the disk must be initialized, formatted, and mounted to a drive letter or mount point just like any other disk.

> **MORE INFO   STRIPING DISKS FOR PERFORMANCE ON LINUX**
>
> Using storage pools allows you to combine disks on Windows for increased throughput and capacity. You can do the same thing on Linux as well using several options. See the following to learn more at: *https://docs.microsoft.com/azure/virtual-machines/linux/configure-raid*.

> **EXAM TIP**
>
> Mounting data disks may come up on the exam. It is important to remember that on Windows, the drive D is mapped to the local resource disk, which is only for temporary data because it is backed by the local physical disk on the host server. The resource disk will be mounted on the / Dev/sdb1 device on Linux, with the actual mount point varying by Linux distribution.

Configure networking

During the virtual machine provisioning process in the portal you can set the following settings using the Networking blade as shown in Figure 3-14.

- The virtual network and subnet and the public IP address
- The network security group for the network interface card (NIC)
- Which public inbound ports should be open (if any)
- Enable accelerated networking
- The option to include the VM in an existing Azure load balancer backend pool

FIGURE 3-14 Specifying the networking options for a virtual machine during creation

MORE INFO NETWORK SECURITY GROUPS

A network security group (NSG) is a networking filter containing a list of security rules that when applied control network traffic. These rules can manage both inbound and outbound traffic. A network security group can be associated to a network interface, the subnet the network interface is in, or both. To simplify management of security rules, it's recommended that you associate a network security group to individual subnets, rather than individual network interfaces within the subnet, whenever possible. You will learn more about NSGs in Chapter 4 Configure and Manage Virtual Networks.

There are several networking features to understand for effectively using Azure Virtual Machines as well as preparing for the exam. In this chapter you will learn some of these concepts, and in Chapter 4 Configure and Manage Virtual Networks you will learn in-depth about virtual networks, network security groups, subnets, IP addresses and DNS management.

MORE INFO APPLICATION SECURITY GROUPS

An application security group (ASG) enables you to define network security policies based on workloads with rules focused on applications instead of IP and network addresses. They provide the capability to group virtual machines with monikers and secure applications by filtering traffic from trusted segments of your network. Like NSGs, you will learn more about ASGs in Chapter 4 Configure and Manage Virtual Networks.

Accelerated networking

Accelerated networking enables single root I/O virtualization (SR-IOV) to a virtual machine, which greatly improves its networking performance. This feature improves performance by bypassing the virtual switch between the host VM and the physical switch. Figure 3-15 shows two deployments: the deployment on the left without accelerated networking and the deployment on the right with accelerated networking enabled.

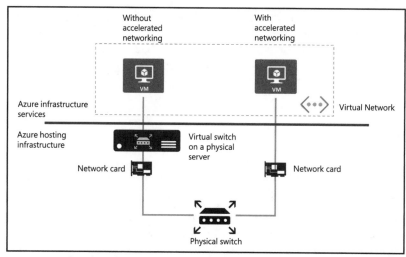

FIGURE 3-15 Virtual machines deployed with and without accelerated networking enabled

Accelerated networking can be enabled at creation time or after the virtual machine is created if the following pre-requisites are followed:

- The VM must be a supported size for Accelerated Networking
- The VM must be a supported Azure Gallery image (and kernel version for Linux)
- All VMs in an availability set or VMSS must be stopped/deallocated before enabling Accelerated Networking on any NIC

Supported sizes:

- Accelerated Networking is supported on most general purpose and compute-optimized instance sizes with 2 or more vCPUs. These supported series are: D/DSv2 and F/Fs
- On instances that support hyperthreading, Accelerated Networking is supported on VM instances with 4 or more vCPUs. Supported series are: D/DSv3, E/ESv3, Fsv2, and Ms/Mms

Supported Windows-based images from the Azure Marketplace:

- Windows Server 2016 Datacenter
- Windows Server 2012 R2 Datacenter

Supported Linux-based images from the Azure Marketplace:

- Ubuntu 16.04
- SLES 12 SP3
- RHEL 7.4
- CentOS 7.4
- CoreOS Linux
- Debian "Stretch" with backports kernel
- Oracle Linux 7.4

To change an existing virtual machine, you must update the network interface. The following example shows how to accomplish this using PowerShell:

```
$nic = Get-AzNetworkInterface -ResourceGroupName "ExamRefRG"  -Name "vmNicName"
$nic.EnableAcceleratedNetworking = $true
$nic | Set-AzNetworkInterface
```

The following example shows how to use the Azure CLI to accomplish the same task:

```
az network nic update \
    --name vmNicName \
    --resource-group ExamRefRG \
    --accelerated-networking true
```

> **MORE INFO LEARNING MORE ABOUT ACCELERATED NETWORKING**
>
> You can learn more about using Accelerated Networking on Windows virtual machines here: *https://docs.microsoft.com/azure/virtual-network/create-vm-accelerated-networking-powershell* or Linux-based VMs here: *https://docs.microsoft.com/azure/virtual-network/create-vm-accelerated-networking-cli.*

Connecting to virtual machines

There are many ways to connect to virtual machines. You should consider options such as connecting to VMs using their public IP addresses and protecting them with network security groups and allowing only the port for the service you are connecting to. You should also understand how to connect to a VM on its private IP address. This introduces additional connectivity requirements such as ExpressRoute, Site-to-Site VPN, or Point-to-Site VPN to put your client on the same network as your VMs. These technologies are discussed in Chapter 4. In this section we'll review the most common tools to connect and manage your VMs.

Connecting to a Windows VM with remote desktop

The default connectivity option for a Windows-based virtual machine is to use the remote desktop protocol (RDP) and a Remote Desktop client such as mstsc.exe. The RDP service listens on TCP port 3389 and provides full access to the Windows desktop. This service is enabled by default on all Windows-based VMs provisioned from the Azure Marketplace. The Azure portal provides a **Connect** button that will appear enabled for virtual machines that have a public IP address associated with them, as shown in Figure 3-16.

FIGURE 3-16 The Connect button for an Azure VM

You can launch a remote desktop session from Windows PowerShell by using the Get-AzRemoteDesktopFile cmdlet. The Get-AzRemoteDesktopFile cmdlet performs the same validation as the Azure portal. The API it calls validates that a public IP address is associated with the virtual machine's network interface. If a public IP exists, it generates an .rdp file consumable with a Remote Desktop client. The .rdp file will have the IP address of the VIP and public port (3389) of the specified embedded virtual machine. There are two parameters that alter the behavior of what happens with the generated file.

Use the Launch parameter to retrieve the .rdp file and immediately open it with a Remote Desktop client. The following example launches the Mstsc.exe (Remote Desktop client), and the client prompts you to initiate the connection.

```
$rgName = "ExamRefRG"
$vmName = "ExamRefVM"
Get-AzRemoteDesktopFile -ResourceGroupName $rgName -Name $vmName -Launch
```

The second behavior is to specify the LocalPath parameter, as the following example shows. Use this parameter to save the .rdp file locally for later use.

```
$rgName = "ExamRefRG"
$vmName = "ExamRefVM"
$Path = "C:\Scratch\ExamRefVM.rdp"
Get-AzRemoteDesktopFile -ResourceGroupName $rgName -Name $vmName -LocalPath $path
```

Connecting to a Linux virtual machine using SSH

The default connectivity option for a Linux-based virtual machine is to use the secure shell (SSH) protocol. This service listens on TCP port 22 and provides full access to a command line shell. This service is enabled by default on all Linux-based VMs. When you click the Connect button on a Linux-based virtual machine with a public IP associated with it you see a dialog advising you to use SSH to connect. Figure 3-17 shows how to use SSH to connect to a virtual machine using the Azure Cloud Shell.

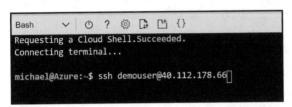

FIGURE 3-17 Using SSH to connect to a virtual machine from the Azure cloud shell

If the virtual machine is configured for password access, SSH then prompts for the password for the user you specified. If you specified the public key for an SSH certificate during the creation of the virtual machine, it attempts to use the certificate from the ~/.ssh folder.

Windows users have many options for connecting using SSH. For example, if you install the Linux subsystem for Windows 10, you will also install an SSH client that can be accessed from the bash command line. You can also install one of many GUI-based SSH clients like PuTTY.

> **MORE INFO OPTIONS FOR USING SSH FROM WINDOWS**
>
> There are plenty of options to connect to your Linux-based virtual machines from Windows. The following link has more detail on SSH certificate management and some available clients at: *https://docs.microsoft.com/azure/virtual-machines/linux/ssh-from-windows.*

Configure monitoring

There are several tools and services in Azure designed to help you monitor different aspects of an application or deployed infrastructure. In addition to the built-in tools, you also can monitor your virtual machines using existing monitoring solutions such as Systems Center Operations Manager, or many other third-party solutions. Let's review some of the built-in capabilities.

Azure diagnostics

There are two levels of VM diagnostics: host and guest. With host diagnostics you can view and act on the data surfaced from the hypervisor hosting your virtual machine. This data is limited to high-level metrics involving the CPU, Disk, and Network. Enabling guest-level diagnostics involves having an agent running on the virtual machine that can collect a richer subset of data.

Azure Diagnostics extension

The Azure diagnostics extension is an agent on both Windows and Linux VMs that provides a rich set of diagnostics data. On Windows, this agent can collect a comprehensive set of performance counter data, event, IIS log files, and even crash dumps. It also provides the ability to automatically transfer this data to Azure Storage as well as surfacing telemetry to the Azure portal for visualization and alerts. The capabilities on Linux are more limited, but they still expose a broad range of performance telemetry to act on for reporting and alerts.

Enabling and configuring diagnostics (Windows)

During the creation of a VM, you can enable both guest operating system diagnostics and boot diagnostics. Diagnostics data for the virtual machine is stored in an Azure storage account. Figure 3-18 shows the Management blade which is where you can enable diagnostics at provisioning time.

FIGURE 3-18 Enabling boot and guest operating system diagnostics during VM creation

You can also enable diagnostics on a VM after it is created as long as the virtual machine is running. Figure 3-19 shows what it looks like to enable the Diagnostics extension on a Windows VM.

FIGURE 3-19 Enabling diagnostics on a Windows VM

After the Diagnostics extension is enabled, you can then capture performance counter data. Using the portal, you can select basic sets of counters by category, as Figure 3-20 shows.

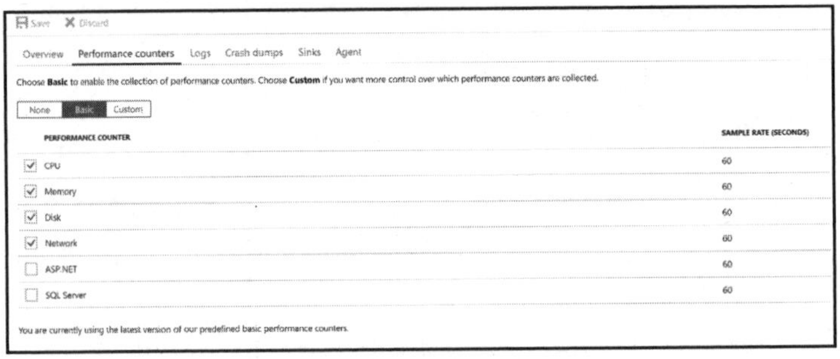

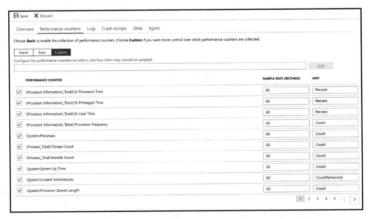

FIGURE 3-20 Configuring the capture of performance counters

You can also configure diagnostics at a granular level by specifying exactly which counters to sample and capture, including custom counters, as Figure 3-21 shows.

FIGURE 3-21 Specifying a custom performance counter configuration

Like capturing performance counters, the Diagnostics extension provides the option of collecting basic event log data, as Figure 3-22 shows. The custom view for capturing event logs supports a custom syntax to filter on certain events by their event source or the value.

FIGURE 3-22 Capturing event logs and levels to capture

Figure 3-23 shows how to configure the extension to automatically transfer IIS web and failed request logs to Azure storage containers for later diagnostics.

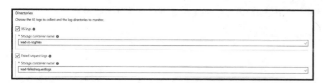

FIGURE 3-23 Capturing event logs and levels to capture

For .NET applications that emit trace data, the extension can also capture this data and filter by the following log levels: All, Critical, Error, Warning, Information, and Verbose, as Figure 3-24 shows.

FIGURE 3-24 Specifying the log level for application logs

Event Tracing for Windows (ETW) provides a mechanism to trace and log events that are raised by user-mode applications and kernel-mode drivers. ETW is implemented in the Windows operating system and provides developers a fast, reliable, and versatile set of event tracing features. Figure 3-25 demonstrates how to configure the Diagnostics extension to capture ETW data from specific sources.

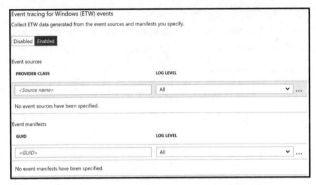

FIGURE 3-25 Collecting Event Tracing for Windows (ETW)

The Azure Diagnostics extension can be configured to monitor processes and automatically capture crash dumps in the event of an unhandled exception, as shown in Figure 3-26. You can choose from mini-crash dumps to full crash dumps. The agent automatically moves the dump files to the Azure Storage container you specify.

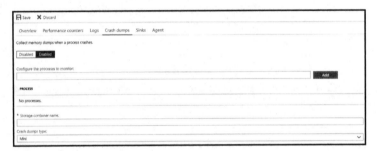

FIGURE 3-26 Configuring process monitoring and crash dump collection

The agent optionally allows you to send diagnostic data to Application Insights, as Figure 3-27 shows. This is especially helpful if you have other parts of an application that use Application Insights natively, so you have a single location to view diagnostics data for your application.

FIGURE 3-27 Sending diagnostics data to Application Insights

The final diagnostics data to mention is boot diagnostics. If enabled, the Azure Diagnostics agent captures a screen shot to a specific Storage account of what the console looks like on the last boot. This helps you understand the problem if your VM does not start. Clicking the Boot Diagnostics link in the portal shows you the last captured screen shot of your VM as well as the serial log of the status of the virtual machine when it booted, as Figure 3-28 shows.

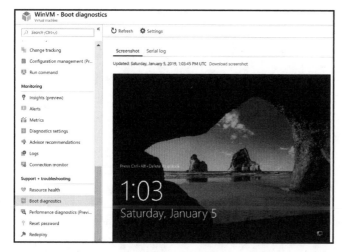

FIGURE 3-28 The screen shot from the last boot for a Windows VM with boot diagnostics configured

Enabling and configuring diagnostics (Linux)

The Diagnostics agent on Linux supports capturing performance metrics, data from the Linux Syslog, as well as rich boot diagnostics data. Like the Windows agent, the Diagnostics extension can be enabled at provisioning time or after the VM is provisioned.

Figure 3-29 shows the basic performance metrics that are available for capture by the Azure Diagnostics agent.

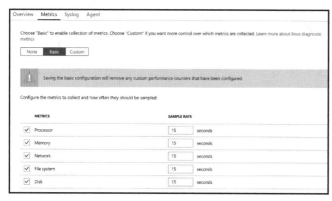

FIGURE 3-29 Enabling diagnostics on a Linux VM

Clicking Custom opens the blade shown in Figure 3-30, which allows much more fine grain control over which metrics to capture.

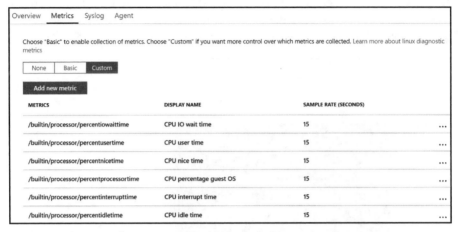

FIGURE 3-30 Custom performance metrics with the Azure Diagnostics agent

Figure 3-31 shows how to configure diagnostic capture for Linux Syslog data.

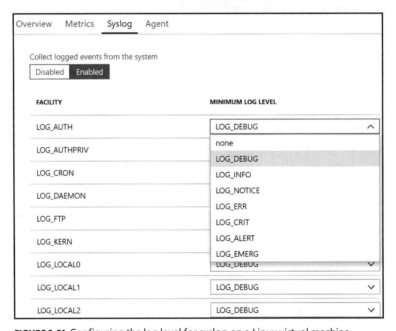

FIGURE 3-31 Configuring the log level for syslog on a Linux virtual machine

Like Windows, boot diagnostics on Linux provides both a screen shot of the console as well as the output of the boot sequence captured in the serial log as shown in Figure 3-32.

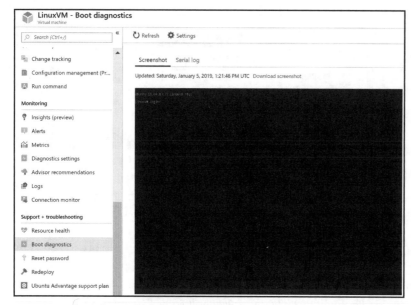

FIGURE 3-32 Boot diagnostics logs for a Linux VM

EXAM TIP

The Azure Diagnostics agent can also be configured through resource manager templates and the command line tools by specifying a configuration file. For the exam you should be aware of the schema of this configuration and how to apply it using automated tools. You can learn more about the diagnostics schema at:

https://docs.microsoft.com/azure/monitoring-and-diagnostics/azure-diagnostics-schema.

Azure Monitor

Azure Monitor maximizes the availability and performance of your applications by delivering a comprehensive solution for collecting, analyzing, and acting on telemetry from your cloud and on-premises environments. It helps you understand how your applications are performing and proactively identifies issues affecting them and the resources they depend on. The Azure Monitor landing page provides a jumping off point to configure other more specific monitoring services such as Application Insights, Network Watcher, Log Analytics, Management Solutions, and so on. Data collected by Azure Monitor fits into one of two types: metrics and logs. Metrics are numerical values that describe some aspect of the system at a point in time. Logs contain different kinds of data organized into records with different properties. Examples of log data include telemetry data such as Azure platform actions, events and trace logs. Figure 3-33 shows some of the various data sources and how they are collected either as metric or log data. The data is consumed, visualized or acted on by various services in Azure.

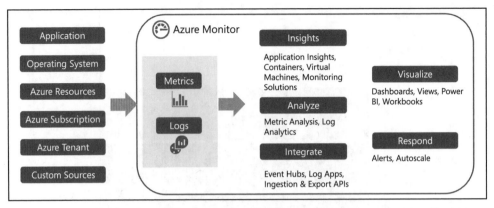

FIGURE 3-33 Azure Monitor data sources for metric and log data and the ways you can act on the data

MORE INFO   AZURE MONITOR

To learn more about the capabilities of Azure Monitor see the following:
https://docs.microsoft.com/azure/monitoring-and-diagnostics/monitoring-overview-azure-monitor.

MORE INFO   AZURE MONITOR FOR VMS (PREVIEW)

Azure Monitor for a VMs is an offering currently in preview that provides new capabilities for monitoring your virtual machines and virtual machine scale sets. You can learn more about the new capabilities here:
https://docs.microsoft.com/azure/azure-monitor/insights/vminsights-overview.

Creating an alert

You create a new alert by clicking Alerts from within the Azure resource configuration blade or from within Azure Monitor, and then click New alert rule. Figure 3-34 shows the Alerts blade from within Azure Monitor.

FIGURE 3-34 The alerts blade from within Azure Monitor

Figure 3-35 shows the Create Rule blade, which prompts for four pieces of information: the resources to monitor, the conditions to alert on, the action groups (which define what action to take when the alert is triggered), and the name and description of the alert.

FIGURE 3-35 The create rule blade after clicking New Alert Rule in Azure Monitor

Clicking the Select button brings up a dialog where you filter on which resource in your subscription to create the alert on. Figure 3-36 shows the Select A Resource blade filtered by the virtual machines resource type. If you do not select a resource type you can filter on different Azure subscription activity log signals to receive alerts on.

FIGURE 3-36 Configuring the criteria for an alert

The next step is to configure the alert criteria by clicking the Add condition button and then selecting the signal to measure. This is the metric to use, the condition, threshold, and the period. The alert shown in Figure 3-37 will trigger an alert when the Percentage CPU metric exceeds 70 percent over a five-minute period.

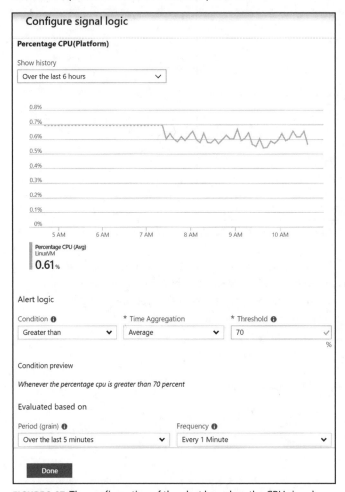

FIGURE 3-37 The configuration of the alert based on the CPU signal

An action group is a collection of actions that should occur in response to an alert being triggered. You can have up to 1000 email actions in an action group. In addition to sending email notifications you can execute the following actions:

- **ITSM** You may have up to 10 IT Service Manager (ITSM) actions with an ITSM connection. The following ITSM providers are currently supported: ServiceNow, System Center Service Manager, Provance, and Cherwell. You can learn more about ITSM connections here: *https://docs.microsoft.com/azure/azure-monitor/platform/itsmc-overview*.

- **Webhook** A webhook allows you to route an Azure alert notification to other systems for post-processing or custom actions. For example, you can use a webhook on an alert to route it to services that send text messages, log bugs, notify a team via chat/messaging services, or do any number of other actions. You can learn more about sending alert information to webhooks at: *https://docs.microsoft.com/azure/monitoring-and-diagnostics/insights-webhooks-alerts.*

- **Runbook** A set of PowerShell code that runs in the Azure Automation Service. See the following to learn more about using Runbooks to remediate alerts at: *https://azure.microsoft.com/blog/automatically-remediate-azure-vm-alerts-with-automation-runbooks/.*

- **Function Apps** A Function App is a set of code that runs "serverless" that can respond to alerts. This functionality requires Version 2 of Function Apps, and the value of the AzureWebJobsSecretStorageType app setting must be set to "files."

- **Logic Apps** A Logic App provides a visual designer to model and automate your process as a series of steps known as a workflow. There are many connectors across the cloud and on-premises to quickly integrate across services and protocols. When an alert is triggered the Logic App can take the notification data and use it with any of the connectors to remediate the alert or start other services. To learn more about Azure Logic Apps visit: *https://docs.microsoft.com/azure/logic-apps/logic-apps-what-are-logic-apps.*

- **SMS** You may have up to 10 SMS actions in an Action Group.

- **Voice** You may have up to 10 Voice actions in an Action Group.

Figure 3-38 shows the various actions that can take place when an alert is triggered.

FIGURE 3-38 Configuring notifications for an alert

Application Insights

Application Insights is used for development and as a production monitoring solution. It works by installing a package into your app, which can provide a more internal view of what's going on with your code. Its data includes response times of dependencies, exception traces, debugging snapshots, and execution profiles. It provides powerful smart tools for analyzing all this telemetry both to help you debug an app, and to help you understand what users are doing with it. You can tell whether a spike in response times is due to something in an app, or some external resourcing issue. If you use Visual Studio and the app is at fault, you can be taken right to the problem line(s) of code, so you can fix it. Application Insights provides significantly more value when your application is instrumented to emit custom events and exception information. You can learn more about Application Insights including samples for emitting custom telemetry at: *https://docs.microsoft.com/azure/application-insights/.*

Network Watcher

The Network Watcher service provides the ability to monitor and diagnose networking issues without logging in to your virtual machines (VMs). You can trigger packet capture by setting alerts and gain access to real-time performance information at the packet level. When you see an issue, you can investigate in detail for better diagnoses. This service is ideal for troubleshooting network connectivity or performance issues.

Azure Log Analytics

Log Analytics is a service that monitors your cloud and on-premises environments to maintain their availability and performance. Log Analytics collects data generated by resources in your cloud and on-premises environments and from other monitoring tool to provide analysis across multiple data sources. Log Analytics provides rich tools to analyze data across multiple sources, allows complex queries across all logs, and can proactively alert you on specified conditions. You can even collect custom data into its central repository, so you can query and visualize it. You can learn more about Log Analytics at: *https://docs.microsoft.com/azure/log-analytics/log-analytics-overview.*

Deploy and configure scale sets

For workloads that support the ability to dynamically add and remove instances to handle increased or decreased demand, VM scale sets (VMSS) should be considered. A VMSS is a compute resource that you can use to deploy and manage a set of identical virtual machines.

By default, a VMSS supports up to 100 instances. However, it is possible to create a scale set up to 1000 instances if they are deployed with the property singlePlacementGroup set to false. A placement group is a construct like an Azure availability set, with its own fault domains and upgrade domains. By default, a scale set consists of a single placement group with a maximum size of 100 VMs. If the scale set property called singlePlacementGroup is set to false, the scale set can be composed of multiple placement groups and has a range of 0-1,000 VMs. When set to the default value of true, a scale set is composed of a single placement group, and has a range of 0-100 VMs.

Using multiple placement groups is commonly referred to as a large-scale set. The single-PlacementGroup property can be set using ARM templates, the command line tools, or during portal creation. Working with large scale sets does have a few conditions to be aware of. If you are using a custom image instead of a gallery image, your scale set supports up to 300 instances instead of 1000. Another scalability factor for consideration is the Azure Load Balancer. The basic SKU of the Azure Load Balancer can scale up to 100 instances. For a large-scale set (> 100 instances) you should use the Standard SKU or the Azure Application Gateway.

Creating a virtual machine scale set (Azure portal)

Figure 3-39 shows a portion of the creation dialog for creating a new VM scale set using the Azure portal. Like other Azure resources, you must specify a name and the resource group to deploy to. All instances of the VMSS will use the same operating system disk image specified here. A scale set can be deployed to an availability zone or an availability set.

FIGURE 3-39 Creating a VM scale set

Figure 3-40 shows further down the blade. This allows you to configure more advanced properties such as scaling beyond 100 instances, Autoscale properties, how virtual machines are spread across fault domains, and networking options such as the virtual network and subnet to use plus which type of load balancer to use. Not shown in the image is a setting that allows the scale set to use managed disks.

FIGURE 3-40 Configuring the instances and the load balancer for a VM scale set

EXAM TIP

The spreading algorithm determines how VMs in the scale set are balanced across fault do-mains. With max spreading, VMs are spread across as many fault domains as possible in each zone. With fixed spreading, VMs are always spread across exactly five fault domains. In the case where fewer than five fault domains are available, a scale set using "Max spreading" will still complete deployment, while a scale set using "Fixed spreading" will fail to deploy.

When Autoscale is enabled, you are presented with a set of configuration options for setting the default rules, as shown in Figure 3-41. Here you can specify the minimum and maximum number of VMs in the set, as well as the actions to scale out (add more) or to scale in (remove instances).

FIGURE 3-41 Configuring Autoscale rules for a virtual machine scale set

The Azure portal creation process does not directly support applying configuration management options like VM extensions. However, they can be applied to a VMSS later using the command line tools or an ARM template.

> **MORE INFO** **VIRTUAL MACHINE SCALE SETS**
>
> You can learn more about virtual machine scale sets here:
> *https://docs.microsoft.com/azure/virtual-machine-scale-sets/.*

Upgrading a virtual machine scale set

During the lifecycle of running a virtual machine scale set you undoubtedly need to deploy an update to the operating system. The VMSS resource property *upgradePolicy* can be set to either the value manual or automatic. If automatic, when an operating system update is available all instances are updated at the same time, which causes downtime. If the property is set to manual, it is up to you to programmatically step through and update each instance using PowerShell with the Update-AzVmssInstance cmdlet or the Azure CLI tools az vmss update-instances command.

> **MORE INFO** **UPGRADING A VIRTUAL MACHINE SCALE SET**
>
> You can learn more about upgrading virtual machine scale sets at:
> *https://docs.microsoft.com/azure/virtual-machine-scale-sets/virtual-machine-scale-sets-upgrade-scale-set.*

Creating a virtual machine scale set (PowerShell)

Creating a VM scale set using PowerShell is very similar to creating a regular virtual machine. You create a VMSS configuration object using the New-AzVmssConfig cmdlet. From there, you either create or retrieve existing dependent resources and set them on the returned configuration object. Typically, virtual machine scale sets use a VM extension to self-configure themselves during the instance startup. The Add-AzVmssExtension cmdlet is used to specify the extension configuration.

The following example is detailed and creates all the resources such as virtual network, load balancer, public IP address, as well as demonstrates how to apply a custom script extension to configure the VM instances on boot.

```
# Create a virtual machine scale set with IIS installed from a custom script extension
$rgName      = "ExamRefRGPS"
$location    = "WestUS"
$vmSize      = "Standard_DS2_V2"
$capacity    = 2

New-AzResourceGroup -Name $rgName -Location $location
# Create a config object
$vmssConfig = New-AzVmssConfig `
    -Location $location `
    -SkuCapacity $capacity `
    -SkuName $vmSize `
    -UpgradePolicyMode Automatic

# Define the script for your Custom Script Extension to run
$publicSettings = @{
    "fileUris" = (,"https://raw.githubusercontent.com/opsgility/lab-support-
public/master/script-extensions/install-iis.ps1");
    "commandToExecute" = "powershell -ExecutionPolicy Unrestricted -File
install-iis.ps1"
}
```

This section of the code adds a new custom script extension to the VM Scale Set configuration object ($vmssConfig). The script will execute automatically as a new node is added to the scale set.

```
# Use Custom Script Extension to install IIS and configure basic website
Add-AzVmssExtension -VirtualMachineScaleSet $vmssConfig `
    -Name "customScript" `
    -Publisher "Microsoft.Compute" `
    -Type "CustomScriptExtension" `
    -TypeHandlerVersion 1.8 `
    -Setting $publicSettings
```

This section specifies the load balancer network configuration, including the public IP address that the load balancer will use, the load balancer and the front end and backend pool of the scale set.

```
$publicIPName = "vmssIP"

# Create a public IP address
$publicIP = New-AzPublicIpAddress `
  -ResourceGroupName $rgName `
  -Location $location `
  -AllocationMethod Static `
  -Name $publicIPName
```

```
# Create a frontend and backend IP pool
$frontEndPoolName = "lbFrontEndPool"
$backendPoolName = "lbBackEndPool"
$frontendIP = New-AzLoadBalancerFrontendIpConfig `
  -Name $frontEndPoolName `
  -PublicIpAddress $publicIP
$backendPool = New-AzLoadBalancerBackendAddressPoolConfig -Name $backendPoolName


# Create the load balancer
$lbName = "vmsslb"
$lb = New-AzLoadBalancer `
  -ResourceGroupName $rgName `
  -Name $lbName `
  -Location $location `
  -FrontendIpConfiguration $frontendIP `
  -BackendAddressPool $backendPool

# Create a load balancer health probe on port 80
$probeName = "lbprobe"
Add-AzLoadBalancerProbeConfig -Name $probeName `
  -LoadBalancer $lb `
  -Protocol http `
  -Port 80 `
  -IntervalInSeconds 15 `
  -ProbeCount 2 `
  -RequestPath "/"


# Create a load balancer rule to distribute traffic on port 80
Add-AzLoadBalancerRuleConfig `
  -Name "lbrule" `
  -LoadBalancer $lb `
  -FrontendIpConfiguration $lb.FrontendIpConfigurations[0] `
  -BackendAddressPool $lb.BackendAddressPools[0] `
  -Protocol Tcp `
  -FrontendPort 80 `
  -BackendPort 80
# Update the load balancer configuration
Set-AzLoadBalancer -LoadBalancer $lb
```

This section of the sample specifies the OS Image and the administrator credentials each node will use when provisioned.

```
# Reference a virtual machine image from the gallery
Set-AzVmssStorageProfile $vmssConfig `
  -ImageReferencePublisher MicrosoftWindowsServer `
  -ImageReferenceOffer WindowsServer `
  -ImageReferenceSku 2016-Datacenter `
  -ImageReferenceVersion latest `
  -OsDiskCreateOption FromImage
```

```
# Set up information for authenticating with the virtual machine
$userName = "azureuser"
$password = "P@ssword!"
$vmPrefix = "ssVM"
Set-AzVmssOsProfile $vmssConfig `
  -AdminUsername $userName `
  -AdminPassword $password `
  -ComputerNamePrefix $vmPrefix
```

In this section of the sample, shows how to specify the virtual network configuration for the scale set.

```
# Create the virtual network resources
$subnetName = "web"
$subnet = New-AzVirtualNetworkSubnetConfig `
  -Name $subnetName `
  -AddressPrefix 10.0.0.0/24


$ssName = "vmssVNET"
$subnetPrefix = "10.0.0.0/16"


$vnet = New-AzVirtualNetwork `
  -ResourceGroupName $rgName `
  -Name $ssName `
  -Location $location `
  -AddressPrefix $subnetPrefix `
  -Subnet $subnet


$ipConfig = New-AzVmssIpConfig `
  -Name "vmssIPConfig" `
  -LoadBalancerBackendAddressPoolsId $lb.BackendAddressPools[0].Id `
  -SubnetId $vnet.Subnets[0].Id


# Attach the virtual network to the config object
$netConfigName = "network-config"
Add-AzVmssNetworkInterfaceConfiguration `
  -VirtualMachineScaleSet $vmssConfig `
  -Name $netConfigName `
  -Primary $true `
  -IPConfiguration $ipConfig
```

This last section shows how to create the scale set using New-AzVmss cmdlet.

```
$scaleSetName = "erscaleset"
# Create the scale set with the config object (this step might take a few minutes)
New-AzVmss `
  -ResourceGroupName $rgName `
  -Name $scaleSetName `
  -VirtualMachineScaleSet $vmssConfig
```

Creating a virtual machine scale set (CLI)

The Azure CLI tools takes a different approach than PowerShell by creating resources like load balancers and virtual networks for you as part of the scale set creation.

```
# Create a VM Scale Set with load balancer, virtual network, and a public IP address
rgName="Contoso"
ssName="erscaleset"
userName="azureuser"
password="P@ssword000114!"
vmPrefix="ssVM"
location="WestUS"
az group create --name $rgName --location $location
az vmss create --resource-group $rgName --name $ssName --image UbuntuLTS \
--authentication-type password --admin-username $userName --admin-password $password
```

The `az vmss create` command allows you to reference existing resources instead of creating them automatically by specifying the resources as parameters if you want to differ from the default behavior. For a VMSS use the `az vmss extension set` command as shown in the following example. The settings.json file should be in the same directory that execute the command.

```
#settings.json
{
  "fileUris": [
    "https://raw.githubusercontent.com/Azure/azure-quickstart-templates/master/
201-vmss-bottle-autoscale/installserver.sh"
  ],
  "commandToExecute": "bash installserver.sh"
}
az vmss extension set --publisher Microsoft.Compute --version 1.8 \
--name CustomScriptExtension --resource-group $rgName --vmss-name $ssName \
--settings @settings.json
```

Skill 3.2: Automate deployment of VMs

The ability to provision virtual machines on-demand using the Azure portal is incredibly powerful. The true power of the cloud, however, is the ability to automatically deploy one or more resources defined in code such as a script or a template. Use cases such as defining an application configuration, and automatically deploying it on-demand, allows teams to be more agile by providing dev/test/production environments in a fast and repeatable fashion. Since the configuration is stored as code, changes to infrastructure can also be tracked in a version control system. In this skill you will learn some of the core capabilities for automating workload deployments in Azure.

Deploy Windows and Linux VMs

Azure Resource Manager templates are authored using JavaScript Object Notation (JSON) and provide the ability to define the configuration of resources like virtual machines, Storage accounts, and so on in a declarative manner. Templates go beyond just providing the ability to create the resources; some resources such as virtual machines also allow you to customize them and create dependencies between them. This allows you to create templates that have capabilities for orchestrated deployments of completely functional solutions.

The Azure team maintains a list of ARM templates with examples for most resources. This list is located at https://azure.microsoft.com/resources/templates/, and is backed by a source code repository in GitHub. If you want to go directly to the source to file a bug or any other reason you can access it at: https://github.com/Azure/azure-quickstart-templates.

The basic structure of a resource manager template has most of the following elements:

```
{
  "$schema": "https://schema.management.azure.com/schemas/2015-01
-01/deploymentTemplate.json#",
  "contentVersion": "1.0.0.0",
  "parameters": { },
  "variables": { },
  "functions": [ ],
  "resources": [ ],
  "outputs": { }
}
```

- **$schema** The URL to the JSON schema that defines the version of the template language.

  For resource group targeted deployments use:

  ```
  http://schema.management.azure.com/schemas/2015-01-01/deploymentTemplate.json#
  ```

  For subscription targeted deployments use:

  ```
  https://schema.management.azure.com/schemas/2018-05
-01/subscriptionDeploymentTemplate.json#
  ```

- **contentVersion**   Version of the template (such as 1.0.0.0). You can provide any value for this element. Use this value to document significant changes in your template. When deploying resources using the template, this value can be used to make sure that the right template is being used.

- **parameters**   Values that are provided when deployment is executed to customize resource deployment.

- **variables**   Values that are used as JSON fragments in the template to simplify template language expressions.

- **functions**   User-defined functions that are available within the template.

- **resources**   Resource types that are deployed or updated in a resource group.

- **outputs**   Values that are returned after deployment.

Defining a virtual network

This skill is focused on learning how to deploy Windows and Linux virtual machines. A prerequisite of deploying a virtual machine is a virtual network. In this example, we'll define the structure of the virtual network using several variables that describe the address space and subnet allocation. The last three variables are additional variables that will be referenced by other resources created later in the section.

```
"ExamRefRGPrefix": "10.0.0.0/16",
"ExamRefRGSubnet1Name": "FrontEndSubnet",
"ExamRefRGSubnet1Prefix": "10.0.0.0/24",
"ExamRefRGSubnet2Name": "BackEndSubnet",
"ExamRefRGSubnet2Prefix": "10.0.1.0/24",
"ExamRefRGSubnet1Ref": "[concat(variables('vnetId'), '/subnets/',
 variables('ExamRefRGSubnet1Name'))]",
"VNetId": "[resourceId('Microsoft.Network/virtualNetworks', variables('VirtualNetworkNa
me'))]",
"VirtualNetworkName": "ExamRefVNET",
```

After the variables are defined you can then add the virtual network resource to the resource's element in your template. The following snippet creates a virtual network named ExamRefVNET, with an address space of 10.0.0.0/16 and two subnets: FrontEndSubnet 10.0.0.0/24 and BackEndSubnet 10.0.1.0/24. Note the syntax to read the value of variables: [variables('variablename')] is used heavily when authoring templates. The virtual network's location is set based on the return value of the built-in resourceGroup() function, which returns information about the resource group the resource is being created or updated in.

```
{
  "name": "[variables('VirtualNetworkName')]",
  "type": "Microsoft.Network/virtualNetworks",
  "location": "[resourceGroup().location]",
  "apiVersion": "2017-06-01",
  "dependsOn": [],
  "properties": {
```

```
      "addressSpace": {
        "addressPrefixes": [
          "[variables('ExamRefRGPrefix')]"
        ]
      },
      "subnets": [
        {
          "name": "[variables('ExamRefRGSubnet1Name')]",
          "properties": {
            "addressPrefix": "[variables('ExamRefRGSubnet1Prefix')]"
          }
        },
        {
          "name": "[variables('ExamRefRGSubnet2Name')]",
          "properties": {
            "addressPrefix": "[variables('ExamRefRGSubnet2Prefix')]"
          }
        }
      ]
    }
  }
```

Defining a network interface

Every virtual machine has one or more network interfaces. To create one with a template, add a variable to the variables section to store the network interface resource name as the following snippet demonstrates:

```
"VMNicName": "VMNic"
```

The following code snippet defines a network interface named WindowsVMNic. This resource has a dependency on the ExamRefVNET virtual network. This dependency will ensure that the virtual network is created prior to the network interface creation when the template is deployed and is a critical feature of orchestration of resources in the correct order. The network interface is associated to the subnet by referencing the ExamRefRG-Subnet1Ref variable.

```
{
    "name": "[variables('VMNicName')]",
    "type": "Microsoft.Network/networkInterfaces",
    "location": "[resourceGroup().location]",
    "apiVersion": "2017-06-01",
    "dependsOn": [
      "[resourceId('Microsoft.Network/virtualNetworks', 'ExamRefVNET')]"
    ],
    "properties": {
      "ipConfigurations": [
        {
          "name": "ipconfig1",
          "properties": {
            "privateIPAllocationMethod": "Dynamic",
            "subnet": {
              "id": "[variables('ExamRefRGSubnet1Ref')]"
            }
```

```
        }
      }
    ]
  }
}
```

Adding a Public IP Address

To add a public IP address to the virtual machine you must make several modifications . The
first is to define a parameter that the user will use to specify a unique DNS name for the public
IP. The following code goes in the parameters block of a template:

```
"VMPublicIPDnsName": {
  "type": "string",
  "minLength": 1
}
```

The second modification is to add the public IP resource itself. Before adding the resource,
add a new variable in the variables section store the name of the public IP resource.

```
"VMPublicIPName": "VMPublicIP"
```

The following snippet shows a public IP address resource with the public IP allocation
method set to dynamic (it can also be set to static). The domainNameLabel property of the
IP address dnsSettings element is populated by the parameter. This makes it easy to specify a
unique value for the address at deployment time.

```
{
  "name": "[variables('VMPublicIPName')]",
  "type": "Microsoft.Network/publicIPAddresses",
  "location": "[resourceGroup().location]",
  "apiVersion": "2017-06-01",
  "dependsOn": [ ],
  "properties": {
    "publicIPAllocationMethod": "Dynamic",
    "dnsSettings": {
      "domainNameLabel": "[parameters('VMPublicIPDnsName')]"
    }
  }
}
```

The next modification is to update the network interface resource that the public IP address is associated with. The network interface must now have a dependency on the public IP

address to ensure it is created before the network interface. The following example shows the addition to the dependsOn array as the following example demonstrates:

```
"dependsOn": [
  "[resourceId('Microsoft.Network/virtualNetworks', 'ExamRefVNET')]",
  "[resourceId('Microsoft.Network/publicIPAddresses', variables('VMPublicIPName'))]"
],
```

The ipConfigurations -> properties element must also be modified to reference the publicI-PAddress resource. The bolded code highlights the addition.

```
"ipConfigurations": [
  {
    "name": "ipconfig1",
    "properties": {
      "privateIPAllocationMethod": "Dynamic",
      "subnet": {
        "id": "[variables('ExamRefRGSubnet1Name')]"
      },
      "publicIPAddress": {
        "id": "[resourceId('Microsoft.Network/publicIPAddresses',
variables('VMPublicIPName'))]"
      },
    }
  }
]
```

Defining a virtual machine resource

Before creating the virtual machine resource, you will add several parameters and variables to define. Each virtual machine requires administrative credentials. To enable a user to specify the credentials at deployment time, add two additional parameters for the administrator account and the password.

```
"VMAdminUserName": {
  "type": "string",
  "minLength": 1
},
"VMAdminPassword": {
  "type": "string",
  "minLength": 1
}
```

Several variables are needed to define the configuration of the virtual machine resource. The following variables define the VM name, operating system image, and the VM size. These should be inserted into the variables section of the template.

```
"VMName": "MyVM",
"VMImagePublisher": "MicrosoftWindowsServer",
"VMImageOffer": "WindowsServer",
"VMOSVersion": "WS2019-Datacenter",
"VMOSDiskName": "VM2OSDisk",
"VMSize": "Standard_D2_v2",
"VM2ImagePublisher": "MicrosoftWindowsServer",
```

```
    "VM2ImageOffer": "WindowsServer",
    "VM2OSDiskName": "VM2OSDisk",
    "VMSize": "Standard_D2_v2"
```

The VM has a dependency on the network interface. It doesn't have to have a dependency on the virtual network, because the network interface itself does. This VM is using managed disks so there are no references to storage accounts for the VHD file. The following code snippet shows a sample virtual machine resource.

```
{
  "name": "[parameters('VMName')]",
  "type": "Microsoft.Compute/virtualMachines",
  "location": "[resourceGroup().location]",
  "apiVersion": "2017-03-30",
  "dependsOn": [
    "[resourceId('Microsoft.Network/networkInterfaces', variables('VMNicName'))]"
  ],
  "properties": {
    "hardwareProfile": {
      "vmSize": "[variables('vmSize')]"
    },
    "osProfile": {
      "computerName": "[variables('VMName')]",
      "adminUsername": "[parameters('VMAdminUsername')]",
      "adminPassword": "[parameters('VMAdminPassword')]"
    },
    "storageProfile": {
      "imageReference": {
        "publisher": "[variables('VMImagePublisher')]",
        "offer": "[variables('VMImageOffer')]",
        "sku": "[variables('VMOSVersion')]",
        "version": "latest"
      },
      "osDisk": {
        "createOption": "FromImage"
      }
    },
    "networkProfile": {
      "networkInterfaces": [
        {
          "id": "[resourceId('Microsoft.Network/networkInterfaces',
variables('VMNicName'))]"
        }
      ]
    }
  }
}
```

There are several properties of a virtual machine resource that are critical to its configuration.

- **hardwareProfile**   This element is where you set the size of the virtual machine. Set the vmSize property to the desired size such as Standard_D2_v2.

- **osProfile**   This element at a basic level is where you set the computerName and adminUsername properties. The adminPassword property is required if you do not specify an SSH key. This element also supports three sub elements: windowsConfiguration, linuxConfiguration and secrets.

- **osProfile, windowsConfiguration**   While the example doesn't use this configuration, this element provides the ability to set advanced properties on Windows VMs. Examples include:

  - **provisionVMAgent**   Enabled by default, but you can disable.

  - **customData**   Specify base-64 encoded data to be added to the VM at creation time. This data can be found in C:\AzureData\CustomData.bin.

  - **timeZone**   Specify the time zone for the virtual machine.

  - **additionalUnattendContent**   Pass unattended install configuration for additional configuration options.

  - **winRM**   Configure Windows PowerShell remoting.

- **osProfile, linuxConfiguration**

  - **disablePasswordAuthentication**   If set to true you must specify an SSH key.

  - **Ssh**, **publicKeys**   Specify the public key to use for authentication with the VM.

- **osProfile, secrets**   This element provides the ability to automatically deploy secrets from an Azure Key Vault.

- **storageProfile**   This element is where OS image is specified, and the OS and data disk configuration are set.

- **networkProfile**   This element is where the network interfaces for the virtual machine are specified.

> *MORE INFO*   **RESOURCE MANAGER TEMPLATE SCHEMA**
>
> Reading through the Azure resource manager template schema is a great way to learn the capabilities of templates. The latest virtual machine schema is published here: *https://docs.microsoft.com/azure/templates/microsoft.compute/2018-10-01/virtualmachines*.

The entire template is available here for reference:

```
{
  "$schema": "https://schema.management.azure.com/schemas/2015-01-01/deploymentTemplate.
json#",
  "contentVersion": "1.0.0.0",
  "parameters": {
    "VMPublicIPDnsName": {
      "type": "string",
      "minLength": 1
    },
    "VMAdminUserName": {
      "type": "string",
      "minLength": 1
    },
```

```
    "VMAdminPassword": {
      "type": "string",
      "minLength": 1
    }
  },
  "variables": {
    "ExamRefRGPrefix": "10.0.0.0/16",
    "ExamRefRGSubnet1Name": "FrontEndSubnet",
    "ExamRefRGSubnet1Prefix": "10.0.0.0/24",
    "ExamRefRGSubnet2Name": "BackEndSubnet",
    "ExamRefRGSubnet2Prefix": "10.0.1.0/24",
    "ExamRefRGSubnet1Ref": "[concat(variables('vnetId'), '/subnets/',
variables('ExamRefRGSubnet1Name'))]",
    "VNetId": "[resourceId('Microsoft.Network/virtualNetworks',
variables('VirtualNetworkName'))]",
    "VirtualNetworkName": "ExamRefVNET",
    "VMPublicIPName": "VMPublicIP",
    "VMNicName": "VMNic",
    "VMName": "MyVM",
    "VMImagePublisher": "MicrosoftWindowsServer",
    "VMImageOffer": "WindowsServer",
    "VMOSVersion": "2019-Datacenter",
    "VMOSDiskName": "VM2OSDisk",
    "VMSize": "Standard_D2_v2"
  },
  "resources": [
    {
      "name": "[variables('VirtualNetworkName')]",
      "type": "Microsoft.Network/virtualNetworks",
      "location": "[resourceGroup().location]",
      "apiVersion": "2017-06-01",
      "dependsOn": [],
      "properties": {
        "addressSpace": {
          "addressPrefixes": [
            "[variables('ExamRefRGPrefix')]"
          ]
        },
        "subnets": [
          {
            "name": "[variables('ExamRefRGSubnet1Name')]",
            "properties": {
              "addressPrefix": "[variables('ExamRefRGSubnet1Prefix')]"
            }
          },
          {
            "name": "[variables('ExamRefRGSubnet2Name')]",
            "properties": {
              "addressPrefix": "[variables('ExamRefRGSubnet2Prefix')]"
            }
          }
        ]
      }
    },
    {
      "name": "[variables('VMNicName')]",
```

```
      "type": "Microsoft.Network/networkInterfaces",
      "location": "[resourceGroup().location]",
      "apiVersion": "2017-06-01",
      "dependsOn": [
        "[resourceId('Microsoft.Network/virtualNetworks', 'ExamRefVNET')]",
        "[resourceId('Microsoft.Network/publicIPAddresses',
variables('VMPublicIPName'))]"
      ],
      "properties": {
        "ipConfigurations": [
          {
            "name": "ipconfig1",
            "properties": {
              "privateIPAllocationMethod": "Dynamic",
              "subnet": {
                "id": "[variables('ExamRefRGSubnet1Ref')]"
              },
              "publicIPAddress": {
                "id": "[resourceId('Microsoft.Network/publicIPAddresses',
variables('VMPublicIPName'))]"
              }
            }
          }
        ]
      }
    },
    {
      "name": "[variables('VMPublicIPName')]",
      "type": "Microsoft.Network/publicIPAddresses",
      "location": "[resourceGroup().location]",
      "apiVersion": "2017-06-01",
      "dependsOn": [],
      "properties": {
        "publicIPAllocationMethod": "Dynamic",
        "dnsSettings": {
          "domainNameLabel": "[parameters('VMPublicIPDnsName')]"
        }
      }
    },
    {
      "name": "[variables('VMName')]",
      "type": "Microsoft.Compute/virtualMachines",
      "location": "[resourceGroup().location]",
      "apiVersion": "2017-03-30",
      "dependsOn": [
        "[resourceId('Microsoft.Network/networkInterfaces', variables('VMNicName'))]"
      ],
      "properties": {
        "hardwareProfile": {
          "vmSize": "[variables('vmSize')]"
        },
        "osProfile": {
          "computerName": "[variables('VMName')]",
          "adminUsername": "[parameters('VMAdminUsername')]",
          "adminPassword": "[parameters('VMAdminPassword')]"
        },
```

```
    "storageProfile": {
      "imageReference": {
        "publisher": "[variables('VMImagePublisher')]",
        "offer": "[variables('VMImageOffer')]",
        "sku": "[variables('VMOSVersion')]",
        "version": "latest"
      },
      "osDisk": {
        "createOption": "FromImage"
      }
    },
    "networkProfile": {
      "networkInterfaces": [
        {
          "id": "[resourceId('Microsoft.Network/networkInterfaces',
 variables('VMNicName'))]"
        }
      ]
    }
  }
 }
 }
 ],
 "outputs": {}
}
```

Configure VHD template

In the storageProfile section of a virtual machine resource you can specify the imageReference element that references an image from the Azure Marketplace.

```
"imageReference": {
    "publisher": "[variables('VMImagePublisher')]",
    "offer": "[variables('VMImageOffer')]",
    "sku": "[parameters('VMOSVersion')]",
    "version": "latest"
}
```

You also can specify a generalized VHD that you have previously created. To specify a user image, you must specify the osType property (Windows or Linux), and the URL to the VHD itself, and the URL to where the disk will be created in Azure storage (osDiskVhdName). The following alternative code snippet demonstrates this (this sample does not build on the previous example):

```
"storageProfile": {
    "osDisk": {
        "name": "[concat(variables('vmName'),'-osDisk')]",
        "osType": "[parameters('osType')]",
        "caching": "ReadWrite",
        "image": {
            "uri": "[parameters('vhdUrl')]"
        },
        "vhd": {
            "uri": "[variables('osDiskVhdName')]"
        },
```

```
        "createOption": "FromImage"
    }
}
```

For context, the following vhdUrl parameter, and osDiskVhdName variable is shown:

```
"vhdUrl": {
    "type": "string",
      "metadata": {
          "description": "VHD Url..."
      }
  }
```

```
"osDiskVhdName": "[concat('http://',parameters('userStorageAccountName'),
'.blob.core.windows.net/',parameters('userStorageContainerName'),'/',
parameters('vmName'),'osDisk.vhd')]"
```

See the following for a complete template example:
*https://docs.microsoft.com/mt-mt/azure/marketplace/cloud-partner-portal/virtual-machine/
cpp-deploy-json-template.*

Deploy from template

You can deploy templates using the portal, the command line tools, or directly using the REST API. Let's start with deploying a template that creates a virtual machine using the portal. To deploy a template from the portal, click the Create Resource button and search for Template Deployment, as shown in Figure 3-42, and select the Template Deployment name from the search results, and then click **Create**.

FIGURE 3-42 The Template Deployment option

From there, you have the option to build your own template using the portal's editor (you can paste your own template in or upload from a file using this option too) or choose from one of the most common templates. Last of all, you can search the existing samples in the quick start samples repository and choose one of them as a starting point. Figure 3-43 shows the various options after clicking the template deployment search result.

FIGURE 3-43 Options for configuring a template deployment

Clicking the Build your own template in the editor option allows you to paste in template code directly. This allows you to author and then deploy them using the portal for simple testing. In Figure 3-44 you can see the Edit template view and the template explained earlier in the chapter.

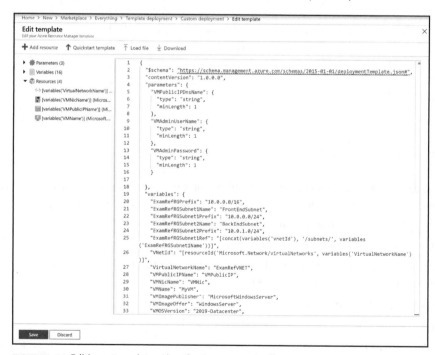

FIGURE 3-44 Editing a template using the Azure portal editor

Clicking save from the previous screen takes you to the page shown in Figure 3-45 where you can specify the resource group, and any parameters needed to deploy the template.

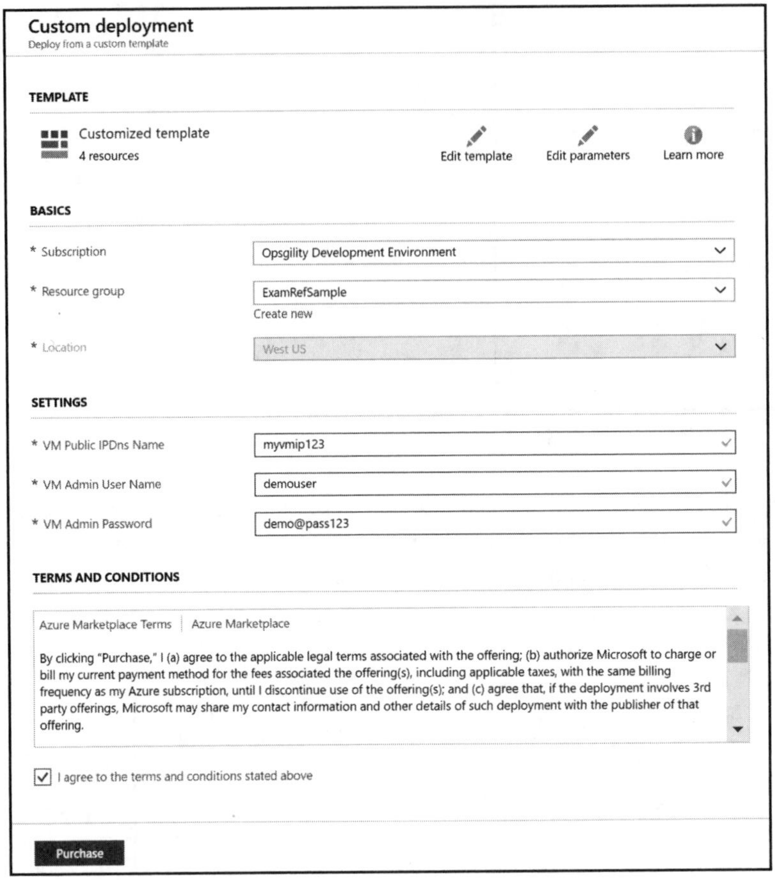

Custom deployment
Deploy from a custom template

TEMPLATE

Customized template
4 resources
Edit template   Edit parameters   Learn more

BASICS

* Subscription — Opsgility Development Environment

* Resource group — ExamRefSample
Create new

* Location — West US

SETTINGS

* VM Public IPDns Name — myvmip123

* VM Admin User Name — demouser

* VM Admin Password — demo@pass123

TERMS AND CONDITIONS

Azure Marketplace Terms | Azure Marketplace

By clicking "Purchase," I (a) agree to the applicable legal terms associated with the offering; (b) authorize Microsoft to charge or bill my current payment method for the fees associated the offering(s), including applicable taxes, with the same billing frequency as my Azure subscription, until I discontinue use of the offering(s); and (c) agree that, if the deployment involves 3rd party offerings, Microsoft may share my contact information and other details of such deployment with the publisher of that offering.

[✓] I agree to the terms and conditions stated above

Purchase

FIGURE 3-45 The template editor view

The edit parameters button allows you to edit a JSON view of the parameters for the template, as shown in Figure 3-46. This file can also be downloaded and is used to provide different behaviors for the template at deployment time without modifying the entire template.

Common examples of using a parameters file:

■ Defining different instance sizes or SKUs for resources based on the intended usage (small instances for test environments for example)

■ Defining different number of instances

■ Different regions

■ Different credentials

Edit parameters

⬆ Load file   ⬇ Download

```
1    {
2      "$schema": "https://schema.management.azure.com/schemas/2015-01-01/deploymentParameters.json#",
3      "contentVersion": "1.0.0.0",
4      "parameters": {
5        "VMPublicIPDnsName": {
6          "value": "myvmip123"
7        },
8        "VMAdminUserName": {
9          "value": "demouser"
10       },
11       "VMAdminPassword": {
12         "value": "demo@pass123"
13       }
14     }
15   }
```

FIGURE 3-46 Editing template parameters using the Azure portal

The last step to creating a template using the portal is to click the Purchase button after reviewing and agreeing to the terms and conditions on the screen.

The Azure command line tools can also deploy templates. The template files can be located locally on your file system or accessed via HTTP/HTTPs. Common deployment models have the templates deployed into a source code repository or an Azure storage account to make it easy for others to deploy the template.

This example uses the Azure PowerShell cmdlets to create a new resource group, specify the location, and then deploy a template by specifying the URL from the Azure QuickStart GitHub repository.

```
# Create a Resource Group
$rgName    = "ExamRefRG"
$location = "WestUs"
New-AzResourceGroup -Name $rgName -Location $location
# Deploy a Template from GitHub
$deploymentName = "simpleVMDeployment"

$templateUri = "https://raw.githubusercontent.com/Azure/azure-quickstart-
templates/master/101-vm-simple-windows/azuredeploy.json"
New-AzResourceGroupDeployment -Name $deploymentName `
            -ResourceGroupName $rgName `
            -TemplateUri $templateUri
```

If the template requires parameters without default values, the cmdlet will prompt you to input their values.

EXAM TIP

The parameters to a template can be passed to the New-AzResourceGroupDeployment cmdlet using the TemplateParameterObject parameter for values that are defined directly in the script as .json. The TemplateParameterFile parameter can be used for values stored in a local .json file. The TemplateParameterUri parameter for values that are stored in a .json file at an HTTP endpoint.

The following example uses the Azure CLI tools to accomplish the same task.

```
#!/bin/bash
# Create the resource group
rgName="Contoso"
location="WestUS"
az group create --name $rgName --location $location
# Deploy the specified template to the resource group
deploymentName="simpleVMDeployment"
templateUri="https://raw.githubusercontent.com/Azure/azure-quickstart-
templates/master/101-vm-simple-linux/azuredeploy.json"
az group deployment create --name $deploymentName  --resource-group $rgName
--template-uri $templateUri
```

EXAM TIP

The parameters to a template can be passed to the az group deployment create command
using the parameters section for values that are defined directly in the script as .json. The
template-file parameter can be used for values stored in a local .json file. The template-uri
parameter can be used for values that are stored in a .json file at an HTTP endpoint.

Modify Azure Resource Manager (ARM) template

Often you will need to modify a template that you have previously used to change the configuration. As previously mentioned, one of the key concepts of using templates to describe your
infrastructure (commonly referred to as infrastructure as code) is so you can modify it and deploy in a versioned manner. To accommodate this behavior Azure Resource Manager supports
two different deployment modes: Complete and Incremental.

In Complete mode, Azure Resource Manager deletes resources that exist in the resource
group that are not in the template. This is helpful if you need to remove a resource from Azure
and you want to ensure your template matches the deployment. You can remove the resource
from the template, deploy using complete mode, and it would be removed.

In Incremental mode, Azure Resource Manager leaves unchanged resources that exist in the
resource group but aren't in the template. It will update the resources in the resource group if
the settings in the template differ from what is deployed.

Incremental is the default mode for the portal and when deploying through the command
line tools or Visual Studio. To use Complete mode, you must use the REST API or the command
line tools with the mode/--mode parameter set to Complete.

The following example deploys a template in Complete mode using PowerShell.

```
New-AzResourceGroupDeployment `
  -Mode Complete `
  -Name simpleVMDeployment `
  -ResourceGroupName ExamRefRG
```

This example deploys a template in Complete mode using the Azure CLI.

```
az group deployment create \
```

```
--name simpleVMDeployment \
--mode Complete \
--resource-group ExamRefRG
```

Save a deployment as an ARM Template

An existing deployment can be exported as a template that you can use to regenerate the environment or to just gain a better understanding of how the deployment is configured. There are two ways of exporting a template from a deployment within a resource group.

The first way is to export the actual template used for the deployment. This method exports the template exactly as it was used, including the values for parameters and variables during the original execution. This approach does not capture any changes made to the deployment after it was deployed. To export this template, navigate to the resource group in the Azure portal and click Deployments, select the deployment to export, and click View Template on the top navigation. Figure 3-47 depicts a deployment selected inside of a Resource Group.

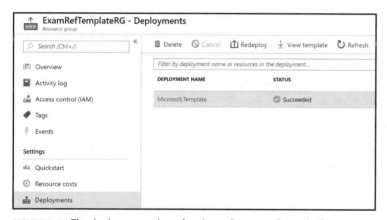

FIGURE 3-47 The deployments view of an Azure Resource Group in the Azure portal

Clicking the View Template link opens in the Template deployment view as shown in Figure 3-48. From here, you can click Download to download the template locally, Deploy to redeploy the template using different parameters, or you can click Add to library to save to your template gallery for later deployment.

FIGURE 3-48 The deployments view of an Azure resource group in the Azure portal

The second approach generates a template that represents the current state of the resource group. The state may have been updated by multiple templates, changes from the portal or changes via the REST API or command line. It may include many hard-coded values and probably not as many parameters as you would expect in a template that was designed for re-usability. This template is useful for redeploying to the same resource group due to the hard-coded values. Using it for other resource groups may require a significant amount of editing. You can access this template by navigating to the resource group and clicking the Automation Script link on the left navigation.

You can also export templates using the command line. The following examples show how to export the actual template using Azure PowerShell and then the Azure CLI.

The following PowerShell code will save the template to the current folder named MyDeployment.json.

```
Save-AzResourceGroupDeploymentTemplate -ResourceGroupName ExamRefRG -DeploymentName
simpleVMDeployment
```

The following CLI code will accomplish the same task, except it will output the template to the console.

```
az group deployment export --name simpleVMDeployment --resource-group ExamRefRG
```

The following code will export all resources in the resource group as a template using the Azure PowerShell cmdlets. In this example ExamRefRG is the name of the resource group.

```
Export-AzResourceGroup -ResourceGroupName ExamRefRG
```

The following code will export all resources in the resource group as a template using the Azure CLI. In this example ExamRefRG is the name of the resource group.

```
az group export --name ExamRefRG
```

Configure location of new VMs

Templates and the command line tools simplify reusability of templates with parameter files. A parameter file is simply a set of names and values that you define separately from the template or script. This makes it easy to design your templates with parameters that can be changed depending on the needs at deployment time and even save the parameters' files separately for increased reusability.

A few of the more common use cases include:

- **Location of Azure resources** Defining the region information in a parameters file makes it easy to reuse a template for any region without having to modify the template itself because the template can just reference the region based on the parameter versus hard-coding it.

- **Virtual machine size** Depending on the environment (dev, test, or production) the expected load may differ greatly.

- **Number of resources**   Like virtual machine size, a development environment may only need a small footprint of the deployment to be functional compared to a full-blown production environment.

- **Tags**   Tagging resources based on cost-center for charge back, or environment is highly simplified using templates and parameter files.

The following example demonstrates an example template file that uses VM scale sets.. In this example, two different parameter files are defined. The dev-env.json template defines values for a development environment with the location specified as WestUS, the vmSize variable set to Standard_DS1, and the instanceCount set to 1.

dev-env.json

```
{
  "$schema": "https://schema.management.azure.com/schemas/2015-01-01/
deploymentParameters.json#",
  "contentVersion": "1.0.0.0",
  "parameters": {
    "location": {
        "value": "WestUS "
    },
    "vmSize": {
        "value": "Standard_DS1"
    },
    "instanceCount": {
        "value": "1"
    }
  }
}
```

The prod-env.json template defines values for a production environment with the location specified as EastUS, the vmSize variable set to Standard_DS3, and the instanceCount set to 4.

prod-env.json

```
{
  "$schema": "https://schema.management.azure.com/schemas/2015-01-01/
deploymentParameters.json#",
  "contentVersion": "1.0.0.0",
  "parameters": {
    "location": {
        "value": "EastUS"
    },
    "vmSize": {
        "value": "Standard_DS3"
    },
    "instanceCount": {
        "value": "4"
    }
  }
}
```

The following code snippet shows how to pass a template file during deployment using PowerShell and reference a parameters file:

```
New-AzResourceGroupDeployment -Name MyDeployment -ResourceGroupName ExamRefRG `
  -TemplateFile c:\MyTemplates\AppTemplate.json `
  -TemplateParameterFile c:\MyTemplates\dev-env.json
```

This example shows how to deploy a template using a parameters file using the Azure CLI.

```
az group deployment create \
  --name MyDeployment \
  --resource-group ExamRefRG \
  --template-file AppTemplate.json \
  --parameters @dev-env.json
```

EXAM TIP

Virtual machine scale sets make it easy to create multiple instances of a virtual machine. To create multiple resources of other resource types such as storage accounts, web apps, and so on, you can use the copy element in conjunction with the copyIndex() **function. Learn more about this feature here:** *https://docs.microsoft.com/azure/azure-resource-manager/resource-group-create-multiple.*

Skill 3.3: Manage Azure VM

So far, this chapter has covered the creation and configuration of virtual machines, including techniques for automatically deploying VMs using templates and the command line tools. This section will focus on post creation tasks such as adding additional storage, adding additional network interfaces, redeploying VMs, changing VM sizes, and moving virtual machines to a different resource group and subscription. The chapter will close on automatic configuration techniques for updating the configuration of the virtual machine itself.

This section covers how to:

- Add data disks
- Add network interfaces
- Manage VM sizes
- Move VMs from one resource group to another
- Redeploy VMs
- Automate configuration management by using PowerShell Desired State Configuration (DSC) and VM Agent by using custom script extensions

Add data disks

Adding a data disk to an existing Azure virtual machine using the Azure portal is almost identical to the creation process. From within the virtual machine configuration blade, click **Disks**, and then click **Add Data Disk**. This action will open the dialog displayed in Figure 3-49. From there, you can choose one of the existing disks that are available to attach, or you can click **Create** to create a new disk that will walk through the create disk user experience.

FIGURE 3-49 The deployments view of an Azure resource group in the Azure portal

If your virtual machine was created with managed disks enabled, you will see the blade displayed in Figure 3-50 for Create Managed Disk. From here you can specify the Name of the disk, the Resource Group, the storage Account Type, and the Source Type.

You can use the following sources to create a new managed disk:

- **Snapshot** If selected, you can browse for snapshots in the current subscription and location.
- **Storage blob** If selected, you can browse storage accounts in all subscriptions you have access to, so you can select the VHD.
- **None (empty disk)** If selected, a new empty VHD is created.

FIGURE 3-50 The Create Managed Disk blade in the Azure portal

If the virtual machine was created with Use Unmanaged Disks selected, you will see the blade to attach an unmanaged disk as shown in Figure 3-51. This blade allows you to create a new empty disk or attach an existing VHD from the same storage account. You can also specify the container and blob name for the new VHD.

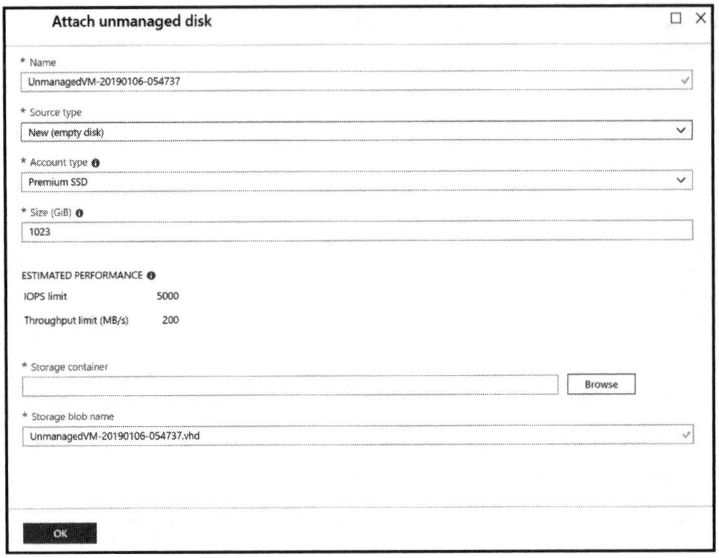

FIGURE 3-51 The Attach Unmanaged Disk blade in the Azure portal

The following example demonstrates how to attach a new managed disk using PowerShell.

```
$dataDiskName = "MyDataDisk"
$location = "WestUS"

# Create the disk configuration
$diskConfig = New-AzDiskConfig -SkuName Premium_LRS -Location $location
-CreateOption Empty -DiskSizeGB 128

# Create the disk
$dataDisk1 = New-AzDisk -DiskName $dataDiskName -Disk $diskConfig
-ResourceGroupName ExamRefRG

# Retrieve the currentVM

$vm = Get-AzVM -Name ExamRefVM -ResourceGroupName ExamRefRG

# Attach the disk
$vm = Add-AzVMDataDisk -VM $vm -Name $dataDiskName -CreateOption Attach
-ManagedDiskId $dataDisk1.Id -Lun 1
```

```
# Update the VM
Update-AzVM -VM $vm -ResourceGroupName ExamRefRG
```

EXAM TIP

If the virtual machine is deployed into an availability zone, use the Zone parameter with the New-AzDiskConfig cmdlet to specify which availability zone to create the disk in if you are creating the disk using PowerShell.

The Azure CLI tools can also accomplish the same task as the following example demonstrates:

```
az vm disk attach \
    -g ExamRefRG \
    --vm-name ExamRefVM \
    --name myDataDisk \
    --new \
    --size-gb 128 \
    --sku Premium_LRS
```

EXAM TIP

If the virtual machine is deployed into an availability zone, the disk is automatically placed into the same zone as the virtual machine using Azure CLI.

Add network interfaces

A network interface enables an Azure virtual machine to communicate with the Internet, Azure, and on-premises resources. Common use cases for having multiple network interfaces are:

- **Network and security function**   Multiple network interfaces enable virtual network appliances such as load balancers, firewalls, and proxy servers.

- **Network isolation**   Common best practices include isolating public facing services from internal networks.

- **Bandwidth isolation**   In certain cases, such as heartbeat signals, it is important to have isolated traffic to guarantee the minimal amount of bandwidth is available to the workload.

To add a new network interface to an Azure virtual machine, click the **Networking** link on the left navigation of the virtual machine configuration blade and then click the **Attach Network Interface** link at the top. The next screen allows you to attach an existing network interface or click Create network interface to create a new one. Figure 3-52 shows the blade for creating a new network interface.

FIGURE 3-52 Creating a new network interface in the Azure portal

After the network interface is created, you must first deallocate the virtual machine before you can attach it. You can deallocate the VM by clicking Stop in the Azure portal or using the command line tools.

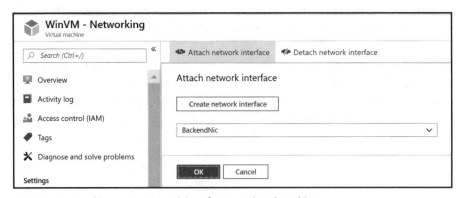

FIGURE 3-53 Attaching a new network interface to a virtual machine

The following example demonstrates how to create and attach a new network interface to an existing virtual machine using PowerShell.

```
$vnetName = "ExamRefVNET" # Ensure your VNET Name matches
$subnetName = "Subnet-1" # Ensure your subnet matches
$rgName = "ExamRefRG"
$vmName = "ExamRefVM"
$nicName="newnic"

# Deallocate the VM first
Stop-AzVm -Name $vmName -ResourceGroupName $rgName

# Retrieve the VM configuration
$vm = Get-AzVm -Name ExamRefVM -ResourceGroupName $rgName

# Get info for the back-end subnet
$myVnet = Get-AzVirtualNetwork -ResourceGroupName $rgName  -Name $vnetName
$backEnd = $myVnet.Subnets|?{$_.Name -eq $subnetName}

# Create a virtual NIC
$newNic = New-AzNetworkInterface -ResourceGroupName $rgName `
    -Name $nicName `
    -Location $location `
    -SubnetId $newNic.Id

# Get the ID of the new virtual NIC and add to VM
$nicId = (Get-AzNetworkInterface -ResourceGroupName $rgName -Name $nicName).Id
Add-AzVMNetworkInterface -VM $vm -Id $nicId -Primary | Update-AzVm
-ResourceGroupName $rgName
```

The following example attaches a network interface using the Azure CLI.

```
vnetName="ExamRefVNET" # Ensure your VNET Name matches
subnetName="Subnet-1" # Ensure your subnet matches
rgName="ExamRefRG"
vmName="ExamRefVM"
nicName="newnic"

az network nic create \
    --resource-group $rgName \
    --name $nicName \
    --vnet-name $ExamRefVNET \
    --subnet $subnetName
az vm nic add -g $rgName --vm-name $vmName --nics $nicName --primary-nic
```

By default, the first network interface attached is defined as the primary network interface. All others are secondary. You can control which network interface you send outbound traffic to; by default, it will be the primary network interface.

MORE INFO   **MULTIPLE NETWORK INTERFACES**

Beyond understanding the basics of adding network interfaces it is important to understand the nuances and constraints in this area. The Azure documentation does a great job of
consolidating and summarizing this information and you can read more about it here:
https://docs.microsoft.com/azure/virtual-network/virtual-network-network-interface-vm.

Manage VM sizes

Azure provides purpose built virtual machine sizes. This means that each family is designed for
specific purposes to make it easier for you to choose the right VM size for the right workload.

The different types are:

- **General purpose**   Offers a balanced CPU-to-memory ratio. Ideal for testing and development, small to medium databases, and low to medium traffic web servers.

- **Compute optimized**   Offers high CPU-to-memory ratio and are good for medium
  traffic web servers, network appliances, batch processes, and application servers.

- **Memory optimized**   Offers high memory-to-CPU ratio that are great for relational
  database servers, medium to large caches, and in-memory analytics.

- **Storage optimized**   Offers high disk throughput and IO, and are ideal for Big Data,
  SQL, NoSQL databases, data warehousing, and large transactional databases. Examples
  include Cassandra, MongoDB, Cloudera, and Redis.

- **GPU optimized**   Specialized virtual machines available with single or multiple NVIDIA
  GPUs. These sizes are designed for compute-intensive, graphics-intensive, and visualization workloads. This article provides information about the number and type of
  GPUs, vCPUs, data disks, and NICs. Storage throughput and network bandwidth are also
  included for each size in this grouping.

- **High performance compute**   Specialized for handling batch processing, molecular
  modeling and fluid dynamics. These 8 and 16 vCPU VMs are built on the Intel Haswell
  E5-2667 V3 processor technology featuring DDR4 memory and SSD-based temporary
  storage. In addition to the substantial CPU power, the H-series offers diverse options for
  low latency RDMA networking using FDR InfiniBand and several memory configurations
  to support memory intensive computational requirements.

Azure virtual machines make it relatively easy to change the size of a virtual machine even
after it has been deployed. There are a few things to consider with this approach.

The first consideration is to ensure that the region your VM is deployed to supports the instance size that you want to change the VM to. In most cases this is not an issue, but if you have
a use case where the desired size isn't in the region the existing VM is deployed to, your only
options are to either wait for the size to be supported in the region, or to move the existing VM
to a region that already supports it.

The second consideration is if the new size is supported in the current hardware cluster your
VM is deployed to. This can be determined by clicking the Size link in the virtual machine con-

figuration blade in the Azure portal of a running virtual machine, as Figure 3-54 demonstrates. If the size is available, you can select it. Changing the size reboots the virtual machine.

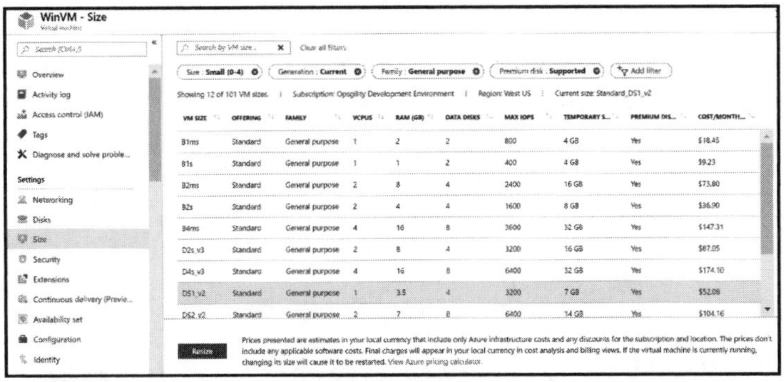

FIGURE 3-54 Changing the size of an Azure virtual machine using the Azure portal

If the size is not available, it means either the size is not available in the region or the current hardware cluster. You can view the available sizes by region at: *https://azure.microsoft.com/regions/services/.* In the event you need to change to a different hardware cluster you must first stop the virtual machine, and if it is part of an availability set you must stop all instances of the availability set at the same time. After all the VMs are stopped, you can then change the size, which moves all the VMs to the new hardware cluster as they are resized and started. The reason all VMs in the availability set must be stopped before performing the resize operation to a size that requires different hardware is that all running VMs in the availability set must use the same physical hardware cluster. Therefore, if a change of physical hardware cluster is required to change the VM size, all VMs must be first stopped and then restarted one-by-one to a different physical hardware cluster.

A third consideration is the form factor of the new size compared to the old size. Consider scaling from a DS3_V2 to a DS2_V2. A DS3_V2 supports up to eight data disks and up to four network interfaces. A DS2_V2 supports up to four data disks and up to two network interfaces. If the VM you are sizing from (DS3_V2) is using more disks or network interfaces then the target size, the resize operation will fail.

Resizing a VM (PowerShell)

Use the Get-AzVMSize cmdlet and pass the name of the region to the location parameter to view all of the available sizes in your region to ensure the new size is available. If you specify the resource group and the VM name, it returns the available sizes in the current hardware cluster.

```
# View available sizes
$location = "WestUS"
Get-AzVMSize -Location $location
```

After you have identified the available size, use the following code to change the VM to the new size.

```
$rgName = "EXAMREGWEBRG"
$vmName = "Web1"
```

```
$size = "Standard_DS2_V2"
$vm = Get-AzVM -ResourceGroupName $rgName -VMName $vmName
$vm.HardwareProfile.VmSize = $size
Update-AzVM -VM $vm -ResourceGroupName $rgName
```

If the virtual machine(s) are part of an availability set, the following code can be used to shut them all down at the same time and restart them using the new size.

```
$rgName = "ExamRefRG"
$vmName = "Web1"
$size = "Standard_DS2_V2"
$avSet = "WebAVSet"
```

Resizing a VM (CLI)

The `az vm list-vm-resize-options` command can be used to see which VM sizes are available in the current hardware cluster.

```
rgName="ExamRefRG"
vmName="Web1"
az vm list-vm-resize-options --resource-group $rgName --name $vmName --output table
```

The `az vm list-sizes` command is used to view all sizes in the region.

```
az vm list-sizes --location westus
```

The `az vm resize` command is used to change the size of an individual VM.

```
az vm resize --resource-group $rgName --name $vmName --size Standard_DS3_v2
```

> **MORE INFO**   **VIRTUAL MACHINE SIZES**
>
> There are a lot of considerations when choosing the correct virtual machine size. For more information on sizes in the context of Windows-based virtual machines see the following: *https://docs.microsoft.com/azure/virtual-machines/windows/sizes*. For the Linux version of the article see the following: *https://docs.microsoft.com/azure/virtual-machines/linux/sizes*.

Move VMs from one resource group to another

Azure provides the ability to move some resources from one subscription to another or from resource group to resource group.

To move a virtual machine using the Azure portal, open the VM blade as shown in Figure 3-55 and click the change link next to the Resource group label or the change button next to the subscription label.

FIGURE 3-55 The virtual machine blade with the change options visible for Resource Group and Subscription

Clicking the change link by the by the resource group name will bring up a new blade as shown in Figure 3-56. This blade shows the resources related to the virtual machine, such as disks, network security groups, network interfaces and so on. From here, you can select the individual resources to move to the destination resource group and the destination resource group.

Since the resource group will change, any existing scripts that target resources in this resource group will no longer work until they have been updated. The portal prompts you to confirm that you are aware of this change before you can continue with the move.

FIGURE 3-56 The move resources blade showing the related resources for a virtual machine

The following example code shows how to use PowerShell to move a resource:

```
# Use Get-AzResource to identify the resource ID value
Get-AzResource -ResourceGroupName ExamRefRG | Format-table -Property ResourceId
# Store the resource ID in a variable
$resourceID = "[your resource id here]"
# Specify the destination resource group and the resource ID to move
Move-AzResource -DestinationResourceGroupName  ExamRefDestRG
-ResourceId $resourceID


# To move to a different subscription, use the -DestinationSubscriptionId parameter
$subscriptionID = "[your subscription id here]"
Move-AzResource -DestinationSubscriptionId $subscriptionID `
    -DestinationResourceGroupName  ExamRefDestRG `
    -ResourceId $resourceID
```

The Azure CLI can accomplish the same task as shown here:

```
# List the resource IDs
az resource list -g ExamRefRG
resourceID="[your resource id here]"
# Move to a different resource group
az resource move --destination-group ExamRefDestRG --ids $resourceID
# Use the --subscription-id parameter to move to a different subscription
subscriptionID="[your resource id here]"
az resource move --destination-group ExamRefDestRG
-destination-subscription-id $suscriptionID --ids $resourceID
```

> **MORE INFO**   **SUPPORTED RESOURCES FOR MOVING**
>
> Not all resources are fully supported moving between resource groups and subscriptions, and there are several caveats regarding virtual machines. See the following for more details: *https://docs.microsoft.com/azure/azure-resource-manager/resource-group-move-resources*.

Redeploy VMs

To help with troubleshooting issues such as RDP or SSH connectivity or application access re-deploying the VM may help. When you redeploy a VM, it moves the VM to a new node within Azure and turns it back on. The Redeploy button is shown in Figure 3-57.

FIGURE 3-57 The redeploy blade in the Azure portal

To redeploy the VM using PowerShell use the Set-AzVM cmdlet as shown here:

```
Set-AzVM -Redeploy -ResourceGroupName ExamRefRG -Name ExamRefVM
```

To redeploy with the Azure CLI tools use the az vm redeploy command.

```
az vm redeploy --resource-group ExamRefRG --name ExamRefVM
```

Automate configuration management

Azure virtual machines have a variety of built-in extensions that can enable configuration management as well as a variety of other operations such as installing software agents and even enabling remote debugging for live troubleshooting purposes. The two most common extensions for configuration management are the Windows PowerShell Desired State Configuration (DSC) extension and the more generic Custom Script Extension. Both extensions can be executed at provisioning time or after the virtual machine has already been started. The Windows PowerShell DSC Extension allows you to define the state of a virtual machine using the PowerShell Desired State Configuration language and apply it as well as perform continuous updates when integrated with the Azure Automation DSC service. The custom script extension can be used to execute an arbitrary command such as a batch file, regular PowerShell script, or a bash script. In addition to these extensions there are also more specific extensions that allow you to configure your virtual machines to use open source configuration management utilities such as Chef or Puppet and many others.

The next step is the Guest config blade, depicted in Figure 3-58. This blade allows the user creating the virtual machine to install a custom script extension such as the custom script extension or one of many others.

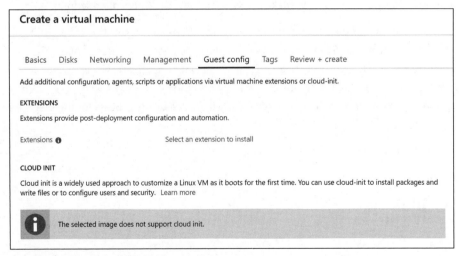

FIGURE 3-58 The Guest config blade in the Azure portal

Figure 3-59 depicts the custom script extension blade that appears when you click the option to select an extension to install.

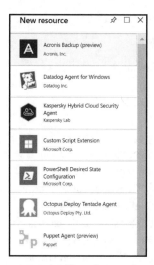

FIGURE 3-59 The select a custom script extension menu

PowerShell Desired State Configuration

PowerShell Desired State Configuration (DSC) allows you to declaratively configure the state of the virtual machine. Using built-in resource providers or custom providers with a DSC script enables you to declaratively configure settings such as roles and features, registry settings, files and directories, firewall rules, and most settings available to Windows. One of the compelling features of DSC is that, instead of writing logic to detect and correct the state of the machine, the providers do that work for you and make the system state as defined in the script.

For example, the following DSC script declares that the Web-Server role should be installed, along with the Web-Asp-Net45 feature. The WindowsFeature code block represents a DSC resource. The resource has a property named Ensure that can be set to Present or Absent. In this example, the WindowsFeature resource verifies whether the Web-Server role is present on the target machine and if it is not, the resource installs it. It repeats the process for the Web-Asp-Net45 feature.

```
Configuration ContosoSimple
{
    Node "localhost"
    {
        #Install the IIS Role
        WindowsFeature IIS
        {
          Ensure = "Present"
          Name = "Web-Server"
        }
        #Install ASP.NET 4.5
```

```
    WindowsFeature AspNet45
    {
      Ensure = "Present"
      Name = "Web-Asp-Net45"
    }
  }
}
```

In addition to the default DSC resources included by default with PowerShell DSC, there is an open source DSC resource kit hosted in GitHub that has many more resources that are maintained and updated by the Windows PowerShell engineering team, and of course you can write your own. To install a custom resource, download it and unzip it into the C:\Program Files\ WindowsPowerShell\Modules folder. To learn about and download the latest DSC resource kit from Microsoft see the following GitHub repo at: *https://github.com/PowerShell/DscResources.*

The example uses the xPSDesiredStateConfiguration module from the DSC resource kit to download a .zip file that contains the website content. This module can be installed using PowerShellGet by executing the following commands from an elevated command prompt:

```
Install-Module -Name xPSDesiredStateConfiguration
```

After the module is installed locally the xPSDesiredStateConfiguration resource is available for use in your script.

```
# ContosoWeb.ps1
configuration Main
{
    # Import the module that defines custom resources
    Import-DscResource -Module xPSDesiredStateConfiguration
    Node "localhost"
    {
        # Install the IIS role
        WindowsFeature IIS
        {
            Ensure       = "Present"
            Name         = "Web-Server"
        }
        # Install the ASP .NET 4.5 role
        WindowsFeature AspNet45
        {
            Ensure       = "Present"
            Name         = "Web-Asp-Net45"
        }
        # Download the website content
        xRemoteFile WebContent
        {
            Uri          = "https://cs7993fe12db3abx4d25xab6.blob.core.windows.net/
public/website.zip"
            DestinationPath = "C:\inetpub\wwwroot"
```

```
        DependsOn        = "[WindowsFeature]IIS"
    }
    Archive ArchiveExample
    {
        Ensure           = "Present"
        Path             = "C:\inetpub\wwwroot\website.zip"
        Destination      = "C:\inetpub\wwwroot"
        DependsOn        = "[xRemoteFile]WebContent"
    }
  }
}
```

Before the DSC script can be applied to a virtual machine, you must use the Publish-Az-VMDscConfiguration cmdlet to package the script into a .zip file. This cmdlet also imports any dependent DSC modules such as xPSDesiredStateConfiguration into the .zip.

```
Publish-AzVMDscConfiguration –ConfigurationPath .\ContosoWeb.ps1
-OutputArchivePath .\ContosoWeb.zip
```

To apply the extension, open the virtual machine blade in the portal and click Extensions. Click Add and then click the PowerShell Desired State Configuration extension as shown in Figure 3-60.

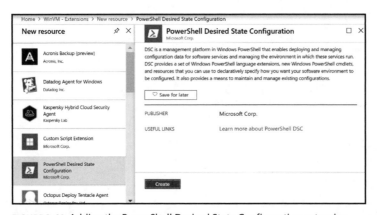

FIGURE 3-60 Adding the PowerShell Desired State Configuration extension

The Configuration Modules or Script field expects the .zip file created by the call to the Publish-AzVMDscConfiguration cmdlet. The Module-Qualified Name of Configuration field expects the name of the script file (with the .ps1 extension) concatenated with the name of the function in the script, which in the example shown in Figure 3-61 is Conto-soWeb.ps1\Main. The PowerShell DSC extension is versioned, in this example we are using version 2.76.

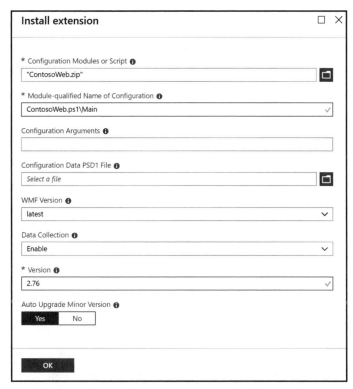

FIGURE 3-61 Configuring the Azure Desired State Configuration extension

One of the powerful features of PowerShell DSC is the ability to parameterize the configuration. This means you can create a single configuration that can exhibit different behaviors based on the parameters passed. The Configuration Data PSD1 file field is where you can specify these parameters in the form of a hashtable. You can learn more about how to separate configuration from environment data at: *https://docs.microsoft.com/powershell/dsc/separatingenvdata.*

The PowerShell DSC extension also allows you to specify whether to use the latest version of the Windows Management Framework (WMF) and to specify the specific version of the DSC extension to use, and whether to automatically upgrade the minor version or not.

> **MORE INFO** **AZURE DESIRED STATE CONFIGURATION EXTENSION VERSION**
>
> See the following to see the current version and change history of the Azure Desired State Configuration extension:
>
> *https://docs.microsoft.com/powershell/dsc/getting-started/azuredscexthistory.*

PowerShell DSC configurations can also be applied programmatically during a PowerShell deployment by using the *Set*-AzVmDscExtension cmdlet. In the example below, the Publish-AzVMDscConfiguration cmdlet is used to publish the packaged script to an existing Azure storage account before applying the configuration using the Set-AzVMDscExtension cmdlet on an existing virtual machine.

```
$rgName = "ExamRefRG"
$location = "WestUS"
$vmName = "ExamRefVM"
$storageName = "dscstorageer1"
$configurationName = "Main"
$archiveBlob = "ContosoWeb.ps1.zip"
$configurationPath = ".\ContosoWeb.ps1"
#Publish the configuration script into Azure storage
Publish-AzVMDscConfiguration -ConfigurationPath $configurationPath `
            -ResourceGroupName $rgName `
            -StorageAccountName $storageName
#Set the VM to run the DSC configuration
Set-AzVmDscExtension -Version 2.76 `
            -ResourceGroupName $rgName `
            -VMName $vmName `
            -ArchiveStorageAccountName $storageName `
            -ArchiveBlobName $archiveBlob `
            -AutoUpdate:$false `
            -ConfigurationName $configurationName
```

The PowerShell DSC extension can also be applied to a virtual machine created through a resource manager template by extending and adding the resource configuration in the virtual machine's resource section of the template. This template takes a parameter to a URL hosting the DSC configuration file (.zip). Typically, these are stored in a storage account or Git repository accessible from the template. For example, the previous example code used Publish-AzVMDscConfiguration to publish to a storage account named dscstorageer1. The resulting URI would be: https://dscstorageer1.blob.core.windows.net/windows-powershell-dsc/ContosoWeb.ps1.zip. The path windows-powershell-dsc was added by the cmdlet.

```
{
    "name": "Microsoft.Powershell.DSC",
    "type": "extensions",
    "location": "[resourceGroup().location]",
    "apiVersion": "2016-03-30",
    "dependsOn": [
      "[resourceId('Microsoft.Compute/virtualMachines', parameters('WebVMName'))]"
    ],
    "tags": {
      "displayName": "WebDSC"
    },
    "properties": {
      "publisher": "Microsoft.Powershell",
      "type": "DSC",
      "typeHandlerVersion": "2.76",
      "autoUpgradeMinorVersion": false,
```

```
      "settings": {
        "configuration": {
          "url": "[parameters('DSCUri'))]",
          "script": "ContosoWeb.ps1",
          "function": "Main"
        },
        "configurationArguments": {
          "nodeName": "[parameters('WebVMName')]"
        }
      },
      "protectedSettings": {
        "configurationUrlSasToken": "[parameters('SasToken')]"
      }
    }
  }
}
```

The previous examples apply the PowerShell DSC configuration only when the extension is executed. If the configuration of the virtual machine changes after the extension is applied, the configuration can drift from the state defined in the DSC configuration. The Azure Automation DSC service allows you to manage all your DSC configurations, resources, and target nodes from the Azure portal or from PowerShell. It also provides a built-in pull server, so your virtual machines will automatically check on a scheduled basis for new configuration changes, or to compare the current configuration against the desired state and update accordingly.

> **MORE INFO**   **AZURE AUTOMATION STATE CONFIGURATION**
>
> For more information on how to automatically apply PowerShell DSC configurations to your virtual machines see:
> *https://docs.microsoft.com/azure/automation/automation-dsc-overview.*

Using the custom script extension

The Azure custom script extension is supported on Windows and Linux-based virtual machines and is ideal for bootstrapping a virtual machine to an initial configuration. To use the Azure custom script extension your script must be accessible via a URI such as an Azure storage account, and either accessed anonymously or passed with a shared access signature (SAS URL). The custom script extension takes as parameters the URI and the command to execute including any parameters to pass to the script. You can execute the script at any time the virtual machine is running.

Using the custom script extension (Azure portal)

To add the custom script extension to an existing virtual machine, open the virtual machine in the portal, click the **Extensions** link on the left, and choose the **Custom Script Extension** option. The script file is specified as well as any arguments passed to the script. Figure 2-18 shows how to enable this extension using the Azure portal.

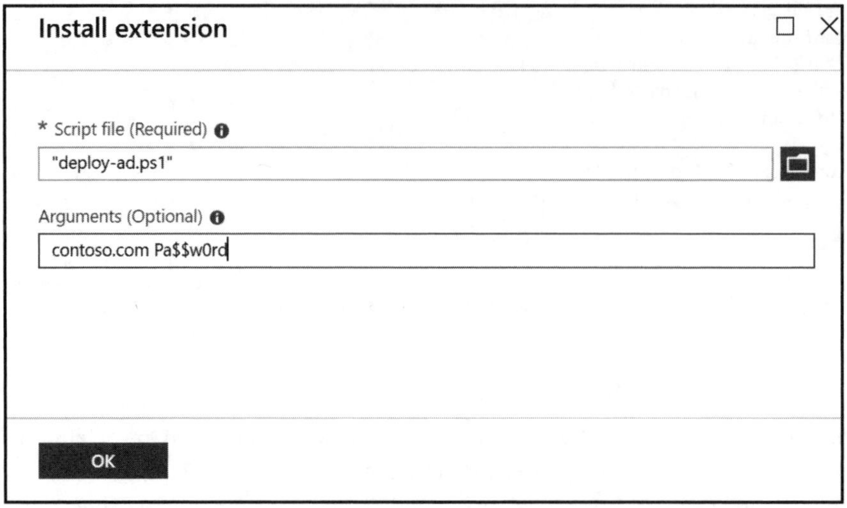

FIGURE 3-62 Specifying the custom script extension configuration

Using the custom script extension (PowerShell)

Both the Azure PowerShell cmdlets and the Azure CLI tools can be used to execute scripts using the custom script extension. Starting with PowerShell, the following script deploys the Active Directory Domain Services role. It accepts two parameters: one is for the domain name and the other is for the administrator password.

```
#deployad.ps1
param(
  $domain,
  $password
)
$smPassword = (ConvertTo-SecureString $password -AsPlainText -Force)
Install-WindowsFeature -Name "AD-Domain-Services" `
              -IncludeManagementTools `
              -IncludeAllSubFeature
Install-ADDSForest -DomainName $domain `
            -DomainMode Win2012 `
            -ForestMode Win2012 `
            -Force `
            -SafeModeAdministratorPassword $smPassword
```

You can use the Set-AzVMCustomScriptExtension cmdlet to run this script on an Azure virtual machine. This scenario can be used for installing roles or any other type of iterative script you want to run on the virtual machine.

```
$rgName     = "ExamRefRG"
$vmName     = "ExamRefVM"
$scriptName = "deploy-ad.ps1"
$domain = "contoso.com"
```

```
$extensionName = "installAD"
$location = "WestUS"
$scriptUri = "https://raw.githubusercontent.com/opsgility/lab-support
-public/master/script-extensions/deploy-ad.ps1" $scriptArgument =
"contoso.com $password"
Set-AzVMCustomScriptExtension -ResourceGroupName $rgName `
                -VMName $vmName `
                -FileUri $scriptUri `
                -Argument "$domain $password" `
                -Run $scriptName `
                -Name $extensionName `
                -Location $location
```

The FileUri parameter of the Set-AzVMCustomScriptExtension cmdlet, accepts the URI to the script, and the Run parameter tells the cmdlet the name of the script to run on the virtual machine. The script can also be specified using the StorageAccountName, StorageAcountKey, ContainerName, and FileName parameters that qualify its location in an Azure storage account.

Using the custom script extension (CLI)

You can also use the custom script extension for Linux-based virtual machines. The following example demonstrates a simple bash script that installs Apache and PHP. The script would need to be uploaded to an accessible HTTP location such as an Azure storage account or a GitHub repository for the custom script extension to access it and apply it to the virtual machine.

```
#!/bin/bash
#install-apache.sh
apt-get update
apt-get -y install apache2 php7.0 libapache2-mod-php7.0
apt-get -y install php-mysql
sudo a2enmod php7.0
apachectl restart
```

The following code example shows how this script can be applied to an Azure Virtual Machine named LinuxVM in the ExamRefRG resource group.

```
rgName="ExamRefRG"
vmName="LinuxVM"
extensionName="InstallApache"
az vm extension set \
  --resource-group $rgName \
  --vm-name $vmName --name customScript \
  --publisher Microsoft.Azure.Extensions \
  --protected-settings ./cseconfig.json
```

The az vm extension set command can take the script to execute as a .json based configuration file as the previous example demonstrates. The contents of this .json file are shown for reference:

```
{
```

```
    "fileUris": [ "https://raw.githubusercontent.com/opsgility/lab-support-public/master/
script-extensions/install-apache.sh" ],
    "commandToExecute": "./install-apache.sh"
}
```

EXAM TIP

There are many other ways of configuring and executing the custom script extension using the Azure CLI tools. The following article has several relevant examples that might be used in an exam, which you can find at: *https://docs.microsoft.com/azure/virtual-machines/linux/ extensions-customscript.*

Like the PowerShell DSC extension, the custom script extension can be added to the resources section of an Azure Resource Manager template. The following example shows how to execute the same script using an ARM template instead of the CLI tools.

```
{
    "name": "apache",
    "type": "extensions",
    "location": "[resourceGroup().location]",
    "apiVersion": "2015-06-15",
    "dependsOn": [
        "[concat('Microsoft.Compute/virtualMachines/', parameters('scriptextensionNa
me'))]"
    ],
    "tags": {
        "displayName": "installApache"
    },
    "properties": {
        "publisher": "Microsoft.Azure.Extensions",
        "type": "CustomScript",
        "typeHandlerVersion": "2.0",
        "autoUpgradeMinorVersion": true,
      "settings": {
        "fileUris": [
          " https://examplestorageaccount.blob.core.windows.net/scripts/apache.sh "
        ],
        "commandToExecute": "sh apache.sh"
      }
    }
}
```

MORE INFO   **TROUBLESHOOTING USING VIRTUAL MACHINE EXTENSION LOGS**

In the event your custom script extension fails to execute it's a good idea to review the log files. On Windows the logs are located at: *C:\WindowsAzure\Logs\Plugins\Microsoft. Compute.CustomScriptExtension.* On Linux the command output is located at: */var/lib/waagent/Microsoft.OSTCExtensions.CustomScriptForLinux-<version>/download/1.*

Skill 3.4: Manage VM Backups

Chapter 2, "Implement and Manage Storage" covered the fundamentals of using the Azure Backup service, such as creating the recovery services vault, backing up and restoring data and creating and configuring backup policies. In this section, we'll cover those topics more closely aligned to virtual machines.

> **This section covers how to:**
> - Configure VM backup
> - Define backup policies
> - Implement backup policies
> - Perform VM restore

Configure VM backup

Chapter 2 discussed using the MARS agent and protecting files and folders with Azure Backup. Azure Backup can also back up one or more virtual machines. This solution provides a way to restore an entire virtual machine, or individual files from the virtual machine, and it is quite easy to set up. To back up a VM in Azure with Azure Backup, navigate to the Recovery Service vault and under Getting Started, click Backup. Select Azure as the location where the workload is running, and virtual machine as the workload to backup and click Backup, as shown in Figure 3-63.

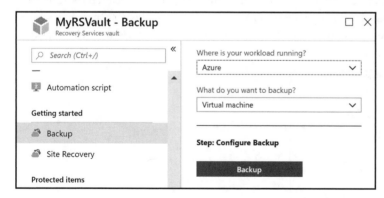

FIGURE 3-63 Configuring Azure Backup to protect virtual machines

The next item to configure is the Backup policy. Here you can create your own policy or choose the default policy. Next, choose the VMs to back up. Only VMs within the same region as the Recovery Services vault are available for backup. Figure 3-64 shows backup user interface with the default policy selected and three virtual machines selected.

FIGURE 3-64 Configuring Azure Backup to backup virtual machines and using the default policy

After the VMs are selected, click the **Enable Backup** button.

When you click the Enable Backup button, behind the scenes the VMSnapshot (for Windows) or VMSnapshotLinux (for Linux) extension is automatically deployed by the Azure fabric controller to the VMs. This allows for snapshot-based backups to occur, meaning that first a snapshot of the VM is taken, and then this snapshot is streamed to the Azure storage associated with the Recovery Services vault. The initial backup is not taken until the day/time configured in the backup policy, however an ad-hock backup can be initiated at any time. To do so, navigate to the Protected Items section of the vault properties, and click Backup items. Then, click Azure Virtual Machine under Backup Management type. The VMs that are enabled for backup are listed here. To begin an ad-hock backup, right-click on a VM and select Backup now, as shown in Figure 3-65.

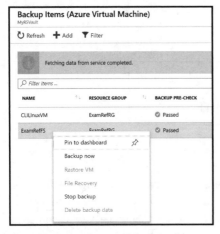

FIGURE 3-65 Starting an ad-hock backup

Backup support for Azure Files and SQL Server in an Azure VM

Azure Backup also directly supports the ability to backup and restore data from Azure Files and SQL Server in an Azure virtual machine. These two features are currently in preview, but it is still a good idea to have a basic understanding of the capabilities as they may eventually appear on the exam.

> **MORE INFO   AZURE FILES AND SQL SERVER IN AN AZURE VM**
>
> Learn about the current capabilities of Azure Backup support for Azure Files here: *https://docs.microsoft.com/azure/backup/backup-azure-files* and SQL Server in an Azure VM here: *https://docs.microsoft.com/azure/virtual-machines/windows/sql/virtual-machines-windows-sql-backup-recovery*.

When to use Azure Backup Server

Azure Backup Server is a stand-alone service that you install on a Windows Server operating system that stores the backed-up data in a Microsoft Azure Recovery Vault. Azure Backup Server inherits much of the workload backup functionality from Data Protection Manager (DPM). Though Azure Backup Server shares much of the same functionality as DPM, Azure Backup Server does not back up to tape and it does not integrate with System Center.

You should consider using Azure Backup server when you have a requirement to back up the following supported workloads:

- Windows Client
- Windows Server
- Linux Servers
- VMWare VMs
- Exchange
- SharePoint
- SQL Server
- System State and Bare Metal Recovery

> **MORE INFO   AZURE BACKUP SERVER PROTECTION MATRIX**
>
> The entire list of supported workloads and the versions supported for Azure Backup Server can be found here: *https://docs.microsoft.com/azure/backup/backup-mabs-protection-matrix*.

Define backup policies

An Azure Backup policy defines how often backups occur and how long the backups are retained. The default policy accomplishes a daily backup at 06:00am and retains backups for 30 days and you can define custom Backup policies. In Figure 3-66 a custom Backup policy is configured that includes Daily, Weekly, Monthly, and Yearly backups, each with their own retention values.

FIGURE 3-66 Configuring a custom backup policy

Implement backup policies

To implement a backup policy, open the policy in the Azure portal and click the Associated items button on the menu shown in Figure 3-67.

FIGURE 3-67 The associated items link for the Azure policy

The associated items blade shown in Figure 3-68 shows all the resources currently associated with the policy.

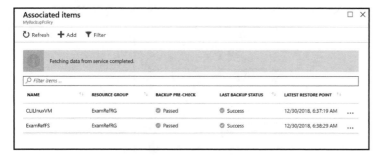

FIGURE 3-68 The associated items for the backup policy

Clicking Add will launch the Backup Goal blade where you can add other virtual machines or file shares to be backed up using the goals defined in the policy.

Perform VM restore

After backing up a virtual machine using Azure Backup there are two methods to restore data.

Restoring a virtual machine

To restore a recovery point as a new virtual machine, open the **Azure Backup** vault and navigate to **Backup Items**, click **Azure Virtual Machine**, and then click the virtual machine you want to restore from the list. The next blade will list all the restore points available for restore as shown in Figure 3-69.

FIGURE 3-69 Available restore points for a virtual machine.

Select the restore point you are interested in and click the **Restore VM** link at the top of the page. From there, you can then restore to a new virtual machine by selecting **Create New**, or you can restore over an existing virtual machine by selecting **Replace** existing.

Figure 3-70 shows the restore VM blade with the option of Create new selected. Here you can specify the virtual machine name, resource group, virtual network, subnet and storage account.

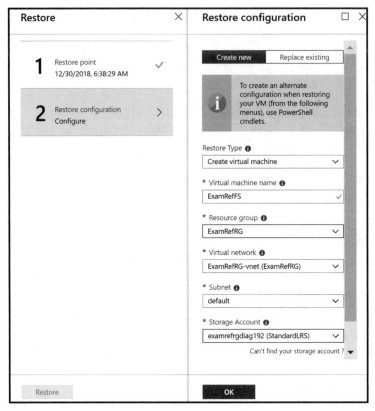

FIGURE 3-70 Restore to a new virtual machine

Restoring files from Azure VM backups

If you just need access to files from the virtual machine, choose the File recovery option at the top of the page shown in Figure 3-68 instead. From there, you can select the recovery point and then download a script that will mount the selected recovery point to another computer as local disks. The disks will remain mounted for 12 hours, so you can recover the needed data.

EXAM TIP

To restore a virtual machine that has encrypted disks you also need to provide the Azure Backup service access to the key vault holding the keys. See the following for more information: *https://docs.microsoft.com/azure/backup/backup-azure-vms-encryption.*

Thought experiment

In this thought experiment, apply what you have learned about this chapter. You can find answers to these questions in the next section.

You are the IT administrator for Contoso and you are tasked with migrating an existing web farm and database to Microsoft Azure. The web application is written in PHP and is deployed across 20 physical servers running RedHat for the operating system and Apache for the web server. The backend consists of two physical servers running MySQL in an active/passive configuration.

The solution must provide the ability to scale to at least as many web servers as the existing solution and ideally the number of web server instances should automatically adjust based on the demand. All the servers must be reachable on the same network, so the administrator can easily connect to them using SSH from a jump box to administer the VMs.

Answer the following questions for your manager:

1. Which compute option would be ideal for the web servers?

2. How should the servers be configured for high availability?

3. What would be the recommended storage configuration for the web servers? What about the database servers?

4. What feature could be used to ensure that traffic to the VMs only goes to the appropriate services (Apache, MySQL, and SSH)?

Thought experiment answers

This section contains the solution to the thought experiment for the chapter.

1. The web servers would be best served by deploying them into a virtual machine scale set (VMSS). Autoscale should be configured on the VMSS to address the requirement of automatically scaling up/down the number of instances based on the demand (CPU) used on the web servers.

2. The web servers should be deployed into their own availability set or availability zone if it is available within the region. The database tier should also be deployed into its own availability set or availability zone.

3. The web servers will likely not be I/O intensive so Standard SSD should be appropriate. The database servers will likely be I/O intensive so Premium SSD is the recommended

approach. To minimize management overhead and to ensure that storage capacity planning is done correctly managed disks should be used in both cases.

4. Use Network Security Groups (NSGs) to ensure that only traffic destined for allowed services can communicate to the VMs.

Chapter summary

This chapter focused heavily on creating and configuring virtual machines in Azure as well as automated deployments using Azure Resource Manager templates and even the command line tools. The chapter wrapped up focusing on backing up and restoring virtual machine data using the Azure Backup service. Let's review some of the key takeaways.

- Each compute family is optimized for either general or specific workloads. You should optimize your VM by choosing the most appropriate size.
- You can create VMs from the portal, PowerShell, the CLI tools, and Azure Resource Manager templates. You should understand when to use which tool and how to configure the virtual machine resource during provisioning and after provisioning. For example, availability sets can only be set at provisioning time, but data disks can be added at any time.
- You can connect to Azure VMs using a public IP address or a private IP address with RDP, SSH, or even PowerShell. To connect to a VM using a private IP you must also enable connectivity such as site-to-site, point-to-site, or ExpressRoute.
- The Custom Script Extension is commonly used to execute scripts on Windows or Linux-based VMs. The PowerShell DSC extension is used to apply desired state configurations to Windows-based VMs.
- A common method of troubleshooting virtual machines with RDP/SSH connectivity or unexplained application issues is to redeploy the virtual machine. Redeploy moves the virtual machine to a different Azure node.
- VM storage comes in Standard HDD, Standard SSD, Premium SSD, with Ultimate SSD in preview. Understanding which tier to choose for capacity and performance planning is important.
- There are unmanaged and managed disks and images. The key difference between the two is with unmanaged disks or images it is up to you to manage the storage account. With managed disks, Azure takes care of this for you, so it greatly simplifies managing images and disks.
- The Azure Diagnostics agent can be enabled on Windows and Linux virtual machines to capture diagnostic, performance, logs and boot diagnostic data.
- You can configure alerts based on metric alerts (captured from Azure Diagnostics) to Activity Log alerts that can notify by email, voice, web hook, SMS, Logic Apps, or even an Azure Automation Runbook.
- Azure Availability Zones provide high availability at the data center level. Azure Availability Sets provide high availability within a data center.

- Managed disks provide additional availability over unmanaged disks by aligning with availability sets and providing storage in redundant storage units.

- Virtual Machine Scale Sets (VMSS), can scale up to 1000 instances. You need to ensure that you create the VMSS configured for large scale sets if you intend to go above 100 instances. There are several other limits to consider too. Using a custom image, you can only create up to 300 instances. To scale above 100 instances, you must use the Standard SKU of the Azure Load Balancer or the Azure App Gateway.

- The Azure Backup service can backup and restore and entire virtual machine and you can also use it for just file recovery to restore files from a recovery point without recreating the entire virtual machine.

CHAPTER 4

Configure and manage virtual networks

The virtual network (or VNet) in Azure provides the foundation for the Azure networking infrastructure. Virtual machines are connected to virtual networks. This connection provides inbound and outbound connectivity, to other virtual machines, to on-premises networks, and to the Internet. Azure provides many networking features which will be familiar to those already experienced in networking, such as the ability to control which network flows are permitted and to control network routing. This allows Azure deployments to implement familiar network architectures, such as network segmentation between layers of an N-tier application.

This chapter focuses on the core capabilities enabling virtual networks to be used flexibly and securely to connect your Azure virtual machines.

Skills in this chapter:

- Implement and manage virtual networking
- Create connectivity between virtual networks
- Configure name resolution
- Create and configure a network security group (NSG)
- Implement Azure load balancer
- Monitor and troubleshoot virtual networking
- Integrate on-premises network with Azure virtual network

Skill 4.1: Implement and manage virtual networking

Azure Virtual Networks (VNets) form the foundation for the Azure Networking infrastructure. Each virtual network allows you to define a network space, comprising one or more IP address ranges. This network space is then carved into subnets. IP addresses for virtual machines, as well as some other services such as an internal Azure Load Balancer, are assigned from these subnets.

Each subnet allows you to define which network flows are permitted (using Network Security Groups), and what network routes should be taken (using User-Defined Routes). Together, these features allow you to implement many common network topologies, such as a DMZ containing a network security appliance, or a multi-tier application architecture with restricted communications between application tiers.

Create and configure a virtual networks and subnets

A virtual network (VNet) is an Azure resource. When creating a VNet, the most important setting to choose is the IP range (or ranges) the VNet will use.

IP ranges are defined using Classless Inter-Domain Routing (CIDR) notation. For example, the range 10.5.0.0/16 represents all IP ranges starting with 10.5 (the /16 indicates that the first 16 bits of the IP address given are fixed, while the remaining bits are variable across the IP range being defined). Each virtual network can use either a single IP range, or multiple disjoint IP ranges.

> **NOTE CIDR NOTATION**
>
> You will need to understand CIDR notation to work effectively with virtual networks in Azure. There are many good explanations to be found online, for example at: *https://devblogs.microsoft.com/premier-developer/understanding-cidr-notation-when-designing-azure-virtual-networks-and-subnets/*

The IP ranges in your VNet are private to that VNet. An IP address in your VNet can only be accessed from within that VNet, or from other networks connected to the VNet.

> **NOTE VIRTUAL NETWORK IP RANGES**
>
> When choosing the IP ranges for your VNet, it is normally a good idea to plan your network space in advance. You will typically want to avoid creating overlaps with other virtual networks, or with on-premises environments, since any overlap will prevent you from connecting these networks together later.

Your VNet IP ranges will typically be taken from the private address ranges defined in RFC 1918. These IP ranges are:

- 10.0.0.0 - 10.255.255.255 (10.0.0.0/8)
- 172.16.0.0 - 172.31.255.255 (172.16.0.0/12)
- 192.168.0.0 - 192.168.255.255 (192.168.0.0/16)

You can also use public, Internet-addressable IP ranges in your VNet. However, this is not recommended, since the addresses within your VNet will take priority, and virtual machines in your Vnet will no longer be able to access the corresponding Internet addresses.

In addition, there are a small number of IP ranges reserved by the Azure platform, and which therefore cannot be used. These are:

- 224.0.0.0/4 (Multicast)
- 255.255.255.255/32 (Broadcast)
- 127.0.0.0/8 (Loopback)
- 169.254.0.0/16 (Link-local)
- 168.63.129.16/32 (Azure-provided DNS)

Subnets

Subnets are used to divide the VNet IP space. Different subnets can have different network security and routing rules, enabling applications and application tiers to be isolated, and network flows between them controlled. For example, consider a typical 3-tier application architecture comprising a web tier, an application tier and a database tier. By implementing each tier as a separate subnet, you can control precisely which network flows are permitted between tiers and from the Internet.

The name of a subnet must be unique within that VNet. You cannot change the subnet name after is has been created.

Each subnet must also define a single network range (in CIDR format). This range must be contained within the IP ranges defined by the VNet. Only IP addresses from within the subnets can be assigned to virtual machines and other resources. Subnets do not have to span the entire VNet address space—they can be a subset, leaving unused space for future expansion.

Azure will hold back a total of 5 IP addresses from each subnet. Like standard IP networks, Azure reserves the first and last IP addresses in each subnet for network identification and for broadcast, respectively. Azure also holds three additional addresses for internal use starting from the first address in the subnet. For example, if the subnet address range is 192.168.1.0/24 then the first available IP address is 192.168.1.4.

If you create a VNet with 10 subnets, you are losing 50 IP addresses to Azure. Careful upfront planning is critical to not cause a shortage of IPs later. Also, the smallest subnet on an Azure VNet is a CIDR /29, which provides three useable IP addresses.

A VNet is not required to have subnets defined, although you are required to define one subnet when creating a VNet using the Azure portal, and a VNet without subnets isn't very useful. VNets typically have multiple subnets, and you can add new subnets to your VNet at any time.

Changes to subnets and address ranges can only be made if there are no devices connected to the subnet. If you wish to make a change to a subnet's address range, you first must delete all the objects in that subnet. If the subnet is empty, you can change the range of addresses to any range that is within the address space of the VNet not assigned to any other subnets.

Subnets can be only be deleted from VNets if they are empty. Once a subnet is deleted, the addresses that were part of that address range are released and available again for use within new subnets that you can create.

Additional virtual network properties

So far, we have focused on the most important properties of each VNet and subnet: the IP address ranges. There are some additional properties and features of VNets and subnets to also be aware of. Table 4-1 provides a summary of the properties supported by virtual networks.

TABLE 4-1 Properties of a virtual Network

Property	Description
Name	The VNet name. It must be unique within the resource group. It is between 2-64 characters, may contain letters (case insensitive), numbers, underscores, periods, or hyphens. Must start with a letter or number and end with a letter, number, or underscore.
Location	Azure location must be the same as the VNet. Each VNet is tied to a single Azure region, and can only be used by resources (such as Virtual Machines) in that region.
Address Space	An array of IP address ranges available for use by subnets.
DDOS Protection	Settings to defines whether additional DDoS protection is provided for resources in the VNet, and if so which protection plan is used.
DHCP Options	Contains an array of DNS servers. If specified, these DNS servers are configured on virtual machines in the virtual network in place of the Azure-provided DNS servers.
Subnets	The list of subnets configured for this VNet.
Peerings	The list of peerings configured for this VNet. Peerings are used to create network connectivity between separate VNets.

Table 4-2 provides a summary of the properties supported by virtual network subnets.

TABLE 4-2 Properties of a virtual network subnet

Property	Description
Name	The subnet name must be unique within the VNet. It is between 2-80 characters, may contain letters (case insensitive), numbers, underscores, periods, or hyphens. Must start with a letter or number. Must end with a letter, number, or underscore.
Address prefix	The IP address range for a subnet, specified in CIDR notation. All subnets must sit within the VNet address space and cannot overlap. Support for multiple IP ranges in a single subnet is currently in preview.
Network security group	Reference to the network security group (NSG) for the subnet. NSGs are essentially firewall rules that can be associated to a subnet and are used to control which inbound and outbound traffic flows are permitted.
Route table	Route table applied to the subnet, used to override the default system routes. These are used to send traffic to destination networks that are different than the routes that Azure uses by default.
Service endpoints (and olicies)	An array of Service Endpoints for this subnet. Service Endpoints provide a direct route to various Azure PaaS services (such as Azure storage), without requiring an Internet-facing endpoint. Service Endpoint Policies provide further control over which instances of those services may be accessed.
Delegations	An array of references to delegations on the subnet. Delegations allow subnets to be used by certain Azure services, which will then deploy managed resources (such as an Azure SQL Database Managed Instance) into the subnet. Access to these resources is private and can be controlled using NSGs. Delegations also support access to and from on-premises networks when hybrid networking is used.
Peerings	The list of peerings configured for this VNet. Peerings are used to create network connectivity between separate VNets.

Creating a virtual network and subnets using the Azure portal

To create a new VNet by using the Azure portal, first click **Create A Resource** and then select **Networking**. Next, click **Virtual Network** as shown in Figure 4-1.

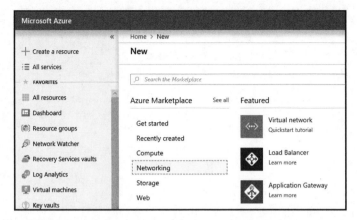

FIGURE 4-1 Creating a virtual network using the Azure portal

The Create Virtual Network blade opens. Here you can provide configuration information about the virtual network. This blade requires the following inputs, as shown in Figure 4-2:

- Name of the virtual network

- Address space to be used for the VNet using CIDR notation

- Subscription in which the VNet is created

- The resource group where the VNet is created

- The location for VNet

- Subnet name for the first subnet in the VNet

- The Address Range of the first Subnet

The blade also allows you to specify some additional settings, relating to DDoS protection, service endpoints and the Azure firewall service.

When creating a VNet using the Azure portal, you can only specify a single IP address range, and you must specify exactly one subnet. You can use the Azure portal to add more IP ranges and subnets after the VNet has been created.

FIGURE 4-2 Create a Virtual Network blade

Once the VNet has completed provisioning, you can review the settings using the Azure portal. Notice the Apps subnet has been created as part of the inputs made and shown in Figure 4-3.

FIGURE 4-3 Virtual network created using the Azure portal

To create another subnet in the VNet, click **+Subnet** on this blade and provide the following inputs, as shown in Figure 4-4:

- Name of the subnet
- The IP address range
- The network security group (if any)
- The route table (if any)
- Which service endpoints to connect from this subnet (if any)
- Which Azure service the subnet should be delegated to (if any)

FIGURE 4-4 Add Subnet blade, used to add a new subnet to an existing virtual network

Creating a virtual network and subnets using Azure PowerShell

The first step in creating a VNet using PowerShell is to build a local array containing an object representing each subnet. In the code example below, the New-AzVirtualNetworkSubnetConfig cmdlet is used to create two local objects that represent two subnets in the VNet. Notice how $subnets = @() creates an array, which is then loaded with each subnet object using the += operator.

```
$subnets = @()
$subnet1Name = "Apps"
$subnet2Name = "Data"
$subnet1AddressPrefix = "10.0.0.0/24"
$subnet2AddressPrefix = "10.0.1.0/24"
$subnets += New-AzVirtualNetworkSubnetConfig -Name $subnet1Name `
                -AddressPrefix $subnet1AddressPrefix
$subnets += New-AzVirtualNetworkSubnetConfig -Name $subnet2Name `
                -AddressPrefix $subnet2AddressPrefix
```

We're now ready to create our VNet, which is achieved using the New-AzVirtualNetwork cmdlet, specifying the VNet name, resource grouplocation, the address space, and the subnet array. You can also pass in multiple address spaces similar to how the subnets are passed in using an array.

```
$rgName      = "ExamRef-RG"
$location    = "Central US"
$vnetAddresssSpace = "10.0.0.0/16"
$VNetName = "ExamRef-vnet"
$vnet = New-AzVirtualNetwork -Name $VNetName `
            -ResourceGroupName $rgName `
            -Location $location `
            -AddressPrefix $vnetAddresssSpace `
            -Subnet $subnets
```

After completing the scripts above, you can retrieve the VNet and subnet properties using the Get-AzVirtualNetwork cmdlet, as shown next.

```
Get-AzVirtualNetwork -Name $VNetName -ResourceGroupName $rgName
```

To add (or remove) a subnet from an existing VNet using Azure PowerShell, first use the Get-AzVirtualNetwork cmdlet to retrieve the current VNet settings into a local object, then make the necessary changes locally, then commit the changes using Set-AzVirtualNetwork. This next example shows how to add a new subnet to the VNet created earlier.

```
$subnet3Name = "Web"
$subnet3AddressPrefix = "10.0.2.0/24"
$vnet = Get-AzVirtualNetwork -Name $VNetName `
    -ResourceGroupName $rgName

$vnet.Subnets += New-AzVirtualNetworkSubnetConfig -Name $subnet3Name `
    -AddressPrefix $subnet3AddressPrefix

Set-AzVirtualNetwork -VirtualNetwork $vnet
```

Creating a virtual network and subnets using the Azure CLI

You can also create and configure VNets and subnets using the Azure CLI using the az network vnet create command. You must specify the address space used by the VNet using the address-prefixes parameter. You can optionally specify your first subnet using the subnet-name and subnet-prefixes parameters.

```
# Create a virtual network (assumes resource group already exists)
az network vnet create --name ExamRef-vnet --resource-group ExamRef-RG
--address-prefixes 10.0.0.0/16 --subnet-name Apps --subnet-prefixes 10.0.1.0/24
```

Following the creation of the VNet, you can create additional subnets using the az network vnet subnet create command.

```
# Create additional subnets
az network vnet subnet create --name Data --vnet-name ExamRef-vnet
--resource-group ExamRef-RG --address-prefix 10.0.2.0/24
```

After running these commands there should be a newly-provisioned VNet named ExamRef-vnet, containing two subnets: Apps and Data. You can verify the VNet settings by retrieving them using the az network vnet show command:

```
# Show virtual network settings
az network vnet show --name ExamRef-vnet --resource-group ExamRef-RG
--output jsonc
```

You've already seen how to use the az network vnet subnet create command to add a new subnet to an existing virtual network. To remove a subnet, use the az network vnet subnet delete command.

> **NOTE SUBNET OPERATIONS**
>
> In Azure PowerShell, adding and removing subnets requires you to first retrieve a local copy of the VNet object, modify this object locally, then submit the modified object back to Azure. In the Azure CLI, these operations work differently. These CLI commands work by creating and deleting the subnets directly, in a single operation, by addressing the subnet as a child resource of the VNet. This approach—exposing certain settings as both a resource property and, at the same time, as a child resource—is quite common across a number of Azure resource types, especially in the Microsoft.Network resource provider.

To modify other VNet settings, use the az network vnet update command, and to modify subnet settings use the az network vnet subnet update command. As with other Azure CLI commands, use the help parameter with each of these commands to see the full list of supported parameters. For example, to modify the address space of our VNet to include an additional IP range, use:

```
az network vnet update --name ExamRef-vnet --resource-group ExamRef-RG
--address-prefixes 10.0.0.0/16 10.10.0.0/16
```

Note that this example specifies the existing address space (10.0.0.0/16) as well as the new address space (10.10.0.0/16).

Configure private IP addresses and network interfaces

VMs in Azure use TCP/IP to communicate with: services in Azure, other VMs you have deployed in Azure, on-premises networks, and the Internet. Just as a physical server uses a network interface card (NIC) to connect to a physical network, virtual machines use a network interface resource (also referred to as a NIC) to connect to a virtual network or the Internet.

There are two types of IP addresses you can use in Azure:

- **Public IP addresses**   Used for communication with the Internet.
- **Private IP addresses**   Used for communication within Azure virtual networks and connected on-premises networks.

This section focuses on how to deploy and manage private IP addresses and network interfaces. Public IP addresses are discussed in the next section.

Network interfaces

Both public and private IP addresses are configured on virtual machines using network interface resources. Therefore, to understand how to use public and private IP addresses with your virtual machine, you first must understand network interfaces. A network interface is a standalone Azure resource. Since its only purpose is to provide network connectivity for virtual machines, it is typically provisioned and deleted with its corresponding virtual machine.

Just as a physical server can have more than one network card, you can associate multiple network interfaces with a single virtual machine. This is a common practice when configuring virtual machines to act as network virtual appliances. These appliances provide network security as well as routing and other features similar to physical network devices in a traditional network.

Table 4-3 details the most important properties of each network interface resource in Azure.

TABLE 4-3 Properties of a network interface

Property	Description
Name	The network interface name. Must be unique within the resource group. it is between 1-80 characters, may contain letters (case insensitive), numbers, underscores, periods, or hyphens. Must start with a letter or number and end with a letter, number, or underscore.
Location	The location of the resource. Must be the same as the location of any virtual network or any virtual machine which the network interface will be connected to.
DNS Settings	If specified, these DNS servers are configured on virtual machines in the virtual network in place of the Azure-provided DNS servers. This setting will override the VNet-level DNS settings, if both are specified.
IP Forwarding	Used to enable IP forwarding on this network interface. It is used for network virtual appliances to allow the virtual machine to receive packets addressed to other networks.
IP Configurations	A list of IP configurations for the network interface. These are the most important settings, containing the public and private IP address properties.
Network Security Group	Used to reference a network security group to be applied to this network interface.
Accelerated Networking	Used to enable accelerated networking (only supported on certain VM sizes).

The most important property of the network interface is the IP configuration. This is where the public and private IP address settings are configured. Each network interface supports an array of IP configurations, which enables each network interface to support multiple IP addresses.

Private IP addresses

Private IP addresses are configured as properties within the IP configurations of the network interface. They are not a separate resource. Each IP configuration specifies a single subnet, and the private IP address is allocated from the address space of that subnet.

There are two methods used to assign private IP addresses: dynamic or static. The default allocation method is dynamic, where the IP address is automatically allocated from the resource's subnet (using an Azure DHCP server).

Dynamic allocation assigns private IP addresses from each subnet in order, starting with the lowest available IP in the subnet IP range. Remember that the first four IP addresses in each subnet are reserved by the Azure platform. For example, if the subnet is 10.10.0.0/24, the first private IP to be allocated will be 10.10.0.4 (because 10.10.0.0 to 10.10.0.3 are reserved).

Dynamically-allocated IP address can change when you stop and start the associated virtual machine. To avoid this, private IP addresses can also be allocated statically. This is used where you want to control which IP address is assigned to a specific server, and for that IP address to remain fixed.

Static private IP addresses are commonly used for:

- Virtual machines that act as domain controllers or DNS servers
- Resources that require firewall rules using IP addresses
- Resources accessed by other apps/resources through an IP address explicitly, rather than a domain name.

To configure a static private IP address, simply specify static IP allocation within the network interface IP configuration, together with the desired IP address. You can specify an existing dynamic private IP address as the static private IP address, or choose a new private IP address. The address must be within the address range of the subnet associated with the IP configuration, and not currently in use.

When changing a private IP address, you may need to manually review and update network settings within the virtual machine. For this reason, it is preferable to plan and specify static private IP addresses in advance when first provisioning the virtual machine.

> **NOTE CONFIGURING STATIC PRIVATE IP ADDRESSES**
>
> Static private IP addresses should only be configured in the Azure network interface resource. They will be assigned to the virtual machine using DHCP, just like with dynamic private IP addresses. Do not configure private IP addresses directly within the virtual machine OS network settings.

Both IPv4 and IPv6 private IP addresses are supported. However, IPv6 support has a number of limitations. VMs cannot communicate between private IPv6 addresses on a VNet, since they can only use IPv6 to receive and respond to inbound traffic from the Internet when using an Internet-facing load balancer.

> **NOTE DYNAMIC AND STATIC PRIVATE IP ASSIGNMENT**
>
> Private IPv4 address assignments can be either dynamic or static. Private IPv6 addresses can only be assigned dynamically.

Enabling static private IP addresses on VMs with the Azure portal

The network interface of a VM holds the configurations of the private IP address. This is known as the IP configuration. Using the Azure portal, you can modify the private IP address allocation method for the IP configuration from dynamic to static. You can also use the Azure portal to manage other network interface settings, such as assigning network security groups, public IP addresses, and adding new IP configurations.

Using the portal, locate the network interface for the VM to be assigned a static IP address. Once the blade loads for the NIC, click on **IP Configurations**, then select the IP configuration you wish to update. The IP Configuration blade is shown in Figure 4-5. Here, you can update the private IP address allocation method to **Static** and specify the static IP address.

FIGURE 4-5 Assigning a Static Private IP Address to a NIC

Enabling static private IP addresses on VMs with PowerShell

When updating an existing network interface resource to use a static IP address, use two PowerShell cmdlets: Get-AzNetworkInterface and Set-AzNetworkInterface. First, use the Get-AzNetworkInterface cmdlet to create a local object representing the network interface. Next, access the IP configurations array of the network interface and modify the appropriate IP configuration object locally, specifying the static IP allocation method and the IP address that should be assigned. Finally, to save your changes to Azure, use the Set-AzNetworkInterface cmdlet.

```
# Update existing NIC to use a Static IP address and set the IP
# Assumes a NIC exists named 'ExamRef-NIC' in resource group 'ExamRef-RG'
# Assumes NIC is associated with a, existing subnet with private IP 10.0.0.5 available
$nic = Get-AzNetworkInterface -Name ExamRef-NIC -ResourceGroupName ExamRef-RG
$nic.IpConfigurations[0].PrivateIpAllocationMethod = "Static"
$nic.IpConfigurations[0].PrivateIpAddress = "10.0.0.5"
Set-AzNetworkInterface -NetworkInterface $nic
```

To change a network interface from static to dynamic assignment, use:

```
# Update existing NIC to use a Dynamic IP address
# Assumes a NIC exists named 'ExamRef-NIC' in resource group 'ExamRef-RG'
$nic = Get-AzNetworkInterface -Name ExamRef-NIC -ResourceGroupName ExamRef-RG
$nic.IpConfigurations[0].PrivateIpAllocationMethod = "Dynamic"
Set-AzNetworkInterface -NetworkInterface $nic
```

Enabling static private IP addresses on VMs with the Azure CLI

To use the Azure CLI to update a network interface to a static private IP address, use one simple command: `az network nic ip-config update`. The name of the network interface and resource group are required, along with the name of the IP configuration to update and the new static IP address.

```
# Update existing NIC to use a Static IP Address and set the IP
# Assumes a NIC exists named 'ExamRef-NIC' in resource group 'ExamRef-RG'
# Assumes NIC has an IP configuration named 'ipconfig1'
# Assumes NIC is associated with a, existing subnet with private IP 10.0.0.5 available
az network nic ip-config update --name ipconfig1 --nic-name ExamRef-NIC
--resource-group ExamRefRG-CLI --private-ip-address 10.0.0.5
```

Note, there is no need to specify the static IP allocation method explicitly—this is implied by specifying the private IP address to use. To specify dynamic IP allocation, use the same command, specifying the IP address as "".

```
# Update existing NIC to use a Dynamic IP Address and set the IP
az network nic ip-config update --name ipconfig1 --nic-name ExamRef-NIC
--resource-group ExamRefRG-CLI --private-ip-address ""
```

Create and configure public IP addresses

Associating a public IP address with a network interface creates an Internet-facing endpoint, allowing your virtual machine to receive network traffic directly from the Internet.

A public IP address is a standalone Azure resource. This contrasts with a private IP address that exists only as a collection of settings on another resource, such as a network interface or a load balancer.

To associate a public IP address with a virtual machine, the IP configuration of the network interface must be updated to contain a reference to the public IP address resource. As a standalone resource, public IP addresses can be created and deleted independently as well as moved from one virtual machine to another.

Basic vs Standard Pricing Tiers

Public IP addresses are available at two pricing tiers (or SKUs): Basic or Standard. All Public IP Addresses created before the introduction of these tiers are mapped to the Basic tier.

The main distinction is that Standard tier Public IP Addresses support zone-redundant deployment, allowing you to use availability zones to protect your deployments against potential outages caused by datacenter-level failures (such as fire, power failure, or cooling failure). There are a number of other important differences between the two tiers, as summarized in Table 4-4.

TABLE 4-4 Comparison of public IP Address Basic and Standard Tiers

Basic Tier	Standard Tier
Supports both static and dynamic allocation methods.	Supports static allocation only.
Open by default for inbound traffic. Use NSGs to restrict inbound or outbound traffic.	Closed by default for inbound traffic. Use NSGs to allow inbound traffic and restrict outbound traffic.
Not zone redundant, but can be assigned to a specific availability zone.	Zone redundant by default, or can instead be assigned to a specific availability zone
Does not support public IP prefixes (discussed later).	Supports public IP prefixes, allowing IP addresses to be assigned from a contiguous IP address block.

Public IP address allocation

As with private IP addresses, public IP addresses support both dynamic and static IP allocation. For the Basic tier, both static and dynamic allocation are supported, the default being dynamic. For the Standard tier, only static allocation is supported.

Under dynamic allocation, an actual IP address is only allocated to the public IP address resource when the resource is in use—that is, when it is associated with a resource such as a running virtual machine. If the virtual machine is stopped (deallocated) or deleted, the IP address assigned to the public IP address resource is released and returned to the pool of available IP addresses managed by Azure. When you restart the virtual machine, a different IP address will most likely be assigned.

If you wish to retain the IP address, the public IP address resource should be configured to use static IP allocation. An IP address will be assigned immediately (if one was not already dynamically assigned). This IP address will never change, regardless of whether the associated virtual machine is stopped or deleted.

Static public IP addresses are typically used in scenarios where a dependency is taken on a particular IP address. For example: commonly used in the following scenarios:

- Where firewall rules specify an IP address.

- Where a DNS record would need to be updated when an IP address changes.

- Where the source IP address is used as a (weak) form of authentication of the traffic source.

- Where an SSL certificate specifies an explicit IP address rather than a domain name.

With private IP addresses, static allocation allows you to specify the IP address to use from the available subnet address range. In contrast, static allocation of public IP addresses does not allow you to specify which public IP address to use. Azure assigns the IP address from a pool of IP addresses in the Azure region where the resource is located.

Public IP address prefixes

When using multiple public IP addresses, it can be convenient to have all of the IP addresses allocated from a single IP range or prefix. For example, when configuring firewall rules, this allows you to configure a single rule for the prefix, rather than separate rules for each IP address.

To support this scenario, Azure allows you to reserve a public IP address prefix. Public IP address resources associated with that prefix will have their IP addresses assigned from that range, rather than from the general purpose Azure pool.

When creating a prefix, specify the prefix resource name, subnet size (for example, /28 for 16 IP addresses), and the Azure region where the IP addresses will be allocated. This feature is currently in preview, so check for the current level of support.

Once the prefix is created, individual public IP addresses can be created that are associated with this prefix. Note that only standard-tier public IP addresses support allocation from a prefix, and thus only static allocation is supported. The IP address assigned to these resources will be taken from the prefix range—you cannot specific a specific IP address from the range.

DNS Labels

The Domain Name System (DNS) can be used to create a mapping from a domain name to an IP address. This allows you to reference IP address endpoints using a domain name, rather than using the assigned IP address directly.

There are four ways to configure a DNS label for an Azure public IP address:

1. By specifying the DNS name label property of the public IP address resource.

2. By creating a DNS A record in Azure DNS or a third-party DNS service hosting a DNS domain.

3. By creating a DNS CNAME record in Azure DNS or a third-party DNS service hosting a DNS domain.

4. By creating an alias record in Azure DNS.

In the first option, you specify the left-most part of the DNS label as a property in the public IP address resource. Azure provides the DNS suffix, which will be of the form `<region>.cloudapp.azure.com`. The DNS label you provide is concatenated with this suffix to form the fully-qualified domain name (FQDN), which can be used to look up the IP address via a DNS query.

For example, if your public IP address is deployed to the Central US region, and you specify the DNS label contoso-app, then the FQDN will be contoso-app.centralus.cloudapp.azure.com.

The major limitation of this first approach is that the DNS suffix is taken from an Azure-provided DNS domain. It does not support the use of your own vanity domain, such as contoso.com. To address this, you will need to use one of the other approaches.

In the second approach, you will have already hosted your vanity domain either in Azure DNS or a third-party DNS service. Using your hosting service, you can create a DNS entry in your vanity domain mapping to your public IP address resource. If you use a DNS A record, which maps directly to an IP address, you will need to update the DNS record if the assigned IP address changes. To avoid this, you will probably prefer to use static rather than dynamic IP allocation.

In the third approach, you start by creating a DNS label for your public IP address. You then create a CNAME record in your vanity domain which maps your chosen domain name to the Azure-provided DNS name. For example, you might map www.contoso.com to contoso-app.centralus.cloudapp.azure.com. This approach has the advantage of avoiding the need for static IP allocation, since the Azure-provided DNS entry updates automatically if the assigned IP address changes. However, the downside of this approach is that the Domain Name System does not support CNAME records at the apex (or root) of a DNS domain, hence while you can create a CNAME record for www.contoso.com, you cannot create one for contoso.com (without the www).

In the fourth approach, your vanity domain must be hosted in Azure DNS. You can then create an alias record, which works the same as an A record, except that rather than specifying the assigned IP address value explicitly in the DNS record, you simply reference the public IP address resource. The assigned IP address is taken from this resource and automatically configured in your DNS alias record. With alias records, the DNS record is automatically updated if the assigned IP address changes, avoiding the need for static IP allocation.

Outbound Internet connections

When a public IP address is assigned to a virtual machine's network interface, outbound traffic to the Internet will be routed through that IP address. The recipient will see your public IP address as the source IP address for the connection.

However, the virtual machine itself does not see the public IP address in its network settings—it only sees the private IP address. Traffic leaves the virtual machine via the private IP address, and Source Network Address Translation (SNAT) is used to map the outbound traffic from the private IP address to the public IP address.

Note that a public IP address is not required for outbound Internet traffic. Even without a public IP address assigned, virtual machines can still make outbound Internet connections. In this case, SNAT is used to map the private IP address to the Internet-facing IP address.

IPv4 and IPv6

Public IP address resources can use either an IPv4 or IPv6 address (but not both). Note that IPv6 support is limited as follows:

- Only the Basic tier is supported.
- Only dynamic allocation is supported.
- Only Internet-facing load balancers (and not virtual machines) can be assigned a public IPv6 address.

Creating a public IP address using the Azure portal

Creating a new public IP address is a simple process when using the portal. Click **New**, and then search for public IP address in the marketplace. Like all resources in Azure, some details will be required, including the name of the resource, the SKU (or pricing tier), the DNS name label, idle time-out, subscription, resource group and location/region. For the Basic SKU, you also specify the IP version and static or dynamic assignment. For the Standard SKU, choose between zone-redundant deployment or a specific availability zone.

The location is critical, as an IP address must be in the same location/region as the virtual machine or other resource that will use it. Figure 4-6 shows the Azure Create Public IP Address Blade.

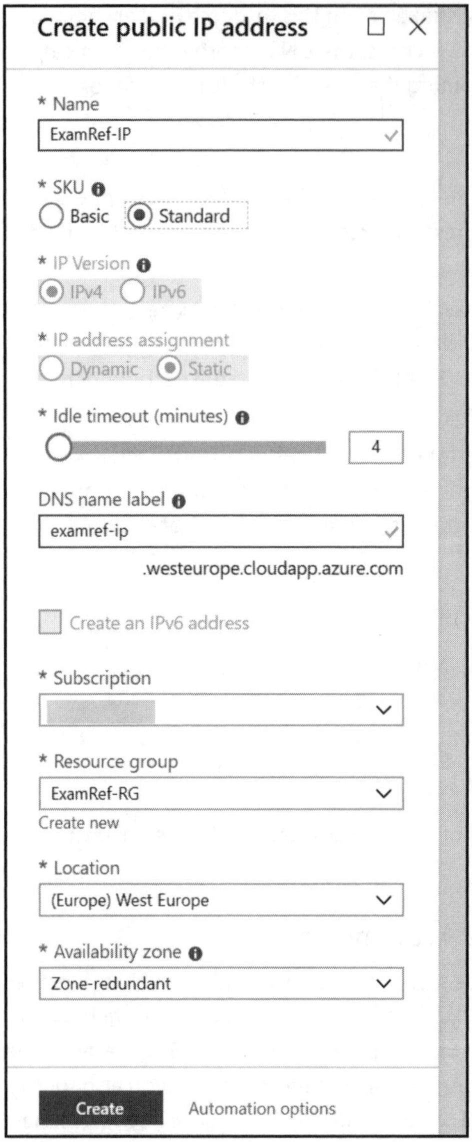

FIGURE 4-6 Creating a Public IP Address in the Azure portal

Creating a public IP address using the PowerShell

To create a new public IP address by using Azure PowerShell, use the New-AzPublicIpAddress cmdlet, as shown in the next example. Each of the IP address properties discussed earlier is specified using an appropriate parameter.

```
# Creating a Public IP Address
# Set Variables
```

```
$publicIpName = "ExamRef-PublicIP1-PS"
$rgName = "ExamRefRG-PS"
$dnsPrefix = "examrefpubip1ps"
$location = "centralus"

# Create the Public IP
New-AzPublicIpAddress -Name $publicIpName `
            -ResourceGroupName $rgName `
            -AllocationMethod Static `
            -DomainNameLabel $dnsPrefix `
            -Location $location
```

Creating a public IP address using the Azure CLI

To create a new public IP address by using the Azure CLI, use the `az network public-ip create` command. Each of the IP address properties discussed earlier is specified using an appropriate parameter. For a full list, use `az network public-ip create -h` to see the inline help.

```
# Creating a Public IP Address
az network public-ip create --name ExamRef-PublicIP1-CLI --resource-group
ExamRefRGCLI --dns-name examrefpubip1cli --allocation-method Static
```

Configure network routes

Network routes control how traffic is routed in your network. Azure provides default routing for common scenarios, with the ability to configure your own network routes where necessary.

System routes

Azure VMs that are added to a VNet can communicate automatically with each other over the network. Even if they are in different subnets or attempting to gain access to the Internet, there are no configurations required by you as the administrator. Unlike typical networking, you will not need to specify a network gateway, even though the VMs are in different subnets. This is also the case for communication from the VMs to your on-premises network when a hybrid connection from Azure to your datacenter has been established.

This ease of setup is made possible by what is known as system routes, which define how IP traffic flows in Azure VNets. The following are the default system routes that Azure will use and provide for you:

- Within the same subnet
- From one subnet to another within a VNet
- VMs to the Internet
- A VNet to another VNet through a VPN gateway
- A VNet to another VNet through VNet peering
- A VNet to your on-premises network through a VPN gateway or ExpressRoute

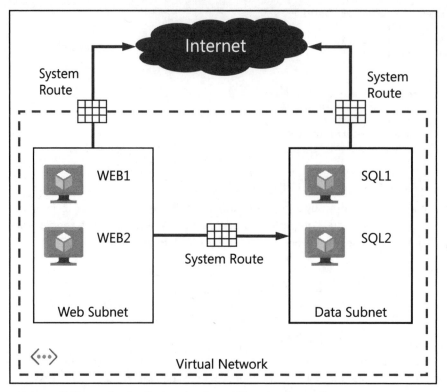

FIGURE 4-7 N-Tier application deployed to Azure VNet using System Routes

Figure 4-7 shows an example of how these system routes make it easy to get up and running. System routes provide for most typical scenarios by default, without you having to make any routing configuration.

User-defined routes

There are some use cases where you will want to configure the routing of packets differently from what is provided by the default system routes. One of these scenarios is when you want to send traffic through a network virtual appliance, such as a third-party load balancer, firewall or router deployed into your VNet from the Azure Marketplace.

To make this possible, you must create what are known as user defined routes (UDRs). The UDR is implemented by creating a route table resource. Within the route table, a number of routes are configured. Each route specifies the destination IP range (in CIDR notation) and the next hop IP address. A variety of different types of next hop are supported. These are:

- **Virtual Appliance**   A virtual machine running a network application such as a load-balancer or firewall. With this next hop type, you also specify the IP address of the appliance, which can be a virtual machine or internal load-balancer for high-availability virtual appliances.

- **Virtual Network Gateway**   Used to route traffic to a VPN Gateway (but not an ExpressRoute Gateway, which uses BGP for custom routes). Since there can be only one VPN Gateway associated with a VNet, you are not prompted to specify the actual gateway resource.

- **Virtual Network**   Used to route traffic within the Virtual Network.

- **Internet**   Used to route a specific IP address or prefix to the Internet.

- **None**   Used to drop all traffic send to a given IP address or prefix.

This route table is then associated with one or more subnets. Traffic originating in the subnet whose destination matches the destination IP range of a route table rule will instead be routed to the corresponding next hop IP address. The service running at this IP address is responsible for all onward routing.

> *NOTE* **ROUTE TABLES**
>
> You can have multiple route tables, and the same route table can be associated to one or more subnets. Each subnet can only be associated to a single route table. All VMs in a subnet use the route table associated to that subnet.

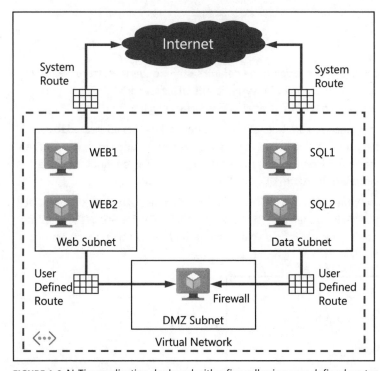

FIGURE 4-8 N-Tier application deployed with a firewall using user defined routes

Figure 4-8 shows a UDR that has been created to direct outbound traffic via a virtual appliance. In this case the appliance is a firewall running as a VM in Azure in the DMZ subnet.

The same appliance can also be used to filter traffic between the Apps and Data subnets. An example route table implementing this design is shown in Figure 4-9.

FIGURE 4-9 Route table rules forcing network traffic through firewall

> **NOTE DEDICATED SUBNETS FOR NETWORK APPLIANCES**
>
> Do not apply a route table to a subnet if the route table contains a rule with a next hop address within that subnet. To do so could create a routing loop. For this reason, virtual network appliances should be deployed to dedicated subnets, separate from the resources that route through that appliance.

IP forwarding

User defined routes (UDR) allow for changing the default system routes that Azure creates for you in an Azure VNet. In the virtual appliance scenario, the UDRs forward traffic to a virtual appliance such as a firewall, which is running as an Azure virtual machine.

By default, a virtual machine in Azure will not accept a network packet addressed to a different IP address. For that traffic to be allowed to pass into that virtual appliance, you must enable IP forwarding on the network interface of the virtual machine. This configuration doesn't typically involve any changes to the Azure UDR or VNet.

IP forwarding can be enabled on a network interface by using the Azure portal, PowerShell, or the Azure CLI. In Figure 4-10, you see that the network interface of the NGFW1 VM has the IP forwarding set as Enabled. This VM is now able to accept and send packets that were not originally intended for this VM.

FIGURE 4-10 IP Forwarding enabled on a virtual appliance

How routes are applied

A given network packet may match multiple route table rules. When designing and implementing custom routes, it's important to understand the precedence rules that Azure applies.

If multiple routes contain the same address prefix, Azure selects the route type, based on the following priority:

1. User defined routes
2. System routes for traffic in a virtual network, across a virtual network peering, or to a virtual network service endpoint
3. BGP routes
4. Other system routes

Within a single route table, a given network packet may match multiple routing rules. There is no explicit precedence order on the rules in a route table. Instead, precedence is given to the rule with the most specific match to the destination IP address.

For example, if a route table contains one rule for prefix 10.10.0.0/16, and another rule for 10.10.30.0/28, then any traffic to IP address 10.10.30.4 will be matched against the second rule in preference to the first.

When troubleshooting networking issues, it can be useful to get a deeper insight into exactly which routes are being applied to a given network interface. The effective routes feature of each network interface allows you to see the full details of every network route applied to that network interface, giving you full insight into how each outbound connection will be routed based on the destination IP address.

Forced tunneling

A special case is when routes are configured with the destination IP prefix 0.0.0.0/0. Given the precedence rules described above, this route controls traffic destined for any IP address is not covered by any other rules.

By default, Azure implements a system route directing all traffic matching 0.0.0.0/0 (and not matching any other route) to the Internet. If you override this route, this traffic is instead directed to the next hop you specify. By using a VPN Gateway as the next hop, you can direct all Internet-bound traffic over your VPN connection to an on-premises network security appliance. This is known as forced tunneling.

Implementing a custom route using the 0.0.0.0/0 prefix has several implications. First, traffic to Azure platform services will also be routed via your custom route. This may add considerable additional latency to these connections. To prevent this, use service endpoints to maintain a direct connection to these services.

Second, you will no longer be able to access resources in your subnet directly from the Internet. Instead, you will need to configure an indirect path, with inbound traffic passing through the next hop device.

Configure user defined routes using the Azure portal

To configure user defined routes, the first step is to create a route table resource. From the Azure portal, click **+Create A Resource**, then click **Networking**, then click **Route Table** to open the **Create Route Table** blade, as shown in Figure 4-11. Fill in the route table name, select the subscription and resource group, and specify the route table location—this must be the same Azure region that the subnets use with this route table.

FIGURE 4-11 The Create Route Table blade in the Azure portal

Having created the route table, the next step is to define the routes. Open the route table blade, and under **Settings** click **Routes** to open the list of routes in the route table. Then click **+Add** to open the **Add Route** blade, as shown in Figure 4-12.

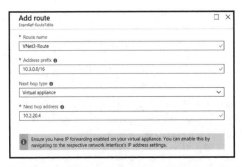

FIGURE 4-12 The Add Route Blade in The Azure Portal

Repeat this process for each custom route in the route table. The list of routes in the route table will be shown in the route table blade, as shown in Figure 4-13.

NAME	ADDRESS PREFIX	NEXT HOP	
VNet3-Route	10.3.0.0/16	10.2.20.4	...

FIGURE 4-13 The list of routes in the route table blade in the Azure portal

The final step is to specify which subnets this route table should be associated with. This can be configured either from the subnet, or from the route table. In the latter case, from the route table blade under **Settings** click **Subnets**, to open the list of subnets associated with the route table. Click **+Associate** to open the **Associate Subnet** blade, as shown in Figure 4-14.

FIGURE 4-14 The Associate Subnet blade for a route table, in the Azure portal

After creating the subnet association, the route table blade will show a list of associated subnets as shown in Figure 4-15.

NAME	ADDRESS RANGE	VIRTUAL NETWORK	SECURITY GROUP	
Default	10.1.0.0/24	VNet1	-	...

FIGURE 4-15 The list of subnets in the route table blade in the Azure portal

To see the effective routes for a given network interface, navigate to the network interface blade in the Azure portal, then click **Effective Routes** to open the **Effective Routes** blade, as shown in Figure 4-16.

Effective routes

SOURCE	STATE	ADDRESS PREFIXES	NEXT HOP TYPE	NEXT HOP TYPE IP ADDRESS	USER DEFINED ROUTE NAME
Default	Active	10.1.0.0/16	Virtual network	-	-
Default	Active	10.2.0.0/16	VNet peering	-	-
Default	Active	0.0.0.0/0	Internet	-	-
Default	Active	10.0.0.0/8	None	-	-
Default	Active	100.64.0.0/10	None	-	-
Default	Active	172.16.0.0/12	None	-	-
Default	Active	192.168.0.0/16	None	-	-
User	Active	10.3.0.0/16	None	10.2.20.4	VNet3-Route

FIGURE 4-16 The list effective routes for the VNet1-VM network interface

Configure user defined routes using Azure PowerShell

To configure user defined routes using Azure PowerShell, follow the same sequence as used for the Azure portal: first create the route table resource by using the New-AzRouteTable cmdlet, then add routes to the route table using the Add-AzRouteConfig cmdlet and commit the changes using the Set-AzRouteTable cmdlet.

Next, associate the route table with the subnet(s). In this case, the subnet must be associated with the route table, not the other way around.

```
# Create the route table resource
$rt = New-AzRouteTable -Name RouteTable1 -ResourceGroupName ExamRef-RG
-Location 'North Europe'

# Add a route to the local route table object
Add-AzRouteConfig -RouteTable $rt `
 -Name Route1 `
 -AddressPrefix 10.3.0.0/16 `
 -NextHopType VirtualAppliance `
 -NextHopIpAddress 10.2.20.4

# Commit the route table back to Azure
Set-AzRouteTable -RouteTable $rt

# Find the VNet and subnet
$vnet = Get-AzVirtualNetwork -Name VNet1 -ResourceGroupName ExamRef-RG
$subnet = $subnet = $vnet.Subnets | where {$_.Name -eq "Default"}

# Update the subnet to specify the route table.
# This cmdlet requires us to re-specify the subnet address prefix, which we take from
 the existing subnet
Set-AzVirtualNetworkSubnetConfig -VirtualNetwork $vnet `
 -Name Default `
 -AddressPrefix $subnet.AddressPrefix `
 -RouteTable $rt

# Commit the VNet back to Azure
Set-AzVirtualNetwork -VirtualNetwork $vnet
```

Azure PowerShell can also be used to retrieve the effective routes for a network interface by using the Get-AzEffectiveRouteTable cmdlet.

```
# Get effective routes for a network interface
Get-AzEffectiveRouteTable -NetworkInterfaceName VNet1-VM `
 -ResourceGroupName ExamRef-RG
```

Configure user defined routes using the Azure CLI

To configure UDRs with the Azure CLI, start by creating the route table resource using the az network route-table create command. Then add routes to the route table using the az network route-table route create command. To associate the route table with a subnet, use the az network vnet subnet update command, specifying the --route-table parameter.

```
# Create route table
az network route-table create --name RouteTable1 --resource-group ExamRef-RG

# Add route(s) to route table
az network route-table route create --name Route1 --route-table-name RouteTable1
```

```
--resource-group ExamRef-RG --address-prefix 10.3.0.0/16
--next-hop-type VirtualAppliance --next-hop-ip-address 10.2.20.4

# Associate route table with subnet
az network vnet subnet update --name default --vnet-name VNet1
--resource-group ExamRef-RG --route-table RouteTable1
```

The Azure CLI can also be used to review effective routes on a network interface, using the `az network nic show-effective-route-table` command.

```
# Get effective routes for a nic
az network nic show-effective-route-table --name VM1-NIC --resource-group ExamRef-RG
```

Skill 4.2: Create connectivity between virtual networks

A virtual network provides a private network space in Azure for your virtual machines. In some scenarios, you may need virtual machines in one virtual network to communicate with virtual machines in another virtual network. This section explains how to achieve this by creating private connections between your virtual networks. There are two kinds of private connections available: VNet Peering, and Site-to-Site VPN connections.

Connectivity between virtual networks is useful in several common scenarios. One example is where applications in different virtual networks need access to a shared service such as a domain controller, a network security appliance, or a gateway. Since each virtual network exists in a single Azure region, another scenario requiring connectivity between virtual networks is for communication between virtual machines in different Azure regions.

> **This section covers how to:**
> - Create and configure VNet peering
> - Create a virtual network gateway and configure VNet to VNet connectivity
> - Verify virtual network connectivity

Create and configure VNet peering

VNet peering allows virtual machines in two separate virtual networks to communicate directly, using their private IP addresses. The VNets can either be in the same Azure region, or separate Azure regions. Peering between VNets in different regions is called *Global VNet peering*. In all cases, traffic between peered VNets travels over the Microsoft backbone infrastructure, not the public Internet.

You can peer VNets in different subscriptions, even if those subscriptions are under different Azure Active Directory tenants (cross-tenant peering is not supported via the Azure portal, you need to use the Azure CLI, PowerShell, or templates).

You can also use VNet peering to connect Resource Manager VNets to the older "Classic" VNets. However, peering between two Classic VNets is not supported (a VNet-to-VNet VPN can be used in this case).

The peered VNets must have non-overlapping IP address spaces. In addition, the VNet address space cannot be modified once the VNet is peered with another VNet.

When peering two Resource Manager VNets, such as VNet1 and VNet2, two peering connections are required – one from VNet1 to VNet2, and one from VNet2 to VNet1.

However, when peering between a Resource Manager VNet and a Classic Vnet, a connection is only made from the Resource Manager VNet.

VNet peering gives the same network performance between VMs as if they were placed in a single, large VNet, while maintaining the manageability that comes from using two or more separate VNets. There is no bandwidth cap imposed on peered VNets. The only limits are those on the VMs themselves, based on VM series and size.

Be aware of the limit of 100 peering connections per VNet. This is a hard limit.

No VNet gateways are required by VNet peering. This avoids the cost, throughput limitations, additional latency and additional incurred complexity associated with using VNet gateways.

Global peering cannot be used to access the frontend IP of an internal Azure load-balancer, or a virtual network gateway, in the remote virtual network. In these cases, a VNet-to-VNet VPN should be used instead. This limitation applies only to global VNet peering between Azure regions, not to VNet peering within an Azure region.

By default, peered VNets appear as a single network for connectivity purposes. That is, there are no restrictions on connectivity between the peered VNets, so virtual machines in peered VNets can communicate with each other as if they were in the same VNet. In addition, the VirtualNetwork service tag (described in Skill 4.4) spans the address space of both peered networks.

Alternatively, you also have the option to limit connectivity—with this option, there is no automatic outbound connectivity between peered VNets, and the VirtualNetwork service tag does not include the address space of the peered VNet. In this case, you control connectivity between peered virtual networks using network security groups.

A simple example of VNet peering is shown in Figure 4-17. This shows two VNets which ave been connected using VNet peering. This allows (for example), the WEB1 virtual machine in VNetA to connect to the MYSQL1 database in VNetB.

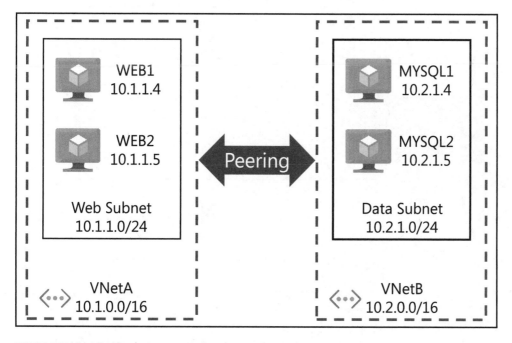

FIGURE 4-17 VNet Peering between two virtual networks

Once peered, traffic between VMs is routed through the Microsoft backbone network. Traffic does not pass over the public Internet, even when using global VNet peering to connect VNets in different Azure regions.

While global VNet peering allows for open connectivity between virtual machines across VNets in different Azure regions, a limitation is that a VM can only connect to the frontend IP address of an internal Azure Load Balancer in the same region. To connect to an internal Azure Load Balancer across regions, a VNet-to-VNet VPN connection is required.

It is important to understand that VNet peering is a pairwise relationship between two virtual networks. To create connectivity across 3 virtual networks (VNetA, VNetB, and VNetC), all 3 pairs must be peered (VNetA to VNetB, VNetB to VNetC and VNetA to VNetC). This is illustrated in Figure 4-18.

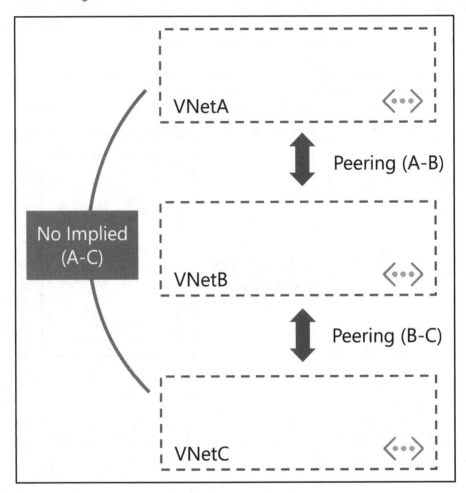

FIGURE 4-18 VNet peerings do not have a transitive relationship

Service chaining and hub-and-spoke networks

A common way to reduce duplication of resources is to use a hub-and-spoke network topology. In this approach, shared resources (such as domain controllers, DNS servers, monitoring systems, and so on) are deployed into a dedicated hub VNet. These services are accessed from multiple applications, each deployed to their own separate spoke VNets.

As you have just seen, VNet peering is not transitive. This means there is no automatic connectivity between spokes in a hub and spoke topology. Where such connectivity is required, one approach is to deploy additional VNet peerings between spokes. However, with a large number of spokes, this can quickly become unwieldy.

An alternative approach is to deploy a network virtual appliance (NVA) into the hub, using user-defined routes (UDRs) to route inter-spoke traffic through the NVA. This is known as *service chaining*, and it enables spoke-to-spoke communication without requiring additional VNet peerings, as illustrated in Figure 4-19.

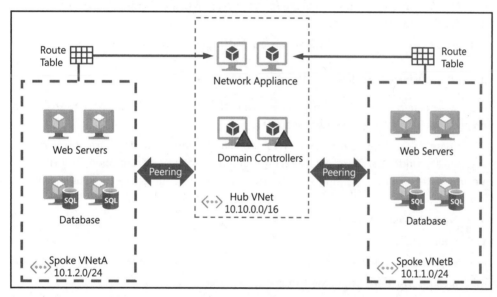

FIGURE 4-19 Service chaining allows for the use of common services across VNet Peerings

To transit traffic from one spoke VNet to another spoke VNet via an NVA in the hub VNet, the VNet peerings must be configured correctly. By default, a peering connection will only accept traffic originating from the VNet to which it is connected. This will not be the case for traffic forwarded between spoke VNets via an NVA in a hub VNet. To permit such traffic, the VNet peerings must enable the **Allow Forwarded Traffic** setting.

Sharing virtual network gateways

Suppose two peered VNets, say VNet-A and VNet-B, wish to send traffic to an external network via a virtual network gateway (this external network could be an on-premises network, or another Azure VNet connected via a site-to-site VPN connection). Rather than deploy two virtual network gateways, it is much simpler and more cost-efficient for both VNets to share a single gateway. This can be achieved, provided both VNets are deployed to the same Azure region, and having the correct configuration of the peering settings.

Suppose the virtual network gateway is deployed to VNet-A, allowing VNet-A to communicate with the external network. By default, only traffic originating in VNet-A is permitted to use this gateway, and the external network is only able to connect to VMs in VNet-A. To allow connectivity between VNet-B and the external network, the following settings must be configured:

- **Use Remote Gateways**   This setting must be enabled on the peering connection from VNET-B to VNET-A. This informs VNET-B of the availability of the gateway in VNET-A. Note that to enable this setting, VNET-B cannot have its own virtual network gateway.

- **Allow Gateway Transit**   This option must be enabled on the peering connection from VNET-A to VNET-B. This permits traffic from VNET-B to use VNET-A's gateway to send traffic to the external network.

Note that in this case, the **Allow Forwarded Traffic** peering option is not required.

Creating a VNet peering using the Azure portal

To create a peering connection between two VNets, the VNets must already have been created and must not have overlapping address spaces.

To create a new VNet peering from VNet1 to VNet2, connect to the Azure portal and locate VNet1. Under **Settings**, click **Peerings**, and then select **+Add** to open the **Add Peering** blade. Use the following settings for a standard peering connection, as shown in Figure 4-20.

- **Name**   VNet1-to-VNet2
- **Peer details**
    - Resource Manager
    - **Subscription**   Select the Subscription for VNet2

    Virtual Network   Choose VNet2

    (Alternatively, you can specify the peer VNet by selecting the **I Know My Resource ID** checkbox and entering the peer VNet resource ID)
- **Configuration**
    - **Allow Virtual Network Access**   Enabled
    - Leave the remaining three checkboxes unchecked

FIGURE 4-20 Adding peering from VNet1 to VNet2 using the Azure portal

Click **OK** to create the peering and return to the **VNet1 – Peerings** view. After refreshing your browser, the VNet peering appears in the portal with the peering status Initiated, as seen in Figure 4-21.

FIGURE 4-21 VNet1-to-VNet2 peering showing status as Initiated in the Azure portal

To complete the VNet peering, you need to create a second peering in the opposite direction, from VNet2 to VNet1. Open VNet2 in the Azure portal, click **Peerings**. Click **+Add** to open the **Add Peering** blade, and fill in as follows next, as shown in Figure 4-22.

- **Name** VNet2-to-VNet1
- **Peer details**
- Resource Manager
- **Subscription** Select the Subscription for VNet1
- **Virtual Network** Choose VNet1
- **Configuration**
  - **Allow Virtual Network Access** Enabled
  - Leave the remaining three boxes unchecked for this example

FIGURE 4-22 Adding Peering from VNet2 to VNet1 using the Azure portal

Once the peering has completed provisioning, it will appear in the portal with the peering status **Connected** to peer network VNet1, as seen in Figure 4-23.

FIGURE 4-23 VNet2-to-VNet1 peering showing as Connected in the Azure portal

Returning to the peering blade of VNet1 shows that the first peering, from VNet1 to VNet2, also now shows a peering status of Connected, as shown in Figure 4-24.

FIGURE 4-24 VNet1-to-VNet2 peering showing as Connected in the Azure portal

Now Vnet1 and VNet2 are peers, and VMs on these networks can communicate with each other, as if this was a single virtual network.

Creating a VNet peering using PowerShell

When creating a new VNet peering using PowerShell, first use the Get-AzVirtualNetwork cmdlet to assign information about the VNet1 and VNet2 into two local objects. Next, use the Add-AzVirtualNetworkPeering cmdlet to create two VNet peerings, from VNet1 to VNet2 and from VNet2 to VNet1. Upon completion, the VNet peering will provision, and move to a connected peering status. You can use the Get-AzVirtualNetworkPeering cmdlet to verify the peering status of the VNets.

```
# Load Vnet1 and VNet2 into local variables
$vnet1 = Get-AzVirtualNetwork `
    -Name VNet1 `
    -ResourceGroupName ExamRef-RG

$vnet2 = Get-AzVirtualNetwork `
    -Name VNet2 `
    -ResourceGroupName ExamRef-RG

# Peer VNet1 to VNet2
Add-AzVirtualNetworkPeering `
   -Name 'VNet1-to-VNet2' `
    -VirtualNetwork $vnet1 `
    -RemoteVirtualNetworkId $vnet2.Id

# Peer VNet2 to VNet1
Add-AzVirtualNetworkPeering `
    -Name 'VNet2-to-VNet1' `
    -VirtualNetwork $vnet2 `
    -RemoteVirtualNetworkId $vnet1.Id

# Check the peering status
  Get-AzVirtualNetworkPeering `
     -ResourceGroupName ExamRef-RG `
     -VirtualNetworkName VNet1 `
     | Format-Table VirtualNetworkName, PeeringState
```

Creating VNet peering using the Azure CLI

To create a VNet peering using the Azure CLI, use the az network vnet peering create command. You can use the az network vnet peering list command to check the peering status.

If the remote VNet is in a different subscription or resource group, you will need to specify the full resource ID of the remote VNet instead of only the name. This resource ID can be found using the az network vnet show command.

```
# Peer VNet1 to VNet2
# Note: if the remote VNet is in a different subscription or resource group,
# specify the full resource ID
az network vnet peering create --name VNet1-to-VNet2 --resource-group
ExamRef-RG --vnet-name VNet1 --allow-vnet-access --remote-vnet  VNet2

# Peer VNet2 to VNet1
# Note: if the remote VNet is in a different subscription or resource group,
# specify the full resource ID
az network vnet peering create --name VNet2-to-VNet1 --resource-group
ExamRef-RG --vnet-name VNet2 --allow-vnet-access --remote-vnet VNet1

#To See the Current State of the Peering
az network vnet peering list --resource-group ExamRef-RG --vnet-name VNet1 -o table
az network vnet peering list --resource-group ExamRef-RG --vnet-name VNet2 -o table
```

Create a virtual network gateway and configure VNET to VNET connectivity

A virtual network gateway allows you to create connections from your virtual network to other networks. When creating a gateway, you must specify if it will be used for VPN connections or ExpressRoute connections. Virtual network gateways used for VPN connections are called a VPN gateways, while those used for ExpressRoute connections are called ExpressRoute gateways.

VPN gateways can be used to create VPN connections, either to on-premises networks or to other virtual networks. A VPN connection with an on-premises network is called a *site-to-site VPN*. These are discussed further in Skill 4.7. A VPN connection between two VNets is called a *VNet-to-VNet connection*.

Connecting virtual networks using VNet-to-VNet connections has several disadvantages over virtual network peering. The VPN gateways add additional cost and complexity. They also add network latency and reduce network bandwidth. In general, VNet peering should be used in preference to VNet-to-VNet connections. VNet-to-VNet connections, however, can be useful in scenarios where VNet peering is not suitable, such as when the additional security of end-to-end encryption is required.

A VNet-to-VNet connection is a type of site-to-site VPN connection, whereas a VPN gateway is used for both VPN endpoints. Therefore, it requires that a VPN gateway be deployed to both VNets.

VPN gateways can only be deployed to a dedicated gateway subnet within the VNet. A gateway subnet is a special type of subnet that can only be used for virtual network gateways. Under the hood, the VPN gateway is implemented using Azure virtual machines (these are not directly accessible and are managed for you). While the minimum size for the gateway subnet is a CIDR /29, the Microsoft-recommended best practice is to use a CIDR /27 address block to allow for future expansion.

VPN Gateways are available in several pricing tiers, or SKUs. The correct tier should be chosen based on the required network capacity, as shown in Table 4-5.

TABLE 4-5 Comparison of VPN gateway pricing tiers

SKU	Max VNet-to-VNet Connections	Max VNet-to-VNet Throughput
Basic	10	100 Mbps
VpnGw1 and VpnGw1Az	30	650 Mbps
VpnGw2 and VpnGw2Az	30	1 Gbps
VpnGw3 and VpnGw3Az	30	1.25 Gbps

> *NOTE* **RE-SIZING VPN GATEWAYS**
>
> You can resize a gateway between the VpnGw1, 2 and 3 tiers. However, you cannot resize a Basic tier gateway. The Basic tier is considered a legacy SKU and does not support all features.

Having created a gateway subnet and VPN gateway in each VNet, the VNets can be connected by creating VPN connections between these gateways. As with VNet peering, two connections must be made—one in each direction—and the virtual networks must have non-overlapping IP address ranges.

Creating a VNet-to-VNet connection between VNets automatically configures the necessary network routes. It also updates the VirtualNetwork service tag (explained in Skill 4.4) to include the IP address space from both VNets, so the default NSG rules will permit open connectivity between connected VNets. Connectivity between VNets can be restricted if necessary by modifying the NSGs.

For increased resilience to datacenter-level failures, virtual network gateways can be deployed to availability zones. This requires the use of dedicated SKUs, called VpnGw1Az, VpnGw2Az, and VpnGw3Az. Both zone-redundant and zone-specific deployment models are supported, and the choice is inferred from the associated public IP address rather than being specified explicitly as a gateway property.

Creating a VPN gateway and VNet-to-VNet connection using the Azure portal

The following steps capture the basic process of creating a VNet-to-VNet connection between two VNets: VNet2 and VNet3. This guide assumes these VNets have been created in advance

- Create gateway subnets on VNet2 and VNet3
- Provision VPN gateways on VNet 2 and VNet3
- Create a connection from the VPN gateway on VNet2 to the VPN gateway on VNet3
- Create a connection from the VPN gateway on VNet3 to the VPN gateway on VNet2

Using the portal, navigate to VNet2 and click the **Subnets** link under **Settings** to open the Subnets blade. Click the **+Gateway Subnet** button and assign an address space using a /27 CIDR. An example is shown in Figure 4-25; you may need to choose a different subnet address range based on the address range assigned to your VNet. Do not modify the other subnet settings.

FIGURE 4-25 Adding a Gateway Subnet to VNet2

Repeat this process to create a similar gateway subnet on VNet3. Once again, choose a /27 gateway subnet IP range within the available address space for VNet3.

Next, provision a VPN gateway for VNet2, as follows. From the Azure portal, click **+Create A Resource**, then click **Networking**, and then select **Virtual Network Gateway**. Complete the Create Virtual Network Gateway blade as follows:

- **Name**   VNet2-GW
- **Gateway type**   VPN
- **VPN Type**   Route-based
- **SKU**   VpnGw1
- **Virtual network**   VNet2 (you may need to set the correct location first)
- **First IP Configuration**   Create New, VNet2-GW-IP
- **Location**   <Same as VNet2>

Do not select the checkboxes for Enable Active-Active Mode or Configure BGP ASN. Figure 4-26 shows the completed gateway settings.

FIGURE 4-26 Creating the Azure VPN gateway for VNet2

Repeat this process to create a similar VPN gateway for VNet3.

The final step is to create the VPN connection between the VPN gateways. Two connections are required, one in each direction. Using the Azure portal, open the blade for the VNet2-GW VPN gateway, and click **Connections**. Then click **+Add** to open the Add Connection blade, and complete the settings as shown in Figure 4-27.

- **Name**   VNet2-to-VNet3
- **Connection type**   VNet-to-VNet
- **First virtual network gateway**   VNet2 (not editable)
- **Second virtual network gateway**   VNet3
- **Shared key (PSK)**   <Choose a secure, random string, and keep a note of it>

FIGURE 4-27   Creating the Connection from VNet2 to VNet3

Now navigate to the VNet3-GW VPN gateway blade and repeat the above process to create a second connection, from VNet3 to VNet2. Be sure to use the same shared key (PSK) as used when creating the first connection.

Both connections will be listed in the Azure portal on the Connections blade of both VPN gateways. After a short time, both should report their status as Connected, as shown in Figure 4-28.

NAME	STATUS	CONNECTION TYPE	PEER	
VNet2-to-VNet3	Connected	VNet-to-VNet	VNet3-GW	...
VNet3-to-VNet2	Connected	VNet-to-VNet	VNet3-GW	...

FIGURE 4-28 VPN connections with status Connected

Creating a VPN Gateway and VNet-to-VNet connection using Azure PowerShell

The process for creating VPN gateways and VNet-to-VNet connections using Azure PowerShell follows the same steps as used by the Azure Portal, like the following script demonstrates.

> **NOTE CREATING A GATEWAY SUBNET**
>
> When creating the gateway subnet, there is no special parameter or cmdlet name to denote that this is a gateway subnet rather than a normal subnet. The only distinction that identifies a gateway subnet is the subnet name, GatewaySubnet.

```
# Script to set up VPN gateways and VNet-to-VNet connection
# Assumes VNet2 and VNet3 already created
# with IP address ranges 10.2.0.0/16 and 10.3.0.0/16 respectively

# Name of resource group
$rg = 'ExamRef-RG'

# Create gateway subnets in VNet2 and VNet3
# Note: Gateway subnets are just normal subnets, with the name 'GatewaySubnet'
$vnet2 = Get-AzVirtualNetwork -Name VNet2 -ResourceGroupName $rg
$vnet2.Subnets += New-AzVirtualNetworkSubnetConfig -Name GatewaySubnet
-AddressPrefix 10.2.1.0/27
$vnet2 = Set-AzVirtualNetwork -VirtualNetwork $vnet2

$vnet3 = Get-AzVirtualNetwork -Name VNet3 -ResourceGroupName $rg
$vnet3.Subnets += New-AzVirtualNetworkSubnetConfig -Name GatewaySubnet
-AddressPrefix 10.3.1.0/27
$vnet3 = Set-AzVirtualNetwork -VirtualNetwork $vnet3

# Create VPN gateway in VNet2
$gwpip2    = New-AzPublicIpAddress -Name VNet2-GW-IP -ResourceGroupName $rg `
  -Location $vnet2.Location -AllocationMethod Dynamic

$gwsubnet2    = Get-AzVirtualNetworkSubnetConfig -Name 'GatewaySubnet' `
  -VirtualNetwork $vnet2

$gwipconf2 = New-AzVirtualNetworkGatewayIpConfig -Name GwIPConf2 `
  -Subnet $gwsubnet2 -PublicIpAddress $gwpip2
```

```
$vnet2gw = New-AzVirtualNetworkGateway -Name VNet2-GW -ResourceGroupName $rg `
  -Location $vnet2.Location -IpConfigurations $gwipconf2 -GatewayType Vpn `
  -VpnType RouteBased -GatewaySku VpnGw1

# Create VPN gateway in VNet3
$gwpip3 = New-AzPublicIpAddress -Name VNet3-GW-IP -ResourceGroupName $rg `
  -Location $vnet3.Location -AllocationMethod Dynamic

$gwsubnet3 = Get-AzVirtualNetworkSubnetConfig -Name 'GatewaySubnet' `
  -VirtualNetwork $vnet3

$gwipconf3 = New-AzVirtualNetworkGatewayIpConfig -Name GwIPConf3 `
  -Subnet $gwsubnet3 -PublicIpAddress $gwpip3

$vnet3gw = New-AzVirtualNetworkGateway -Name VNet3-GW -ResourceGroupName $rg `
  -Location $vnet3.Location -IpConfigurations $gwipconf3 -GatewayType Vpn `
  -VpnType RouteBased -GatewaySku VpnGw1

# Create Connections
New-AzVirtualNetworkGatewayConnection -Name Vnet2-to-VNet3 `
  -ResourceGroupName $rg `
  -Location $vnet2.Location `
  -VirtualNetworkGateway1 $vnet2gw `
  -VirtualNetworkGateway2 $vnet3gw `
  -ConnectionType VNet2VNet `
  -SharedKey "secretkey123"

New-AzVirtualNetworkGatewayConnection -Name Vnet3-to-VNet2 `
  -ResourceGroupName $rg `
  -Location $vnet3.Location `
  -VirtualNetworkGateway1 $vnet3gw `
  -VirtualNetworkGateway2 $vnet2gw `
  -ConnectionType VNet2VNet `
  -SharedKey "secretkey123"
```

Creating a VPN gateway and VNet-to-VNet connection using the Azure CLI

The process for creating VPN gateways and VNet-to-VNet connections using Azure PowerShell follows the same steps as used by the Azure Portal, as the following script demonstrates.

Once again, the gateway subnet is created simply by specifying the name GatewaySubnet when creating a normal subnet.

In this case, the public IP address required by the VPN gateway must be created beforehand, rather than being created implicitly when creating the gateway.

```
# Create VPN gateways and VNet-to-VNet connection between VNet1 and VNet2
in resource group ExamRef-RG-CLI
# Assumes VNet2 and VNet3 already created,
# with IP address ranges 10.2.0.0/16 and 10.3.0.0/16
# and locations NorthEurope and WestEurope, respectively
```

```
# Create gateway subnets in VNet2 and VNet3
az network vnet subnet create --name GatewaySubnet --vnet-name VNet2
--resource-group ExamRef-RG-CLI --address-prefixes 10.2.1.0/27
az network vnet subnet create --name GatewaySubnet --vnet-name VNet3
--resource-group ExamRef-RG-CLI --address-prefixes 10.3.1.0/27

# Create public IP addresses for use by VPN gateways
az network public-ip create --name VNet2-GW-IP --resource-group
ExamRef-RG-CLI --location NorthEurope
az network public-ip create --name VNet3-GW-IP --resource-group
ExamRef-RG-CLI --location WestEurope

# Create VPN gateways in VNet2 and VNet 3
az network vnet-gateway create --name VNet2-GW --resource-group
ExamRef-RG-CLI --gateway-type vpn --sku VpnGw1 --vpn-type RouteBased
--vnet VNet2 --public-ip-addresses VNet2-GW-IP --location NorthEurope

az network vnet-gateway create --name VNet3-GW --resource-group
ExamRef-RG-CLI --gateway-type vpn --sku VpnGw1 --vpn-type RouteBased
--vnet VNet3 --public-ip-addresses VNet3-GW-IP --location WestEurope

# Create connections between VPN gateways
az network vpn-connection create --name VNet2-to-VNet3 --resource-group
ExamRef-RG-CLI --vnet-gateway1 VNet2-GW --vnet-gateway2 VNet3-GW
--shared-key secretkey123 --location NorthEurope

az network vpn-connection create --name VNet3-to-VNet2 --resource-group
ExamRef-RG-CLI --vnet-gateway1 VNet3-GW --vnet-gateway2 VNet2-GW
--shared-key secretkey123 --location WestEurope
```

Verify virtual network connectivity

There are many reasons why a connection between VNets might not work as expected. For example:

- A peering connection may not have enabled the Allow Virtual Network Connectivity option.

- Network security groups may be configured to block the traffic.

- The peering or VNet-to-VNet connection may not have been established successfully.

- Network settings (e.g. firewall settings) within the VMs may be obstructing traffic.

- User-defined routes (UDRs) may be misconfigured to route traffic incorrectly.

- A network virtual appliance (NVA) used to bridge traffic between spokes in a hub-and-spoke network architecture may be misconfigured.

There are several ways to verify connections between VNets:

- The simplest way is to check if VMs in each VNet can communicate with each other, for example by trying to create an RDP or SSH connection between them.

- Verify the status of the peerings connections or VNet-to-VNet connections.

Network troubleshooting, including troubleshooting VPN connections, is covered in greater depth in Skill 4.6.

Skill 4.3: Configure name resolution

Humans work with names, but computers prefer IP addresses. Fundamentally, DNS is about mapping names to IP addresses; to make name-based rather than IP-based networking possible. Simplifying somewhat, a client makes a DNS query containing a domain name, and receives a response containing the IP address for that name.

Almost everywhere you look, you'll see DNS scenarios. From browsing the web, to smartphone apps, to IoT devices, to database lookups within an application, DNS is everywhere. Because DNS is so universal, it is especially important that DNS services offer exceptionally high availability and low latency, since the impact of DNS failures or delays will be widespread.

Azure DNS provides a high performance, highly-available DNS service in Azure. It can be used for two separate DNS scenarios:

1. Providing Internet-facing name resolution for a public DNS domain by hosting the corresponding DNS zone.

2. Providing internal name resolution between virtual machines within or between virtual networks.

In addition, Azure provides the ability to control which DNS servers are configured on your virtual machines, allowing you to use your own DNS servers instead of the Azure-provided service.

> **This section covers how to:**
> - Configure Azure DNS
> - Configure custom DNS settings
> - Configure private DNS zones

Configure Azure DNS

This section describes how Azure DNS is configured to host Internet-facing domains. We start with a summary of how the domain name system works, since understanding DNS is a prerequisite to understanding Azure DNS.

How DNS Works

To properly understand the various DNS services and features available in Azure, it is first necessary to understand how the domain name system works. In particular, it is important to understand the different roles played by recursive and authoritative DNS servers, and how a DNS query is routed to the correct DNS name servers using DNS delegation.

First, it's important to understand the distinction between a domain name, and a DNS zone. The Internet-facing domain name system is a single global name hierarchy. A domain name is just a name within that hierarchy. Owning a domain name gives you the legal right to control the DNS records within that name, and any sub-domains of that name.

You purchase a domain name from a domain name registrar. The registrar then lets you control which name servers receive the DNS queries for that domain, by letting you configure the NS records for the domain.

A DNS zone is the representation of a domain name in an *authoritative DNS server*. It contains the collection of DNS records for a given domain name. The service hosting the DNS zone lets you manage the DNS records within the zone, and hosts the data on authoritative name servers, which answers DNS queries with DNS responses based on the configured DNS records.

In Azure, you can purchase domain names using the App Service Domains service. DNS zone hosting is provided by Azure DNS.

The DNS settings on the user's device point to a *recursive DNS server*, also sometimes known as a *local DNS service* (or LDNS), or simply as a *DNS resolver*. The recursive DNS service is typically hosted by your company (if you're at work) or by your ISP (if you're at home). There are also public recursive DNS services available, such as Google's 8.8.8.8 service. The recursive DNS service doesn't host any DNS records, but it allows your device to off-load most of the work associated with resolving DNS queries.

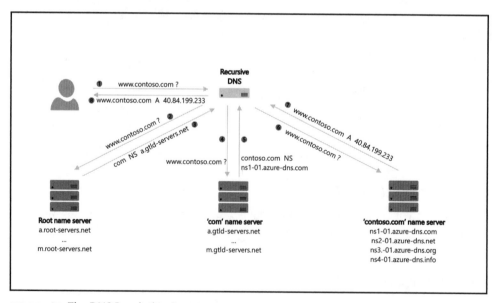

FIGURE 4-29 The DNS Resolution Process

To understand the role of recursive and authoritative DNS servers, consider Figure 4-29, which describes the DNS resolution process for a single DNS query, www.contoso.com:

1. Your PC makes a DNS query to its locally-configured recursive DNS server. This query is simply a packet sent over UDP port 53, although TCP can also be used (typically when responses are too big to fit in a UDP packet).

2. Let's assume the recursive DNS server has just been switched on, so there is nothing in its cache. It passes the query to one of the root name servers (the addresses of the root name servers are pre-configured). The root name servers are authoritative name servers—they host the actual DNS records for the root zone. A zone is simply the data representing a node in the DNS hierarchy.

3. The root name servers don't know anything about the contoso.com DNS zone. They do, however, know where you can find the com zone. So, they return a DNS record of type NS, which tells the recursive DNS server where to find the com zone.

4. The recursive server tries again, this time calling the com name servers. Again, these are authoritative name servers, this time for the com zone.

5. These name servers don't recognize www.contoso.com, but they do have NS records that define where the contoso.com DNS zone can be found.

6. The recursive server tries again, this time calling the authoritative contoso.com name servers.

7. These servers *are* authoritative for the contoso.com DNS zone. And, there is a record on these servers matching the www record name. The server does recognize the www.contoso.com query name and returns the A record response that maps this name to an IP address.

8. The recursive server then returns this result back to the client.

The recursive DNS server can also follow a chain of CNAME records (which map one DNS name to another name). And the recursive DNS server also caches the responses it receives, so that it can respond more quickly next time. The duration of the cache is determined by the TTL (time-to-live) property of each DNS record.

The domain name system is a distributed system, where one set of servers can refer queries to another set using NS records. The process we've just seen to map a query name to a result perhaps via a long chain of authoritative DNS servers is called DNS *name resolution*.

The NS records tell clients on the Internet where to find the name servers for a given DNS zone. The NS records for a DNS zone are configured in the parent zone, and a copy of the records is also present in the child zone. Setting up these NS records is called *delegating* a DNS domain.

A *fully-qualified domain name* (FQDN) is a domain name containing all components all the way up to the root zone. Strictly speaking, a fully-qualified name ends with a "." (i.e. www-dot-contoso-dot-com-DOT), which represents the root zone, although by convention the trailing "." is often omitted.

Reverse DNS is the ability to map an IP address to a name (as opposed to name to IP address, which is what normal DNS provides). Some applications use reverse DNS as a weak form of authentication. For example, it's commonly used in email spam-scoring algorithms.

Reverse DNS lookups use a completely independent DNS hierarchy from the forward lookups. The reverse lookup for www.contoso.com does not sit in the contoso.com zone. It instead sits in a separate DNS zone hierarchy based on reversed IP addresses. For example, suppose www.contoso.com resolves to IP address 1.2.3.4. Then the reverse lookup for the IP address 1.2.3.4 will typically be a record named 4 in the DNS zone 3.2.1.in-addr.arpa, giving a FQDN 4.3.2.1.in-addr.arpa (notice the reversed IP address.)

Reverse DNS lookup zones are controlled by whomever owns the IP subnet. The reverse DNS lookup zone for an IP block you own can be hosted in Azure DNS. Public IP addresses in Azure reside in Microsoft-owned IP blocks, and hence the reverse DNS lookups use Microsoft-managed reverse DNS lookup zones.

There's nothing in the domain name system to ensure the reverse lookup maps to the same name as was used in the forward lookup. That's achieved simply by the correct configuration in both forward and reverse lookup zones.

DNS services in Azure

There are several DNS-related services and features in Azure—an overview of each is given below. The first three items are Azure services, which you consume by creating service-specific resources that you will be billed for. The remaining three items are Azure features, which you configure using settings on other resource types, such as a virtual network, public IP address, or network interface.

- **Azure DNS**   Allows you to host your DNS domains in Azure. It provides the ability to create and manage the DNS records for your domain and provides name servers, which answer DNS queries for your domain from other users on the Internet.

    Azure DNS also supports private DNS zones, which are used for intranet-based name resolution for VM to VM lookups, including support for some scenarios not supported by the Azure-provided DNS service, which we'll come to shortly. Private DNS zones are currently in preview.

- **Azure Traffic Manager**   An intelligent DNS service that uses DNS to implement global traffic management. Where Azure DNS always provides the same DNS response to any given DNS query, in Azure Traffic Manager the same query may result in one of several possible responses, depending on a number of factors which you control, such as where the end-user is located or which of your service endpoints is currently available. This enables you to route traffic intelligently between Azure regions, or between Azure deployments and on-premises deployments.

    Understanding Traffic Manager is out of scope for the AZ-103 exam.

- **App service domains**   llows purchasing of domain names, which can then be hosted in Azure DNS. This service is integrated with Azure App Service, but can be used for any domain registration, even if App Service is not being used.

- **Azure-provided DNS**   Sometimes called Internal DNS, it allows the VMs in your virtual network to find each other, using DNS queries based on the hostname of each VM. The DNS queries are internal (private) to the virtual network.

- **Recursive DNS**   A service provided by Azure for DNS name resolution from your Azure VMs or other Azure services. You can also configure your VMs to use your own DNS server instead. This is sometimes informally called bring your own DNS. This is common when joining your VMs to a domain controller.

- **Reverse DNS**   Provides the ability to configure the reverse DNS lookup for an Azure-assigned public IP address. (Reverse DNS lookup zones for IP blocks you own can be hosted in Azure DNS).

Creating and delegating a DNS Zone to Azure DNS

A DNS zone is a resource in Azure DNS. Creating a DNS zone resource allocates authoritative DNS name servers to host the DNS records for that zone. Azure DNS can then be used to manage those DNS records. DNS queries directed to those DNS name servers receive a DNS response based on the DNS records configured at that time.

You do not have to own the corresponding domain name before creating a DNS zone in Azure DNS. You can create a DNS zone with any name, except for names on the public suffix list (see *https://publicsuffix.org/*). You can also create more than one DNS zone resource with the same DNS zone name, so long as they are in different resource groups. In this case, the DNS zones will be allocated to separate DNS name servers, so no conflict arises.

You can test your DNS records by directing DNS queries directly to the assigned DNS name servers for your zone. For general use, however, your DNS zone should be delegated from the parent zone. This requires you to own the corresponding domain name.

Before you can delegate your DNS zone to Azure DNS, you first need to know the names of the name servers assigned to your zone. These can be obtained using the Azure portal, PowerShell, or CLI after the DNS zone resource has been created. You can't predict in advance which name server pool will be assigned to your DNS zone. You need to create the DNS zone, and then check.

The assigned name servers will vary between zones, so if you're setting up multiple zones in Azure DNS you need to check the name servers on each one. Don't assume that the name servers will be the same across all your zones.

Each domain name registrar has their own DNS management tool allowing you to set the name server (NS) records for a domain. In the registrar's DNS management page, edit the NS records and replace the NS records with the ones Azure DNS assigned.

When delegating a domain to Azure DNS, you must use the name server names provided by Azure DNS. You should always use all four name server names, regardless of the name of your domain. Domain delegation does not require the name server name to match your domain name.

Azure DNS treats child zone as entirely separate zones. Delegating a child zone therefore follows the same process as delegating the parent zone:

1. Create the child zone resource.

2. Identify the name servers for the child zone. These will be different to the name servers assigned to the parent zone.

3. Create NS records in the parent zone to delegate the child zone. The name of the NS records should be the child zone name (excluding the parent zone name suffix), and the RDATA in the NS records should be the child zone name servers.

Managing DNS records in Azure DNS

Each record in the domain name system includes the following properties:

- **Name** The name of the DNS record is combined with the name of the DNS zone, to form the fully-qualified domain name (FQDN). For example, the record www in zone contoso.com corresponds to the FQDN www.contoso.com.

- **Type** The type of DNS record determines what data is associated with the record and what purpose it is used for. A list of record types supported by Azure DNS is provided in Table 4-6.

- **TTL** The TTL (or Time-to-Live) tells recursive DNS servers how long a DNS record should be cached.

- **RDATA** The data returned for each DNS record. The type of data returned depends on the DNS record type. For example, an A record will return an IPv4 address, whereas a CNAME record returns another domain name.

The collection of records in a DNS zone with the same name and the same type is called a *resource record set* (or *RRSet*, or in Azure DNS, simply a *record set*). Records in Azure DNS are managed using record sets. Record sets are a child resource of the DNS zone, and can contain up to 20 individual DNS records. The name, type and TTL are configured on the record set, and the RDATA is configured on each DNS record within the record set.

To create a DNS record set at the root (or *apex*) of a DNS zone, use the record set name "@". For example, the record set named "@" in the zone contoso.com will resolve against queries for contoso.com. You can also use "*" in the record set name to create wildcard records (subject to DNS wildcard matching rules).

Azure DNS supports all commonly-used DNS record types. The full list of supported record types, together with a description of each, is provided in Table 4-6.

TABLE 4-6 DNS Record Types in Azure DNS

DNS Record Type	Remarks
A	Used to map a name to an IPv4 address.
AAAA	Used to map a name to an IPv6 address.
CAA	Used to specify which certificate authorities can issue certificates for a domain. Note that CAA records are not currently available in the Azure portal, so they must be configured using the Azure CLI or Azure PowerShell.
CNAME	Provides a mapping from one DNS name to another. The DNS standards do not allow CNAME records at the zone apex. In addition, you cannot create a CNAME record with the same name as a record of any other record type, and CNAME record sets only support a single DNS record rather than a list of records. These are DNS RFC constraints, not Azure DNS limitations.
MX	Used for mail server configuration.
NS	An NS record set at the zone apex containing the name servers for the DNS zone is required by the DNS standards. This is created for you when the DNS zone is created. It can be edited, for example to add additional records when co-hosting a DNS zone with more than one provider, but not deleted. You can create additional NS record sets to delegate child zones.
PTR	Used for reverse DNS lookups in reverse lookup zones.
SOA	An SOA record is required at the apex of every zone. This is created and deleted with the DNS zone resource.
SRV	SRV records are used for service discovery for a wide range of services, from Kerberos to Minecraft to the Session Initiation Protocol used for Internet telephony. Note that the Service and Protocol parameters are specified as part of the record set name, for example: _service._protocol.media.contoso.com. Some DNS services prompt you to enter these values separately, then merge them to form the record set name. With Azure DNS, you need to specify them as part of the record set name, but they are not entered separately.
TXT	Used for a wide range of applications, including email Sender Policy Framework (SPF).

> **NOTE SPF RECORDS**
>
> Sender Policy Framework (SPF) records are used to identify legitimate mail servers for a domain and help prevent spam. The SPF record type was deprecated by RFC7208, which states that the TXT record type should be used for SPF records.

Alias records

Azure DNS offers integration with other services hosted in Azure via Alias records.

With conventional DNS records, you explicitly specify the target, such as the IP address of an A record. If the IP address changes, you need to update the DNS record accordingly.

Alias records allow you to define the target of the DNS record *implicitly*, by referencing another Azure resource. The value of the DNS record is populated automatically based on the resource it references and is updated automatically if that resource changes.

Alias records can reference three different resource types:

- An A or AAAA record can reference a public IP address, of type IPv4 or IPv6 respectively

- A, AAAA, or CNAME record can reference a Traffic Manager profile. This exposes the dynamic, traffic-managed name resolution of the Traffic Manager directly within a record in your DNS domain. Prior to this feature, you had to create a CNAME record from your domain to a record in the trafficmanager.net domain provided by Azure Traffic Manager.

- An A, AAAA or CNAME record can also reference another record in the same DNS zone. This lets you create synchronized records with ease.

Alias records are a very useful way to address a number of scenarios.

First, Alias records allow you to avoid orphaned DNS records. A common problem with DNS systems is that records are not cleaned up when the services they reference are deleted. The DNS record is left dangling. With Alias records, the DNS record no longer resolves once the underlying service is deleted.

Second, as we have already discussed, by updating automatically when underlying resources change, Alias records reduce your management overhead and help you avoid accidental application downtime.

Third, since Alias records enable you to avoid using a CNAME record when using a vanity domain name with Azure Traffic Manager, they enable you to implement a traffic-managed record at the apex of your domain.

Creating DNS zones and DNS records using the Azure portal

To create a DNS zone, click **+Create A Resource**, then **Networking**, then click **DNS Zone** to open the **Create DNS Zone** blade. Fill in the blade by specifying the DNS domain name as the DNS zone resource name, and selecting your resource group, as shown in Figure 4-30.

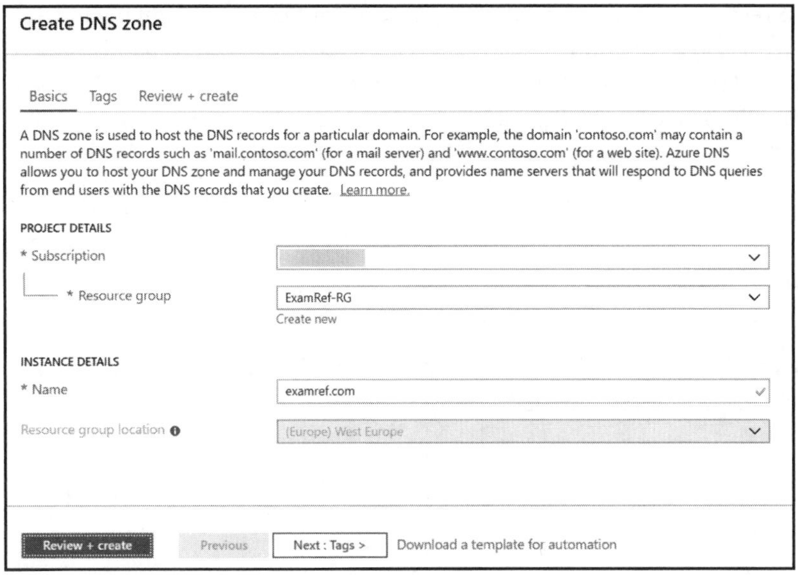

Create DNS zone
Basics
Tags
Review + create
A DNS zone is used to host the DNS records for a particular domain. For example, the domain 'contoso.com' may contain a number of DNS records such as 'mail.contoso.com' (for a mail server) and 'www.contoso.com' (for a web site). Azure DNS allows you to host your DNS zone and manage your DNS records, and provides name servers that will respond to DNS queries from end users with the DNS records that you create. Learn more.
PROJECT DETAILS
* Subscription
* Resource group
ExamRef-RG
Create new
INSTANCE DETAILS
* Name
examref.com
Resource group location
(Europe) West Europe
Review + create
Previous
Next : Tags >
Download a template for automation

FIGURE 4-30 Creating a DNS zone using the Azure portal

> ***NOTE*** **DNS ZONES AND AZURE REGION**
>
> **When creating a DNS zone, the location field only specifies the resource group location. It does not apply to the DNS zone resource itself, which is global rather than regional.**

Once the DNS zone has been created, open the DNS zone blade. The Azure DNS name servers assigned to the zone are listed in the essentials panel, as highlighted in Figure 4-31.

examref.com
DNS zone
Search (Ctrl+/)
Overview
Activity log
Access control (IAM)
Tags
Diagnose and solve problems
Record set
Move
Delete zone
Refresh
Resource group (change)
examref-rg
Subscription (change)
Visual Studio Enterprise – MPN
Subscription ID
41811f87-4f0d-44d0-bec9-a9b162257403
Name server 1
ns1-03.azure-dns.com.
Name server 2
ns2-03.azure-dns.net.
Name server 3
ns3-03.azure-dns.org.
Name server 4
ns4-03.azure-dns.info.

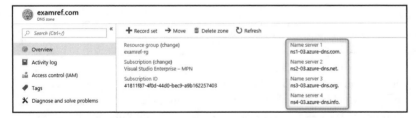

FIGURE 4-31 The DNS zone blade, highlighting the Azure DNS name servers assigned to this zone

To set up DNS delegation for the DNS zone, these name servers must be listed in the corresponding NS records in the parent zone. If the domain name was purchased using the Azure App Service Domains service, this will be done automatically. Otherwise, this must be configured at the DNS registrar where the domain name was purchased.

To create a DNS record in a new record set, click **+Record Set** to open the **Add Record Set** blade. If there is an existing record with the same name and type as the record you wish to create, you should instead click on the existing record set and add the new record there. To create a pair of A records with name www (giving the fully-qualified domain name www.examref.com), fill in the blade with the following values, as shown in Figure 4-32.

- **Name** www
- **Type** A
- **Alias record set** No
- **TTL** 1 hour (or choose your own value)
- **IP Addresses** Enter A record IP addresses, one for each DNS record in the record set.

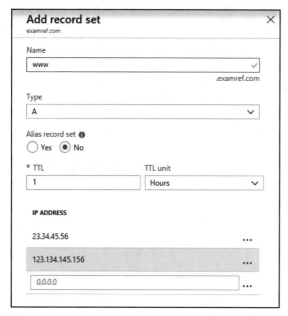

FIGURE 4-32 The Add Record Set blade

Suppose now you wish to create a DNS record at the zone apex (so the fully-qualified domain name is simply the DNS zone name examref.com), pointing to a dynamically-allocated public IP address. Click **+Add Record Set** again and complete the **Add Record Set** blade with the following settings, as shown in Figure 4-33.

- **Name** @ (this is a DNS convention for records at the zone apex)
- **Type** A
- **Alias record set** Yes
- **Choose subscription** Choose the subscription containing the public IP address
- **Azure resource** Choose the public IP address resource
- **TTL** 1 hour (or choose your own value)

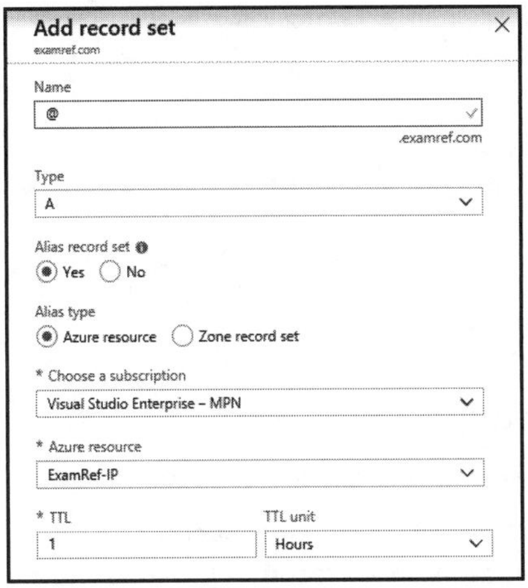

FIGURE 4-33 The Add Record Set blade for an Alias record set

Creating DNS zones and DNS records using Azure PowerShell

DNS Zones and record sets are created using the New-AzDnsZone and New-AzDnsRecordSet cmdlets, respectively.

You can specify DNS records when creating the record set, or you can create an empty record set and add DNS records afterward, using the Get-AzDnsRecordSet, Add-AzDnsRecordConfig, and Set-AzDnsRecordSet cmdlets.

You can use a similar sequence to remove DNS records from an existing record set, using the Get-AzDnsRecordSet, Remove-AzDnsRecordConfig, and Set-AzDnsRecordSet cmdlets. Note that when removing a record, you must specify all RDATA fields for the resource type and they must all be an exact match to an existing record.

```
# Create a DNS zone
New-AzDnsZone -Name examref.com -ResourceGroupName ExamRef-RG

# Create a record set containing a single record
New-AzDnsRecordSet -Name www -RecordType A `
        -ZoneName examref.com `
        -ResourceGroupName ExamRef-RG `
        -Ttl 3600 `
        -DnsRecords (New-AzDnsRecordConfig -IPv4Address "1.2.3.4")

# Create a record set at the zone apex containing multiple records
$records = @()
$records += New-AzDnsRecordConfig -IPv4Address "1.2.3.4"
$records += New-AzDnsRecordConfig -IPv4Address "5.6.7.8"
New-AzDnsRecordSet -Name '@' -RecordType A `
        -ZoneName examref.com `
        -ResourceGroupName ExamRef-RG `
        -Ttl 3600 `
        -DnsRecords $records
```

```
# Add a new record to and remove an existing record from an existing record set
$recordset = Get-AzDnsRecordSet -Name www -RecordType A `
          -ZoneName examref.com `
          -ResourceGroupName ExamRef-RG
Add-AzDnsRecordConfig -RecordSet $recordset -IPv4Address "5.6.7.8"
Remove-AzDnsRecordConfig -RecordSet $recordset -IPv4Address "1.2.3.4"
Set-AzDnsRecordSet -RecordSet $recordset

# View records
Get-AzDnsRecordSet -ZoneName examref.com -ResourceGroupName ExamRef-RG
```

Creating DNS Zones and DNS Records using the Azure CLI

To create a DNS zone using the Azure CLI, use the `az network dns zone create` command.

To manage DNS records, first create an empty record set using the `az network dns record-set A create` command. In this case, A represents the DNS A record type—substitute a different record type as required.

DNS records are then added and removed using the `az network dns record-set a add-record` and `az network dns record-set a remove-record` commands (again, substituting the required record type).

DNS records can be listed using the `az network dns record-set list` command, which returns a list of records of all record types.

```
# Create a DNS zone
az network dns zone create --name examref.com --resource-group ExamRef-RG

# Create an empty record set of type 'A'
az network dns record-set a create --name www --zone-name examref.com
--resource-group ExamRef-RG --ttl 3600

# Add A records to the above record set
az network dns record-set a add-record --record-set-name www
--zone-name examref.com --resource-group ExamRef-RG --ipv4-address 1.2.3.4
az network dns record-set a add-record --record-set-name www
--zone-name examref.com --resource-group ExamRef-RG --ipv4-address 5.6.7.8

# Remove an A record from the record set
az network dns record-set a remove-record --record-set-name www
--zone-name examref.com --resource-group ExamRef-RG --ipv4-address 1.2.3.4

# View records
az network dns record-set list --zone-name examref.com
--resource-group ExamRef-RG -o table
```

Importing and Exporting DNS zone files using the Azure CLI

A DNS zone file is a text file that contains details of every DNS record in the zone. It follows a standard format, making it suitable for transferring DNS records between DNS systems. Using a zone file is a quick, reliable, and convenient way to transfer a DNS zone into or out of Azure DNS.

Azure DNS supports importing and exporting zone files by using the `az network dns zone import` and `az network dns zone export` commands. Since zone files are processed client-side in the CLI itself, zone file import and export are not available via any other Azure DNS tools, such as PowerShell, the Azure portal, or even the Azure DNS SDKs or REST API.

Importing a zone file will create a new zone in Azure DNS if one does not already exist. If the zone already exists, the record sets in the zone file are merged with the existing record sets.

SOA parameters are taken from the imported zone file, except for the host property, for which the value assigned by Azure DNS is retained. Similarly, for the NS record set at the zone apex, which contains the Azure DNS name servers assigned to the zone, the TTL is always taken from the imported zone file, but the name server names are taken from the zone in Azure DNS.

```
# Export a DNS zone file
az network dns zone export --name examref.com --resource-group ExamRef-RG --file-name
"examref.com.txt"

# Import a DNS zone file (to different resource group)
az network dns zone import --name examref.com --resource-group ExamRef2-RG --file-name
"examref.com.txt"
```

Configure custom DNS settings

When a virtual machine connects to a virtual network, it receives its IP address via DHCP. As part of that DHCP exchange, DNS settings are also configured in the VM. By default, VMs are configured to use Azure's recursive DNS servers. These provide name resolution for Internet-hosted domains, plus private VM-to-VM name resolution within a virtual network.

The hostname of the VM is used to create a DNS record mapping to the private IP address of the VM. You specify the hostname—which is simply the VM name—when you create the virtual machine. Azure specifies the DNS suffix, using a value that is unique to the virtual network. These suffixes end with internal.cloudapp.net. The hostname and DNS suffix together form the unique fully-qualified domain name.

Name resolution for these DNS records is private—they can only be resolved from within the virtual network. The DNS suffix is configured as a lookup suffix within each VM, so names can be resolved between VMs within the virtual network using the hostname only.

This built-in DNS service uses the IP address: 168.63.129.16. This is a special static IP address that is reserved by the platform for this purpose. This IP provides both the authoritative DNS service for Azure-provided DNS as well as Azure's recursive DNS service, which is used to resolve Internet DNS names from Azure VMs.

Bring your own DNS

Alternatively, you can configure your own DNS settings, which will be configured on the VMs instead during the DHCP exchange. This enables you to specify your own DNS servers, either in Azure or running on-premises. With your own DNS servers, you can support any DNS scenario, including scenarios not supported by the Azure-provided service. Example scenarios requiring you to use your own DNS servers include name resolution between VMs in different virtual networks, name resolution between on-premises resources and Azure virtual machines, reverse DNS lookup of internal IP addresses, and name resolution for non-Internet-facing domains, such as domains associated with Active Directory.

You should not specify your own DNS settings within the VM itself, since the platform is then unaware of the settings you have chosen. Instead, Azure provides configuration options within the virtual network settings. These DNS server settings are at the virtual network level, and apply to all VMs in the virtual network.

You can also specify VM-specific DNS server settings within each network interface. This takes precedence over settings at the virtual network level. Where multiple VMs are deployed in an availability set, setting DNS servers at the network interface, all VMs in the availability set are updated. The DNS servers applied are the union of the network interface-level DNS servers from across the availability set.

> *NOTE* **DNS NAME SERVER SETTINGS**
>
> Custom DNS settings can be configured at the VNet level, and the network interface level, but not at the subnet level. To use specific settings for an individual subnet, you must configure those settings on each network interface in the subnet.

You can use these DNS settings to direct your VMs' DNS queries to any DNS servers you choose. They can point to IP addresses of on-premises servers, such as an Active Directory Domain Controller or network appliance, a DNS service running in an Azure Virtual Machine, or anywhere else on the Internet.

If you use your own DNS servers, those servers will need to offer a recursive DNS service, otherwise name resolution for Internet domains from your virtual machines will break. If you point the DNS settings directly at an Internet-based recursive DNS service, such as Google 8.8.8.8, then you will not be able to perform VM-to-VM lookups.

> *NOTE* **RESTART VIRTUAL MACHINES WHEN CHANGING DNS SETTINGS**
>
> If you make changes to the DNS settings at the virtual network level, any affected virtual machines must restart to pick up the new settings. If you make changes to DNS settings and the network interface level, the affected VM (or VMs across the availability set, if used) will restart automatically to pick up the new settings.

One challenge when using your own DNS servers is that you will need to register each VM in your DNS service. To do this, you can configure the DNS service to accept Dynamic DNS queries, which the VM will send when it boots. This allows the VMs to register with the DNS server automatically. A problem with this approach is that the DNS suffix in the Dynamic DNS query must match the DNS zone name configured on the DNS server, and Azure does not support configuring the DNS suffix via the Azure platform settings. As a workaround, you can configure the correct DNS suffix within each VM yourself, using a start-up script.

Configure custom DNS settings using the Azure portal

To configure the DNS servers on a VNet, open the virtual network blade, and then click on **DNS Servers** under **Settings**, as seen in Figure 4-34. You can then enter the DNS servers you wish this VM to use. After saving your changes, you need to restart the VMs in the VNet to pick up the change.

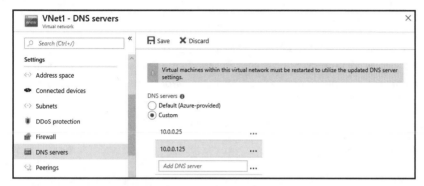

FIGURE 4-34 Custom DNS servers for a virtual network configured using the Portal

The steps to configure the DNS servers on an individual VM are similar. Open the blade for the VM's network interface, and then click on **DNS Servers** under **Settings**, as seen in Figure 4-35. You can then enter the DNS servers you wish this VM to use. Note that VMs in an availability set will adopt the union of DNS servers from network interfaces across the availability set. After saving your changes, your VM (or VMs in the availability set) will automatically restart to pick up the change.

FIGURE 4-35 Custom DNS servers for a network interface configured using the Portal

Configure custom DNS settings using Azure PowerShell

To configure custom virtual network DNS settings when creating a virtual network using Azure PowerShell, use the DNSServer parameter of the New-AzVirtualNetwork cmdlet.

```
# Create a virtual network with custom DNS settings
New-AzVirtualNetwork -Name VNet1 `
  -ResourceGroupName ExamRef-RG `
  -Location "North Europe" `
  -AddressPrefix 10.1.0.0/16 `
  -DNSServer 10.0.0.4,10.0.0.5 `
  -Subnet (New-AzVirtualNetworkSubnetConfig `
    -Name Default `
    -AddressPrefix 10.1.0.0/24)
```

To change the custom DNS settings on an existing VNet, use the Get-AzVirtualNetwork cmdlet to create a local object representing the VNet. Modify the DNS settings locally on this object, then commit your changes using the Set-AzVirtualNetwork cmdlet. Existing VMs must be restarted to pick up the change.

```
# Modify the DNS server configuration of an existing VNet
$vnet = Get-AzVirtualNetwork -Name VNet1 `
  -ResourceGroupName ExamRef-RG

$vnet.DhcpOptions.DnsServers.Clear()
$vnet.DhcpOptions.DnsServers.Add("10.10.200.1")
$vnet.DhcpOptions.DnsServers.Add("10.10.200.2")

Set-AzVirtualNetwork -VirtualNetwork $vnet

# Restart the VMs in the VNet to pick up the DNS change (example for 1 VM)
$vm = Get-AzVM -Name VNet1-VM -ResourceGroupName ExamRef-RG
Restart-AzVM -Id $vm.Id
```

When creating a virtual machine using Azure PowerShell, there is no option to specify the DNS settings. To change the custom DNS settings on the network interface of an existing VM, use the Get-AzNetworkInterface cmdlet to create a local object representing the network interface. Modify the DNS settings locally on this object, then commit your changes using the Set-AzNetworkInterface cmdlet. This will cause the VM (or VMs in the availability set) to restart automatically to pick up the change.

```
# Update the DNS settings on a network interface
$nic = Get-AzNetworkInterface `
      -Name VM1-NIC `
      -ResourceGroupName ExamRef-RG

$nic.DnsSettings.DnsServers.Clear()
$nic.DnsSettings.DnsServers.Add("8.8.8.8")
$nic.DnsSettings.DnsServers.Add("8.8.4.4")

# Commit the DNS change. This will cause VM (or VMs in Availability Set) to restart
Set-AzNetworkInterface -NetworkInterface $nic
```

Configure custom DNS settings using the Azure CLI

Use the dns-servers parameter to specify custom DNS servers when creating a virtual network using the az network vnet create command.

```
# Create a virtual network using custom name servers (uses default subnet)
az network vnet create --name VNet1 --resource-group ExamRef-RG --address-prefixes
10.0.0.0/16 --dns-servers 8.8.8.8 8.8.4.4
```

To modify the DNS server configuration on an existing VNet, use the az network vnet update command. Use the dns-servers parameter to specify custom DNS settings, and the remove parameter to remove the custom DNS servers and revert to the Azure-provided DNS defaults. VMs must be restarted to pick up the change.

```
# Set custom DNS servers on a VNet
az network vnet update --name VNet1 --resource-group ExamRef-RG --dns-servers 10.0.0.254
```

```
# Remove custom DNS servers from a VNet
az network vnet update --name VNet1 --resource-group ExamRef-RG
--remove DHCPOptions.DNSServers
```

To modify the DNS server configuration on an existing VM, use the az network nic update command. NIC-level DNS settings are aggregated across availability sets, and VMs must be restarted to pick up the change.

```
# Set custom DNS servers on a NIC
az network nic update --name VM1-NIC --resource-group ExamRef-RG
--dns-servers 8.8.8.8 8.8.4.4
```

Configure private DNS zones

In addition to supporting Internet-facing DNS domains, Azure DNS also supports private DNS domains as a Preview feature. This provides an alternative approach to name resolution within and between virtual networks.

By using private DNS zones, you can use your own custom domain names, including DNS suffix, rather than the Azure-provided DNS suffix, without the overhead or complexity of running your own DNS servers.

The service supports automatic registration of VMs into the private zone, but only from a single virtual network, called the *registration VNet*. This must be registered with the DNS zone before any VMs are created.

If you want to resolve VM names from multiple virtual networks, the VMs in any other networks must be registered with the service manually (or via a custom automation). Name resolution between VNets is independent of connectivity between VNets, so peering your virtual networks or setting up a VNet-to-VNet connection is not required.

Name resolution is supported from up to 10 virtual networks. These are called *resolution VNets*. The zone name is not registered with the VMs as a DNS search suffix, so you will need to register it yourself or use fully-qualified domain names in your DNS queries.

Create private DNS zones using Azure PowerShell or the Azure CLI

As a preview feature, there are several limitations. Most notably, you cannot configure private DNS zones using the Azure portal—you need to use Azure PowerShell or the Azure CLI.

With Azure PowerShell, specify the ZoneType Private parameter to create a private DNS zone with the New-AzDnsZone cmdlet. Use the RegistrationVirtualNetwork and ResolutionVirtualNetwork parameters to specify the virtual networks.

```
# Create a private DNS zone
$vnet1 = Get-AzVirtualNetwork -Name VNet1 -ResourceGroupName ExamRef-RG
$vnet2 = Get-AzVirtualNetwork -Name VNet2 -ResourceGroupName ExamRef-RG

New-AzDnsZone -Name contoso.local `
  -ResourceGroupName ExamRef-RG `
  -ZoneType Private `
  -RegistrationVirtualNetwork $vnet1 `
  -ResolutionVirtualNetwork $vnet2
```

With the Azure CLI, specify zone-type private when creating a DNS zone with the az network dns zone create command to create a private zone. Use the --registration-vnets and --resolution-vnets parameters to specify the virtual networks, using either the network name or resource ID.

```
# Create a private DNS zone
az network dns zone create --name contoso.local --resource-group ExamRef-RG
--zone-type private --registration-vnets VNet1 --resolution-vnets VNet2
```

Once created, you can manage DNS records in a private DNS zone using the Azure portal, PowerShell, or CLI, in the same way as for public DNS zones. Only manually-registered DNS entries are visible using these tools—the DNS records corresponding to the automatically-registered VMs in the registration VNet are not available.

Skill 4.4: Create and configure a network security group (NSG)

Network security groups (NSGs) allow you to control which network flows are permitted into and out of your virtual networks and virtual machines. Each NSG contains lists of inbound and outbound rules, which give you fine-grained control over exactly which network flows are allowed or denied.

> **This section covers how to:**
> - Create security rules
> - Associate NSG to a subnet or network interface
> - Identify required ports
> - Evaluate effective security rules

Create security rules

A network security group (NSG) is a standalone Azure resource, which acts as networking filter. Each NSG contains a list of security rules. These are used to allow or deny inbound or outbound network traffic, depending on the properties of that traffic such as protocol, IP address, and port. To apply the NSG, it is associated with either a subnet or with a specific VM's network interface.

NSG rules

NSG rules define which traffic flows are allowed or denied by the NSG. Table 4-7 describes the properties of an NSG rule.

TABLE 4-7 NSG properties

Property	Description	Constraints	Considerations
Name	The name of the rule.	Must be unique within the region. Must end with a letter, number, or underscore. Cannot exceed 80 characters.	You can have several rules within an NSG, so make sure you follow a naming convention that allows you to identify the purpose of each rule.
Protocol	The network protocol the rule applies to.	TCP, UDP, or *.	Using * as a protocol includes ICMP as well as TCP and UDP. In the Azure portal, select 'Any' instead of '*'.
Source port range(s)	Source port range(s) to match for the rule.	Single port number from 1 to 65535, port range (example: 1-65535), a list of port or port ranges, or * (for all ports).	The source ports could be ephemeral so unless your client program is using a specific port, use * in most cases. Try to reduce the number of rules by specifying multiple ports or port ranges in a single rule.
Destination port range	Destination port range(s) to match for the rule.	Single port number from 1 to 65535, port range (example: 1-65535), a list of port or port ranges, or * (for all ports).	Try to reduce the number of rules by specifying multiple ports or port ranges in a single rule.
Source address prefix(es)	Source address prefix(es) or service tag(s) to match for the rule.	Single IP address (example: 10.10.10.10), IP subnet (example: 192.168.1.0/24), a service tag, a list of the above, or * (for all addresses).	Consider using ranges, service tags, and lists to reduce the number of rules. The IP addresses of Azure VMs can also be specified implicitly using application security groups.
Destination address prefix(es)	Destination address prefix(es) or service tag(s) to match for the rule.	Single IP address (example: 10.10.10.10), IP subnet (example: 192.168.1.0/24), a service tag, a list of the above, or * (for all addresses).	Consider using ranges, default tags, and lists to reduce the number of rules. The IP addresses of Azure VMs can also be specified implicitly using application security groups.
Direction	Direction of traffic to match for the rule.	Inbound or outbound.	Inbound and outbound rules are processed separately, based on traffic direction.

TABLE 4-7 Continued

Property	Description	Constraints	Considerations
Priority	Rules are checked in the order of priority. Once a matching rule is found, no more rules are tested.	Unique Number between 100 and 4096. Uniqueness is only within this NSG.	Consider creating rules jumping priorities by 100 for each rule to leave space for new rules you might create in the future.
Action	Type of action to apply if the rule matches.	Allow or Deny.	Keep in mind that if an allow rule is not found for a packet, the packet is dropped.

> **NOTE NSG RULE PRIORITY**
>
> NSG Rules are enforced based on their Priority. Priority values start from 100 and go to 4096 (and from 65001 to 65003 for default rules). Rules will be read and enforced starting with 100 then 101, 102, and so on. When a rule is found that matches the traffic under consideration, the rule is applied, and all further processing stops—subsequent rules are disregarded.
>
> For example, suppose you had an inbound rule that allowed TCP traffic on any port with a priority of 250 and another that denied TCP traffic on Port 80 with a priority of 125. An inbound TCP connection on port 80 would be denied, since the deny rule has a lower priority value and would be applied before the allow rule is considered.

Service Tags

Many Azure services are accessed via Internet-facing endpoints. These endpoints can change over time, for example as new Azure regions are built. This makes it difficult to use NSG rules to control access to those services—it's hard to identify the list of IP ranges to use, and even harder to keep the list up-to-date.

To address this problem, Azure provides service tags. These are platform-defined shortcuts that map to the IP ranges of various Azure services. The IP ranges associated with each service tag are updated automatically whenever the IP addresses used by the service change.

Service tags are used in NSG rules as a quick and reliable way of creating rules that control traffic to each service. Typically, they are used in outbound rules to control which other Azure services the VMs in a VNet can or cannot access.

Note that service tags control access to the service, but not to a specific resource within that service. For example, a service tag might be used in an NSG rule allowing a VM to connect to Azure storage. This rule cannot control which account in Azure storage the VM will attempt to use.

Service tags are provided for around 20 Azure services, and the list is growing. Here are some of the most commonly-used service tags.

- **VirtualNetwork** controls access to the virtual network address space where the NSG is assigned. It refers to the entire virtual network (not just the subnet), plus all connected virtual networks and any on-premises address space connected via Site-to-Site VPN or ExpressRoute (which we discuss in the next Skill section of this course).

Note that the network address space of peered virtual networks is only included if the Allow Virtual Network Access property is set to Enabled.

- **Internet**   Denotes the public Internet address space. This includes the Internet-facing Azure IP address ranges, used for public IP addresses and Azure platform services.

- **AzureCloud**   Denotes the Azure datacenter public IP space. This service tag can be scoped to a specific Azure region, for example by specifying `AzureCloud.EastUs`.

- **AzureLoadBalancer**   Denotes the IPs where Azure load balancer health probes will originate. Traffic from these addresses should be allowed for any load-balanced VMs. Note that this service tag cannot be used to control traffic coming through the load balancer from elsewhere. This traffic can be filtered using the originating source IP, which is not modified as it passes through the Azure load balancer

- **AzureTrafficManager**   Performs a similar role for Azure Traffic Manager. It is used to allow traffic from the source IP addresses of Traffic Manager health probes.

- **Storage**   Represents the IP addresses used by the Azure Storage service. As with the Azure Cloud Service Tag, the Storage service tag can be region scoped. For example, you can specify `Storage.WestUS` to only allow access to Storage accounts in the West US region.

- **The Sql**   Represents the IP addresses used by the Azure SQL Database service. This service tag can also be scoped to a specific region.

Default rules

All NSGs have a set of default rules. You cannot add to, edit, or delete these default rules. However, since they have the lowest possible priority, they can be overridden by other rules which you create.

The default rules allow and disallow traffic as follows:

- **Virtual network**   Traffic originating and ending in a virtual network is allowed both in inbound and outbound directions.

- **Internet**   Outbound traffic is allowed, but inbound traffic is blocked.

- **Load balancer**   Allows Azure load balancer to probe the health of your VMs and role instances. If you are not using a load balanced set, you can override this rule.

> **NOTE LOAD BALANCER TRAFFIC**
>
> The Load Balancer default rule uses the AzureLoadBalancer service tag. This applies only to Azure load balancer health probes, which originate at the load balancer. It does not apply to traffic received through the load balancer, which retain their original source IP address and port.

Table 4-8 shows the default inbound rules for each NSG.

TABLE 4-8 Default Inbound Rules

Name	Priority	Source	Source Port	Destination	Destination Port	Protocol	Access
AllowVNetInBound	65000	VirtualNetwork	Any	VirtualNetwork	Any	Any	Allow
AllowAzureLoad BalancerInBound	65001	AzureLoadBalancer	Any	Any	Any	Any	Allow
DenyAllInBound	65500	Any	Any	Any	Any	Any	Deny

Table 4-9 shows the default outbound rules for each NSG.

TABLE 4-9 Default Outbound Rules

Name	Priority	Source	Source Port	Destination	Destination Port	Protocol	Access
AllowVNet OutBound	65000	VirtualNetwork	Any	VirtualNetwork	Any	Any	Allow
AllowInternet OutBound	65001	Any	Any	Internet	Any	Any	Allow
DenyAllOutBound	65500	Any	Any	Any	Any	Any	Deny

Application security groups

As you have seen, NSG rules are like traditional firewall rules, and are defined using source and destination IP blocks. They enable you to segment your network traffic into application tiers, by segmenting your application tiers into separate subnets.

This creates some management challenges. The IP blocks for each subnet must be carefully planned in advance. To allow for additional servers to be added in future, each subnet must be bigger than you really need, making inefficient use of the IP space. And if you make a subnet too small and run out of space, it can be time-consuming to reconfigure the network to free up additional space, especially without application downtime. Also, each subnet requires a separate NSG, making it difficult to get an overall picture of the permitted and blocked traffic at an application level.

Application security groups (ASGs) address these challenges by offering an alternative approach to network segmentation. They allow you to achieve the same goal of segmenting your application into separate tiers, and strictly controlling the permitted network flows between tiers. But they avoid the need to associate each tier with a separate subnet, and therefore all the challenges associated with planning and managing subnets fall away. With ASGs, you define which application tier each VM belongs to explicitly, rather than implicitly based on the subnet in which the VM has been placed. All VMs can be placed in a single subnet, and a single NSG is used to define all permitted network flows between application tiers. Since a single subnet is used, the IP space can be managed much more flexibly. And since there is a single NSG, with rules referring to named application tiers, the network rules are easier to understand, and can all be managed in one place.

Figure 4-36 shows an example. We have a standard 3-tier application architecture, with web servers, application servers, and database servers. These servers have been grouped by associating each server with the appropriate application security group. All servers are placed in the same subnet, without having to think about how the network space is subdivided. A single network security group contains rules defining the permitted traffic flows between application tiers.

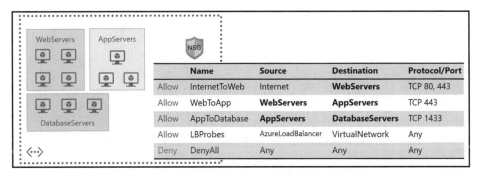

FIGURE 4-36 Using application security groups to simplify subnet and NSG management

Application security groups enable you to configure network security as a natural extension of an application's structure, allowing you to group virtual machines and define network security policies based on those groups. You can reuse your security policy at scale without the manual maintenance of explicit IP addresses. The platform handles the complexity of explicit IP addresses and multiple rule sets, allowing you to focus on your business logic.

Configuring application security groups is straightforward:

1. First, you create an application security group resource for each server group. This resource has no properties, other than its name, resource group, and location.

2. Next, you associate the network interface from each VM with the appropriate application security group. This defines which group (or groups) each VM belongs to.

3. Finally, you define your network security group rules using application security group names instead of explicit IP ranges. This is similar to how rules are configured using named service tags.

Create an NSG using the Azure portal

To create an NSG using the portal, first click **Create A Resource**, then **Networking**, then select **Network Security Group**. Once the Create Network Security Group blade loads you will need to provide a name, the subscription where your resources are located, the resource group for the NSG and the location (this must be the same as the resources you wish to apply the

NSG). In Figure 4-37, the NSG will be created to allow HTTP traffic into the Apps subnet and be named AppsNSG.

FIGURE 4-37 Creating a network security group using the Azure Portal

After the NSG has been created, open the NSG Overview blade as shown in Figure 4-38. Here, you see that the NSG has been created, but there are no inbound or outbound security rules beyond the default rules.

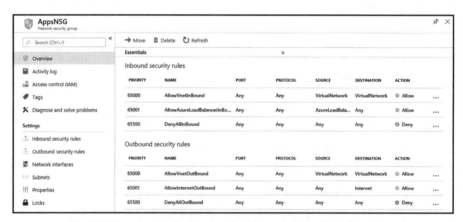

FIGURE 4-38 The NSG Overview blade, showing the inbound and outbound security rules

The next step is to create the inbound rule for HTTP and HTTPS traffic. Under the **Settings** area, click on **Inbound Security Rules**, then click **+Add** to open the Add Inbound Security Rule panel. Notice how the panel has both Basic and Advanced modes, depending on the level of control required. To allow HTTP/HTTPS traffic on Port 80 and 443, fill in the settings as shown in Figure 4-39:

- **Source**   Any
- **Source Port Ranges**   *
- **Destination**   VirtualNetwork
- **Destination Port Ranges**   80,443

- **Protocol** TCP
- **Action** Allow
- **Priority** 100
- **Name** Allow_HTTP_HTTPS
- **Description** Allow HTTP and HTTPS inbound traffic on ports 80 and 443

Once all the settings have been filled in, click the **Add** button to create the NSG rule.

> *NOTE* **APPLYING NSGS TO VIRTUAL NETWORKS**
>
> The destination IP ranges refers to the VirtualNetwork. This allows the NSG to be applied to any subnet in any VNet, and avoids coupling the NSG to a specific IP range. Traffic will only be permitted to those subnets where the NSG is applied.

FIGURE 4-39 Adding an Inbound Rule to allow HTTP traffic

Once the inbound rule has been saved, it will appear in the portal. Review your rule to en-sure it has been created correctly.

Create an NSG using Azure PowerShell

To create an NSG and configure the rules by using Azure PowerShell, you need to use the New-AzNetworkSecurityRuleConfig and New-AzNetworkSecurityGroup PowerShell cmdlets together.

```
# Create array to contain NSG rules
$rules = @()
# Build a new Inbound Rule to Allow TCP Traffic on Port 80 or 443 to the Subnet,
```

```
and add to the $rules array
$rules += New-AzNetworkSecurityRuleConfig -Name Allow_HTTP_HTTPS `
                    -Description "Allow HTTP and HTTPS
                      inbound on ports 80 and 443" `
                    -Access Allow `
                    -Protocol Tcp `
                    -Direction Inbound `
                    -Priority 100 `
                    -SourceAddressPrefix * `
                    -SourcePortRange * `
                    -DestinationAddressPrefix VirtualNetwork `
                    -DestinationPortRange 80,443
# Create an NSG, including the new inbound rules
$nsg = New-AzNetworkSecurityGroup -ResourceGroupName ExamRef-RG `
                    -Location centralus `
                    -Name AppsNSG `
                    -SecurityRules $rules
```

Create an NSG using the Azure CLI

Creating an NSG using the Azure CLI is a multi-step process, just as it was with the portal and PowerShell. First, use the `az network nsg create` command to create the NSG. Once created, use the `az network nsg rule create` command to add each NSG rule.

```
# Create the NSG
az network nsg create --name AppsNSG --resource-group ExamRef-RG

# Create the NSG Inbound Rule allowing TCP traffic on Port 80
az network nsg rule create --name Allow_HTTP_HTTPS --nsg-name AppsNSG
--resource-group ExamRef-RG --direction Inbound --priority 100
--access Allow --source-address-prefixes "*" --source-port-ranges "*"
--destination-address-prefixes "VirtualNetwork" --destination-port-ranges 80 443
--description "Allow HTTP and HTTPS inbound on ports 80 and 443" --protocol TCP
```

Associate NSG to a subnet or network interface

NSGs are used to define the rules of how traffic is filtered for your IaaS deployments in Azure. We have seen how to create NSG resources and define the NSG rules. However, these NSGs by themselves are not effective until they are associated with a resource in Azure.

NSGs can be associated with network interfaces (NICs) which are associated to the VMs, or they can be associated with a subnet. Each NIC or subnet can only be associated with a single NSG. However, a single NSG can be associated with multiple NICs and/or subnets.

When associating an NSG with a NIC, it applies to all IP configurations in that NIC. All inbound and outbound traffic to and from the NIC must be allowed by the NSG. It is possible to have a multi-NIC VM, and you can associate the same or different NSG to each Network Interface.

Alternatively, NSGs can be associated with a subnet, in which case they apply to all traffic to and from resources in that subnet. This approach is useful when applying the same rule across multiple VMs.

Associating an NSG with a subnet using the Azure portal

We have seen how to create an NSG and how to add an inbound rule for HTTP and HTTPS traffic. Yet, this NSG has not been associated with any subnets or NICs, and so is not in effect.

The next task will be to associate it with the Apps subnet. You can use either the NSG blade or the virtual network subnet blade for this task; we'll use the former.

In the NSG blade of the Azure portal, click the subnets link to show the list of subnets currently associated with the NSG (this should be empty at this stage). Click **+Associate** to open the Associate Subnet blade. The portal will ask for two configurations: the virtual network, and the subnet. Note that you can only select virtual networks in the same Azure region as the NSG. In Figure 4-40, the virtual network ExamRefVNET and subnet Apps has been selected.

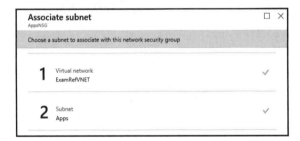

FIGURE 4-40 The ExamRefVNET virtual network and Apps subnet have been selected

After being saved, the rules of the NSG are now being enforced for all network interfaces that are associated with this subnet. This will allow inbound TCP traffic on ports 80 and 443 for all VMs that are connected to this subnet. Of course, you need to have a webserver VM configured and listening on ports 80 or 443 to respond.

Associating an NSG with a subnet using Azure PowerShell

To associate an NSG with a subnet using Azure PowerShell the subnet configuration must be updated to reference the NSG. This is achieved in three steps:

1. Use Get-AzVirtualNetwork to retrieve a local object representing the VNet.

2. Identify the desired subnet within the VNet object and update the subnet configuration to reference the NSG.

3. Use Set-AzVirtualNetwork to save the updated VNet configuration back to Azure.

```
#Associate the Rule with the Subnet Apps in the Virtual Network ExamRefVNET-PS
$vnet = Get-AzVirtualNetwork -Name ExamRef-vnet -ResourceGroupName ExamRef-RG

# Find the 'Apps' subnet
$subnet = $vnet.Subnets | where {$_.Name -eq "Apps"}

# Modify the 'Apps' subnet to reference the NSG
# Assumes $nsg is already populated from the earlier script or via
Get-AzNetworkSecurityGroup
$subnet.NetworkSecurityGroup.Id = $nsg.Id

Set-AzVirtualNetwork -VirtualNetwork $vnet
```

In step 2 above, you can also use the Set-AzVirtualNetworkSubnetConfig cmdlet to update the subnet configuration. However, this requires you to specify the AddressPrefix for the subnet, even if this has already been defined.

Associating an NSG with a subnet using the Azure CLI

To associate an NSG with a subnet using the Azure CLI, use the az network vnet subnet update command.

```
# Associate the NSG with the ExamRef-vnet Apps Subnet
az network vnet subnet update --name Apps --vnet-name ExamRef-vnet
--resource-group ExamRef-RG --network-security-group AppsNSG
```

This example specifies the NSG by name, which assumes the NSG resource is in the same resource group as the VNet. If the NSG is in a different resource group, specify the full NSG resource ID instead.

To remove an NSG from a subnet, use the same command, specifying empty double quotes ("") as the NSG name.

Identify required ports

When defining NSGs, it can be a challenge to identify all the network flows that an application requires. Certain flows, such as from a middle tier to a database tier, will be obvious to anyone familiar with the application architecture. Other flows, however, such as DNS lookups, connections to Active Directory, or checks against licensing or key management servers, are less obvious, but still critical.

Azure provides two very useful tools which can help you identify the network flows used by a running application. These are the Service Map and NSG flow logs.

Service Map

The Service Map is a Log Analytics solution. It helps you document the network flows from a running application. It works by installing two agents on each server: the Microsoft Monitoring Agent (MMA) and the Dependency Agent. Both agents are available for Windows and Linux. There is no requirement that the application be running in Azure—it can also be used for on-premises applications.

Service Map provides rich reporting of dependencies and network flows, including traffic volumes and internal application processes. Machines can be grouped to provide a logical view that reflects the application architecture. Of interest when configuring NSGs is the Failed Connections view (Figure 4-41), which shows network flows that cannot be completed. This may indicate a missing or mis-configured NSG rule.

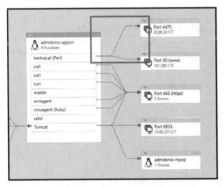

FIGURE 4-41 A Service Map example, showing a failed connection

To get started with the Azure Service Map, from the Azure portal click **Create A Resource** and install the **Service Map** solution from the Azure Marketplace. As the Service Map is a Log Analytics solution, you will need to create a Log Analytics workspace, or reference an existing workspace.

The next step is to on-board your VMs to Log Analytics. This will also install the Microsoft Monitoring Agent (MMA) on each VM. Open the log analytics workspace, and under **Workplace Data Sources**, click **Virtual Machines** to see a list of virtual machines together with their on-boarding status, as shown in Figure 4-42.

NAME	OMS CONNECTION	OS	SUBSCRIPTION	RESOURCE GROUP	LOCATION
DemoVM	This workspace	Windows	41811f87-4f0d-44d0-be...	DemoRG	westeurope
ExamRef-VM1	Not connected	Linux	41811f87-4f0d-44d0-be...	ExamRef-RG	northeurope

FIGURE 4-42 The virtual machines list under Log Analytics data sources

Click the virtual machine to on-board, which will open a separate blade, then click **Connect**, as shown in Figure 4-43. After a short delay to install the MMA, the virtual machine will be connected to the Log Analytics workspace.

FIGURE 4-43 Connecting a virtual machine to Log Analytics

Next, for the Service Map solution, an additional VM extension called the Dependency Agent must be installed. This can be installed in many ways, including a standalone installer, PowerShell DSC, or via a PowerShell script, as shown below:

```
# Deploy the Dependency agent to every VM in a Resource Group
$version = "9.4"
$ExtPublisher = "Microsoft.Azure.Monitoring.DependencyAgent"
$OsExtensionMap = @{ "Windows" = "DependencyAgentWindows"; "Linux" =
"DependencyAgentLinux" }
$rmgroup = "ExamRef-RG"

Get-AzVM -ResourceGroupName $rmgroup |
ForEach-Object {
    ""
    $name = $_.Name
    $os = $_.StorageProfile.OsDisk.OsType
    $location = $_.Location
    $vmRmGroup = $_.ResourceGroupName
    "${name}: ${os} (${location})"
    Date -Format o
    $ext = $OsExtensionMap.($os.ToString())
    $result = Set-AzVMExtension -ResourceGroupName $vmRmGroup -VMName $name
-Location $location `
    -Publisher $ExtPublisher -ExtensionType $ext -Name "DependencyAgent"
-TypeHandlerVersion $version
    $result.IsSuccessStatusCode
}
```

Deployment is now complete. It's best to leave several days to gather data, since some network flows may not be used frequently.

To view the Service Map, click **Solutions** within the Log Analytics workspace, then click on the Service Map solution. On the Overview blade, a summary tile should show the number of virtual machines on-boarded, as shown in Figure 4-44.

FIGURE 4-44 The Service Map solution overview

Finally, click the Service Map summary tile to open the Service Map. An example is shown in Figure 4-45. From here, you can browse processes and connections for each VM.

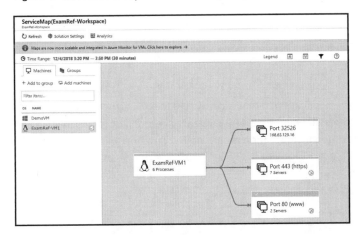

FIGURE 4-45 The Service Map for ExamRef-VM1

NSG flow logs

NSG flow logs are a form of Azure diagnostic logs. They record both allowed and denied network flows in and out of an NSG. By analyzing NSG flow logs, you can understand which traffic flows your application is using, and which flows are being requested by an application, but blocked by your NSG. You can then review if the NSG rules should be updated to allow or deny these flows.

An example flow log is shown next. It is written in JavaScript Object Notation (JSON), and starts with metadata such as the timestamp and resource ID of the NSG generating the log. Then, for each NSG rule, the log gives a list of FlowTuples that describe the flow itself.

```
{
    "time": "2018-05-01T15:00:02.1713710Z",
    "systemId": "<Id>",
    "category": "NetworkSecurityGroupFlowEvent",
    "resourceId":
"/SUBSCRIPTIONS/<Id>/RESOURCEGROUPS/<rg>/PROVIDERS/MICROSOFT.NETWORK/
NETWORKSECURITYGROUPS/MYVM-NSG",
    "operationName": "NetworkSecurityGroupFlowEvents",
    "properties": {
        "Version": 1,
        "flows": [
            {
                "rule": "UserRule_default-allow-rdp",
                "flows": [
                    {
                        "mac": "000D3A170C69",
                        "flowTuples": [
                            "1525186745,192.168.1.4,10.0.0.4,55960,3389,T,I,A"
                        ]
                    }
                ]
            }
        ]
    }
}
```

Each FlowTuple describes the application of that security rule to a particular network flow. The fields in the FlowTuple are described in Table 4-10. (An enhanced v2 flow log format is currently in Preview, giving additional information regarding the duration and data volume of each flow.)

TABLE 4-10 NSG Flow Log FlowTuple Fields

Example data	What data represents	Explanation
1542110377	Time stamp	The time stamp of when the flow occurred, in UNIX EPOCH format. In the previous example, the date converts to May 1, 2018 at 2:59:05 PM GMT.
10.0.0.4	Source IP address	The source IP address that the flow originated from. 10.0.0.4 is the private IP address of the VM you created in Create a VM.
13.67.143.118	Destination IP address	The destination IP address that the flow was destined to.
44931	Source port	The source port that the flow originated from.
443	Destination port	The destination port that the flow was destined to. Since the traffic was destined to port 443, the rule named UserRule_default-allow-rdp, in the log file processed the flow.
T	Protocol	Whether the protocol of the flow was TCP (T) or UDP (U).
O	Direction	Whether the traffic was inbound (I) or outbound (O).
A	Action	Whether the traffic was allowed (A) or denied (D).

Analyzing large flow logs can be a substantial task. To make this easier, the Traffic Analytics solution for Log Analytics can be used to analyze the logs and summarize the data in a variety of easy-to-consume reports.

Before using NSG Flow Logs, your subscription must be registered to use the Microsoft. Insights resource provider. You can register the resource provider using the Azure portal, by clicking **All Services**, then **Subscriptions**. Choose your subscription to open the Subscription blade, then click **Resource Providers**. Find the Microsoft.Insights resource provider (as shown in Figure 4-46) and register it if necessary.

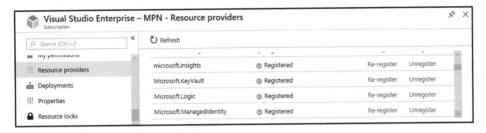

FIGURE 4-46 Registering the Microsoft.Insights Resource Provider

You can also register the resource provider using PowerShell:

```
# Register the Microsoft.Insights Resource Provider
Register-AzResourceProvider -ProviderNamespace Microsoft.Insights
```

Or, you can register the resource provider using the Azure CLI:

```
# Register the Microsoft.Insights Resource Provider
az provider register --namespace Microsoft.Insights
```

Another pre-requisite is to create a storage account to store the NSG Flow Logs. In the Azure Portal, click **Create A Resource**, then **Storage**, then **Storage Account**, and fill in the Create Storage Account blade, specifying the storage account name and other settings. For more details on creating storage accounts, see Chapter 2.

NSG Flow Logs are one of many network diagnostics features provided by Azure Network Watcher. In the Azure portal, select **All Services**, then enter **Network Watcher** in the search filter, then click **Network Watcher** in the results to open the Network Watcher blade. The Network Watcher service is enabled automatically in any region where you have deployed a virtual network.

Within the Network Watcher blade in the Azure portal, click **NSG Flow Logs**. A list of NSGs is shown, together with the flow log and traffic analytics status for each NSG (see Figure 4-47).

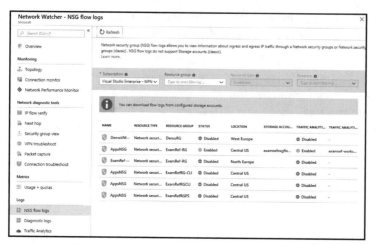

FIGURE 4-47 NSG Flow Logs view in Network Watcher, showing the Flow Log status for each NSG

To enable NSG Flow Logs, click on an NSG to open the Flow Logs Settings blade (Figure 4-48). Within this blade, you can enable NSG Flow Logs and select the storage account used to store the logs. You can also optionally enable Traffic Analytics, and select the Log Analytics workspace used by this solution.

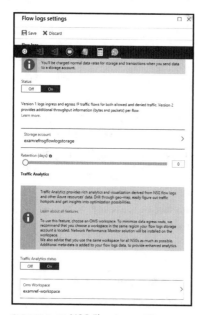

FIGURE 4-48 NSG Flow Log settings

Evaluate effective security rules

When troubleshooting networking issues, it can be useful to get a deeper insight into exactly how NSGs are being applied. When NSG rules are defined using service tags and application security groups, instead of explicit IP addresses or prefixes, it sometimes isn't clear whether a particular flow matches a particular rule, or not.

The Effective Security Rules view is designed to provide this insight. It allows you to drill into each NSG rule and see the exact list of source and destination IP prefixes that have been applied, regardless of how the NSG rule was defined.

To access the Effective Security Rules view, your virtual machine must be running. This is because the data is taken directly from the configuration of the running VM.

View effective security rules using the Azure portal

Using the Azure portal, open the Virtual Machine blade, then click **Networking**. This will show the networking settings, including the NSG rules (and includes a convenient link to add new rules). At the top of this blade, click **Effective Security Rules** (as highlighted in Figure 4-59) to open the Effective Security Rules blade.

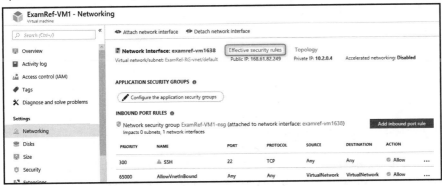

FIGURE 4-49 Azure Virtual Machine Networking blade

At first sight, the Effective Security Rules blade (Figure 4-50) looks very similar to the Networking blade shown previously. It shows the name of the network interface and associated NSGs, together with a list of NSG rules.

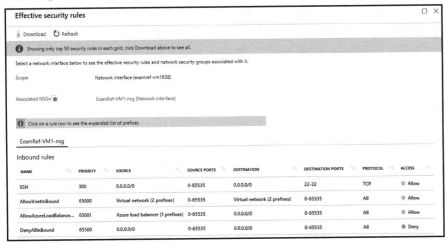

FIGURE 4-50 Azure Virtual Machine Networking blade

The difference becomes clear when you click on one of the NSG rules. This opens an additional pane, showing the exact source and destination IP address prefixes used by that rule. For example, in Figure 4-51, you can see the exact list of 122 IP address prefixes used for outbound Internet traffic.

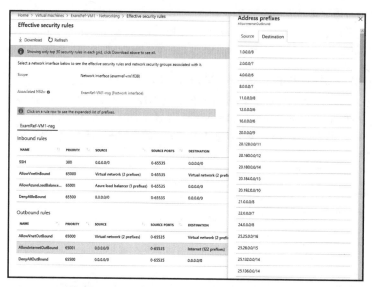

FIGURE 4-51 Effective Security Rules showing Internet address prefixes

Having access to the exact list of address prefixes for each NSG rule allows you to investigate networking issues without fear of any ambiguity over how NSG rules are defined.

View effective security rules using Azure PowerShell

Effective security rules are also available using Azure PowerShell, using the Get-AzEffective-NetworkSecurityGroup cmdlet. This cmdlet returns an object containing all effective rules for a given network interface, including NSGs at both the subnet and network interface level.

```
# Get effective security rules for a NIC
Get-AzEffectiveNetworkSecurityGroup -NetworkInterfaceName
examref-vm1638 -ResourceGroupName ExamRef-RG
```

View effective security rules using the Azure CLI

Effective security rules are also available using the Azure CLI, using the az network nic list-effective-nsg command.

When using the table output format, the results show a summary of the NSG rules but do not show the individual IP address prefixes. Using a verbose output format such as JSON gives the full output, including IP address prefixes.

```
# Get effective security rules for a NIC
az network nic list-effective-nsg --name examref-vm1638 --resource-group ExamRef-RG
--output json
```

Skill 4.5: Implement Azure load balancer

Azure Load Balancer is a fully-managed load-balancing service, used to distribute inbound traffic across a pool of backend servers running in an Azure virtual network. It can receive traffic on either Internet-facing or Intranet-facing endpoints, and supports both UDP and TCP traffic.

Azure Load Balancer operates at the transport layer (OSI layer 4), routing inbound and outbound connections at the packet level. It does not terminate TCP connections, and thus does not have visibility into application-level constructs. For example, it cannot support SSL offloading, URL path-based routing, or cookie-based session affinity (for these, see "Application Gateway" in Skill 3.1.)

Azure Load Balancer provides low latency and high throughput, scaling to millions of network flows. It also supports automatic failover between backend servers based on health probes, enabling high availability applications.

> **This section covers how to:**
> - Configure internal load balancer, load balancing rules, and public load balancer
> - Manage Azure load balancing

Configure internal load balancer, load balancing rules, and public load balancer

The deployment of Azure Load Balancer involves the coordinated configuration of several groups of settings. These settings work together to define the overall load balancer behavior.

Basic and Standard Load Balancer tiers

Azure Load Balancer is available in two pricing tiers, or SKUs: Basic and Standard. They offer different levels of scale, features, and pricing. Table 4-11 provides a comparison of the main feature differences between the Basic and Standard tiers.

TABLE 4-11 Comparison between Standard and Basic Load Balancer Tiers

	Standard	Basic
Availability Zones	Supports zone-specific or zone-redundant deployments including cross-zone load-balancing	Not supported
Backend Pools	Up to 1,000 servers, any mix of VMs, availability sets, and VM Scale Sets, in the same VNet	Up to 100 servers, must be VMs in the same availability set or a single VM Scale Set
Health Probes	TCP, HTTP, HTTPS	TCP, HTTP
Diagnostics	Rich metrics via Azure Monitor, including byte and packet counters, health probe status, connection attempts, outbound connection health, and more	Azure Log Analytics for public load balancer only; alerts, backend pool health count
Security	Closed by default. Whitelist permitted inbound flows using Network Security Groups	Open by default. Can optionally restrict flows using Network Security Groups
Outbound Connectivity	Supports multiple outbound IP addresses, configurable via outbound rules	Single outbound IP, not configurable
Other Features	Supports HA Ports, TCP Reset on idle timeout, faster management operations	N/A
Pricing	Based on number of rules and data processed	Free
SLA	99.99% for data path with two healthy VMs	None

For a complete comparison of Basic and Standard Load Balancer tiers, see: *https://docs. microsoft.com/en-us/azure/load-balancer/load-balancer-overview#skus*.

Frontend IP configuration

Azure Load Balancer supports two modes: *internal load balancer* or *public load balancer*. In each case, the frontend IP configuration defines the endpoint upon which the load balancer receives incoming traffic.

- **Internal load balancer**   Used to load-balance traffic for Intranet-facing applications, or between application tiers. The frontend IP configuration references a subnet, and an IP address from that subnet is allocated using either dynamic or static assignment to the load balancer.

- **Public load balancer**   Used to load-balance traffic for Internet-facing applications. The frontend IP configuration references a separate public IP address resource, which is used to receive inbound traffic.

When used with IaaS VMs, each load balancer can support multiple frontend IP configurations. This allows it to receive traffic on multiple IP addresses, to load-balance traffic for multiple applications. All frontend configurations, however, must be of the same type, internal or public.

A public load balancer must be associated with a public IP address resource. If the load-balancer uses the standard pricing tier, then the public IP address must also use the standard pricing tier. Standard tier load balancers support both zone specific and zone redundant deployment options. The choice of deployment option is taken from the associated public IP address, rather than being specific explicitly in the load balancer properties.

Backend configuration

The backend pool defines the backend servers over which the load balancer will distribute incoming traffic.

When using a basic-tier load balancer, this backend pool must comprise either a single virtual machine, virtual machines in the same availability set, or a VM scale set (traffic will be distributed to all virtual machines in the VM scale set). You cannot distribute traffic to multiple virtual machines unless they are members of the same availability set or VM scale set.

With a standard-tier load-balancer, these restrictions are lifted. Backend pools can comprise a combination of virtual machines, across availability sets and VM scale sets.

Health Probes

Azure Load Balancer supports continual health probing of backend pool instances, to determine which instances are healthy and able to receive traffic. The load balancer will stop sending traffic flows to any backend pool instance that is determined to be unhealthy. Unhealthy instances continue to receive health probes, so the load balancer can resume sending traffic to that instance once it returns to a healthy state.

Azure Load Balancer supports three types of health probes:

- **TCP** Probes attempt to initiate a connection by completing a three-way TCP hand-shake (SYN, SYN-ACK, ACK). If successful, the connection is then closed with a four-way handshake (FIN, ACK, FIN, ACK).
- **HTTP** Probes issue an HTTP GET with a specified path.
- **HTTPS** Probes are similar to HTTP probes, except that a TLS/SSL wrapper is used. HTTPS probes are only supported on the standard-tier load balancer.

All three probe types must also specify the probe port, or the interval. The minimum probe interval is five seconds in length, and the minimum consecutive probe failure threshold is two seconds. For HTTP and HTTPs probes, the probe path must also be given.

And endpoint is marked unhealthy if:

- For HTTP or HTTPS probes only, the endpoint returns an HTTP status code other than 200 OK.
- The probe endpoint closes the connection using a TCP reset.
- The probe endpoint fails to respond during the timeout period, for a consecutive number of requests. The number of failed requests required to mark the endpoint unhealthy is configurable.

Configuring a dedicated health check page, such as /healthcheck.php, enables each backend server to implement custom application logic to decide whether it is healthy. Checking the availability of a backend database is an example of this.

When configuring network security groups (NSGs) for backend servers, it is important to allow both inbound traffic and probe traffic. Azure Load Balancer does not modify the source IP address of inbound traffic, so inbound traffic rules should be configured as if the load balancer was not in use. Whitelisting inbound probe traffic is achieved by allowing traffic originating from the AzureLoadBalancer service tag.

Load-balancing rules

Similar to Azure Application Gateway, load-balancing rules are used to connect the frontend IP configuration to the backend server pool, and to a health probe. Unlike App Gateway, there is no separate backend HTTP settings configuration; any additional HTTP settings are defined directly within the load-balancing rule itself. These include frontend and backend ports, idle timeout, protocol (TCP or UDP), and IP version (IPv4 or IPv6).

The load-balancing rule also allows you to configure how inbound connections are distributed between backend instances. There are three options:

- **None**   Traffic is distributed based on a 5-tuple hash of source IP, destination IP, source port, destination port, and protocol. This is the default option.
- **Source IP**   Traffic is distributed based on a 2-tuple hash of source and destination IP only.
- **Source IP and Protocol**   Traffic is distributed based on a 3-tuple hash of source IP, destination IP, and protocol.

Under the default option, new TCP sessions from a given client might be routed to a different backend endpoint, since the source port will have changed. By excluding the source port from the load-balancing algorithm, the Source IP and Source IP Protocol options provide consistent mappings between client and individual backend servers across separate connections. This is useful in applications where traffic between the client and server uses more than one connection or protocol. Media uploads that use both a TCP session to control and monitor the upload, as well as UDP packets to upload the media data are examples.

Inbound NAT Rules

You have seen how Azure Load Balancer can be configured to distribute inbound traffic across a pool of backend servers. Another common scenario is where a connection must be made to a specific backend server via the load balancer frontend. This is useful for gaining access to a specific server, such as when diagnosing a problem, without exposing a new endpoint on that server.

The direct connectivity to individual servers is achieved by creating a *port mapping* from the frontend to a specific backend server. This mapping is also known as an *inbound NAT rule*. Each inbound NAT rule specifies a frontend IP address, frontend port, protocol (TCP or UDP), backend server, and backend port. Once enabled, traffic received by the frontend IP on the designated frontend port is directed to the specified backend server and port.

Network Security Group configuration

The final step in configuring the Azure load balancer is to ensure that Network Security Groups (NSGs) are correctly configured. These NSGs can be associated with the subnet containing the backend virtual machines, or with their network interfaces. Two inbound security rules are required.

First, an inbound rule must permit traffic from the end users to the backend servers. Even though traffic passes through the load balancer, this does not change the source IP of the inbound traffic, hence the rule must reference the end user source IP address and port range.

A second inbound rule must permit traffic originating from the load balancer health probe. The IP addresses from which the health probes originate are defined in the AzureLoadBalancer service tag, which should be used to define the source IP address range for this rule.

> *NOTE* **LOAD BALANCERS AND NETWORK SECURITY GROUPS**
> Standard-tier load balancers use standard-tier public IP addresses, which are by default closed to inbound traffic. When using a standard-tier load balancer, traffic *must* be whitelisted using NSGs. In contrast with basic-tier load balancers, traffic *should* be whitelisted using NSGs, but will also flow if NSGs are not used.

Create an Azure load balancer using the Azure Portal

To use the Azure load balancer, the administrator must first provision the resource, which includes the frontend IP configuration. After this step has been completed, you can create the backend pool, the heath probes, and finally the load balancing rule.

To create the load balancer in the portal, click **+Create a resource**, followed by **Networking**, then click **Load Balancer**. This will open the **Create Load Balancer** blade, as shown in Figure 4-52. Complete the blade as follows:

- **Name**   Provide a name for the load balancer resource.
- **Type**   Choose between Public or Internal.
- **SKU**   Select the pricing tier: Basic or Standard.
- **Public IP address (public load balancers only)**: Choose an existing public IP address resource, or create a new one. Standard-tier load balancers must use standard-tier public IP addresses.
- **Virtual network, subnet and IP assignment   (internal load balancers only)**: Choose the virtual network and subnet from which the frontend IP address will be allocated, and choose between static and dynamic allocation.
- **Availability zone**   (standard-tier load balancers only): For public load balancers, the availability zone is configured as part of the public IP address configuration. For internal load balancers, it is explicitly specified.

- **Subscription, resource group, and location** Specify as required.

FIGURE 4-52 Creating a Load Balancer with the Azure Portal

After the load balancer has been created, the next steps are to create the backend pool, the health probe, and finally the load-balancing rule.

To create a backend pool, open the load balancer blade in the Azure Portal, then click **Backend Pools**, followed by **+Add**. This opens the **Add Backend Pool** blade, as shown in Figure 4-53. Specify the backend pool name and, for a standard load balancer, select the virtual machines (and their IP addresses) to include in the backend pool. For basic load balancers, you will need to choose between adding an individual virtual machine, an availability set, or a VM scale set.

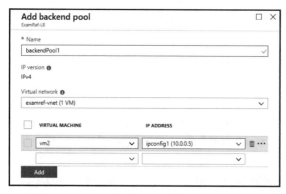

FIGURE 4-53 Creating a backend pool and adding virtual machines, using a standard load balancer

To create a health probe, navigate to the load balancer blade and click **Health Probes** followed by **+Add**. This opens the **Add Health Probe** blade as shown in Figure 4-54. Specify the health probe name, together with the protocol, port, probe interval, and consecutive probe failures threshold.

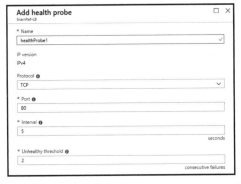

FIGURE 4-54 Creating a health probe in Azure Load Balancer

The final step is to configure a load balancing rule, which links the frontend IP configuration to the backend pool, specifying the health probe and other load balancing settings. From the load balancer blade, click **Load Balancing Rules**, followed by **+Add**. This opens the **Add Load Balancing Rule** blade, as shown in Figure 4-55. Choose the frontend IP configuration, backend pool, and health probe selected earlier. For HTTP traffic, select **TCP**, specify port **80** for both the frontend and backend ports, select **None** for session persistence, and leave the idle time-out at the default (4 minute) value.

> **NOTE** **FLOATING IP**
>
> The last setting, Floating IP (direct server return), is only recommended when load-balancing traffic for a SQL Server AlwaysOn Availability Group listener. For other scenarios, the Floating IP setting should be left disabled.

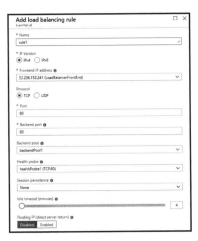

FIGURE 4-55 Creating a load balancing rule in Azure load balancer

The final step is to ensure NSGs are configured to allow incoming traffic and health probe traffic. With this in place, if the VMs added to the backend pool are configured with a web server, you should be able to connect to the public IP address of the load balancer and see the webpage.

Create an Azure load balancer using PowerShell

Creating an Azure load balancer using PowerShell involves several steps. In the case of a public load balancer, the public IP address must be created. Next, the frontend IP configuration, backend pool, health probe, and load balancing rule are configured, each as a separate local object. The load balancer itself is created using these local objects to specify the load balancer configuration.

```
# Set Variables
$rgName = "ExamRef-RG"
$location = "West Europe"

# Create the Public IP
$publicIP = New-AzPublicIpAddress `
    -Name ExamRefLB-IP `
    -ResourceGroupName $rgName `
    -AllocationMethod Static `
    -Location $location

#Create Frontend IP Configuration
$frontendIP = New-AzLoadBalancerFrontendIpConfig `
    -Name ExamRefFrontEnd `
    -PublicIpAddress $publicIP

# Create Backend Pool
$beAddressPool = New-AzLoadBalancerBackendAddressPoolConfig `
    -Name ExamRefBackEndPool

#Create HTTP Probe
$healthProbe = New-AzLoadBalancerProbeConfig `
    -Name HealthProbe `
    -RequestPath '/' `
    -Protocol http `
    -Port 80 `
    -IntervalInSeconds 5 `
    -ProbeCount 2

#Create Load Balancer Rule
$lbrule = New-AzLoadBalancerRuleConfig `
    -Name ExamRefRuleHTTPPS `
    -FrontendIpConfiguration $frontendIP `
    -BackendAddressPool  $beAddressPool `
    -Probe $healthProbe `
    -Protocol Tcp `
    -FrontendPort 80 `
    -BackendPort 80

#Create Load Balancer
$lb = New-AzLoadBalancer `
```

```
-ResourceGroupName $rgName `
-Name ExamRefLB `
-Location $location `
-FrontendIpConfiguration $frontendIP `
-LoadBalancingRule $lbrule `
-BackendAddressPool $beAddressPool `
-Probe $healthProbe
```

Having created the load balancer, the next step is to add virtual machines to the backend pool. When using Azure PowerShell, the process is not to add a virtual machine or network interface to the backend pool, but rather the other way around, by adding a reference to the backend pool to the network interface of the VM. This is similar to the process used to add virtual machines to an App Gateway backend pool.

The following PowerShell script shows how to add a virtual machine to a load balancer backend pool. Note that when updating the IP configuration of the network interface, all existing IP configuration settings must be re-stated, otherwise they will be lost.

```
# Set Variables
$rgName = "ExamRef-RG"
# Add VM1 to the LB backend pool
# First, get the VM. Then get the NIC based on the VM ID
$vm1 = Get-AzVM -Name VM1 -ResourceGroupName $rgName
$vm1nic = Get-AzNetworkInterface -ResourceGroupName $rgName `
    | where {$_.VirtualMachine.Id -eq $vm1.Id}

# Get the LB and backend pool (skip if you have these already)
$lb = Get-AzLoadBalancer `
    -Name ExamRefLB `
    -ResourceGroupName $rgName

$beAddressPool = Get-AzLoadBalancerBackendAddressPoolConfig `
    -Name ExamRefBackEndPool `
    -LoadBalancer $lb

# Update the IP config of the NIC to reference the backend pool of the
Application Gateway
# Note: This is NOT an incremental change. You need to specify ALL settings of
the IP config
#       Exisiting settings (such as public IP addresses) will be lost if not
re-specified.
#       This example re-specifies the subnet only (this is mandatory)
$ipconfig = Get-AzNetworkInterfaceIpConfig `
    -Name ipconfig1 `
    -NetworkInterface $vm1nic

Set-AzNetworkInterfaceIpConfig `
    -Name ipconfig1 `
    -NetworkInterface $vm1nic `
    -SubnetId $ipconfig.Subnet.Id `
    -LoadBalancerBackendAddressPoolId $beAddressPool.Id

# Commit the change
Set-AzNetworkInterface -NetworkInterface $vm1nic
```

The final step is to ensure NSGs are configured to allow incoming traffic and health probe traffic. With this in place, if the VMs added to the backend pool are configured with a web server, you should be able to connect to the public IP address of the load balancer and see the webpage.

Create an Azure load balancer using the Azure CLI

The same configurations are required when creating a load balancer by using the Azure CLI when creating load balancers in the portal or by using PowerShell. First, for public load balancers only, create the public IP address that the load balancer will use. Next, create the load balancer itself, using the az network lb create command. This step also creates the frontend IP configuration and backend pool. The load balancer is then updated to incrementally add the health probe and load balancing rule.

```
# Creating a Public IP Address
az network public-ip create --name ExamRefLB-IP --resource-group
ExamRef-RG --allocation-method Static --location westeurope

#Create Load Balancer
az network lb create --name ExamRefLB --resource-group ExamRef-RG
--location westeurope --backend-pool-name ExamRefBackEndPool
--frontend-ip-name ExamRefFrontEnd --public-ip-address ExamRefLB-IP

#Create HTTP Probe
az network lb probe create --name HealthProbe --lb-name ExamRefLB
--resource-group ExamRef-RG --protocol http --port 80 --path /
--interval 5 --threshold 2

#Create Load Balancer Rule
az network lb rule create --name ExamRefRule --lb-name ExamRefLB
--resource-group ExamRef-RG --protocol Tcp --frontend-port 80
--backend-port 80 --frontend-ip-name ExamRefFrontEnd
--backend-pool-name ExamRefBackEndPool --probe-name HealthProbe
```

Having created the load balancer, the next step is to add virtual machines to the backend pool. As with Azure PowerShell, the Azure CLI implements this by adding a reference to the backend pool to the network interface of the VM. This is more straightforward with the Azure CLI than it is with PowerShell, since incremental update of the network interface is supported. Note that the name (or resource ID) of the network interface attached to the VM is required.

```
# Add the Web Servers to the Backend Pool
az network nic ip-config address-pool add --address-pool ExamRefBackEndPool
--lb-name ExamRefLB --resource-group ExamRef-RG --nic-name vm1-nic
--ip-config-name ipconfig1
```

The final step is to ensure that NSGs are configured to allow incoming traffic and health probe traffic. With this in place, if the VMs added to the backend pool are configured with a web server, you should be able to connect to the public IP address of the load balancer and see the webpage.

Troubleshoot load balancing

Basic- and standard-tier load balancers also support additional diagnostic logs to enable common troubleshooting scenarios. These logs are different between the basic and standard tiers.

Basic-tier load balancer metrics and diagnostics

The basic tier load balancer provides the following diagnostic logs:

- **Alert event logs**   These logs record load balancer alert events. They are written whenever a load balancer alert is raised (max every 5 minutes).
- **Health probe logs**   These logs allow you to investigate the status of health probes for backend servers. They are written whenever there is a change in health probe status.
- **Metrics**   Used to track common load balancer metrics.

To enable basic-tier load-balancer logs, open the load balancer blade in the Azure Portal, select **Diagnostic Logs** and click **Turn On Diagnostics** to open the diagnostics configuration blade, shown in Figure 4-56.

FIGURE 4-56 Configuring diagnostics logs in a basic-tier load-balancer

Having configured the diagnostics logs, they can be downloaded for offline analysis or analyzed using Log Analytics.

Standard-tier load balancer metrics and diagnostics

The standard load balancer also supports diagnostics, via metrics routed automatically to Azure Monitor. Available metrics include byte count, packet count, health probe status, SYN count (for new connections), and more. Azure monitor supports charting and alerting based on these metrics. In addition, they are exposed as *multi-dimensional* metrics, meaning that charts and alerts can be built using filtered views. An example is filtered based on protocol, source IP, or port. An example chart is shown in Figure 4-57.

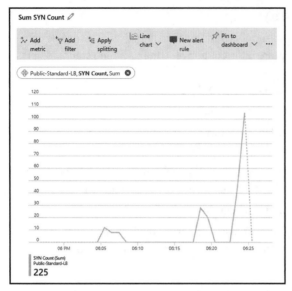

FIGURE 4-57 Azure Monitor chart showing standard load balancer SYN count

Skill 4.6: Monitor and troubleshoot virtual networking

Azure offers numerous features and services to enable you to monitor your network and investigate network issues. These features provide a wide range of diagnostic and alerting capabilities. A good understanding of the range of features available will enable you to investigate network issues quickly and effectively.

> **This section covers how to:**
> - Monitor on-premises connectivity
> - Use network resource monitoring
> - Use Network Watcher
> - Troubleshoot external networking
> - Troubleshoot virtual network connectivity

Monitor on-premises connectivity

Azure Network Performance Monitor (NPM) is a network monitoring solution for hybrid networks. It enables you to monitor network connectivity and performance between various points in your network, both in Azure and on premises. It can provide reports of network performance and raise alerts when network issues are detected.

NPM provides three services:

- **Performance Monitor**   Used to monitor connectivity between various points in your network, both in Azure and on-premises. You can monitor nodes at both ends, gather data on connectivity, packet loss, latency, and available network paths.

- **Service Connectivity Monitor**   Used to monitor outbound connectivity from nodes on your network to any external service with an open TCP port, such as web sites, applications, or databases. This measures latency, response time, and packet loss, enabling you to determine whether poor performance is caused by network or application issues.

- **ExpressRoute**   Used to monitor end-to-end connectivity between your on-premises network and Azure, over ExpressRoute. This service can auto-discover your ExpressRoute network topology. It can then tracking your ExpressRoute bandwidth utilization, packet loss, and latency. These are measured at the circuit, peering and Azure virtual network level.

NPM also provides a dashboard giving an overview of the network status. as well as detailed per-service charts and reports.

Deploying Network Performance Monitor

NPM is a Log Analytics solution. Log Analytics agents are installed on each node used to measure network connectivity and performance. These agents perform synthetic transactions over either TCP or ICMP to measure network performance. Data gathered from these agents is channeled into a Log Analytics workspace. NPM analyzes this data to provide both reporting and alerting.

NPM can be installed from the Azure Marketplace (from the Azure Portal, click **+Create A Resource** and search for **Network Performance Monitor**). It is also available from Network Watcher, an Azure service that acts as a hub for a wide range of network monitoring and diagnostic tools. You will be required to create a Log Analytics workspace or select an existing workspace to use. Be sure to deploy your Log Analytics workspace to one of the regions supported by Network Performance Monitor, as listed at: *https://docs.microsoft.com/azure/azure-monitor/insights/network-performance-monitor#supported-regions*.

Having deployed NPM, the monitoring agents must be installed and configured. The choice of where to install the agents depends on your network topology and which parts of your network you plan to measure. To monitor a given network link, agents should be installed on servers at both ends of that link. To monitor connections between subnets, an agent on at least one server in each subnet is required.

To install the NPM monitoring agent on an Azure virtual machine, simply open the Log Analytics workspace, and click **Virtual Machines** (under **Workspace Data Sources**) to see a list of virtual machines and the status of their Log Analytics connection (Figure 4-58). From there, click on a VM and click **Connect** to add the VM to Log Analytics. After a few minutes, refresh the list of virtual machines to see the updated list.

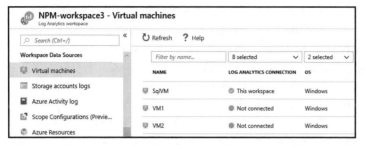

FIGURE 4-58 Connecting Azure Virtual Machines to a Log Analytics workspace

To connect on-premises servers with Log Analytics, you need to install the Log Analytics agent. Open the Log Analytics Workspace, then click **View Solutions** under Configure Monitoring Solutions. Select the NPM solution and click the **Solution Requires Additional Configuration** tile, as shown in Figure 4-59.

FIGURE 4-59 Solution Requires Additional Configuration tile in Network Performance Monitor

Here you will find options to download and install the Log Analytics agent, the workspace IDs and keys needed to configure the agent, and a PowerShell script to open the necessary firewall ports, as shown in Figure 4-60.

FIGURE 4-60 Network Performance Monitor Configuration

Having installed and configured the agents, ensure that Network Security Groups and on-premises firewalls are configured to allow the agents to communicate. The default port used is TCP 8084.

Finally, on the left-nav, complete the Network, Subnetworks, and Nodes sections to describe your network topology, as shown in Figure 4-61. This allows you to define the networks and subnets in your network and identify which monitoring nodes sit within each network segment.

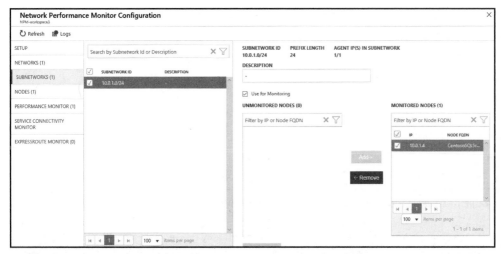

FIGURE 4-61 Network Performance Monitor Network and Subnet Configuration

Performance Monitor

Performance Monitor enables you to monitor packet loss and latency between your endpoints, both in Azure and on-premises. A VM or server running the Log Analytics agent is required at both ends of each monitored connection.

To configure Performance Monitor, first complete the Performance Monitor tab on the Setup section of the Network Performance Monitor Configuration blade. This allows you to specify TCP or ICMP-based monitoring.

Next, use the Performance Monitor section to define your monitoring rules. Each rule requires you to specify the source and destination networks, and the network protocol. You can also choose whether to enable health monitoring events based on defined criteria, and whether to raise alerts based on those events. An example Performance Monitor rule is shown in Figure 4-62.

FIGURE 4-62 Example Performance Monitor Rule Configuration

Once configured, Performance Monitor will continually gather data from the Log Analytics agents, enabling both reporting and alerts. Figure 4-63 gives an example of a packet loss and latency chart from Performance Monitor.

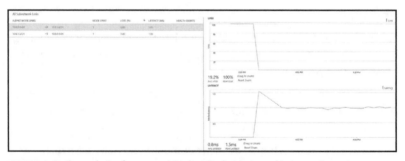

FIGURE 4-63 Example Performance Monitor Packet Loss and Latency Report

Service Connectivity Monitor

Service Connectivity Monitor is used to test outbound connectivity from your network to open a TCP port, such as a website, application, or database. It supports pre-configured endpoints for Microsoft Office365 and Dynamics. You can also configure custom tests to arbitrary endpoints.

To use the pre-configured endpoints, select the Service Connectivity Monitor tab from the setup section of the Network Performance Monitor Configuration blade, as shown in

Figure 4-64. Select the services to monitor, click **+Add Agents** to choose which of your network nodes should monitor these services, then click **Save And Continue**.

FIGURE 4-64 Configuring Service Connectivity Monitor for Microsoft Services

Now move to the Service Connectivity Monitor section, on the left-nav. This shows the existing tests and allows you to configure custom tests. Figure 4-65 shows a custom test to check the availability of the Azure management portal, at *https://portal.azure.com*.

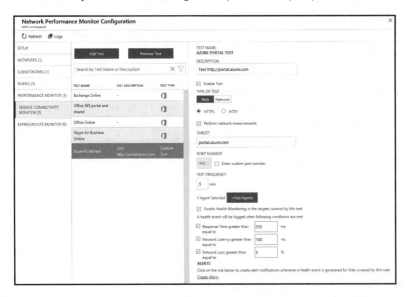

FIGURE 4-65 Configuring a custom test in Service Connectivity Monitor

Once configured, Service Connectivity Monitor will generate packet loss and network performance charts (showing latency and response times) for each tested endpoint. Figure 4-66 provides an example chart.

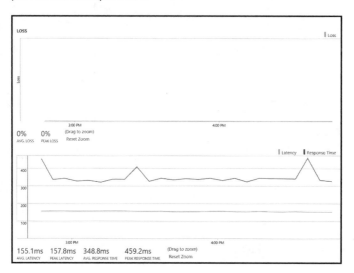

FIGURE 4-66 Packet loss and network performance charts from Service Connectivity Monitor

ExpressRoute Monitor

ExpressRoute Monitor allows you to monitor end-to-end network connectivity and performance between on-premises and Azure endpoints over ExpressRoute connections. It can auto-detect ExpressRoute circuits and your network topology, and track bandwidth utilization, packet loss and network latency. Reports are available for each ExpressRoute circuit or peering, and also for each Azure virtual network using ExpressRoute.

To configure ExpressRoute Monitor, use the ExpressRoute Monitor section of the Network Performance Monitor Configuration blade (see Figure 4-67). First, ExpressRoute resources (such as gateways and circuits) are identified in your subscriptions. Next, the monitoring for each peering can be enabled, configuring health events and choosing monitoring agents.

FIGURE 4-67 Configuring ExpressRoute Monitor

Once configured, it takes 30-60 minutes for the first ExpressRoute reporting data to become available. Several reports and charts are available, including bandwidth utilization, latency, and packet loss for each ExpressRoute circuit and for each peering. A network topology view shows network connections and status (Figure 4-68). Log Analytics alerts can be configured for a wide range of events, such as high latency, packet drops, high and low utilization, and more.

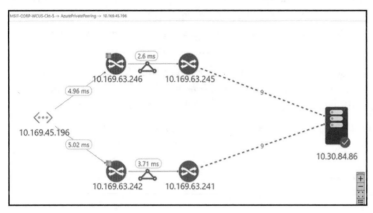

FIGURE 4-68 Network Topology view in ExpressRoute Monitor

Use network resource monitoring

Earlier in this chapter, you saw how Application Gateways and Azure load balancers emit diagnostic logs, which can be used for detailed insight into the status of each service. These logs can be captured in a storage account, streamed to an EventHub, or integrated with an Azure Log Analytics workspace, which enables customized queries and log-based alerting. In the case of App Gateway, you also saw how the Azure Application Gateway Analytics Log Analytics solution provides a pre-configured dashboard and charts showing App Gateway status.

Diagnostic logs are also available for a number of other networking resources, including Traffic Manager, Azure DNS, and Network Security Groups. In each case, they give deeper insight into the status and operation of each service, as well as supporting log-based alerts through Log Analytics. In the case of NSGs, the Traffic Analytics Log Analytics solution provides detailed reports giving insight into the successful and blocked traffic flows into and out of your Azure services.

Use Network Watcher

Network Watcher provides a central hub for a wide range of network monitoring and diagnostic tools. These tools are valuable across a wide range of network troubleshooting scenarios, and also provide access to other tools listed in this skill section, such as the Network Performance Monitor and Connection Monitor.

Deploying Network Watcher

Network Watcher is enabled as a single instance per Azure region. It is not deployed like a conventional Azure resource, although it does appear as a resource in a resource group.

Any subscription containing a virtual network resource will automatically have Network Watcher enabled. Otherwise, it can be enabled via the Azure Portal, under All Services, Network Watcher, which also shows the Network Watcher status per region. It can also be deployed via the command line (using the New-AzNetworkWatcher cmdlet or the az network watcher configure command), which unlike the Azure Portal gives control over the resource group used.

Some of the Network Watcher tools require the Network Watcher VM extension to be installed on the VM being monitored. This extension is available for both Windows and Linux VMs. It is installed automatically when using Network Watcher via the Azure Portal.

The Network Watcher VM extension can also be installed via Azure PowerShell:

```
# Install Network Watcher VM extension
Set-AzVMExtension `
    -ResourceGroupName ExamRef-RG `
    -Location "West Europe" `
    -VMName VM1 `
    -Name networkWatcherAgent `
    -Publisher Microsoft.Azure.NetworkWatcher `
    -Type NetworkWatcherAgentWindows `
    -TypeHandlerVersion 1.4
```

It can also be installed via the Azure CLI:

```
# Install Network Watcher VM extension
az vm extension set --vm-name VM1 --resource-group ExamRef-RG
--publisher Microsoft.Azure.NetworkWatcher --version 1.4
--name NetworkWatcherAgentWindows --extension-instance-name NetworkWatcherAgent
```

IP Flow Verify

The IP Flow Verify tool provides a quick and easy way to test if a given network flow will be allowed into or out of an Azure virtual machine. It will report whether the requested traffic is allowed or blocked, and in the latter case which NSG rule is blocking the flow. It is a useful tool for verifying that NSGs are correctly configured.

It works by simulating the requested packet flow through the NSGs applied to the VM. For this reason, the VM must be in a running state.

To use IP Flow Verify via the Azure Portal, open Network Watcher and click IP Flow Verify. Select the VM and NIC to verify, and specify the protocol, direction, and remote and local IP addresses and ports, as shown in Figure 4-69.

FIGURE 4-69 Using Network Watcher IP Flow Verify

IP Flow verify can also be used from PowerShell, using the `Test-AzNetworkWatcherIPFlow` cmdlet, or the Azure CLI, using the `az network watcher test-ip-flow` command.

Next Hop

The Next Hop tool provides a useful way to understand how a VM's outbound traffic is being directed. For a given outbound flow, it shows the next hop IP address and type, and the route table ID of any user-defined route in effect. Possible next hop types are:

- Internet
- VirtualAppliance
- VirtualNetworkGateway
- VirtualNetwork
- VirtualNetworkPeering
- VirtualNetworkServiceEndpoint
- None (this is used for user-defined routes)

To use Next Hop via the Azure Portal, open Network Watcher and click **Next Hop**. Select the source VM, NIC and IP address, and the destination address, as shown in Figure 4-70. The destination can be any IP address, either on the internal network or the Internet.

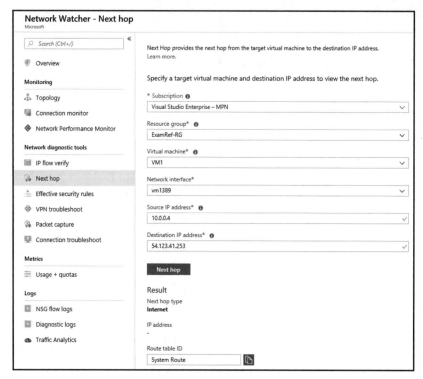

FIGURE 4-70 Using Network Watcher Next Hop

Next Hop can also be used from PowerShell using the `Get-AzNetworkWatcherNextHop` cmdlet, or the Azure CLI using the `az network watcher show-next-hop` command.

Packet Captures

The Packet Capture tool allows you to capture network packets entering or leaving your virtual machines. It is a powerful tool for deep network diagnostics.

You can capture all packets, or a filtered subset based on protocol and local and remote IP addresses and ports. You can also specify the maximum packet and overall capture size, and a time limit (captures start almost immediately once configured).

Packet captures are stored as a file on the VM or in an Azure storage account, in which case NSGs must allow access from the VM to Azure storage. These captures are in a standard format, and can be analyzed off-line using common tools such as WireShark or Microsoft Message Analyzer.

To use the Packet Capture tool, open Network Watcher and click on **Packet Capture**, then click **+Add**. Select the VM, give the capture a name, and specify the destination, packet and total size, time limit, and filters. An example is shown in Figure 4-71.

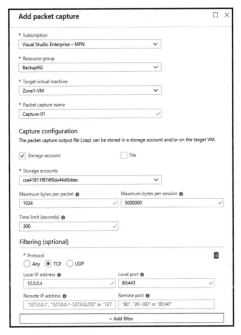

FIGURE 4-71 Using Network Watcher Packet Capture

Packet Capture can also be used from PowerShell. The following script shows how to start a packet capture, check packet capture status, and stop a packet capture.

```
# Get the Network Watcher resource
$nw = Get-AzResource | Where {$_.ResourceType `
    -eq "Microsoft.Network/networkWatchers" -and $_.Location -eq "WestEurope" }

$networkWatcher = Get-AzNetworkWatcher `
    -Name $nw.Name `
    -ResourceGroupName $nw.ResourceGroupName

# Get the storage account to store the capture in
$storageAccount = Get-AzStorageAccount `
    -Name examref-storage `
    -ResourceGroupName ExamRef-RG

# Set up filters
$filter1 = New-AzPacketCaptureFilterConfig `
    -Protocol TCP `
        -RemoteIPAddress "1.1.1.1-255.255.255.255" `
    -LocalIPAddress "10.0.0.3" `
    -LocalPort "1-65535" `
    -RemotePort "20;80;443"

$filter2 = New-AzPacketCaptureFilterConfig `
    -Protocol UDP

# Get the VM
$vm = Get-AzVM -Name VM1 -ResourceGroupName ExamRef-RG
```

```
# Start the packet capture
New-AzNetworkWatcherPacketCapture `
    -NetworkWatcher $networkWatcher `
    -TargetVirtualMachineId $vm.Id `
    -PacketCaptureName "PacketCaptureTest" `
    -StorageAccountId $storageAccount.id `
    -TimeLimitInSeconds 60 `
    -Filter $filter1, $filter2

# Check packet capture status
Get-AzNetworkWatcherPacketCapture `
    -NetworkWatcher $networkWatcher `
    -PacketCaptureName "PacketCaptureTest"

# Stop packet capture
Stop-AzNetworkWatcherPacketCapture `
    -NetworkWatcher $networkWatcher `
    -PacketCaptureName "PacketCaptureTest"
```

You can also use Packet Capture from the Azure CLI, as shown in the following script:

```
# Start packet capture
az network watcher packet-capture create --name PacketCaptureTest2
--resource-group ExamRef-RG --vm VM1 --time-limit 300
--storage-account examref-storage --filters '[ { "protocol":
"TCP","remoteIPAddress":"1.1.1.1-255.255.255.255","localIPAddress":"10.0.0.3","remotePo
rt":"20"} ]'

# Get packet capture status
az network watcher packet-capture show-status --name PacketCaptureTest2
--location WestEurope

# Stop packet capture
az network watcher packet-capture stop --name PacketCaptureTest2
--location WestEurope
```

Network Topology

The Network Topology view in Network watcher provides a diagrammatic view of the resources in your virtual network. It is not a diagnostic or alerting tool. It is a quick and easy way to review your network resources and manually check for misconfiguration.

A limitation of the tool is that it only shows the topology within a single virtual network. All common network resource types are supported, although for Application Gateways, only the backend pool connected to the network interface is shown.

To use Network Topology via the Azure Portal, open Network Watcher and click **Topology**. Select the resource group and virtual network, and the topology will be shown.

An example topology is given in Figure 4-72. In this example, you can see that the NSG has been misconfigured, since it is configured on VM1, but not on VM2. An NSG should be added to VM2 or moved to the subnet level.

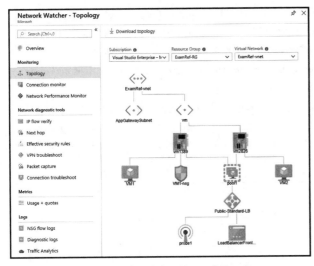

FIGURE 4-72 Using Network Watcher Network Topology

The underlying topology data can be downloaded in JSON format via Azure PowerShell or the Azure CLI, using the `Get-AzNetworkWatcherTopology` cmdlet or the `az network watcher show-topology` command, respectively.

Troubleshoot external networking

We have already seen how the Network Performance Monitor provides a range of powerful features to monitor and diagnose issues across both Azure and on-premises networks, including detailed analytics for ExpressRoute connections.

Another pair of useful tools to investigate issues with external networks are the Connection Monitor and Connection Troubleshoot tools in Network Watcher. These are discussed in the next section: "Troubleshoot virtual network connectivity."

In this section we discuss another feature of Network Watcher, VPN Troubleshoot, which is designed specifically to diagnose problems with VPN connections.

Do not forget—for simple validation that a VPN connection is working, it's also always worthwhile trying to connect between VMs on either end of VPN tunnel, using standard tools such as `tcping`.

VPN Troubleshoot

The VPN Troubleshoot feature in Network Watcher provides automated diagnostics of Azure VPN gateways and connections. The results provide a detailed report on gateway health and connection health, providing accurate pointers on common issues enabling informed remediations.

VPN Troubleshoot only supports route-based VPN gateways (not policy-based gateways or ExpressRoute gateways). It supports both IPsec Site-to-Site VPNs and Vnet-to-Vnet connections; it does not support ExpressRoute connections or Point-to-Site connections.

During the troubleshooting process, logs are written to a storage account. This account must be created before starting the troubleshooting process.

To use VPN Troubleshoot via the Azure Portal, first open **Network Watcher**, followed by clicking **VPN Troubleshoot**. Select the storage container for the troubleshooting logs, then select which VPN resources to troubleshoot, as shown in Figure 4-73. Finally, click **Start Troubleshooting**.

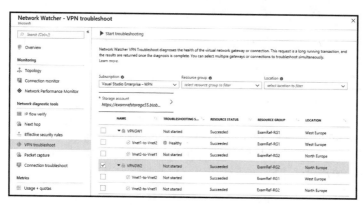

FIGURE 4-73 Using Network Watcher VPN Troubleshoot

The troubleshooting process takes a few minutes to run. Once complete, the results will be shown at the bottom of the page, as shown in Figure 4-74.

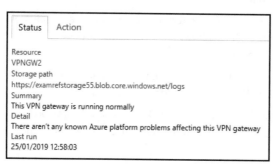

FIGURE 4-74 Network Watcher VPN Troubleshoot Results

VPN Troubleshoot can also be accessed via PowerShell, as demonstrated in the following script. In this example, troubleshooting is run on a VPN connection. It can also be run on a VPN gateway.

```
# Get the Network Watcher resource
$nw = Get-AzResource | Where {$_.ResourceType `
    -eq "Microsoft.Network/networkWatchers" -and $_.Location -eq "WestEurope" }

$networkWatcher = Get-AzNetworkWatcher `
    -Name $nw.Name `
    -ResourceGroupName $nw.ResourceGroupName

# Create a storage account and container for logs
# (You could also use an existing account/container)
$sa = New-AzStorageAccount `
    -Name examrefstorage `
    -SKU Standard_LRS `
    -ResourceGroupName ExamRef-RG `
    -Location "WestEurope"

Set-AzCurrentStorageAccount -ResourceGroupName $sa.ResourceGroupName
-Name $sa.StorageAccountName

$sc = New-AzureStorageContainer -Name logs

# Get the connection to troubleshoot
$connection = Get-AzVirtualNetworkGatewayConnection `
    -Name Vnet1-to-Vnet2 `
    -ResourceGroupName ExamRef-RG1

# Start VPN Troubleshoot
Start-AzNetworkWatcherResourceTroubleshooting `
    -NetworkWatcher $networkWatcher `
    -TargetResourceId $connection.Id `
    -StorageId $sa.Id `
    -StoragePath "$($sa.PrimaryEndpoints.Blob)$($sc.name)"
```

VPN Troubleshoot can also be accessed via the Azure CLI. In these example commands, values in { } should be replaced with the output of earlier commands.

```
# Crate a storage account and container for logs
# (You could also use an existing account/container)
az storage account create --name examrefstorage --location westeurope
--resource-group ExamRef-RG --sku Standard_LRS
az storage account keys list --resource-group ExamRef-RG
--account-name examrefstorage
az storage container create --account-name examrefstorage
--account-key {storageAccountKey} --name logs

# Start VPN Troubleshoot
# Note: Assumes storage account and VPN connection are in the same resource group
# If not, specify using full resource IDs instead
# Use JSON output, since table output does not show the actual troubleshooting result
az network watcher troubleshooting start --resource-group ExamRef-RG
--resource Vnet1-to-Vnet2 --resource-type vpnConnection
--storage-account examrefstorage --storage-path
https://examrefstorage.blob.core.windows.net/logs --output json
```

Troubleshoot virtual network connectivity

A number of the tools we have already seen can be useful for troubleshooting connectivity issues between and within virtual networks. Network Watcher offers two more tools that are particularly useful in this scenario: Connection Troubleshoot and Connection Monitor.

Connection Troubleshoot

Connection Troubleshoot is a Network Watcher feature designed to allow you to test the connectivity between an Azure VM or an App Gateway and another endpoint—either another Azure VM, or an arbitrary Internet or Intranet endpoint. This diagnostic tool can identify a range of problems, including guest VM issues, such as guest firewall configuration, low memory or high CPU, Azure configuration issues such as Network Security Groups blocking traffic, or routing issues diverting traffic. It can also diagnose other network issues, such as DNS failures.

To use Connection Troubleshoot from the Azure Portal, open **Network Watcher** then click **Connection Troubleshoot**. Specify the source VM, then specify the destination, either as another VM or by giving a URI, FQDN, or IPv4 address. Specify the protocol to use (either TCP or ICMP). For TCP, you can specify the destination port, and, under **Advanced Settings**, the source port. An example configuration is shown in Figure 4-75.

FIGURE 4-75 Network Watcher Connection Troubleshoot configuration

The test takes a few minutes to run. Upon completion, the results will be shown at the bottom of the page. An example output is shown in Figure 4-76.

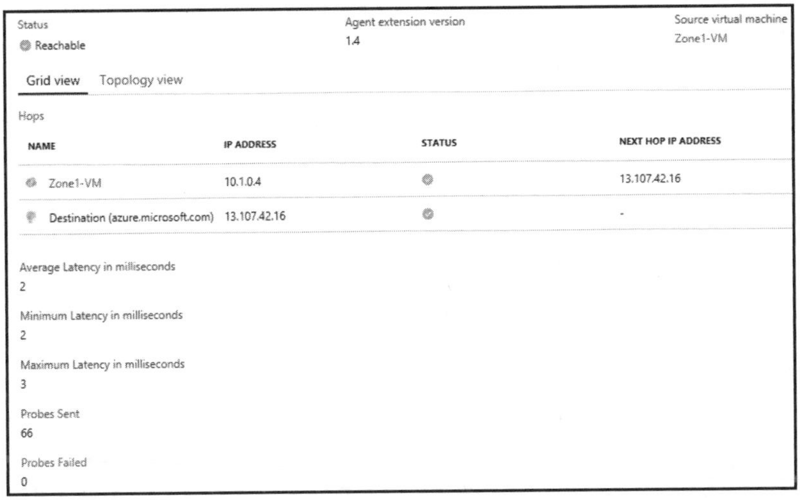

FIGURE 4-76 Network Watcher Connection Troubleshoot results

Connection Troubleshoot is also available via PowerShell, using the `Test-AzNetworkWatcherConnectivity` cmdlet, and via the Azure CLI, using the az network watcher az `network watcher test-connectivity` command.

Connection Monitor

The Connection Monitor in Network Watcher is similar to Connection Troubleshoot, in that it uses the same mechanism to test the connection between an Azure VM or App Gateway and another endpoint. The difference is that Connection Monitor provides ongoing connection monitoring, whereas Connection Troubleshoot only provides a point-in-time test.

Data from Connection Monitor is surfaced in Azure Monitor. Charts show key metrics such as round-trip time and probe failures. Azure Monitor can also be used to configure alerts, triggered by connection failures or a drop in performance.

To use Connection Monitor via the Azure Portal, open **Network Watcher**, then click **Connection Monitor**. A list of active monitored connections is shown. Click **+Add** to create a new monitored connection, then fill in the connection settings. The settings are the same as for Connection Troubleshoot, plus the probe frequency. An example is shown in Figure 4-77.

FIGURE 4-77 Network Watcher Connection Monitor configuration

The monitored connection will be listed on the Connection Monitor blade within Network Watcher. Click on a monitored connection to open the results panel, as shown in Figure 4-78. The chart shows average round-trip time and % probe failures. Click on the chart to view the data in Azure Monitor. From there, alerts can be configured based on these metrics exceeding thresholds you define. The table below the chart shows the current connection status—clicking on each line gives further details about the status, which is similar to the results obtained from Connection Troubleshoot.

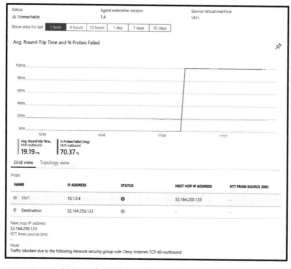

FIGURE 4-78 Network Watcher Connection Monitor status

Skill 4.7: Integrate on-premises network with Azure virtual network

Many Azure deployments require connectivity between the on-premises network and the Azure VNet. This integrated network is called a *hybrid network*.

Hybrid networks are commonly used for Intranet applications, which may be hosted in Azure but only accessed from the on-premises network. They are also used by Azure applications that require access to an on-premises resource, such as a database.

Hybrid networks provide connectivity between the private IP space of the on-premises network and the private IP space of the Azure VNet. The VNet can be thought of as an extension of the existing on-premises network. The concept is similar to extending the on-premises network to a new office location.

> **This section covers how to:**
> - Create and configure Azure VPN Gateway
> - Create and configure site-to-site VPN
> - Configure Express Route
> - Verify and troubleshoot on-premises connectivity

Create and configure Azure VPN Gateway

A virtual network gateway allows you to create connections from your virtual network to other networks. When creating a gateway, you must specify if it will be used for VPN connections or ExpressRoute connections. Virtual network gateways used for VPN connections are called a VPN gateway, while those used for ExpressRoute connections are called ExpressRoute gateways.

Earlier in this chapter we saw how VPN gateways can be used to connect one Azure VNet to another. They can also be used to create VPN tunnels between Azure VNets and on-premises networks—this is called a site-to-site VPN. They can also be used as a hub for point-to-site networks, where individual machines connect to an Azure VNet via the VPN client on the machine.

Gateway subnets

VPN gateways can only be deployed to a dedicated gateway subnet within the VNet. A gateway subnet is a special type of subnet that can only be used for virtual network gateways. Under the hood, the VPN gateway is implemented using Azure virtual machines (these are not directly accessible and are managed for you). While the minimum size for the gateway subnet is a CIDR /29, the Microsoft-recommended best practice is to use a CIDR /27 address block to allow for future expansion.

A VPN connection between an on-premises network and an Azure VNet can only be established if the network ranges do not overlap. Network address ranges should be planned carefully to avoid restricting future connectivity options.

Gateway SKUs

VPN Gateways are available in several pricing tiers, or SKUs. The correct tier should be chosen based on the required network capacity, as shown in Table 4-12.

TABLE 4-12 Comparison of VPN Gateway Pricing Tiers

SKU	Max Site-to-Site VPN Connections	Throughput
Basic	10	100 Mbps
VpnGw1 and VpnGw1Az	30	650 Mbps
VpnGw2 and VpnGw2Az	30	1 Gbps
VpnGw3 and VpnGw3Az	30	1.25 Gbps

> **NOTE RESIZING VPN GATEWAYS**
>
> You can resize a gateway between the VpnGw1, 2, and 3 tiers. You cannot, however, resize a Basic tier gateway.

BGP

Border Gateway Protocol (BGP) is a standard used in the Internet to exchange routing information between networks. BGP can be optionally enabled on your VPN gateway, if the on-premises gateway also supports it. If used, it enables the VPN gateway and the on-premises gateway to exchange routing information automatically, avoiding the need to configure routes manually.

BGP also enables high availability redundant connections (see next section) advanced features such as transit routing across multiple networks. It is also used where a VPN connection is used as a failover in case the primary connection, using ExpressRoute, were to fail.

High Availability

By default, each VPN gateway is deployed as two VMs in an active-standby configuration. To reduce downtime in the event the active instance fails, an active-active configuration can also be used (not supported for Basic SKU gateways). In this mode, both gateway instances have their own public IP addresses, and two connections are made to the on-premises VPN endpoint.

Dual on-premises VPN endpoints can also be used. This requires BGP to be enabled, and works with both active-standby or active-active VPN gateways. Combining dual on-premises endpoints with active-active VPN gateways provides a fully-redundant configuration, avoiding single points of failure, as shown in Figure 4-79. In this configuration, Traffic will be distributed over all four VPN tunnels.

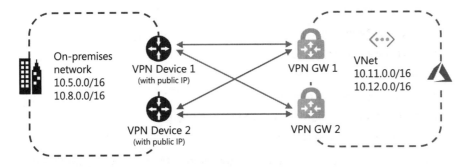

FIGURE 4-79 Dual on-premises VPN endpoints connected to active-active VPN gateways

For increased resilience to datacenter-level failures, virtual network gateways can be deployed to availability zones. This requires the use of dedicated SKUs, called VpnGw1Az, VpnGw2Az, and VpnGw3Az. Both zone-redundant and zone-specific deployment models are supported, the choice being inferred from the associated public IP address rather than being specified explicitly as a gateway property.

Create a VPN Gateway using the Azure Portal

Before creating the VPN gateway, first create the gateway subnet. Using the Azure Portal, navigate to your virtual network and click the **Subnets** link under **Settings** to open the subnets blade. Click the **+Gateway Subnet** button and assign an address space using a /27 CIDR, as seen in Figure 4-80. Do not modify the other subnet settings.

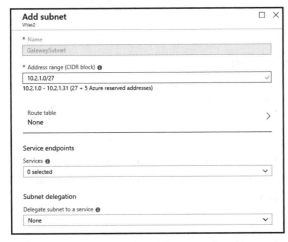

FIGURE 4-80 Adding a Gateway Subnet to a virtual network

Next, provision a VPN gateway as follows. From the Azure Portal, click **+Create A Resource**, then click **Networking,** and then select **Virtual Network Gateway**. Complete the **Create Virtual Network Gateway**' blade as follows:

- **Name** VNet-GW

- **Gateway type** VPN

- **VPN Type** Route-based

- **SKU** VpnGw1

- **Virtual Network** <choose your VNet>

- **First IP Configuration** Create New, VNet-GW-IP

- **Location** <Same as your VNet>

Do not select the checkboxes for **Enable Active-Active Mode** or **Configure BGP ASN**'. Figure 4-81 shows the completed gateway settings.

FIGURE 4-81 Creating an Azure VPN Gateway

Create a VPN Gateway using PowerShell

The process for creating VPN gateways and VNet-to-VNet connections using Azure PowerShell follows the same steps as used by the Azure Portal, as the following script demonstrates.

> **NOTE** **GATEWAY SUBNETS**
>
> When creating the gateway subnet, there is no special parameter or cmdlet name to denote that this is a gateway subnet rather than a normal subnet. The only distinction that identifies a gateway subnet is the subnet name, GatewaySubnet.

```
# Script to set up VPN gateways and VNet-to-VNet connection
# Assumes VNet1 is already created, with IP address ranges 10.1.0.0/16

# Name of resource group
$rg = 'ExamRef-RG'

# Create gateway subnet in VNet1
# Note: Gateway subnets are just normal subnets, with the name 'GatewaySubnet'
$vnet1 = Get-AzVirtualNetwork`
    -Name VNet1 `
```

```
    -ResourceGroupName $rg

$vnet1.Subnets += New-AzVirtualNetworkSubnetConfig `
    -Name GatewaySubnet `
    -AddressPrefix 10.1.1.0/27

$vnet1 = Set-AzVirtualNetwork `
    -VirtualNetwork $vnet1

# Create VPN gateway in VNet1
$gwpip = New-AzPublicIpAddress `
    -Name VNet1-GW-IP `
    -ResourceGroupName $rg `
    -Location 'North Europe' `
    -AllocationMethod Dynamic

$gwsubnet   = Get-AzVirtualNetworkSubnetConfig `
    -Name 'GatewaySubnet' `
    -VirtualNetwork $vnet1

$gwipconf = New-AzVirtualNetworkGatewayIpConfig `
    -Name GwIPConf `
    -Subnet $gwsubnet `
    -PublicIpAddress $gwpip

$vnet1gw = New-AzVirtualNetworkGateway `
    -Name VNet1-GW `
    -ResourceGroupName $rg `
    -Location 'North Europe' `
    -IpConfigurations $gwipconf `
    -GatewayType Vpn `
    -VpnType RouteBased `
    -GatewaySku VpnGw1
```

Create a VPN Gateway using the Azure CLI

The process for creating VPN gateways using the Azure CLI follows similar steps. First the public
IP address and gateway subnet are created, followed by the gateway itself. Once again, the
gateway subnet is created simply by specifying the name 'GatewaySubnet' when creating a
normal subnet.

In this case, the public IP address required by the VPN gateway must be created beforehand, rather than being created implicitly when creating the gateway.

```
# Create VPN gateway in VNet1 (already created, with IP address ranges 10.1.0.0/16)

# Create gateway subnets in VNet2 and VNet3
az network vnet subnet create --name GatewaySubnet --vnet-name VNet1
--resource-group ExamRef-RG --address-prefixes 10.1.1.0/27

# Create public IP addresses for use by VPN gateway
az network public-ip create --name VNet1-GW-IP --resource-group ExamRef-RG
--location NorthEurope
```

```
# Create VPN gateway in VNet1
az network vnet-gateway create --name VNet1-GW --resource-group ExamRef-RG
--gateway-type vpn --sku VpnGw1 --vpn-type RouteBased --vnet VNet1
--public-ip-addresses VNet1-GW-IP --location NorthEurope
```

Create and configure site-to-site VPN

Site-to-site VPNs enable on-premises networks to be connected to an Azure virtual network. This connection enables on-premises servers and Azure VMs to communicate over their private network space, without being exposed to the Internet.

Site-to-Site connections are established between your VPN on-premises device and an Azure VPN gateway. Traffic flows over the public Internet, enclosed in a secure, encrypted tunnel between these two endpoints. The underlying VPN encryption method used is IPsec IKEv2. An example is illustrated in Figure 4-82.

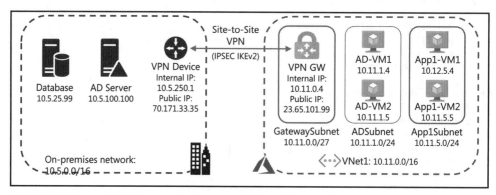

FIGURE 4-82 Site-to-site VPN connection between Azure and On-Premises

Supported VPN devices

A wide range of on-premises VPN devices is supported for Azure Site-to-Site VPNs, from many device manufacturers. A full list, including links to configuration instructions, is given in the Azure documentation (see *https://docs.microsoft.com/azure/vpn-gateway/vpn-gateway-about-vpn-devices*). For certain devices, Azure also provides configuration scripts to automate the setup process.

If you do not have access to a hardware VPN device, a software-based device can be used, such as Microsoft Routing and Remote Access Service (RRAS) on Windows, or OpenSWAN on Linux.

Multi-Site networks

Each VPN gateway can support multiple Site-to-Site VPN connections. This is called a *multi-site connection*. Multi-site connections are commonly used to connect an Azure virtual network to multiple on-premises sites. They can also be used to create VPN connections to other Azure virtual networks in cases where VNet peering is not available (see Skill 4.2).

To use a multi-site connection, a route-based VPN is required. Since each VNet supports only a single VPN gateway, all connections share the available bandwidth. In Figure 4-83, you see an example of a network with three sites and two VNets in different Azure regions.

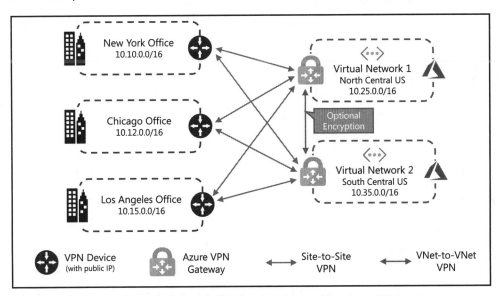

FIGURE 4-83 Multi-Site Site-to-Site Network with three locations and two Azure VNets

Create a Site-to-Site VPN using the Azure Portal

Before creating a Site-to-Site VPN connection, ensure that your on-premises VPN device is supported and deployed with a static Internet-facing IPv4 address. Plan your network so that on-premises and Azure address spaces do not overlap, then deploy your Azure VPN gateway as described earlier.

Next, deploy a local network gateway resource in Azure. This resource represents your on-premises network and is where details of that network (such as IP prefixes and the gateway IP address) are configured. In the Azure Portal, click **+Create A Resource** and search for **ocal network gateway**, and click to open the **Create Local Network Gateway** blade as shown in Figure 4-84. Fill in the blade as follows:

- **Name**   Choose a name for the local network gateway resource.
- **IP address**   The Internet-facing IP address of your on-premises VPN gateway.
- **Address space**   The on-premises network address space.
- **Configure BGP settings**   Leave unchecked, unless using BGP.
- **Subscription**, **resource group and location**   Choose any values. The location does not have to match the location of your VPN gateway.

FIGURE 4-84 Create Local Network Gateway

Next, configure your on-premises VPN device. You will need to specify a shared key (choose any sufficiently random, secret value) and the public IP address of the Azure VPN gateway. Use the configuration guides or configuration scripts available from the Azure documentation pages, if available for your device.

Next, create the VPN connection in Azure. Open the blade for your VPN gateway, and click **Connections** to see the list of current connections. Then click **+Add** to open the **Add Connection** blade, as shown in Figure 4-85. Fill in the blade as follows:

- **Name**   Choose a name for the connection
- **Connection type**   Site-to-site (IPsec)
- **Virtual network gateway**   The currently selected Azure VPN gateway (fixed)
- **Local network gateway**   Choose your local network gateway resource
- **Shared key (PSK)**   Enter the same value as used on-premises

- **Subscription, resource group, and location** These are taken from the VPN gateway (fixed)

FIGURE 4-85 Add VPN Connection

The VPN connection will now be created. The connection status can be seen in the Connections list for the VPN gateway. The status will initially be **Updating**, and after a few moments it should change to **Connected** once the connection is established, as shown in Figure 4-86.

FIGURE 4-86 VPN Connection status Connected

Configure a Site-to-Site VPN using Azure PowerShell

The process for creating a Site-to-Site VPN using Azure PowerShell follows the same steps required for the Azure Portal. We assume you have already planned your network, deployed your on-premises VPN device, and created your VPN gateway in Azure, as described earlier. The follow script shows how to create the local network gateway and the VPN connection.

```
# Create local network gateway
$localnw = New-AzLocalNetworkGateway `
    -Name LocalNetGW `
    -ResourceGroupName ExamRef-RG `
    -Location "West Europe" `
    -GatewayIpAddress "53.50.123.195" `
    -AddressPrefix "10.5.0.0/16"
```

```
# Get VPN gateway
$gateway = Get-AzVirtualNetworkGateway `
    -Name VPNGW1 `
    -ResourceGroupName ExamRef-RG

# Create the connection
$conn = New-AzVirtualNetworkGatewayConnection `
    -Name OnPremConnection `
    -ResourceGroupName ExamRef-RG `
    -Location 'West Europe' `
    -VirtualNetworkGateway1 $gateway `
    -LocalNetworkGateway2 $localnw `
    -ConnectionType IPsec `
    -SharedKey "abc123"
```

Configure a Site-to-Site VPN using the Azure CLI

The process for creating a Site-to-Site VPN using the Azure CLI follows the same steps as the Azure Portal and Azure PowerShell. The following script shows how to create the local network gateway and the VPN connection, assuming the on-premises VPN device and Azure VPN gateway have already been deployed.

```
# Create Local Network Gateway
az network local-gateway create --gateway-ip-address 53.50.123.195
--name LocalNetGW --resource-group ExamRef-RG --local-address-prefixes 10.5.0.0/16

# Create VPN Connection
az network vpn-connection create --name OnPremConnection -resource-group
ExamRef-RG --vnet-gateway1 VPNGW1 --location WestEurope --shared-key abc123
--local-gateway2 LocalNetGW
```

Configure ExpressRoute

ExpressRoute is a secure and reliable private connection between your on-premises network and the Microsoft cloud. The connection is provided by a third-party network provider who has partnered with Microsoft to offer ExpressRoute services. This third party is known as the *ExpressRoute provider*.

Unlike a Site-to-Site VPN, network traffic using ExpressRoute uses your provider's network and does not pass over the Internet. The latency and bandwidth for an ExpressRoute circuit is therefore more predictable and stable because traffic stays on your provider's network.

Another key difference between ExpressRoute connections and Site-to-Site VPN connections is that Site-to-Site VPN connections only provide connectivity to your Azure VNet, whereas ExpressRoute provides connectivity to all Microsoft cloud services. This includes Azure VNets, Azure platform services (such as CosmosDB), and Microsoft services outside of Azure such as Office 365 and Dynamics 365.

Connectivity models

ExpressRoute connectivity can be established in one of three ways. The capabilities and features of ExpressRoute are the same in each case.

- If your network already has a presence at a co-location facility with a cloud exchange, your co-location provider can establish a virtual cross-connection with the Microsoft Cloud. This provides either a layer 2 or a managed layer 3 connection.

- Your connectivity provider may be able to provide a point-to-point ethernet connection from their network to your on-premises network. Again, this approach offers either a layer 2 or managed layer 3 connection.

- Finally, your existing IPVPN WAN provider may be able to integrate ExpressRoute into your WAN, if they are registered as an ExpressRoute provider. In this case, your provider will typically offer managed layer 3 connectivity.

These connectivity options are shown in Figure 4-87.

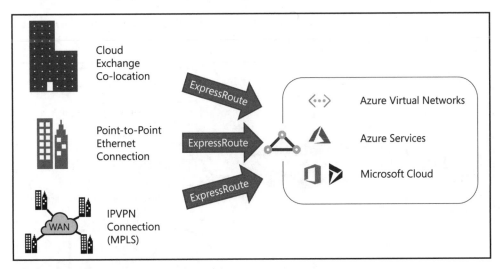

FIGURE 4-87 ExpressRoute connectivity models

Circuits and peering

An ExpressRoute circuit is an Azure resource used to represent the logical connection between your on-premises network and Microsoft. Each circuit is identified by a GUID called a *service key* (s-key), which is shared with your connectivity provider.

Each circuit has a fixed bandwidth, and a specific peering location. The available bandwidth options are 50 Mbps, 100 Mbps, 200 Mbps, 500 Mbps, 1 Gbps, 2 Gbps, 5 Gbps, and 10 Gbps. This bandwidth can be either metered or unlimited:

- **Metered**   All inbound data transfer is free of charge, and all outbound data transfer is charged based on a pre-determined rate. Users are also charged a fixed monthly port fee (based on high-availability dual ports).

- **Unlimited**   All inbound and outbound data transfer is free of charge. Users are charged a single fixed monthly port fee (based on high-availability dual ports).

New ExpressRoute circuits offer two peering options, also known as routing domains: Private or Microsoft Peering. Each circuit can use either one or both peerings. These peerings are shown in Figure 4-88.

- **Azure Private Peering**   Provides connectivity over the Intranet address space into your Azure virtual network. This peering is considered a trusted extension of your core network into Azure.

- **Microsoft Peering**   Provides connectivity over the Internet address space into Microsoft services such as Office 365, Dynamics 365, and Internet-facing endpoints of Azure platform (PaaS) services.

Older circuits may use a third peering model, Azure Public Peering, which provides connectivity to Azure PaaS services only. This is deprecated for new circuits.

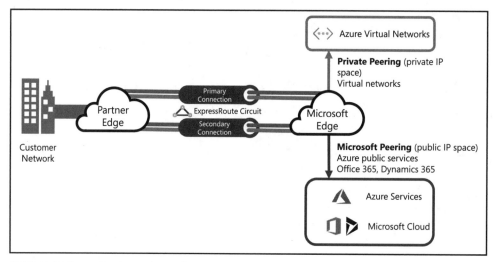

FIGURE 4-88 ExpressRoute peering options

Each ExpressRoute circuit has two connections from your network edge to two Microsoft edge routers, configured using BGP. Microsoft requires dual BGP connections from your edge to each Microsoft edge router. You can choose not to deploy redundant devices or ethernet circuits at your end; however, connectivity providers use redundant devices to ensure that your connections are handed off for high availability to Microsoft in a redundant manner. Figure 4-89 shows a redundant connectivity configuration.

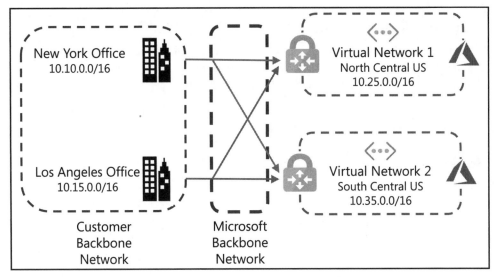

FIGURE 4-89 Multiple cities connected to ExpressRoute in two Azure regions

Global availability and ExpressRoute Premium

ExpressRoute is only available in certain cities throughout the world, so it is important to check with your local providers to determine availability. For a list of ExpressRoute providers and their supported locations, see: *https://docs.microsoft.com/azure/expressroute/expressroute-locations*.

By default, each ExpressRoute circuit enables connectivity to Microsoft data centers within a geopolitical region. For example, a connection in Amsterdam gives you access to all Microsoft datacenters in Europe.

With the ExpressRoute Premium add-on, connectivity is extended to all Microsoft datacenters worldwide. This add-on also raises the number of routes permitted for the Azure Private Peering from 4,000 to 10,000. It also increases the number of virtual networks that can be connected to each ExpressRoute circuit, from 10 to between 20 and 100 (depending on the bandwidth of the circuit).

Creating an ExpressRoute circuit

To create an ExpressRoute circuit using the Azure Portal, click **+Create a resource**, then **Networking**, then **ExpressRoute** to open the Create ExpressRoute blade (Figure 4-90). Specify the circuit name, provider and peering location, then specify the bandwidth, billing model, and whether or not the ExpressRoute Premium add-on is required. Finally, specify the subscription, resource group, and resource location.

FIGURE 4-90 Creating an ExpressRoute circuit

The ExpressRoute circuit will be created. The resource overview blade will show the provider status as Not Provisioned, and also shows the service key. Copy the service key and share it with your ExpressRoute provider. The provider status will change to Provisioning and finally to Provisioned once the provider setup is complete.

Next, you need to provision either Azure Private Peering or Microsoft Peering for your circuit. From the ExpressRoute circuit blade, click **Peerings**, and select the type of peering to configure. Fill in the BGP ASN, and subnets as promoted, and then save the configuration.

For Microsoft Peering, you may see the status Validation Needed for the advertised public IP prefixes. This is because Microsoft needs to validate that you own these IP prefixes before updating their routing to use the ExpressRoute connection. In this case, use the Azure Portal to raise a support ticket to perform the validation.

Connecting virtual networks to ExpressRoute

Virtual networks are connected to ExpressRoute circuits using an ExpressRoute gateway. An ExpressRoute gateway is a virtual network gateway, created with the ExpressRoute option (rather than the VPN option, used to create VPN gateways). Just as with VPN gateways, the ExpressRoute gateway must be created in the gateway subnet of the virtual network.

Once the ExpressRoute gateway is created, it can be connected to the ExpressRoute circuit. The process is the same as adding a VPN connection to a VPN gateway, except that the ExpressRoute connection type is selected, and the ExpressRoute circuit specified. The circuit must be enabled by your connectivity provider and have Azure Private Peering enabled beforehand.

Verify and troubleshoot on-premises connectivity

To verify connectivity or troubleshoot connectivity between on-premises networks and Azure:

- Verify the status and configuration of all VPN connections, virtual network gateways, ExpressRoute connections, or ExpressRoute circuits involved.
- For ExpressRoute, try to reset a failed circuit using the Get-AzExpressRouteCircuit and Set-AzExpressRouteCircuit PowerShell cmdlets, as described at: *https://docs.microsoft. com/azure/expressroute/reset-circuit*.
- Try to connect between an on-premises server and an Azure VM, and vice-versa, such as using SSH or TCP.
- Use standard network tools such as tcping or tracert to confirm connectivity between networks.
- Use the Azure network diagnostics tools described in Skill 3.3.

Thought experiment

In this thought experiment, apply what you have learned about this objective. You can find answers to these questions in the next section.

Your company, Contoso, wishes to lift and shift an existing HR application to Azure. The application architecture comprises two web servers, and a database tier implemented using three servers in a SQL Server Always-On Availability Group. The web application uses an in-memory session state that requires each user to be consistently routed to the same web server instance.

The application should be accessible only to the company Intranet, and not exposed to the Internet.

In addition, Contoso has already migrated several other applications to Azure. A recent finance review, however, has highlighted the increasing of Azure spend, and your manager has identified the duplication of infrastructure components (such as domain controller virtual machines) across each migrated application as a potential area where savings can be made. Each of these applications is managed by a separate team, and the team should have administrative access only to their application.

1. How should the web tier be load-balanced?

2. How should the database tier be load-balanced?

3. How can you restrict network traffic between application tiers, and prevent on-premises uses from having direct access to the database tier?

4. How should the application be integrated into the company Intranet, avoiding exposing an Internet endpoint?

5. How can you reduce costs by consolidating duplicated components?

6. How does your design maintain administrative separation between applications?

Thought experiment answers

This section contains the solution to the thought experiment for the chapter.

1. The web tier should be load-balanced using Application Gateway. This option is chosen in preference to Azure load balancer because it supports cookie-based session affinity, which enables each user to be consistently routed to the same backend server. The App Gateway will be deployed in a separate subnet of the same virtual network that is used to host the web tiers and database tiers of the HR application (each tier uses a separate subnet). NSGs associated with each subnet are used to restrict network flows, such as to ensure that only the web tier has access to the database.

2. The database tier should be load balanced using Azure Load Balancer. The load balancer will be configured with an internal (Intranet) IP address only. Since the load balancer is being used as a SQL Server Always-On Availability Group Listener, the Floating IP (Direct Server Return) option should be enabled.

3. Network security groups should be used to restrict inbound and outbound traffic for the subnets used by each application tier. Optionally, application security groups can be used to simplify the IP address management and reduce the number of subnets and NSGs required.

4. Connectivity between the application and the on-premises network can be achieved in two ways. The simplest option is to establish a Site-to-Site VPN between the on-premises network and the Azure virtual network. This creates an encrypted tunnel (over the Internet) linking the two networks together. A compatible om-premises VPN device with a static Internet-facing IPv4 address is required, together with a VPN gateway in Azure

(hosted in a dedicated gateway subnet). Alternatively, an ExpressRoute connection can be used. This provides a more reliable and consistent connection over a dedicated connection from a connectivity provider. In this case, an ExpressRoute gateway is used to connect the ExpressRoute circuit to the Azure virtual network.

5. A dedicated VNet should be created to contain common services (such as Active Directory servers), which are consumed by multiple applications. Each application should remain in its own VNet, which should only contain application-specific components. The application VNets should be peered with the shared services VNet, in a hub-and-spoke configuration (with the shared services VNet as the hub). This peering will give the applications network access to the shared components.

6. Because each application retains its own VNet containing all application-specific components, there is no loss of isolation or control for the application owners. These application components can even be deployed in separate subscriptions, making separate role-based access and billing straightforward. Peering of Resource Manager VNets is supported across subscription boundaries.

Chapter summary

This chapter covered many of the advanced networking features available in Azure. Below are some of the key takeaways from this chapter.

- Azure virtual networks (VNets) are isolated networks using a private IP address space.
- Virtual networks are divided into subnets, which allow you to isolate workloads.
- Azure reserves the first 4 and last IP address in each subnet. The first IP address allocated to VMs is therefore typically the .4 IP address.
- Private IP addresses for a VM are assigned from a subnet and configured as settings on the IP configuration of a network interface resource.
- A VM can be associated with one or more network interfaces, and each network interface can contain multiple IP configurations.
- Private IP addresses support two allocation methods: dynamic or static. Dynamic IP addresses are released when the VM is stopped (deallocated).
- Public IP addresses are managed as a standalone resource, which can be associated with a network interface IP configuration.
- Public IP addresses support two pricing tiers (SKUs). The Basic tier supports dynamic and static assignment and provides open connectivity (which can be restricted using NSGs). The Standard tier supports zone-redundant deployments, use static allocation only, and is closed by default (access is enabled using NSGs).
- User Defined Routes (UDRs) change the default behavior of subnets allowing you to direct outbound traffic to other locations. Typically, traffic is sent through a virtual appliance such as a firewall.

- If a UDR is used to send traffic to a virtual appliance, IP forwarding must be enabled on the NIC of the virtual appliance VM.

- Routing outbound Internet traffic via a VPN connection to a network security device is known as forced tunneling.

- The effective routes for each network interface can be reviewed to help diagnose routing issues.

- VNets can be connected using either VNet peering or VNet-to-VNet VPN connections.

- To connect two VNet, they must have non-overlapping IP address spaces.

- Virtual networks can be connected using VNet peering. This is supported both within a region or across regions.

- By default, peered VNets appear and perform as a single network. There is an option to limit connectivity, in which case NSG rules must be used to define the permitted connections.

- VNet peering allows VMs to see each other as one network, but their relationships are non-transitive. If VNETA and VNETB are peered and VNETB and VNETC are peered VNETA and VNETC are not peered.

- A common approach is to use a hub and spoke network architecture, in which separate spoke VNets are used by each application, peered to a hub VNet containing a network virtual appliance (NVA). The peering connections must enable Allow Forwarded Traffic.

- Using VNet peering to provide access to a central VNet containing shared services, such as Active Directory domain controllers, is known as service chaining.

- Alternatively, virtual networks can be connected using a VNet-to-VNet VPN connection.

- A virtual network gateway can be used to create VPN connections between virtual networks (and is then called a VPN gateway).

- The size of the VPN gateway should be chosen based on the throughput required.

- The GatewaySubnet is a special subnet that is only used for virtual network gateways.

- A VPN gateway can be shared by peered VNets. The peering connections must enable the settings to Use Remote Gateway (on the peering towards the gateway) and Allow Gateway Transit (on the peering from the gateway).

- Both global VNet peering and VNet-to-VNet VPN connections route traffic between Azure regions over the Microsoft backbone network, not the public Internet.

- Azure DNS provides an authoritative DNS service for hosting Internet-facing domains.

- DNS zones in Azure DNS must be delegated from the parent domain. This is achieved by setting up appropriate NS records in the parent domain, pointing to the name servers assigned by Azure DNS.

- DNS records in Azure DNS are managed using record sets, which are the collection of records with the same name and the same type.

- DNS records at the zone apex use the record name @. You cannot create records with the CNAME record type at the zone apex.

- Azure DNS Alias records allow DNS records to reference other Azure resources, such as a public IP address.

- DNS zone files are a standard format used to transfer DNS records between DNS systems. DNS zone files can only be imported into or exported from Azure DNS by using the Azure CLI.

- Azure-provided DNS, also known as Internal DNS, provides VM-to-VM DNS lookups within a virtual network.

- Alternatively, a customer can implement their own DNS servers, which can be configured either at the VNet or the network interface level.

- Azure DNS also supports private DNS zones, which can also be used to enable VM-to-VM DNS lookups.

- Network security groups are used to create firewall rules to control network flows.

- NSGs can be applied at the subnet level, or on individual VM network interfaces.

- Each NSG includes a list of default rules, which can be overridden using user-defined rules. Rules are applied in priority order (processing stops at the first rule matching the traffic in question).

- Source and destination IP address ranges in NSG rules can be specified explicitly using CIDR ranges.

- IP address ranges can also be specified using service tags which are platform shortcuts for the IP ranges for key Azure services. Commonly-used service tags include VirtualNetwork, Internet, AzureCloud, Storage, and SQL.

- IP address ranges can also be specified using application security groups (ASGs). ASGs allow NSG rules to be defined for groups of VMs without needing to allocate the VMs into separate subnets.

- Tools to help identifying the required NSG rules include service map and NSG flow logs.

- Effective security rules can be reviewed for each network interface. This allows you to see the exact IP ranges used by each service tag and ASG.

- Azure Load Balancer (ALB) is a fully-managed, high performance load-balancing service for TCP and UDP traffic. It operates at the transport layer (OSI Layer 4). Unlike App Gateway, it does not have visibility into application-level traffic.

- ALB can be deployed with either a public (Internet) or private (Intranet) frontend IP address.

- ALB comes in two pricing tiers (SKUs): Basic or Standard. The Standard tier supports availability zones, larger and more flexible backend pools, and a number of other features. The Basic tier is free of charge.

- An ALB load-balancing configuration comprises frontend IP configuration, backend pool, health probes, and load-balancing rule.

- ALB also supports port forwarding, using inbound NAT rules. This maps a specific frontend port to a specific backend port on a specific backend server.

- Network Performance Monitor provides monitoring for hybrid networks. It supports performance monitor (for monitoring connections between two endpoints), connectivity monitor (to monitor outbound connections to a given IP or FQDN), and ExpressRoute monitor to monitor ExpressRoute connections.

- Network Watcher is a central hub providing access to a wide range of networking tools in Azure.

- IP Flow Verify is a Network Watcher feature used to test if a given network flow is allowed in or out of an Azure VM.

- Next Hop is used to determine the next hop address and routing rule for a given network flow.

- Packet Captures enables network traffic on a given VM to be captured, either locally or to an Azure storage account.

- Network Topology creates a diagrammatic representation of the resources in your virtual network.

- VPN Troubleshoot provides automated, in-depth troubleshooting of VPN connections.

- Connection Troubleshoot allows you to test the connectivity between two Azure VMs, or between a VM and an arbitrary external endpoint.

- Connection Monitor enables long-term connection monitoring, using similar diagnostics as used by Connection Troubleshoot.

- Site-to-Site VPN connections provide connectivity between an on-premises network and an Azure virtual network, using an encrypted tunnel over the public Internet.

- VPN gateways are virtual network gateways deployed with gateway type VPN. They are used to terminate site-to-site VPN connections.

- Site-to-Site VPNs support BGP routing and active-active gateways and connections to enable high availability.

- A wide variety of physical (and software) devices are supported as the on-premises Site-to-Site VPN endpoint. The device must have an Internet-facing static IPv4 address.

- A local network connection is an Azure resource used to represent the on-premises VPN device and network in Azure.

- An ExpressRoute connection provides connectivity between an on-premises network an Azure virtual network, using a dedicated connection from a connectivity provider.

- You can connect to ExpressRoute either via your co-location facility provider, via a point-to-point ethernet connection, or by extending your IPVPN WAN.

- ExpressRoute provides Microsoft Peering (connectivity to Azure PaaS endpoints, and other Microsoft services) or Private Peering (connectivity to Azure virtual networks). The former uses Internet address and the latter uses Intranet addresses. Azure Public Peering, for Azure PaaS services only, is deprecated for new ExpressRoute circuits.

- ExpressRoute circuits provide different levels of bandwidth, from 50Mbps to 10Gbps. They also provide redundant connections.

- ExpressRoute circuits are connected to an Azure virtual network using an ExpressRoute gateway (a virtual network gateway of type ExpressRoute).
- By default, ExpressRoute provides connectivity to all Microsoft datacenters in a given geopolitical region. The ExpressRoute Premium Add-On extends coverage to all datacenters, globally. It also increases the number of private peering routes and the number of virtual networks, which can be connected to a circuit.

## CHAPTER 5

Manage identities

M icrosoft has long been a leader in the identity space. This leadership goes back to the introduction of Active Directory (AD) with Windows 2000 before the cloud even existed. Microsoft moved into cloud identity with the introduction of Azure Active Directory (Azure AD), which is now used by over five million companies around the world. The adoption of Office 365 led to this extended use of Azure AD. These two technologies, however, have very different purposes, with AD primarily used on-premises and Azure AD primarily used for the cloud.

Microsoft has poured resources into making AD and Azure AD work together. The concept is to extend the identity that lives on-premises to the cloud by synchronizing the identities. This ability is provided by a technology named Azure AD Connect. Microsoft has also invested in extending those identities to enable scenarios such as single sign-on by using Active Directory Federation Services (ADFS), which is deployed in many large enterprises.

Microsoft has continued pushing forward by developing options for developers to leverage Azure AD for their applications. Microsoft provides the ability for developers to extend a company's Azure AD to users outside of the organization. The first option is known as Azure AD B2C (Business to Consumer). This allows consumers to sign into applications by using their social media accounts, such as a Facebook ID. A complementary technology, known as Azure AD B2B (Business to Business), extends Azure AD to business partners.

As the cloud becomes more popular and Azure AD adoption continues to pick up, there are some legacy applications that require you to use the traditional AD, even in the cloud. For this, Microsoft has developed a service called Azure AD Domain Services. This allows for traditional Kerberos and LDAP functionality in the cloud without deploying Domain controllers into an Azure virtual network.

This area of the AZ-103 exam is focused on the management of identities by using Azure Active Directory, as well as implementing and managing hybrid identities.

Skills covered in this chapter:

- Skill 5.1: Manage Azure Active Directory (AD)
- Skill 5.2: Manage Azure AD objects (users, groups, and devices)
- Skill 5.3: Implement and manage hybrid identities
- Skill 5.4: Implement multi-factor authentication (MFA)

Skill 5.1: Manage Azure Active Directory (AD)

Azure Active Directory (Azure AD) has several features beyond user and group management, such as the ability to add one or more custom domains to an Azure AD tenant. Azure AD also provides, user experience controls such as self-service password reset (SSPR) and the ability to perform ongoing access reviews to ensure compliance with policies through Azure AD access reviews. There are also controls to manage the potential risk associated with user logins through Azure AD Identity Protection, the management of devices with AD Join, and the management of data stored on these devices with Enterprise State Roaming.

This section covers how to:

- Add custom domains
- Configure Azure AD Identity Protection, Azure AD Join, and Enterprise State Roaming
- Configure self-service password reset
- Implement conditional access policies
- Manage multiple directories
- Perform an access review

Add custom domains

Creating an Azure AD requires an initial domain name in the form of domainname.onmicrosoft.com. This name cannot be changed or deleted, but it is possible to add a registered Internet domain name to your Azure AD. Companies typically have domain names they use to do business and users who sign in by using their AD Domain name. Adding custom domain names to Azure AD allows you to assign user names familiar to users. This means they can log in by using their email address, like billg@contoso.com, instead of billg@contoso.onmicrosoft.com.

The process to add a customer domain is simple:

- Add the custom domain name to your directory.
- Add a DNS entry for the domain name at the domain name registrar.
- Verify the custom domain name in Azure AD.

To add a custom domain by using the Azure portal, open the Azure AD that you wish to add a custom domain to. Next, select **Custom Domain Names** followed by **+Add Custom Domain**, then enter a domain name, such as contoso.com. Upon completion, you can see a screen resembling the screen shown in Figure 5-1 with instructions on adding a DNS record to your authoritative NS server that Azure will use to verify you are the owner of the domain.

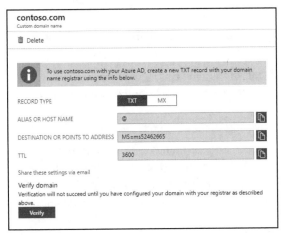

FIGURE 5-1 Add a custom domain to Azure AD

After the records are added with your registrar, click **Verify**, and the domain is added to the list of domains that can be used with this Azure AD.

> **NOTE ADD AND VERIFY YOUR CUSTOM DOMAIN**
>
> You should add your custom domain and verify it prior to synchronizing the directory to an on-premises Active Directory. This allows your users to log in to Azure AD by using their on-premises credentials.

Note that you can verify your custom domains with either a TXT or MX record. It is also important to remember that you can take some time for DNS records to propagate after making any updates with your registrar.

After you have verified the domain, you may want to set it as the primary domain. In Azure AD, the onmicrosoft.com domain is the primary default. By setting the primary domain to a custom domain you can ensure new users are created in the desired domain namespace. When you set the primary domain, existing users are not affected, and their user names may still need to be updated.

To set the primary domain, select the custom domain that you want to be the primary followed by the *make primary* command and confirm your change.

Configure Azure AD Identity Protection, Azure AD Join, and Enterprise State Roaming

Azure AD Identity Protection, Azure AD Join, and Enterprise State Roaming are features of Azure Active Directory that allow you to manage both user and device identity while protected the data that those identities access.

Azure AD Identity Protection

Azure Active Directory Identity Protection is a feature of the Azure AD Premium P2 edition that enables you to:

- Detect potential vulnerabilities affecting your organization's identities
- Configure automated responses to detected suspicious actions that are related to your organization's identities
- Investigate suspicious incidents and take appropriate action to resolve them

Enabling Azure AD Identity Protection requires a global administrator to onboard the service. After the service has been on-boarded into an Azure AD tenant, if can be managed by users with the global administrator and security administrator roles in Azure AD. Users with the security reader role will be able to access the service but cannot make configuration changes.

To enable Azure AD Identity Protection, browse to the Azure portal as a global administrator and search for Azure AD Identity Protection in the Azure Marketplace. After selecting the service, you can create it as shown in Figure 5-2.

FIGURE 5-2 Enabling Azure AD Identity Protection

The configuration of Azure AD Identity Protection is performed by browsing to the service in the Azure portal. Through the portal you can configure the MFA registration policy, sign-in risk policy, and user risk policy for the Azure AD tenant.

The multi-factor authentication registration policy allows you to apply organization-wide policy to all users or select individuals and groups within your Azure AD tenant. To configure this policy, browse to Azure AD Identity Protection in the Azure portal and select MFA registration to open the Policy Settings blade. From this blade you can select the users that are included and or/excluded from the policy as shown in Figure 5-3.

FIGURE 5-3 Select users and groups for MFA registration policy

After selecting your users and/or groups you can then set the type of access you want to enforce as shown in Figure 5-4.

FIGURE 5-4 Select controls to be enforced for the MFA registration policy

Finally, you can set the state of your policy to On or Off as shown in Figure 5-5.

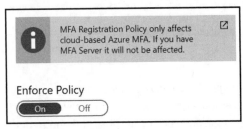

FIGURE 5-5 Select the state of the MFA registration policy

Configuring the sign-in risk policy is done through the Sign-In Risk policy blade of Azure AD Identity Protection. When configuring the policy, you will first select the users and/or groups the policy applies to.

Next, you will select the sign-in risk level for the policy as shown in Figure 5-6.

FIGURE 5-6 Select the sign-in risk level for the sign-in risk policy

Select the controls to be enforced and then the enforcement state can be set to On or Off.

Configuring the user risk policy is performed in the User risk policy blade of Azure AD Identity Protection. When configuring the policy, you will first select the users and/or groups the policy applies to.

Next, you will select the user risk level that will be associated with the policy as shown in Figure 5-7.

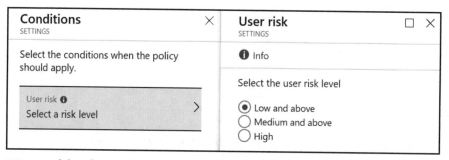

FIGURE 5-7 Select the user risk level for the user risk policy

Select the controls to be enforced and then the enforcement state can be set to On or Off.

Azure AD Join

Azure Active Directory includes the ability to manage device identity which enables single sign-on to devices and the applications and services managed through Azure Active Directory that are accessed from that device. Managed devices include both enterprise and bring-your-own-device (BYOD) scenarios. This allows users to work from any device, including personal devices, all while protecting corporate intellectual property with the necessary regulatory and compliance controls.

Azure AD Join allows you to control these devices, the applications installed and access from them, and how those applications interact with your corporate data.

When associating devices with Azure AD, you have two options: registering a device or joining a device. Registration of devices would be appropriate for personal devices while joining devices is useful for corporate-owned devices.

In either case, associating a device with Azure AD allows you to manage a device's identity. Note that this identity can be managed independently of a user's identity. This provides a great degree of flexibility as devices can be enabled or disabled without affecting a user account. Azure AD Join is an extension of device registration which changes the local state of the device. When a device is Azure AD Joined, users can sign in to the device using an organizational account instead of a personal account.

Registration of devices in Azure AD can be combined with a mobile device management solution such as Microsoft Intune as well. This allows for additional attributes from the device to be tracked in Azure AD (*e.g.* device OS version, device state including whether the device is rooted or jailbroken, etc.). Those attributes can then be used to build and enforce conditional access policies which can further secure corporate data.

Device registration is configured in Azure AD under **Devices** and then **Device Settings**. From this screen, you can set the configuration for an entire Azure AD tenant as seen in Figure 5-8.

FIGURE 5-8 Configure device registration settings

From this screen, you can configure the following settings:

- **Users may join devices to Azure AD**   This setting allows you to select the users and groups that can join devices to Azure AD. This setting only applies to Azure AD Join on Windows 10 devices. The default value is **All** and can be changed to **Selected** or **None**.

- **Additional local administrators on Azure AD joined devices**   With Azure AD Premium, you can choose which users are granted local administrator rights to the device. Global Administrators and the device owner are granted local administrator rights by default. The default value is **None** and can be changed to **Selected**. If the value is **Selected**, any users added here are also added to the Device Administrators role in Azure AD.

- **Users may register their devices with Azure AD**   Allow users to register their devices with Azure AD (Workplace Join). Enrollment with Microsoft Intune or Mobile Device Management for Office 365 requires Device Registration. If you have configured either of these services, ALL will be selected, and the button associated with the setting will be disabled.

- **Require Multi-Factor Auth to join devices**   Multi-factor authentication is recommended when adding devices to Azure AD. When set to **Yes**, users that are adding devices from the internet must first use a second method of authentication. Prior to enabling this setting, you must ensure that multi-factor authentication is configured for the users that are able to register devices and that those users have gone through MFA setup. This setting is only applicable to Azure AD Join on Windows 10 and BYO device registration for Windows 10, iOS and Android.

- **Maximum number of devices per user**   This setting designates the maximum number of devices that an individual user can have in Azure AD. If the quota is reached, the user will not be able to add a device until one of their existing devices is removed. Valid values for this setting are 5, 10, 20, 50, 100, and Unlimited.

- **Users may sync settings and app data across devices**   With Azure AD Premium you can select a subset of your users through the **Selected** value and enable the Enterprise State Roaming feature for them the feature can be enabled or for **All** users or **None**.

After the directory has been configured, you can begin registering devices. For Azure AD Join, there are several requirements for devices, including Windows versions. The requirements for Windows versions are driven by the type of Azure AD Join – hybrid or non-hybrid. Non-hybrid Azure AD Join is applicable to devices that are not joined to an on-premises Active Directory while hybrid Azure AD Join is applicable to devices that are joined to an on-premises directory. For hybrid Azure AD Join, an IT administration must perform the join to Azure AD.

For non-hybrid Azure AD Join, Windows 10 Professional and Windows 10 Enterprise devices can be joined to a directory. For hybrid Azure AD Join scenarios, you can join current Windows devices such as Windows 10 and Windows Server 2016. There is support for a hybrid join with down-level devices as well including Windows 7, Windows 8.1, Windows Server 2008 R2, Windows Server 2012, and Windows Server 2012 R2.

Enterprise State Roaming

Enterprise State Roaming is available for Windows 10 devices and allows users to synchronize user settings and application data through Azure AD. While this feature is like the consumer settings sync that has been in Windows since Windows 8, it does offer several benefits when considering protecting corporate data on client devices, including separation of consumer and corporate data, encryption of roaming data, and better management with the ability to monitor which devices are synchronizing data and turn off synchronization per-device when needed. For a device to use Enterprise State Roaming, the device must be Azure AD Joined. Once joined, both hybrid and non-hybrid joined devices can leverage the feature.

When Enterprise State Roaming is enabled, Azure Rights Management (Azure RMS) is used to encrypt the data before it leaves the device and all data is encrypted in transit and at rest. This differs once again from consumer sync in that a data is encrypted where in consumer sync only sensitive information such as credentials is encrypted. The license used for Azure RMS is a limited use license which is used just for encryption and decryption of data. Microsoft customers can purchase a full Azure RMS license to gain access to additional functionality such as document protection and bring-your-own-key (BYOK) support

Enterprise State Roaming data is stored in an Azure region that most closely aligns with the country or region value set in Azure Active Directory. This value is set at the time the directory is created and cannot be changed later. There are three geographies that are used to partition roaming data – North America, Europe, the Middle East and Africa (EMEA), and Asia-Pacific (APAC). Microsoft may store the roaming data in one or more Azure regions within a geography.

Roaming data includes Windows settings and application data. Windows settings such as the theme, browser settings for both Internet Explorer and Microsoft Edge, passwords, language settings and other common Windows settings are synchronized while application data includes data from Universal Windows apps which write their data to a roaming folder in the user profile. The synchronization of application data is dependent on the application developer to leverage the roaming feature of Windows 10.

Enterprise State Roaming is enabled through the Azure AD admin center and the Azure Portal. To enable Enterprise State Roaming, select **Azure Active Directory**, then **Devices**, and **Enterprise State Roaming** (see Figure 5-9). The user enabling the service can select which users can sync settings and data, with the ability to select all users or a subset of users in the directory.

FIGURE 5-9 Configure Enterprise State Roaming

Configure self-service password reset

Self-service password reset (SSPR) allows users to reset their password in Azure AD, including the ability to optionally write the password back to an on-premises environment when properly licensed and configured by using password writeback and Azure AD Connect. SSPR allows users to change their password, reset their password when they cannot sign in, and unlock their account all without the intervention of an IT administrator.

Each scenario above address either cloud-only or hybrid users; licensing varies as well. Table 5-1 details each scenario, the type of user it applies to, and any required licenses.

TABLE 5-1 Self-service password reset license requirements

Scenario	User Type	License Requirements
Password Change	Cloud-only user.	Included in all editions of Azure AD
Password Reset	Cloud-only user	Azure AD Basic, Azure AD Premium P1, Azure AD Premium P2
Password Change/Unlock/Reset	Hybrid user	Azure AD Premium P1, Azure AD Premium P2

SSPR can be enabled through the Azure Portal by browsing to your Azure AD tenant and then selecting Password reset. When enabling SSPR (see Figure 5-10), you can scope the functionality to a group, so you can roll out the feature in waves as users are onboarded into the service. As a part of configuration, you will also select the authentication methods for SSPR: email, mobile phone, office phone, and/or security questions. Finally, you will configure registration options, whether registration is required to use SSPR and the number of days for reconfirmation.

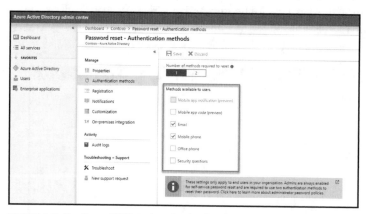

FIGURE 5-10 Configure SSPR Authentication methods

Implement conditional access policies

Security is a concern for every organization using the cloud. As service providers take on more responsibilities for physical network security controls, organizations using Azure AD still maintain full control over their users and how those users interact with the services that use Azure AD for authentication and authorization. Focusing on who can access your organization's resources, along with how the resources are accessed, allows you to maintain a cloud-first, mobile-first security posture.

With Azure AD conditional access policies, you can implement automated access control decisions for allowing access to your cloud applications after a user has authenticated that are based on conditions. Conditions are evaluated in real-time, based on signals from the users' login included device, location, and the application they are accessing. This information is evaluated against Microsoft's data set of global logins to Azure AD and your organizational policies. Optionally, session risk can also be evaluated, and effective security controls applied to the authentication attempt. This can include MFA challenges, of even denying access based on the input signals and conditions. Only after passing through the rules associated with conditional access can a user access their application. Cloud applications, such as Office 365, and even on-premises applications can be protected by Azure AD conditional access.

A conditional access policy is a definition of an access scenario using the pattern: *when this happens, then do this*. *When this happens* is the entry point, or trigger, for a conditional access policy. This is where the conditions that will be evaluated are defined. *Then do this* refers to the response of a policy. This is where the access controls of the policy are applied to the request. Conditional access does not grant authorization to a cloud application or override user rights within an application once they have accessed it. That still occurs through user assignments to an application registration in Azure AD. Conditional access allows you to define the conditions under which that access should be granted.

To create a conditional access policy, at a minimum you need to configure the assignments for users/groups and cloud apps (*when this happens*). You must also supply at least one access control (*then do this*). The assignment conditions for users/groups and cloud apps are mandatory. If needed, you can define additional conditions beyond the mandatory set such as associating a sign-in risk, mandating a device platform, or defining the locations associated with a policy.

When creating conditional access polices, you will also have access to both *include* and *exclude* rules. There are policies that will lock you out of your Azure AD tenant if not properly configured. You should carefully evaluate policies that affect complete sets such as all users, all groups, or all cloud apps and apply exclusions accordingly. It is a best practice to test policies with non-production or test users first to evaluate their impact before assigning them to your standard users.

Using conditional access requires an Azure AD Premium P1 or P2 (or equivalent EM + S) license.

When you create a new policy, there are no users, groups, apps, or access controls selected. A policy must include these items before it can be finalized. As stated, these are mandatory items. If no users or groups are assigned to a policy, the policy will never be triggered and if you do not select any access controls there is nothing for the policy to do.

Conditional access policies are managed through the Azure portal. They items can be found by browsing to your Azure AD tenant and selecting Conditional access policies. From here, you can create and manage existing policies. An example of the **+New Policy Blade** is shown in Figure 5-11 with users and groups, cloud apps, and access controls highlighted.

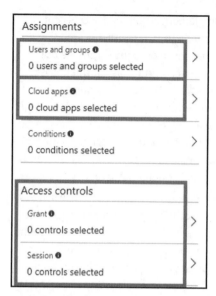

FIGURE 5-11 Configure conditional access policy

When selecting cloud apps, you can apply the policy to all cloud apps in the Azure AD tenant or only selected apps (see Figure 5-12). You cannot select an app that is not registered in the directory.

FIGURE 5-12 Configure conditional access policy Cloud apps

Available conditions include:

- **Sign-in risk**   The likelihood that the sign-in is coming from someone other than the user. The risk level can be high, medium or low. This feature requires an Azure AD Premium 2 license.

- **Device platforms**   The platform the user is signing in from. Available platforms include Android, iOS, Windows Phone, Windows, and macOS.

- **Locations**   The location (determined using IP address range) the user is signing in from.

- **Client apps (preview)**   The software the user is using to access the cloud app. Valid selections include Browser and Mobile apps and desktop clients.

- **Device state (preview)**   Whether the device the user is signing in from is Hybrid Azure AD Joined or marked as compliant. Compliant devices are devices that are Intune compliant and will be excluded from the evaluation of the policy.

When configuring access controls, you can block access or grant access with additional requirements such as requiring multi-factor authentication or requiring an approved client application from Microsoft.

Approved client apps can be used to control access from Android and iOS devices when using the device platform condition. The setting applies to the following apps:

- Microsoft Azure Information Protection
- Microsoft Edge
- Microsoft Excel
- Microsoft Flow
- Microsoft Intune Managed Browser
- Microsoft Invoicing
- Microsoft Kaizala
- Microsoft Launcher
- Microsoft OneDrive
- Microsoft OneNote
- Microsoft Outlook
- Microsoft Planner
- Microsoft PowerApps
- Microsoft Power BI
- Microsoft PowerPoint
- Microsoft SharePoint
- Microsoft Skype for Business
- Microsoft StaffHub
- Microsoft Stream

- Microsoft Teams
- Microsoft To-Do
- Microsoft Visio
- Microsoft Word
- Microsoft Yammer

Policies can be enabled and disabled as needed and Microsoft also supplies a What if tool which can be used to evaluate which policies will apply to one or more users or groups under certain conditions. The What if tool (see Figure 5-13) can only evaluate enabled conditions against enabled policies.

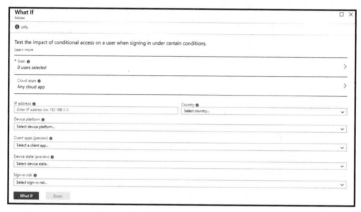

FIGURE 5-13 Conditional access What if tool

Manage multiple directories

Each Azure AD tenant (or directory) is managed as an independent resource. There is no parent-child relation between directories, although users from one directory can be invited to another directory through Azure AD B2B features.

As each tenant is an independent resource, directories can be created and deleted as needed. This also means that each directory can have independent administers and role assignments. Deleting an existing directory can affect resources outside of the directory. For example, when deleting a directory where external users are present, those users will no longer be able to access any applications or resources that have been shared with them as you will need to remove both the users and the association to the underlying resources (for example, a resource group in Azure).

Finally, each directory can be synchronized independently as well. This means if you have two domains on-premises that need to be synchronized to two different Azure AD tenants, you have the flexibility you need when implementing hybrid identity in Azure AD.

Managing directories may include deleting directories or even an entire Azure AD tenant. When deleting a tenant, global administrator rights are required. When a directory is deleted, all the resources or objects within that directory are deleted as well.

There are several prerequisites that must be satisfied prior to directory deletion, specifically:

- There can be no existing users or groups except for the single global admin.
- There can be no enterprise application registrations in the directory.
- There are no MFA providers linked to the directory.
- There are no subscriptions for Azure, Office 365, or other Microsoft SaaS services associated with the directory.

Perform an access review

Azure AD access reviews allow organizations to better manage privileged role assignments, group memberships for Azure AD security and Office 365 groups, and access to cloud apps registered in Azure AD.

Access reviews can be used to recertify access for not just your employees, but also external users who have been invited into an Azure AD tenant. When combined with Azure AD Privileged Identity Management, role assignments for administrative users who are assigned Azure AD roles or Azure subscription roles can also be recertified.

Azure AD access reviews require an Azure AD Premium P2 or EM + S E5 license. Access reviews can be created by browsing to the Azure portal and accessing the Access reviews service. You must onboard to the service before performing any configuration through the Onboard blade and clicking **Onboard Now** (see Figure 5-14 for a screen shot).

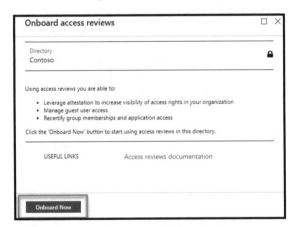

FIGURE 5-14 Onboard to Azure AD Access Reviews

From the Access reviews blade you can proceed to select or create a program and create controls.

To create a program, you will need to supply a name and a description. Programs allow you to group controls and the access reviews (see Figure 5-15) associated with a control together. This allows to you scope reviews to initiatives within your organization and offers easier reporting based on program. You can create new programs as needed, however a program cannot be deleted if it has any controls associated with it.

To create a control, you will need to supply:

- Review name
- Optional description
- Start date
- Frequency: One time, Weekly, Monthly, Quarterly, or Annually
- Duration
- End: Never, End by, or Occurrences. When selecting Occurrences, you will enter the number of occurrences for the review.
- Users that the access review applies to
- Program the control applies to
- Reviews that will perform the reviews.

FIGURE 5-15 Creating an access review

When creating a review and selecting the users to review, you will also select a scope for the review. Valid scopes include Guest users only and Everyone. You will also define the type of users to review, either users assigned to an application or members of a group.

There are advanced controls available within an access review which allow the creator to configure whether or not the results of the review should be applied automatically, what should happen if a reviewer does not respond, and whether or not a justification is required when an approver allows continued to access to a group or application.

FIGURE 5-16 Creating an access review Upon completion and Advanced settings

After a review has been created, reviewers will action the review through the Azure portal or through the Access panel. Reviews for Azure AD roles and Azure resource roles are performed in the Azure portal, as these reviews are created through Privileged Identity Management (PIM), whereas all other reviews occur in the Access panel.

To see the pending access reviews, click the Review Access link in the email or Sign in on the Azure AD access panel as shown in Figure 5-17.

FIGURE 5-17 Example Access review email

From there, you can perform the review for yourself (or for others) depending on the control configuration of the access review. Within an individual access review, you will see names of the users who the review is applicable to. It is possible to see only your name in the list of users if the review applies to your own access. For each user in the list, you will approve or deny the access of the user. You may be asked to supply additional data based on how the review was configured. For instance, the review may require that a reason is supplied for approval.

When a user's access is removed as a part of a review, their access isn't removed immediately. It can be removed automatically when the review is completed or when an admin stops the views. This means that approvers can return to an in-progress review and update their response if needed.

Skill 5.2: Manage Azure AD Objects

In an Azure AD tenant there are users, groups, and devices that are controlled through the features of Azure AD discussed in this chapter. In this section we will focus on managing users and groups throughout their lifecycle, how to manage device settings, and how to perform bulk updates to users using automation tooling such as PowerShell.

Create users and groups

Recall that there are two types of users in Azure AD – cloud-only users and users synchronized from an on-premises directory. How you create a user varies based on where that user is sourced from with cloud-only users created and managed exclusively in Azure AD while synchronized identities are created and managed in the source system. For example, to update an attribute for a user created in an on-premises Active Directory and synchronized to Azure AD, that attribute must be updated on-premises first and then synchronized to Azure AD through Azure AD Connect. In the case of cloud-only users, attributes can be updated directly in Azure AD.

You can create cloud-only users through the Azure Portal, Azure PowerShell, and the Azure CLI. You can also interact with users through the Graph API as well if you are developing solutions that interact with Azure AD. When creating new users, you must have Global administrator or user administrator rights within the directory.

To create cloud-only users from the Azure Portal, browse to your Azure AD tenant as a user with rights to create users and select the Users blade followed by **+New User**. An example of this blade is shown in Figure 5-18. Note that you can also add guest users to your directory through the Azure portal as well.

FIGURE 5-18 New user blade in the Azure portal

Creating cloud-only groups is a similar experience and can be performed from the Azure Portal, Azure PowerShell, the Azure CLI, and the Graph API. To create a group in Azure portal, browse to your Azure AD tenant and select the Groups blade followed by **+New Group**. An example of the New Group blade is shown in Figure 5-19.

FIGURE 5-19 New Group blade in the Azure portal

When creating a new group, there are several factors that dictate the type of group that is created and how that group behaves in Azure AD and associated workloads such as Office 365.

You will first select the type of group you are creating. This is a required field. There are currently two values you can select from: Security and Office 365. A Security group is used to manage members' access to shared resources such as resources in Azure and items in Office 365. An Office 365 group if a part of the wider Office 365 service where membership to Office 365 resources such as a shared Outlook inbox and a SharePoint site are managed. Note that even if you are creating groups in an Azure AD tenant that is not associated with an Office 365 subscription you will still see the option to create an Office 365 group.

The group name is also a required field. While group description is not required, it is recommended that you always include a description to make it easier to find and identify the purpose of a group later.

Membership type allows you to select from one of three values:

- **Assigned**   This value allows you to select one or more users and add them to the group. Adding and removing users is performed manually.

- **Dynamic user**   This value allows you to use dynamic group rules to automatically add and remove members.

- **Dynamic device**   This value allows you use dynamic group rules to automatically add and remove devices.

For both dynamic user and dynamic device-based groups, the rules associated with the group are evaluated on an ongoing basis. If a user or device has an attribute that matches the rule, that user or device is added to the group. If an attribute changes and the user or device no longer matches the criteria for group membership, the entity will be removed. Membership processing is not immediate. If an error occurs while processing a membership rule, an error is surfaced on the group page in the Azure portal. You can always view the current processing status from the group page.

It is important to note that you can create a dynamic group for users or devices, but not both at the same time. You also cannot use user attributes in device-based rule. It is possible to change the membership type of a group after it has been created, which provides an opportunity to transition from a static (or assigned) membership model to a dynamic membership model or vice-versa.

When creating dynamic groups, rules can be edited in the simple rule format, where you will build the query and conditions through select lists or they can be built in the advanced editor where you can build complex rules with conditional logic. In the example shown in Figure 5-20, a dynamic user group is being created which will automatically update its membership based on the department attribute and its value in Azure AD.

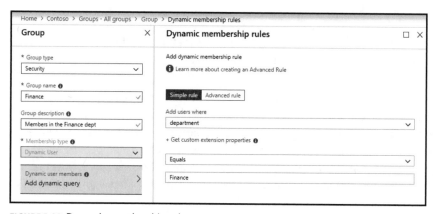

FIGURE 5-20 Dynamic membership rules

Dynamic groups require an Azure AD Premium P1 (or equivalent EM + S) license.

Manage user and group properties

As users and groups are used, they may need updates to their attributes (or properties). This may be simple updates such as changing a users' Job title or adding and removing members from an existing group.

Cloud-only users and groups can be updated using the same management tools that are available for creation: Azure Portal, Azure PowerShell, Azure CLI, and the Graph API. Figure 5-21 shows an example of the user update screens from the Azure portal that can be accessed by browsing to your Azure AD tenant, selecting Users, then a User, and clicking Edit.

FIGURE 5-21 Edit User blade in the Azure portal

Groups can be managed through the Azure Portal by browsing to your Azure AD tenant, selecting **Groups**, a group, and then **Properties**, **Members**, or **Owners**, depending on the type of update you want to make. When editing a group, you will not be able to change the group type (change a Security group to an Office 365 group) but you will be able to update the Group Name, Group Description, and in some cases the Membership Type as shown in Figure 5-22.

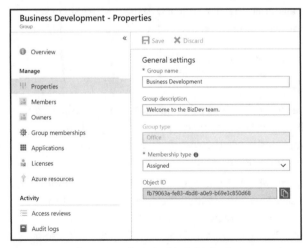

FIGURE 5-22 Edit group properties blade in the Azure portal

Manage device settings

Registered and joined devices in Azure AD can be managed in two areas in the Azure Portal. The first is by browsing to your Azure AD tenant in the Azure portal and selecting Devices followed by All Devices. The second is through the Devices blade for an individual user. With either option you will be able to search for devices using the device name as a filter, view a detailed overview of any registered and joined devices, and perform common device management tasks.

To enable and disable devices you must be a global administrator. Disabling a device prevents a device from accessing Azure AD resources. Note that this does not prevent the user from accessing resources in general, only from accessing resources from that disabled device. Figure 5-23 shows the disable menu.

FIGURE 5-23 Disable device menu from the All Devices blade in the Azure portal

Deleting devices is similar to enabling or disable a device. Again, the user performing the update must be a global administrator. Deleting a device prevents a device from accessing your Azure AD resources and removes all details that are attached to the device (BitLocker keys for Windows devices). Deleting a device represents a non-recoverable activity and is not recommended unless it is required.

Perform bulk user updates

The Azure portal can be helpful for one-time operations but is not suited for making programmatic updates to users in bulk. Tools like PowerShell can be quicker at making bulk updates and are better suited for the task. Example tasks include creating and updating users and groups in batches, bulk updates to user properties, and bulk removes.

When approaching user updates with PowerShell, you need to be mindful of the module you use and the versions of those modules. There are multiple modules available that can be used to update users, including the Azure Active Directory v1 (or MSOL cmdlets) and the Azure Active Directory v2 (or AzureAD cmdlets). The Azure Active Directory v2 cmdlets are also referred to as the Azure Active Directory PowerShell Module Version for Graph.

These cmdlets can be used for Azure AD administrative tasks such as user management, domain management, and for configuring single sign-on. To begin using the module, you will first need to install the module from the PowerShell Gallery (or PSGallery) using the `Install-Module` command.

The AzureAD module is available through the PowerShell Gallery.

```
# Install the module
Install-Module AzureAD
```

After the module has been installed, you can import the module to a PowerShell session using `Import-Module`.

```
# Import the module
Import-Module AzureAD
```

Using a user with rights to manage users you can use the Connect-AzureAD cmdlet to establish a connection with your Azure AD tenant.

```
# Store a credential (username/password)
$AzureAdCred = Get-Credential

# Connect to public cloud
Connect-AzureAD -Credential $AzureAdCred
```

The following PowerShell script demonstrates how users could be created in bulk by using a CSV file.

```
# Simple CVS
# DisplayName,UPN,MailNickname,GivenName,Surname,UsageLocation,Password

$users = Import-CSV .\users.csv
foreach ($user in $users) {
    # Define password profile
    $PasswordProfile = New-Object -TypeName Microsoft.Open.AzureAD.Model.PasswordProfile
    $PasswordProfile.Password = $user.Password


    # Create new user
    New-AzureADUser `
      -DisplayName $user.DisplayName `
      -GivenName $user.GivenName `
      -SurName $user.Surname `
      -UserPrincipalName $user.UPN `
      -MailNickname $user.MailNickname `
      -UsageLocation $user.UsageLocation `
      -PasswordProfile $PasswordProfile `
      -AccountEnabled $true
}
```

In this next example, you will see how to create Security groups in bulk using a CSV too.

```
# Simple CVS
# DisplayName,Description

$groups = Import-CSV .\groups.csv
foreach ($group in $groups) {
    New-AzureADGroup `
```

```
      -Description $group.Description `
      -DisplayName $group.DisplayName `
      -MailNickName $group.MailNickName `
      -MailEnabled $false `
      -SecurityEnabled $true
}
```

Skill 5.3: Implement and manage hybrid identities

Integrating an on-premises AD with Azure AD is the lifeblood for hybrid cloud deployments. This section focuses on how to accomplish this by using Azure AD Connect and then leveraging that setup to provide more complex scenarios, such as password synchronization and write-back.

> **This section covers how to:**
> - Install and configure Azure AD Connect
> - Configure federation and single sign-on
> - Manage Azure AD Connect
> - Manage password sync and writeback

Install and configure Azure AD Connect

Azure AD Connect, or AAD Connect is Microsoft's tool for integrating on-premises directories with Azure AD and is the cornerstone of hybrid identity in the Microsoft cloud. Being able to use your on-premises identities with Azure AD means you have a common identity for access all your resources, regardless of whether they are in the cloud or on-premises. AAD Connect is the current iteration of Microsoft's identity synchronization tooling for Azure AD and the replace for DirSync and AAD Sync.

Preparing for Directory Synchronization

Prior to installing AAD Connect, there are several prerequisites across Active Directory and Azure AD that you must be aware of in addition to the requirements of the AAD Connect software itself.

Within Azure AD, you will want to ensure that the user name suffix for your on-premises users has been added and verified as a custom domain in Azure AD. For example, if your user's logon to their devices with a user name ending in @contoso.com, you will want to have contoso.com added as a custom domain in Azure AD. This allows your users to synchronize from on-premises and keep the same user name. If you do not verify the domain prior to synchronization, users will be created in Azure AD in the onmicrosoft.com namespace. Next, you will need to verify the number of objects that you intend to synchronize to Azure AD. When you verify your first domain, the object limit will be increased from 50k to 300k objects. If you need more than 500k objects you will need a license beyond the free tier of Azure AD.

After you have added a custom domain and verified you are within the synchronization limits for your Azure AD tenant, it is recommended that you fix any potential errors in your on-premises directory with IdFix. IdFix is a Microsoft provided tool which will identify errors in your on-premises directory and help you fix them. IdFix detects a number of errors and in some cases can automatically fix them as well. Common errors include the detection of illegal characters such as a leading and trailing spaces in mail addresses and illegal characters in user principal names. It also detects duplicate entries, formatting errors, length errors, and null value errors. Note that these attributes may work in your on-premises directory today, but should be fixed before you perform any synchronization activities as they will not be compatible with Azure AD.

IdFix can be used to perform the updates for any errors it finds, however you may wish to perform those updates in another manner (*e.g.* through a custom PowerShell script) where you can exercise more control. You can run IdFix as many times as needed as you assess your environment and its readiness for synchronization to Azure AD.

For your on-premises directory itself, you must be at both a forest functional level and AD schema version of Windows Server 2003 or later. This requirement only applies to the schema version, and not your domain controllers themselves which can run any version of Windows Server. There are some optional features of Azure AD such as password write which require Windows Server 2008 R2 or later for your domain controllers.

Finally, there are the requirements for AAD Connect itself. AAD Connect must be installed on Windows Server Standard or higher and requires a server with a GUI, which means it is not supported for installation on Windows Server Core. AAD Connect can be installed on a domain controller, however this is not required nor is it recommended. AAD Connect must be installed on a domain member.

Inbound projections, or identities, from your on-premises directory are stored in a Microsoft SQL Server database. A default installation of AAD Connect using the Express settings will install SQL Server 2012 Express LocalDB which has a 10GB size limit and will limit the number of objects that you can manage (approximately 100k objects). There are also potentially availability and recovery concerns in larger environments when using SQL Express. It is possible to use a separate SQL Server instance (shared or dedicated) for your identity database and storage. When using an external SQL Server, SQL Server 2008 or later is required. While the SQL Server can be shared with other workloads, it is only supported to have a SQL instance associated with one synchronization engine at a time. This means you cannot use the same SQL instance for hosting databases for both AAD Connect and FIM/MIM.

To install AAD Connect, you will also need access to several accounts. A local administrator account is required to install AAD Connect along with the credentials for a Global administrator in the Azure AD tenant which you will be establishing a synchronization relationship with. When AAD Connect is installed with defaults, a Connector Account is also created in the on-premises directory which is used to read and write information to and from Active Directory. To create this account as a part of AAD Connect installation, the credentials for an Enterprise Administrator are required. Optionally, the Connector Account can be pre-created by an administrator prior to the installation of AAD Connect which would negate the need for Enterprise Administrator credentials during installation.

You should also be aware of DNS resolution requirements. AAD Connect requires both intranet and internet DNS resolution and must be able to resolve both your on-premises Active Directory and the public Azure AD endpoints.

> **NOTE AZURE AD CONNECT PREREQUISITES**
>
> The full and current list of prerequisites for Azure AD Connect can be found at:
> *https://docs.microsoft.com/azure/active-directory/hybrid/how-to-connect-install-prerequisites.*

Installing AAD Connect

The AAD Connect installer is linked through the Azure Active Directory service in the Azure Portal and can be downloaded directly from the Microsoft Download Center at *https://go.microsoft.com/fwlink/?LinkId=615771*. The download (see Figure 5-24) is a single MSI. To install AAD Connect, download the installer to the target server and run the executable.

FIGURE 5-24 Download Azure AD Connect link in the Azure portal

There are two phases to the installation of AAD Connect: the installation of the agents and the associated tooling such as PowerShell on older versions of Windows Server and the required versions of the .NET Framework which is then followed by the configuration of synchronization between your on-premises domain and Azure AD (see Figure 5-25).

To begin the installation, execute the installer on the target server. Recall that you will need the credentials for a Global administrator in your target Azure AD and optionally the credentials for an Enterprise Administrator account if you have not already created the Connector Account.

FIGURE 5-25 Microsoft Azure AD Connect Setup

After agreeing to the terms and conditions, you will select a custom or express installation. Selecting **Use Express Settings** will configure synchronization for all identities in the local formation, configure password hash synchronization (see Figure 5-26), enable auto-upgrade of AAD Connect, and initiate synchronization as soon as the installer completes. Choosing a custom installation offers the opportunity to specific a custom installation location, use an existing SQL instance, specific existing service accounts, and specify custom sync groups.

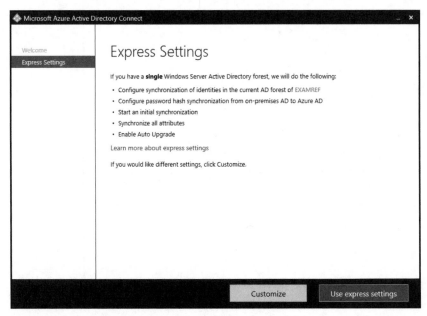

FIGURE 5-26 Microsoft Azure AD Connect Setup Express Settings

With the installation of required components complete, you will proceed to the second phase of the installation–the configuration of synchronization.

You will first select how users will sign-in to Azure AD (see Figure 5-27). Valid options are:

- **Password Hash Synchronization**   This option allows users to sign in to Azure AD using the same user name and password that they use on-premises. This is also known as a simple or same sign-on model.

- **Pass-Through Authentication**   This option enables Azure AD to authenticate users using your on-premises identity infrastructure.

- **Federation With AD FS**   This option allows users to sign-in with AD FS as a federated identity provider. With this option, after users in federated domains have been resolved through home realm discovery in Azure AD they will be redirected to the target identity provider.

- **Federation with PingFederate**   This option allows users to sign-in with PingFederate. With this option, after users in federated domains have been resolved through home realm discovery in Azure AD they will be redirected to the target identity provider.

- **Do Not Configure**   This option allows you to perform federated authentication with a federated identity provider which is not AD FS or PingFederate but is in the Azure AD Identity Provider Compatibility Docs located at *https://www.microsoft.com /download/ details.aspx?id=56843*.

You can optionally enable single sign-on for domain-joined desktops without the use of AD FS (see Figure 5-27).

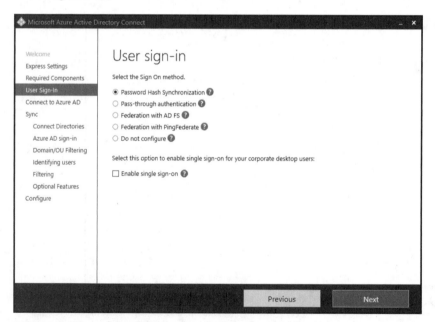

FIGURE 5-27 Microsoft Azure AD Connect Configuration User sign-in

Next, you will enter the credentials for a Global administrator in your target Azure AD (see Figure 5-28). This is required to enable synchronization and establish the relationship between your on-premises directory and Azure AD. You will not be able to proceed beyond this screen without the required credentials.

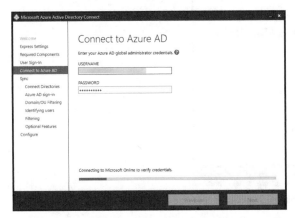

FIGURE 5-28 Microsoft Azure AD Connect Configuration Connect to Azure AD

You can now connect to your local Active Directory forest(s) and select one or more domains for synchronization (see Figure 5-29). This is the phase of the configuration where the Connector Account is created or where you will select an existing Active Directory account. When creating a new account, the credentials for an Enterprise Administrator are required.

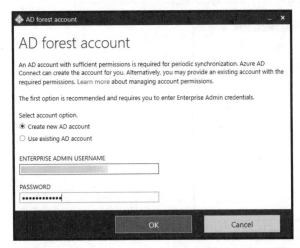

FIGURE 5-29 Microsoft Azure AD Connect Configuration AD forest account

The after adding your domain(s), the configuration wizard (see Figure 5-30) will enumerate the verified domains in your target Azure AD tenant and allow you to select the attribute that you will use from your on-premises directory to project to Azure AD as the user principal name (or sign-in name). By default, this will be a straight translation from your on-premises userPrincipalName to userPrincipalName. In cases where your on-premises userPrincipalName is not internet routable or does not match the verified domain suffix in Azure AD, you are afforded the opportunity to select the appropriate attribute.

FIGURE 5-30 Microsoft Azure AD Connect Configuration Azure AD sign-in configuration

For each directory that you added previously in the wizard, you will have the opportunity select which domains and OUs you will synchronize. This is an opportunity to prune the number of objects that will synchronize to Azure AD. If you have objects which do not need to be projected to Azure AD, do not synchronize them. For example, service accounts that are dedicated to on-premises workloads may not need to exist in the cloud. Figure 5-31 shows an example configuration where only a single OU will be synchronized to Azure AD.

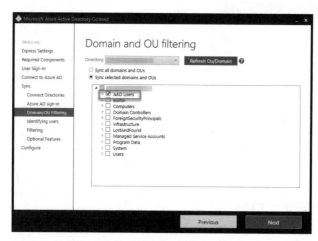

FIGURE 5-31 Microsoft Azure AD Connect Configuration Domain and OU filtering

To match users on-premises to their cloud identity, AAD Connect needs to know how to uniquely identify users in your directories on-premises (see Figure 5-32). If you have multiple forests or domains and users are represented more than once, this is where you will inform AAD Connect how to identify the source identity. You will also select how users should be matched in Azure AD through a source anchor. You can select any attribute in your on-premises directory as the anchor attribute but note that the configuration cannot be altered after it is set.

FIGURE 5-32 Microsoft Azure AD Connect Configuration Uniquely identifying your users

You will next configure any optional filters for users and devices (see Figure 5-33). This allows you to synchronize a subset of users which may be appropriate for a pilot deployment or if you have objects you want to synchronize that are spread across multiple OUs and mixed with objects you do not want to synchronize.

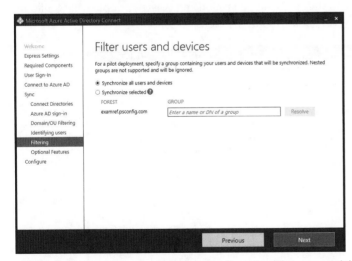

FIGURE 5-33 Microsoft Azure AD Connect Configuration Filter users and devices

Finally, you will have the opportunity to configuration any optional features (see Figure 5-34). For example, if you are going to configure SSPR with password writeback, this is where the feature would be enabled in Azure AD Connect. This screen will not have some options enabled if they are not available in your environment. For example, you will not be able to synchronize Exchange attributes if you do not have Exchange deployed and your on-premises schema extended.

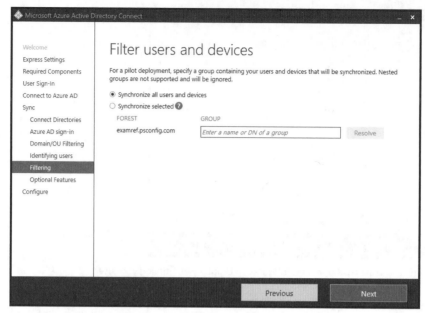

FIGURE 5-34 Microsoft Azure AD Connect Configuration Optional features

With the configuration complete, you can now commit it and finalize the configuration of AAD Connect. You can choose to start the synchronization immediately or optionally configure the AAD Connect tooling to run in staging mode (see Figure 5-35).

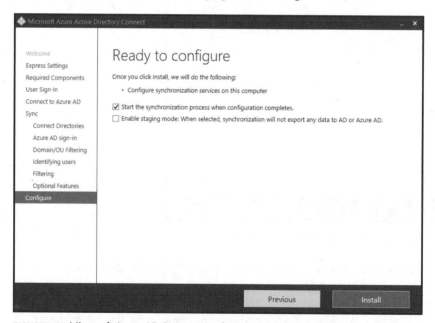

FIGURE 5-35 Microsoft Azure AD Connect Configuration Ready to configure

If this is your first AAD Connect installation, do not select **Enable Staging Mode**. Staging mode is used for high availability with AAD Connect or to test new configuration changes without impacting your existing synchronization jobs. When AAD Connect is running in staging mode, no outbound projections are made from AAD Connect to Azure AD or your on-premises directory (in the case of writeback) but all inbound rules and projections do run.

Selecting **Install** will enable synchronization for your Azure AD tenant and configure the management agents in AAD Connect. The Azure AD Connect Health agent for sync will also be installed at this time. After the installation is complete and a full synchronization has run, the users and groups from the on-premises AD appear in the Azure AD portal sourced from Windows Server AD.

FIGURE 5-36 Azure Active Directory synchronized users

Configure federation and single sign-on

Azure AD Connect can help you implement multiple forms of authentication for an Azure AD tenant, including federated single-sign on as well as single-sign on when using Password synchronization or Pass-through authentication.

Azure AD Connect single sign-on

Prior to configuring a domain in Azure AD for single sign-on with AAD Connect, you will need to add a custom domain and that domain will need to be verified. To deploy this feature, you also need to deploy AAD Connect to a Windows Server running Windows Server 2012 R2 or later and TLS 1.2 will need to be enabled. The server must also be a domain member of the same Active Directory forest as the users whose passwords you will need to validate.

Configuring single-sign on (see Figure 5-37) for use with Password synchronization or Pass-through authentication needs to be completed once for each forest that is being synchronized to Azure AD. To configure this feature, an account is created in the on-premises Active Directory and you will configure client machines to support single-sign on. Pass-through authentication is a tenant wide configuration, meaning it will apply to all of the custom (or managed) domains in your tenant. This also means that if you change the configuration later, such as on a staging server, it is possible to impact the configuration of your production deployment of AAD Connect.

FIGURE 5-37 Microsoft Azure Active Directory Connect User sign-in

To begin, you will select the appropriate sign-on method and then **Enable Single Sign-On** (see Figure 5-38). Then, for each domain that you will enter the credentials of an administrator with Domain Administrator rights to enable the creation of the new authentication broker accounts.

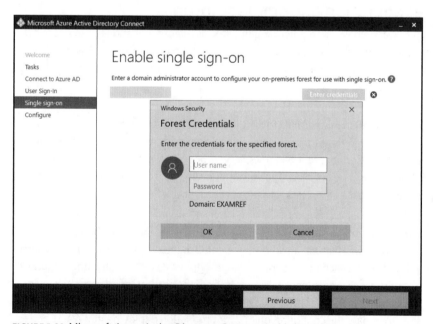

FIGURE 5-38 Microsoft Azure Active Directory Connect Enable single sign-on

After SSO has been enabled, you will be able to view the configuration change in the Azure Portal (see Figure 5-39).

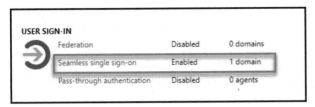

FIGURE 5-39 Seamless single sign-on enabled in Azure AD

Password Hash Synchronization (PHS) and Pass-through authentication (PHA) vary slightly in the deployment of additional on-premises components. As a part of configuration with PHA, an agent will be installed on the local server where AAD Connect is running. This agent brokers the connection between Azure AD and your on-premises directory when users attempt to authenticate to Azure AD. By default, only one agent is deployed, but you can deploy additional agents to other servers in your environment to enable high availability. It is recommended that you deploy at least three of these authentication agents and not more than 12 can be deployed per tenant.

After configuring single-sign on in Azure AD Connect you will also need to enable clients for single sign-on. The configuration varies based on the client operating system and browser.

For Windows clients using Internet Explorer, this can be done through Group Policy by adding the site https://autologon.microsoftazuread-sso.com to the Local Intranet Zone in Internet Explorer through the Site to Zone Assignment List Group Policy that can be found at User Configuration\Administrative Templates\Windows Components\Internet Explorer\Internet Control Panel\Security Page\Site to Zone Assignment List. You also need to enable the **Allow Updates To Status Bar Via Script** through Group Policy. This configuration is required for clients to successfully authenticate because by default Windows clients will not send Kerberos tickets to fully qualified domain names.

For other browsers, such as Firefox, Google Chrome, and Safari on macOS, refer to the configuration documentation at: *https://docs.microsoft.com/ azure/active-directory/hybrid/ how-to-connect-sso-quick-start#browser-considerations*.

This configuration only works for users that are:

- Signed in to a domain joined device. Note the device does not need to be Azure AD Joined.

- Directly connected to the domain at the time they authenticate to Azure AD. This means that for users that are off the network (*e.g.* remote workers not a on VPN) seamless SSO will not be possible with this method.

- Accessing cloud apps that support modern authentication. Legacy authentication protocols are not supported with this method.

Azure AD Connect Federation

Azure AD Connect can also assist in the deployment of Active Directory Federation Services (or AD FS) and its associated roles if you do not have it deployed already. This is an optional part of the Azure AD Connect installation process. This potentially makes it easier to get AD FS installed and configured if you do not have any existing federation infrastructure or you are looking for any automated installation mechanism for AD FS. If there is already an AD FS infrastructure deployed, Azure AD Connect can perfectly integrate it as well.

Before configuring AD FS through Azure AD Connect, ensure that you have the following in place:

- A Windows Server 2012 R2 or later server for the federation server with remote management enabled

- A Windows Server 2012 R2 or later server for the Web Application Proxy server with remote management enabled

- An SSL certificate for the federation service name you intend to use (for example sts.examref.com)

- The credentials of a domain administrator

For the Web Application Proxy (WAP) server(s), you may need to perform additional configuration if they are not domain joined. From the server which you are going to run the AAD Connect installation and configuration wizard, you will need to add each WAP server to the TrustedHosts list for WSMan (Web Services for Management). This can be done by running the following command replacing the <DMZServerFQDNs> value with the value of your WAP server. If you have multiple WAP servers, you can use a comma separated list of servers as well.

```
Set-Item WSMan:\localhost\Client\TrustedHosts -Value <DMZServerFQDNs> -Force
-Concatenate
```

The SSL certificate you will provide to the installation wizard must be an X509 certificate and the identity of the certificate must match the federation service name. The identity can be a SAN extension or common name of the certificate. Certificates with multiple SAN entries are supported as are wildcard certificates. Note that the installation wizard will not provision this certificate for you and you must obtain it prior to configuration.

Finally, for both the Federation server(s) and any WAPs you must have DNS records in place. You can use split-brain DNS for your federation services (*e.g.* point internal clients to your Federation server(s) and external clients to your WAPs). Your internal DNS must use an A record or Windows authentication will not function properly. If you are deploying a highly-available AD FS environment, ensure that the DNS entries point to the load-balanced endpoints for each segment.

To being configuration of AD FS federation with AAD Connect, select **Federation With AD FS** on the User sign-in screen (see Figure 5-40) in the configuration wizard.

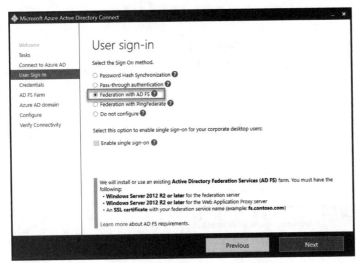

FIGURE 5-40 Configure Federation with AD FS in the Microsoft Azure Active Directory Connect installation wizard

Next, you will supply the credentials of a domain administrator (see Figure 5-41).

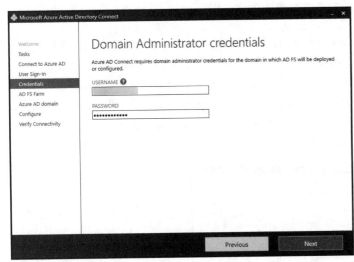

FIGURE 5-41 Microsoft Azure Active Directory Connect installation wizard Domain administrator credentials

From this point, the wizard varies. You will select whether you are configuring a new AD FS farm or using an existing farm. If you are configuring a new farm, you will need to supply the SSL certificate that meets the requires as stated above. For an existing farm, you will specify the server name for the primary server in the AD FS farm (see Figure 5-42).

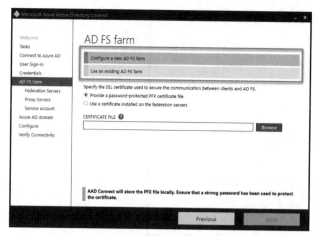

FIGURE 5-42 Microsoft Azure Active Directory Connect installation wizard AD FS farm

For the remainder of the example, we will focus on creating a new AD FS farm. On the next screens, you will add each of the Federation servers and each WAP. The selection of WAP servers is optional for the purposes of the wizard but recommended for a full AD FS deployment where users will be authentication from external locations.

After adding your servers, you will specify the AD FS service account (see Figure 5-43). The installation wizard can create a new group Managed Service Account (group MSA), use an existing group MSA, or use a domain account. When creating a new account, you will need to supply the credentials of an Enterprise Administrator and for existing accounts you will supply the account name or the account credentials. If you have Windows Server 2012 domain controllers and your AD FS member servers belong to the same domain, it is recommend to use a group MSA.

FIGURE 5-43 Microsoft Azure Active Directory Connect installation wizard AD FS service account

Next, you will select the domain you will federate. On the first run of the configuration wizard, you can only select one domain. If you run the AAD Connect wizard again later, you can then select additional domains (Figure 5-44).

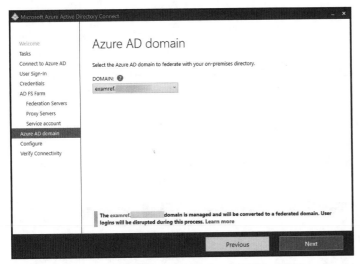

FIGURE 5-44 Microsoft Azure Active Directory Connect installation wizard Azure AD domain

If you have not previously verified the domain, for example in cases where the custom domain has been added as a part of the AAD Connect installation wizard, you will need to verify the domain before proceeding. Once you are ready to configure (see Figure 5-45), click the Configure button. After configuration has completed, you can test connectivity or re-run the AAD Connect wizard to add additional federated domains.

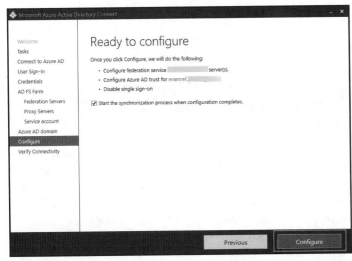

FIGURE 5-45 Microsoft Azure Active Directory Connect installation wizard Ready to configure

Manage Azure AD Connect

Azure AD Connect can be managed through several tools including the AAD Connect installation wizard and PowerShell.

The most common will be running the installation wizard again to update or alter an existing configuration. For example, to change the user sign-in method or to add a new on-premises directory for synchronization you would simply run the wizard again.

You can find the installation wizard in the Start Menu named Azure AD Connect or on the Desktop for the user that installed the tool. When you launch the wizard, the synchronization service scheduler will be paused. This means that no synchronizations (*e.g.* delta synchronizations from your on-premises directory to Azure AD) will occur until the configuration updates are complete or the wizard is closed.

You will see a screen like the one in Figure 5-46. If you have deployed AD FS you will have even more options.

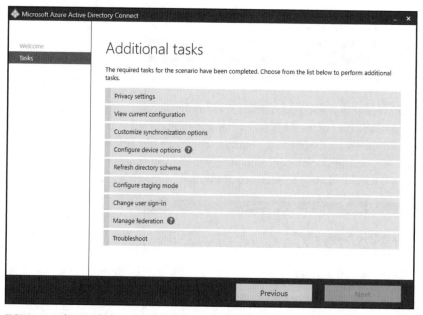

FIGURE 5-46 Azure AD Connect installation wizard being run a second time

Choosing Customize Synchronization Options and make bold will allow you to make changes to the current configuration. The options you see running the wizard a second time will be a subset of the options that were available in the initial installation. From this option, you can add more directories, update domain and organizational unit (or OU) filtering, remove group filtering, and change optional features such as enabling or disabling password writeback, group writeback, and Azure AD app and attribute filtering.

If you update the schema in your on-premises Active Directory forest you can use the Refresh directory schema option to update the schema for one or more directories to enable synchronization of newly created attributes.

The configure staging mode will allow you to enable or disable staging mode on the server. Staging mode can used for enabling high-availability, testing and deploying new configuration changes, and introducing new Azure AD Connect servers prior to decommissioning or retiring an existing server.

Finally, you can also change the user sign-in method to and from password hash sync, pass-through authentication, or federation. When changing sign-in methods, there can be disruptions to user connectivity.

Using PowerShell, you can use the ADSync module to view and update settings for the synchronization service, such as altering the sync schedule or manually initiating synchronizations.

To use the ADSync module, open a PowerShell prompt as an administrator on the server where AAD Connect is installed and import the module.

```
Import-Module ADSync
```

You can view the existing sync schedule with the Get-ADSyncScheduler cmdlet, as shown in Figure 5-47.

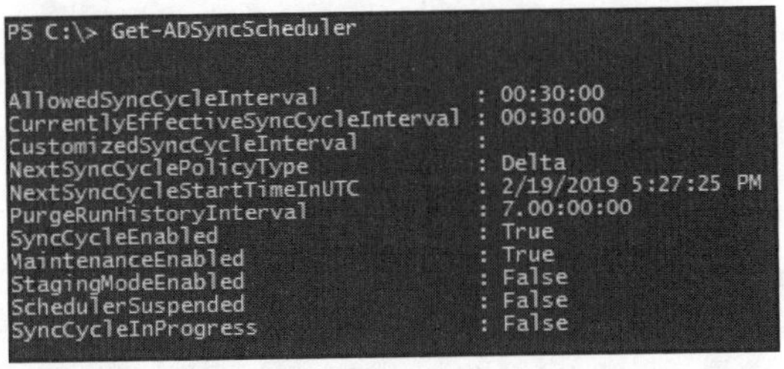

FIGURE 5-47 Get-ADSyncScheduler output

By default, synchronization occurs every 30 minutes. If you need to alter the schedule, use the Set-ADSyncScheduler cmdler. For example, you could run the following command to set the scheduler to sync every hour.

```
Set-ADSyncScheduler -CustomizedSyncCycleInterval 01:00:00
```

To view the current sync status, use the Get-ADSyncConnectorRunStatus cmdlet.

To initiate a full or incremental synchronization, you can use the Start-ADSyncSyncCycle cmdlet and specify the PolicyType parameter. A PolicyType of Initial will start a full sync and while a PolicyType of Delta will start an incremental sync. Use the Get-ADSyncConnector-RunStatus cmdlet to view the status.

Manage password sync and writeback

AAD Connect supports a feature known as Password Hash Synchronization (PHS). With PHS, AAD Connect can be used to synchronize user passwords to Azure AD where they can then be leveraged for authentication. This is useful in scenarios where you want to allow users to sign-in to Azure AD with the same credentials they use on-premises but do not have the associated infrastructure to support federation or you do not require single sign-on.

The passwords that are synchronized to Azure AD are not sent or stored in clear text. They are instead a hash of a hash of a user's password from your on-premises Active Directory.

PHS is enabled through the AAD Connect installation wizard on the User sign-in screen (Figure 5-48).

FIGURE 5-48 Microsoft Azure Active Directory Connect User sign-in

There is no additional configuration required to leverage the feature. PHS is a one-way synchronization from your on-premises directory to Azure AD. This means there is a delay between when a password is changed on-premises and when that change is reflected in Azure AD as synchronization must occur for the updated password to be written to the cloud.

For environments where PHS is configured, cloud passwords are set to never expire. Combined with the previously mentioned delay in synchronization, there are cases where a user will be able to authenticate to the cloud apps that use Azure AD as their identity provider with their old password until synchronization occurs. To force a synchronization manually, you can use the Start-ADSyncSyncCyle cmdlet.

Password writeback is a feature of Azure AD and AAD Connect that allows users to change their password in the cloud and have that password written back to an on-premises directory while adhering to your organization's password policies and security controls. Password writeback is a user-friendly feature and provides immediate feedback to users as it is a synchronous operation.

Password writeback requires one of the following licenses:

- Azure AD Premium P1
- Azure AD Premium P2
- Enterprise Mobility + Security E3 or A3
- Enterprise Mobility + Security E5 or A5
- Microsoft 365 E3 or A3
- Microsoft 365 E5 or A5
- Microsoft 365 F1

Password writeback also supports additional controls which ensure that password change requests adhere to your organizational policy. For example, when a user or administrator initiates a password reset, the password is checked for history, complexity, age, and any other filters you have in place on-premises. As resets are a synchronous operation, users are immediately informed of the status of their reset.

When password writeback is enabled, administrators will have the ability to change user passwords through the Azure Portal as well.

Password writeback is enabled through AAD Connect and by configuring self-service password reset (or SSPR). To enable writeback through AAD Connect, open the installation wizard and browse to the Optional Features page. From that page, select the box next to **Password Writeback** (highlighted in Figure 5-49) and click Next. On the **Ready To Configure** page, select **Configure** and wait for the process to finish.

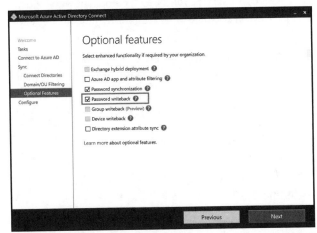

FIGURE 5-49 Azure AD Connect installation wizard option features view

With password writeback enabled in Azure AD Connect, browse to your Azure AD tenant in the Azure Portal as a Global administrator and open the Password Reset blade and then choose on-premises integration. Set the option for Write Back Passwords To Your On-Premises directory to **Yes** and optionally set the option for Allow Users To Unlock Accounts Without Resetting Their Passwords to **Yes**. When complete, click **Save**.

Skill 5.4: Implementing multi-factor authentication (MFA)

Multi-Factor Authentication (MFA) is a security enhancement that is applicable to authentication for users and devices in Azure Active Directory (Azure AD) where users must present additional information before they can authenticate to services that use Azure AD as an identity provider. MFA is also sometimes referred to as two-step or two-factor (2FA) authentication because it is a discrete step, separate from the entry or presentation of credentials during the authentication of a user. While MFA can include more than two factors, the implementation in Azure is strictly a two-factor implementation.

In its most basic form, MFA requires two or more of the following authentication methods:

- Something you know, for example a password or a pin.
- Something you have, for example a smart card or a mobile phone.
- Something you are, for example your fingerprint, which is unique to you.

MFA requires that your credentials come from two or more different sources to enhance security. For example, a user with MFA attempting to authenticate to the Azure mobile app will need their user name and password as well as a second factor such as a one-time pin generated by the Microsoft Authenticator app.

For organizations that need to be compliant with industry standards, such as PCI DSS version 3.2, MFA is a must-have capability to authenticate users. Beyond being compliant with industry standards, enforcing MFA to authenticate users can also help organizations to mitigate credential theft attacks.

MFA in Azure AD is provided through Azure Multi-Factor Authentication. Azure MFA helps safeguard access to data and applications that use Azure AD as an identity provider while maintaining simplicity for users with administrator-controlled functionality such as conditional MFA.

> **This section covers how to:**
> - Configuring Azure MFA
> - Configuring user accounts for MFA
> - Configure advanced MFA features, including:
>   - Trusted IPs
>   - Conditional access policies
>   - Fraud alerts
>   - One-time bypass
>   - Identity Protection

Multi-Factor Authentication

Before implementing MFA in Azure AD, there are several considerations. MFA is both a service that is configured through Azure AD and a feature that is assigned to users through an Azure AD license which includes usage rights for Azure MFA. Assigning your users a license that includes the features of MFA is not enough–you must also configure the service to meet your organizational requirements.

The MFA service comes in multiple versions:

- Multi-Factor Authentication for Office 365 and Multi-Factor Authentication for Microsoft 365 Business
- Multi-Factor Authentication for Azure AD Administrators
- Azure Multi-Factor Authentication

Azure MFA for Office 365/Microsoft 365 is a version of the MFA service that works only with Office 365 applications and is managed through the Microsoft 365 administrative portal. Azure MFA for Azure AD Administrators is available for Global Administrators of an Azure AD tenant for no charge. Azure MFA is the full or complete version of MFA, and doesn't have any limitations that are imposed when using just Azure MFA for Office 365 or Azure MFA for Azure AD Administrators.

> **NOTE   AZURE MFA FEATURE COMPARISON**
>
> For a feature comparison of the available versions of Azure MFA, refer to the documentation at: *https://docs.microsoft.com/azure/active-directory/authentication/concept-mfa-licensing#feature-comparison-of-versions*.

Azure MFA is included with Azure Active Directory Premium (both P1 and P2) licenses and other suites with equivalent licensing such as Enterprise Mobility + Security E3/E5. For some time, Azure MFA also could be purchased in a consumption model, but that is no longer possible, and the only way to obtain usage rights for Azure MFA is through the previously mentioned license.

Azure MFA per-user entitlements (licenses) enable the Azure MFA service, which then has two variations that vary in functionality. Azure MFA can be run purely in the cloud, and there is also an on-premises MFA server that can be deployed. PIN mode, one-time bypass, and caching are features that are exclusive to Azure MFA Server. The ability to remember MFA for trusted devices is exclusively to MFA in the cloud.

> **NOTE   AZURE MFA SERVER**
>
> Azure MFA Server one-time bypass is discussed later in this chapter.

Configure Azure MFA

Configuring Azure MFA in the cloud begins with ensuring you meet the perquisites. In addition to obtaining user licensing that includes the MFA features of Azure AD, you will also need a Global Administrator account to access and configure the service.

> **NOTE   AZURE MFA SERVER DEPLOYMENT GUIDANCE**
>
> Throughout this section, we refer to the configuration of Azure MFA in the cloud. For specific deployment guidance of Azure MFA Server on-premises, refer to the documentation at *https://docs.microsoft.com/azure/active-directory/authentication/howto-mfaserver-deploy.* Features that are exclusive to MFA Server will be called out.

The MFA service requires the configuration of one or more authentication methods. The authentication methods that you select as a part of the configuration of the MFA service will drive how much information your users need to provide to successfully authenticate through Azure AD and the MFA service.

The authentication methods available for use with Azure MFA are:

- **Password**   This is the password of the user in Azure AD. This is a required authentication method and cannot be disabled.
- **Call to Phone**   Through this method a voice call is made through an automated calling service to the user's registered phone number. The user will answer the call and press # to verify the call.
- **Text Message To Phone**   In this method an SMS is sent to the user's registered mobile phone number. The SMS message contains a code that must be entered to authenticate to Azure AD.
- **Notification Through Mobile App**   This authentication method allows a user to register the Microsoft Authenticator app with Azure AD during registration and receive

push notifications on their iOS or Android mobile device for each MFA-enforced authentication to Azure AD.

- **Verification Code From Mobile App Or Hardware Token** This method allows users to use the Microsoft Authenticator app or a compatible third-party application to generate one-time pins (OTP). The application generating the pin is a software token that generates OATH verification codes. In the case of hardware tokens, Azure AD supports the use of OATH-TOTP SHA-1 tokens of both the 30 and 60 second varieties.

NOTE **HARDWARE TOKENS**

The use of hardware tokens is currently in preview.

NOTE **AUTHENTICATION METHOD BEST PRACTICE**

Consider configuring two or more authentication methods in addition to a password (which cannot be removed) when configuring the MFA service. Users may not have access to all of their methods at the time of authentication and having more than one method available will provide your users with more flexibility. For example, when a user is at their desk, they may not be able to receive calls on their mobile device, but they do have access to their office phone. In this case, it may be desirable to have Call To Phone and SMS or mobile app notifications configured.

You can also control the use of app passwords when configuring the MFA service. There may be applications that users authenticate through Azure Ad to access, but they do so with a non-browser-based application that cannot perform modern authentication. For example, users in your organization may access their Office 365 mailbox hosted in Exchange Online through a third-party email client that does not use modern authentication. In this case, you must allow users to create app passwords in the MFA service. It is also possible to leverage Azure MFA to block authentication attempts to applications that do not support modern authentication by blocking the ability to create app passwords. By default, app passwords are disabled and must be enabled as a part of the configuration of the MFA service.

NOTE **APP PASSWORD AUTHENTICATION**

If your organization uses federated identity with Azure AD (for example, with AD FS), be aware that the use of app passwords circumvents federation because the authentication occurs only in Azure AD.

To configure authentication methods (or verification options), or disallow the use of app passwords in the MFA service, browse to your Azure AD tenant in the Azure Portal and select the MFA blade as shown in Figure 5-50.

FIGURE 5-50 MFA in the Azure Portal

NOTE **NAVIGATING TO AZURE AD IN THE AZURE PORTAL**

If you do not see the Azure Active Directory service in the left navigation, you can find it by selecting All Services. There is also a dedicated URL for the quick management of Azure AD at *https://aad.portal.azure.com*.

From the MFA blade, click **Additional Cloud-Based MFA Settings** as shown in Figure 5-51.

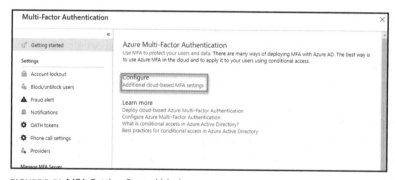

FIGURE 5-51 MFA Getting Started blade

A new tab will open in your browser and you will be taken to the Service Settings tab for the MFA service. From this tab, you can configure:

- App passwords
- Trusted IPs

- Verification methods
- Device remember/re-authentication settings

> **NOTE TRUSTED IPS**
>
> The configuration of Trusted IPs is discussed later in this chapter.

Configure the service as needed based on your organization's requirements, and click **Save** to persist the configuration, as shown in Figure 5-52.

FIGURE 5-52 MFA service settings tab

Configure user accounts for MFA

Before or after the configuration of the service settings for Azure MFA is complete, licenses can be assigned to users. In many cases, it is desirable to first configure the MFA service, onboard several test users to verify the configuration is performing as desired, and then onboard your remaining users.

MFA can be enabled for users in three ways:

- **Changing user state**   This is the most common method to enable MFA and works for both MFA in the cloud and MFA server. In this configuration, a license is assigned to each user who requires MFA and MFA is enabled for the account until the state is changed to disabled.

- **Through conditional access policies** In this configuration, receive MFA challenges based on administrator-defined rules that allow or deny access to applications in Azure AD.

- **Through Azure AD Identity Protection** In this configuration, risk policies in Azure AD conditionally enforce MFA authentication based on the sign-in risk associated with the authentication attempt.

To configure MFA for your users by changing user state, browse to Azure Active Directory in the Azure Portal and select the Users blade as shown in Figure 5-53.

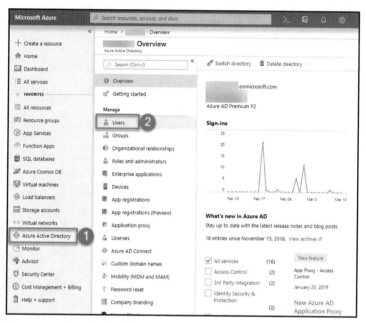

FIGURE 5-53 Azure Active Directory service and Users blade

From the All Users blade, select **Multi-Factor Authentication** in the toolbar as shown in Figure 5-54.

FIGURE 5-54 Azure Active Directory All users blade

A new browser tab will open, and you will be taken to the Users tab of the MFA service as shown in Figure 5-55.

FIGURE 5-55 MFA service users tab

From the user settings screen, you can view the MFA status (user state) for your users. The user settings screen also supports filtering user attributes and roles through the Views drop-down. This includes filtering by Sign-in allowed users, Billing administrators, Global administrators, Password administrators, Service administrators, and User management administrators. It is also possible to further filter the list of users by user state, including Any, Enabled, or Enforced.

When a user's state is *Disabled*, the user is not enrolled in MFA. When MFA is enabled for a user, their state changes to *Enabled*. Even though a user has been enabled for the MFA service, they have not yet performed registration (for example, setting their mobile or configuring other authentication methods). After a user has completed the registration process for Azure MFA, their state will change to *Enforced*.

> **IMPORTANT   REGISTERING USERS FOR MFA**
>
> When you have enabled MFA for a user, it is critical that they register for the MFA service as soon as possible if they are not yet registered. MFA cannot be enforced for a user until that user has completed registration. Enabling MFA for your users should be a coordinated effort between Azure AD administrators, your support desk, and your users. Users must be trained on how to register for the service, and how authentication to Azure AD applications will change with MFA in place.
>
> Users can register for the MFA service before a license is assigned at *https://aka.ms/mfasetup*. This is recommended in most cases as your users will transition directly to Enforced when MFA is enabled on their accounts. By pre-registering your users, you can ensure that that users are given time to understand the MFA service and provided the proper training.

To update the state for a single user, select the user, and under quick steps select **Enable** to configure the user for MFA, as shown in Figure 5-56.

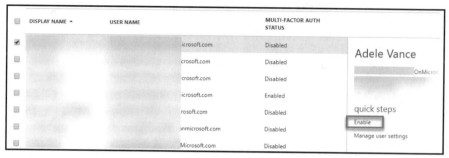

	DISPLAY NAME ▲	USER NAME	MULTI-FACTOR AUTH STATUS	
☑		icrosoft.com	Disabled	**Adele Vance**
☐		crosoft.com	Disabled	OnMicros
☐		crosoft.com	Disabled	
☐		icrosoft.com	Enabled	
☐		rosoft.com	Disabled	quick steps
☐		nmicrosoft.com	Disabled	Enable
☐		Microsoft.com	Disabled	Manage user settings

FIGURE 5-56 MFA service users tab

At the prompt, select **Enable Multi-Factor Auth** as shown in Figure 5-57.

About enabling multi-factor auth

Please read the deployment guide if you haven't already.

If your users do not regularly sign in through the browser, you can send them to this link to register for multi-factor auth: https://aka.ms/MFASetup

enable multi-factor auth   cancel

FIGURE 5-57 Enable Multi-Factor Auth for a single user

After the update has been made the user's state will change to Enabled. Selecting the same user, you will now see that the options under Quick Steps have changed and Disable and Enforce are now options. In most cases, users in the enabled state will be prompted to perform registration on their next authentication attempt and be transitioned to a user state of Enforced. It is also possible for an administrator to force a user state of Enforced even if a user has not completed registration. In either case (whether in an Enabled state or an Enforced state), the user must still go through registration.

> **NOTE MANUALLY MOVING USERS TO ENFORCED STATE**
>
> Do not ever move users directly to the Enforced state. This can cause non-browser-based applications to stop working, because the user has not yet registered and will not have any app passwords configured.

It is also possible to perform bulk updates to user state using PowerShell or a CSV uploaded through the MFA service. CSV updates can only be used to enable or disable MFA for existing users, not to add new users to Azure AD. To perform CSV updates, from the Users tab in the MFA service, select the **Bulk Update** button, as shown in Figure 5-58.

FIGURE 5-58 Enable multi-factor auth for a single user

In the prompt that appears, you can download a sample file or upload an existing CSV. The format for the CSV is two columns:

- **Username**   Where the value is the UPN of the user
- **MFA Status**   Where the status is the desired user state of Enabled or Disabled

    For example:

```
Username, MFA Status
chris@opsgility.com, Enabled
paul@opsgility.com, Disabled
shane@opsgility.com, Disabled
jonathan@opsgility.com, Enabled
abu@opsgility.com, Enabled
```

When uploading a file, it will be verified where a check is performed to validate UPNs and the MFA Status column.

To perform updates using PowerShell, you will need the MSOnline module. In an administrator-elevated PowerShell prompt, first install the module. After installing the module, you can connect to the online service using the Connect-MsolService cmdlet.

```
Install-Module MSOnline
Connect-MsolService
```

Create an array of users or retrieve the users from an existing data store, such as a CSV or a SQL database. In this example, we will use an array:

```
$users = "chris@opsgility.com", "jonathan@opsgility.com", "abu@opsgility.com"
foreach ($user in $users) {
  $st = New-Object -TypeName Microsoft.Online.Administration.
StrongAuthenticationRequirement
  $st.RelyingParty = "*"
  $st.State = "Enabled"
  $sta = @($st)
  Set-MsolUser -UserPrincipalName $user -StrongAuthenticationRequirements $sta
}
```

The user state is set through the State property on the object of type Microsoft.Online. Administration.StrongAuthenticationRequirement, and the Set-MsolUser cmdlet is used to update the MFA settings for each user.

Azure MFA advanced features

So far, we have examined some of the basic settings to onboard to the Azure MFA service, and how to also onboard users to the service. There are several configuration items in the Azure MFA service that can be used to improve the user experience for users who are subject to MFA authentication.

The features of Azure MFA that we will review are:

- Trusted IPs
- Conditional Access Polices
- Fraud Alerts
- One-time bypass
- Azure Active Directory Identity Protection

Azure Active Directory Identity Protection requires Azure Active Directory Premium P2 licensing while the other features are available with either an Azure Active Directory Premium P1 or P2 license.

Configure Trusted IPs

One or more IP address ranges can be associated with the MFA service. When this is done, MFA is bypassed for authentication attempts from those configured ranges. This functionality is typically used to allow users on your Intranet or your internal network to authenticate to Azure AD applications without the additional verification step introduced with MFA. This way, users on your corporate network, or flagged network segments, can access required services in a more streamlined manner while they will still have to perform MFA when they are off the network or authenticating to Azure AD from an unknow network segment.

In addition to specifying a range of trusted IP addresses, you can also configure the MFA service to bypass MFA for federated users in your Azure AD tenant by including a custom claim from your identity provider to Azure AD after the user has authenticated in the federated identity provider. For example, if you federate a custom domain using AD FS, users who authenticate through AD FS can bypass MFA for authentication attempts that originate from within the corporate network.

Trusted IPs are configured through the MFA service settings. To access the service settings, in the Azure Portal browse to the Azure Active Directory service and select the MFA blade as shown in Figure 5-59.

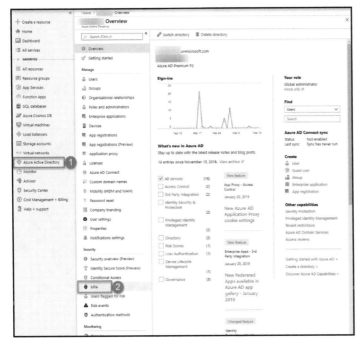

FIGURE 5-59 MFA in the Azure Portal

From the MFA blade, click **Additional Cloud-Based MFA Settings**, as shown in Figure 5-60.

FIGURE 5-60 MFA Getting Started blade

On the **Service Settings** tab, in the **Trusted IPSA** section, enter one or more IP address ranges using CDIR notation. For example, if your on-premises clients are in the segment 10.1.0.0/16, enter that value in the text box, as shown in Figure 5-61. You can enter multiple ranges if needed.

To bypass MFA for federated users signing in from the corporate network, select the **Skip Multi-Factor Authentication For Requests From Federated Users On My Intranet** check box.

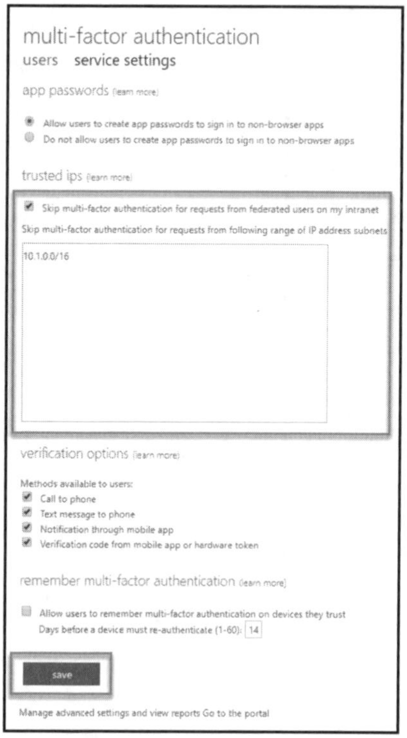

FIGURE 5-61 MFA service settings Trusted IPS

To persist the configuration, click **Save**.

> **NOTE MFA SERVICE SETTINGS LIMITS**
>
> You can enter up to 50 IP addresses/address ranges in Service Settings when configuring Azure MFA.

If you have selected the **Skip multi-factor authentication for requests from federated users on my intranet** check box, you must also add inject an additional claim for users authenticating through your federated identity provider. If you are using AD FS, this can be done by adding a new claim rule. The format of the claim is:

```
c:[Type== "http://schemas.microsoft.com/ws/2012/01/insidecorporatenetwork"] =>
issue(claim = c);
```

Configure Conditional Access Policies

One of more conditional access policies can be configured to all your users to bypass MFA authentication based on the logic that is defined in the conditional access policy.

To configure a new conditional access policy, browse to the **Azure Active Directory** service in the Azure Portal and select the **Conditional Access** blade, as shown in Figure 5-62.

FIGURE 5-62 Azure Active Directory service in the Azure Portal

From the **Policies** blade, click **New Policy** as shown in Figure 5-63.

FIGURE 5-63 Conditional Access Policies

Enter a name for your policy. In the example shown in Figure 5-64, the policy name will be **Enforce MFA**.

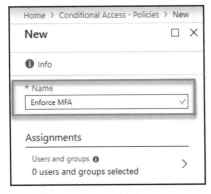

FIGURE 5-64 New policy blade

In the Assignments blade, select the Users And Groups that the policy will apply to as shown in Figure 5-65. Note that you can select users and groups the policy will apply to in the Include tab and you can also select users or groups to exclude from the policy through the Exclude tab. It is possible with some policies to lock yourself out of your tenant and in some cases it is recommended that you leave at least one user who has access rights to manage policy excluded from restrictive policies. You can select multiple users and multiple groups if needed. Click **Done**.

FIGURE 5-65 New policy blade Users and groups

Next, select the applications the policy will apply to, as shown in Figure 5-66. You can select **All Cloud Apps** or individual applications that are registered in your Azure AD tenant. It is also possible to exclude one or more cloud apps from a policy through the Exclude tab. Any apps selected on the Exclude tab are exempt from the policy. Click **Done**.

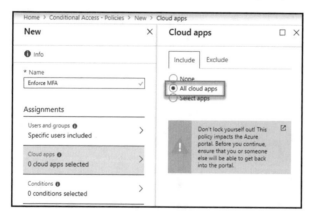

FIGURE 5-66 New policy blade Cloud apps

If you have any conditions you would like to configure, these can be done in the Conditions section. For example, if you have configured trusted IP ranges or defined locations based on country or geographic region, using the named locations feature of conditional access, you can apply the conditional logic here. You can also use the sign-in risk level from Azure Active Directory Identity Protection as a trigger for a condition. For the example provided, there will be no additional conditions, and the policy will simply trigger off of group membership for all cloud apps.

In the Grant blade under the Access controls section of the New policy blade, select **Grant Access** and the check box for **Require Multi-Factor Authentication**, as shown in Figure 5-67. Click **Select**.

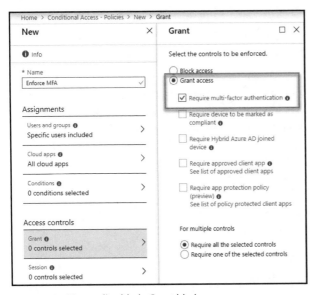

FIGURE 5-67 New policy blade Grant blade

In the New Policy blade, select **On** for Enable Policy, and click **Create** to save the new policy, as shown in Figure 5-68.

FIGURE 5-68 New policy Enable policy

The policy will be validated and then created. After several seconds you will receive a notification in the Portal that the policy has been successfully created, as shown in Figure 5-69. After the policy is created, it can still take several minutes before it takes effect.

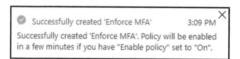

FIGURE 5-69 New policy successfully created

Configure Fraud Alerts

Fraud alerts in Azure MFA allow users to report what they suspect are fraudulent attempts to access their applications. For example, if a user that is configured for verification through the

Microsoft Authenticator app receives a push notification when they are not attempting to sign in to a service, it may be a bad actor attempting to access the user's applications. Remember, MFA challenges a user for their configured authentication methods only after a valid password has been provided, so if the user is not the one logging in, there is a very good chance that the user's credentials have been compromised.

To configure fraud alerts, browse to **Azure Active Directory** in the Azure Portal and select the **MFA** blade, as shown in figure 5-70.

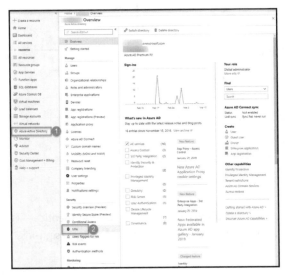

FIGURE 5-70 MFA in the Azure Portal

From the MFA blade, select **Fraud Alert**, as shown in Figure 5-71.

FIGURE 5-71 Fraud alert in the Azure Portal

To enable fraud alerts, turn the **Allow Users To Submit Fraud Alerts** button to **On**, as shown in Figure 5-72. You can also automatically block a user who reports fraud. If you configure this setting, the user account will be blocked and will remain blocked from all authentication attempts to Azure AD for 90 or until their account is unblocked by an administrator. This can be a good setting to leave enabled, as it will prevent fraudulent authentication attempts to all the cloud applications that a user can authenticate to using Azure AD.

There is also an option to configure a **Code to report fraud during initial greeting**. This code is used during voice verification. For example, if you set the value to **1**, when a user receives a voice call for verification, they can press 1# and the fraud attempt will be reported. When the service is configured as needed, click **Save**.

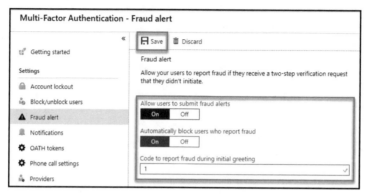

FIGURE 5-72 Fraud alert in the Azure Portal

After the service is configured, users can report fraud through the Microsoft Authenticator app or through the phone. Administrators can view fraud reports in the Azure AD sign-ins report.

Configure One-time Bypass

One-time bypass allows an administrator to exempt a user from MFA authentication for a short period of time. This can be useful if a user does not have access to their authentication method and your administrators still have a method to verify users are who they say they are. For example, if a user is configured for voice verification but their phone is stolen, they would not be able to perform two-step verification until they procure a new mobile phone and register their phone number in the MFA service.

> **IMPORTANT   ONE-TIME BYPASS AND AZURE MFA SERVER**
>
> One-time bypass is a feature of Azure MFA that is only available through the on-premises MFA Server.

To configure one-time bypass, browse to the **MFA** blade in the Azure Active Directory Service through the Azure Portal, as shown in Figure 5-73.

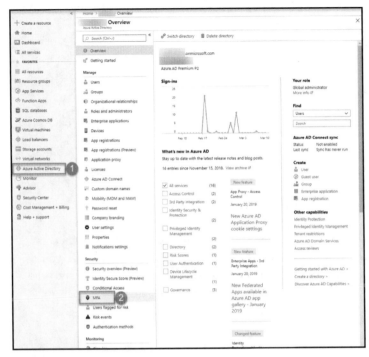

FIGURE 5-73 MFA in the Azure Portal

In the MFA service, select the **One-Time Bypass** blade, as shown in Figure 5-74.

FIGURE 5-74 One-Time Bypass blade in the MFA service

To create a bypass for a user, click the **Add** button. In the **Add One-Time Bypass** blade, enter the user principal name (also known as UPN or sign-in name) for a user, the number of seconds the bypass will be valid for, and a reason that will be captured with the bypass request. Click **Ok** to enable the bypass, as shown in Figure 5-75.

FIGURE 5-75 Add one-time bypass blade in the MFA service

The bypass will immediately be enabled and begin counting down. To view past bypass requests, browse to the **One-Time Bypass** blade in the MFA service. From this blade, you can add a new bypass as well as view current and past bypass requests. For current and valid requests, you can cancel them using the **Cancel** link, as shown in Figure 5-76.

FIGURE 5-76 One-Time Bypass blade in the MFA service

Configure Identity Protection

Azure Active Directory Identity Protection is a premium feature of Azure Active Directory, which requires Azure Active Directory Premium P2 licenses. Azure AD Identity Protection has features that are beyond the scope of MFA, and in this section, we will focus on the MFA registration policy feature of Azure AD Identity Protection.

The MFA registration policy can be used to assist in the rollout and implementation of Azure MFA through the creation of a policy that will enforce MFA registration for your users. Note that this policy is a feature of Azure AD Identity Protection and is not the same as a conditional access policy. The MFA registration policy enforces registration for the selected users and groups while conditional access can optionally enforce MFA for authentication to select cloud apps. For example, by enabling the MFA registration policy, you can ensure that all your users have registered for MFA and provided the needed inputs to configure their verification methods before you implement MFA. This can lower the burden on support staff and if left in place will enforce MFA registration for new users as well.

To configure the MFA registration policy, browse to the Azure AD Identity Protection service in the Azure Portal. There are multiple ways to access the service and, in the example, shown in Figure 5-77 you can browse to **All Services**, search for **Identity**, and then select the service.

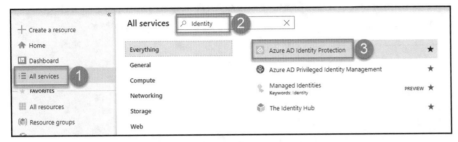

FIGURE 5-77 Azure AD Identity Protection in All services

> **NOTE   ENABLING AZURE AD IDENTITY PROTECTION**
>
> If you have not enabled Azure AD Identity Protection, you will need to do so before configuring the MFA registration policy. Guidance for enabling the service can be found at: *https://docs.microsoft.com/azure/active-directory/identity-protection/enable.*

In the Identity Protection service, select the **MFA Registration** blade, as shown in Figure 5-78.

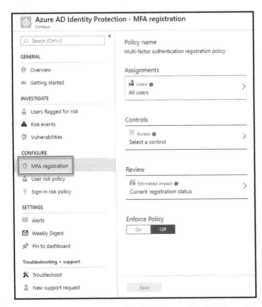

FIGURE 5-78 Azure AD Identity Protection MFA registration blade

To configure the policy, select the users for which you would like to enforce registration. In a manner like a conditional access policy, you can exclude users from the registration policy too. Select your users and/or groups, click **Select**, and then **Done**.

In the Access control blade, select **Require Azure MFA Registration** and click **Select**, as shown in Figure 5-79.

FIGURE 5-79 Azure AD Identity Protection Require Azure MFA registration

In the Estimated Impact blade, you can view the current state of MFA registration in your Azure AD tenant. as shown in Figure 5-80.

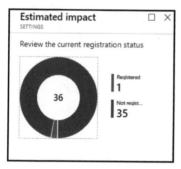

FIGURE 5-80 Azure AD Identity Protection Estimated impact

To enable the policy, turn the **Enforce Policy** switch to **On**, and click **Save**, as shown in Figure 5-81.

FIGURE 5-81 Azure AD Identity Protection enable MFA registration policy

After the policy has been successfully saved, you will see a notification in the portal as shown in Figure 5-82.

FIGURE 5-82 Azure AD Identity Protection enable MFA registration policy successfully

Thought experiment

In this thought experiment, apply what you have learned. You can find answers to these questions in the next section.

You are the administrator for Trey Research Pharmaceuticals. As a leader in the design and manufacturing of cutting-edge treatments for cancer patients, Trey Research needs to ensure that the users within the organization are protected as they access cloud apps from Microsoft such as Office 365 and external cloud apps including Salesforce CRM for their sales department.

Trey Research needs to ensure cloud identity implementation has the following features:

1. When users log in to Office 365 and Salesforce they should be redirected to an existing on-premises AD FS Farm. For disaster recovery purposes when the AD FS Farm is unavailable users should be able to log in to their cloud apps with the same user name and password that they use on-premises.

2. Users in the research department are all members of a security group. Users in this group handle sensitive data and must use multi-factor authentication (MFA) when accessing cloud apps.

3. Due to the sensitive nature of the intellectual property that users in the research group interact with; Trey Research would like to implement period reviews to verify group membership.

4. To make it easier for users to manage their credentials, Trey Research would like users to be able to update their passwords both on-premises and in the cloud.

Thought experiment answers

This section contains the answers to the thought experiment for the chapter.

1. Add and verify a custom domain in Azure AD that matches the on-premises user principal name suffix. Install Azure AD Connect and configure domain federation so that users are redirected to the on-premises AD FS farm when they attempt to login to Office 365. To meet the requirements for disaster recovery, configure Azure AD Connect with password hash synchronization. In the event the AD FS farm is unavailable, a global

administrator can configure the domain from a federated to a managed domain that allows the users to login to Azure AD authenticated cloud apps with the same user name and password they use on-premises.

2. A global administrator should enable Azure AD Identity Protection and configure a multi-factor authentication registration policy that requires MFA for the Research security group.

3. From the Access reviews service, an administrator should create a new access review for the Research security group in the default program. When configuring the access review, the administrator will need to select the recurrence rules for the review and any necessary reviewers.

4. An administrator should re-run the Azure AD Connect installation wizard and enable password writeback in the Optional features section of the wizard. This can be done by opening the wizard, selecting Customize synchronization options and proceeding through the wizard to the Optional features screen where Password writeback can be selected. After reconfiguring Azure AD Connect, a global administrator should configure self-service password reset through the Azure AD Portal by browsing to the Azure AD tenant.

Chapter summary

Below are some of the key takeaways from this chapter:

- Custom domains can be added to Azure AD, such as contoso.com, but there is always a default onmicrosoft.com domain.

- Azure AD Identity Protection enables administrators to configuration Azure AD tenant-wide policies for multi-factor authentication, sign-in risk, and user risk.

- Windows 10 can be added to Azure AD as a device to be managed, enabling BYOD or corporate cloud only deployments with Azure AD Join.

- Azure AD Join enables administrators to manage device identity independently of users. For example, dynamic security groups can be created based on device attributes and then conditional access policies could be applied to those groups.

- Downstream Windows clients can be managed through Azure AD using Azure AD hybrid join.

- Enterprise State Roaming allows Windows 10 clients to synchronize settings and application data securely across multiple corporate devices.

- Conditional access is a feature of Azure AD which allows administrators to control access to cloud applications through additional checks such as user location, the device the user is accessing the cloud app from, and more.

- Multiple Azure AD tenants can be created and managed through Azure. This includes creating new directories and deleting existing directories.

- Users and groups can be created through the Azure Portal, Azure PowerShell, the Azure CLI, and the Graph API.

- Users and groups can be managed in bulk with tools like PowerShell.

- Azure AD supports hybrid identity scenarios with Azure AD Connect.

- Azure AD supports federated logins and single-sign on. When federated identity is not required, Azure AD also single sign-on with both password hash synchronization and pass-through authentication.

- Self-service password reset can be combined with the password writeback features of Azure AD Connect to allow users to reset their passwords from the cloud while adhering to on-premises password standards.

- Many advanced features of Azure AD require Azure AD Premium P1 or Azure AD Premium P2 licenses. When considering Azure AD features, administrators need to be aware of the licensing boundaries.

Index

M

Manage Alert Rules, 40
Manage Azure Active Directory, 410, 413, 421
Manage Azure AD Connect, 448
Manage VM Backups, 269
Management Group , 72
Maximum number of devices per user, 416
MFA, ix, 409, 412-413, 416, 419, 423, 452-465, 467-476
Microsoft Open Licensing, 2
Microsoft Peering, 398, 401, 406
Microsoft Resellers, 2
Microsoft Teams, 422
Microsoft To-Do, 422
Microsoft Visio, 422
Microsoft Word, 422
Microsoft Yammer, 422
Multi-Site networks, 393

N

Network Performance Monitor, 369, 375, 381, 406
Network Security Group configuration, 361
Network Security Groups, 207, 343, 361
Network Topology, 380
networkProfile, 235-236, 239
New Alert Rule, 122, 219
New ExpressRoute, 398
New Group, 427
New Policy, 465, 468
New Policy Blade, 419
New User, 426
NewAzResourceGroup, 70
Next Hop, 377, 406

O

Operating System Disk, 198
Operations Management Suite, 160
Outbound Internet connections, 295

P

Packet Captures , 378
parameters, 16-17, 19-23, 29, 31, 49-50, 65-69, 71, 74, 96, 100, 107-108, 118, 125, 134, 137-138, 144, 183, 185, 194-195, 209, 229-231, 233-236, 238-240, 242-248, 263-268, 286-287, 327, 333, 338

PEERING CONNECTIONS, 306
PEERING LIMITS, 306
Performance Monitor, 371-372
Performance Tiers, 102
Preview Features, 169

R

ReadOnly, 76-77, 201-202
Receive, 139
Replace, 147, 273
Require Azure MFA Registration, 474
RESIZING VPN GATEWAYS, 388
Resource Group , 72
RESOURCE MANAGER TEMPLATE SCHEMA, 236
Resource Providers, 170, 353
RESOURCE TYPES, 30
Restoring a virtual machine, 273
Route Table, 302
Routes, 302

S

Save, 5
Security, viii, xv, 8, 24-25, 55, 62, 84-87, 90, 92-97, 112, 115, 182-183, 185-187, 206-207, 209, 251, 257, 279, 281-282, 285, 288, 290, 301, 305, 307, 314, 320, 338-339, 341-345, 347-349, 351-357, 360-361, 402, 404-405, 412, 418-419, 423, 427, 429, 431, 450-453, 475-476
Selected Networks, 111, 113
Settings, 27, 69, 302-303, 315, 335, 344, 354, 389, 415
SHARED IMAGE GALLERY, 188
Sharing virtual network gateways, 309
Solution Requires Additional Configuration, 370
SPECIFYING REPLICATION AND PERFORMANCE TIER SETTINGS, 103
SPF RECORDS, 327
Standard Load Balancer, 357
Standard Pricing Tiers Public, 292
Start Troubleshooting, 382
Storage Account,, 353
Storage Explorer, 108-109, 116, 119, 128, 131, 133, 143, 175
Storage Sync Agent After, 154
storageProfile, 235-236, 239
SUBNET OPERATIONS, 287, 318
Subscription, 2, 21, 23, 27, 29, 35, 37, 59-60, 69, 152, 283, 310-311, 353, 362, 394-395